Changing Women in a Changing Society

Changing Women in a Changing Society

Edited by Joan Huber

The University of Chicago Press
Chicago and London

This work also appeared as volume 78, number 4
(January 1973), of American Journal of Sociology,
under the guest editorship of Joan Huber and
published by the University of Chicago Press.

The University of Chicago Press, Chicago 60637
The University of Chicago Press, Ltd., London

International Standard Book Number:
0-226-35644-2 (clothbound)
Library of Congress Catalog Card Number: 72-96342

CONTENTS

Editor's Introduction[1]

Joan Huber
University of Illinois, Urbana

One of the men who evaluated manuscripts for this issue was surprised that "the good gray *AJS*" wanted to publish articles on women. That women are currently a subject of sociological interest has apparently surprised many people. Indeed, as sociologists we have suffered a series of collective shocks as we discovered that some of the natives in our pluralist consensual society were growing restless. In the early sixties we learned that poverty persisted in the affluent society. As the decade continued, blacks, teenagers, and women showed signs of getting out of hand; by the seventies some of the elderly were also becoming noisy. Confronted by events, sociologists typically try to make up for lost time by producing a spate of research or speculation on the latest hot topic. Although we probably know more about the total society than any other group of specialists, we are apparently unable to anticipate major sources of discontent. Why are we so often taken by surprise when some outraged group begins to complain?

Social conflict is likely to occur when some group feels that it is not getting its fair share of rewards. Sociologists often fail to spot probable sources of conflict because our stratification theories are outmoded. We need new theoretical spectacles. For the most part, our notions about stratification are a response to the ideas of Marx. The major strata that we study are descended from Marx's two great classes: the entrepreneurs and the proletariat. Aware of the shift to an employee society, we typically use the categories of white-collar and blue-collar occupations in social and political analysis. Some sociologists then conclude that classes are not very important anymore because the rapid rise of real income and the spread of educational opportunity cause the life styles of blue-collar and white-collar employees to converge; the entire society is becoming middle class. Even sociologists who show deep awareness of persistent economic inequalities in American society are not certain which classes are potentially important as conflict groups. The difficulty is that categories based on collar color no longer tell us enough about what we need to know to make sense of what is going on.

What is most wrong with stratification theory today is the assumption

[1] Those who are sympathetic to the women's movement will be grateful to the *American Journal of Sociology* for devoting an issue to reporting research about women. For their enormous help, I am deeply grateful to Florence Levinsohn and William H. Form, and to the many persons who read and evaluated the 79 manuscripts received.

Joan Huber

that the family remains the basic unit of analysis. That the family has changed with industrialization has not escaped notice, but the changes have never been systematically integrated into stratification theory. Owing in part to rapid technological change, certain strata within the family are systematically disadvantaged by the occupational reward system. The women's movement is a sign that it is possible to have a party with class interests which cuts across traditional class lines. The treatment of women in the sociology texts indicates that sociologists are not aware of this. Women are discussed as part of family and almost never as part of market institutions. Indeed, the categories of race, sex, and age are usually excluded from the topic of stratification in the introductory texts, in which the discussion of race is usually an atheoretical documentation of discrimination in every aspect of American life; sex refers to fads, fashions, and fancies in coital behavior; and age, to social isolation. Any discussion of stratification which makes no attempt to explain the market situation of persons in any of these categories is bound to be thin and unsatisfying.

The preoccupation with the family as the primary agent of stratification has also led to the idea that we live in an achievement society, even though a substantial majority of all Americans suffers restricted opportunity because of an ascribed status. Any woman, for example, whose daily routine includes changing diapers and dishing out the applesauce is doing semi-skilled blue-collar work, regardless of her own educational attainment or the SES level of her husband. A trick of definition—the work is unpaid—allows us to maintain the fiction that this kind of outcome doesn't really count. The anomaly that half of all Americans are expected to do blue-collar work regardless of talent and training is not discussed in the stratification texts. In the labor force, blacks clearly suffer from purposeful discrimination. Women, teenagers, and the elderly suffer from protection. They are excluded from or restricted in labor market participation for their own good because certain jobs might injure their health, interfere with their education, or damage their morals. The intent of the protective laws was manifestly benign, but the consequence is to protect a privileged position for middle-aged males by hamstringing possible competitors.

The main factor in the rise of the women's movement is the perception of occupational discrimination. Women sensed what was going on long before male sociologists became aware of it. The perception was rooted in awareness of two important technological and demographic changes. First, control of pregnancy is not only possible but is increasingly viewed as desirable. A woman who produces a sizable number of children is likely to be defined as socially irresponsible. The average American woman now has her last child when she is only 27, and she may well feel that devoting much of the rest of her life to domestic service for one adult male will keep her busy mainly with busywork.

Second, in contrast with the early part of the century, when women usually worked only until they married or had children, women today tend to return to work when their children are partly grown. By 1970 more than half of all women worked, in contrast with about 80% of men. Comparing full-time workers in the same occupations, women earn only about three-fifths of the wages of men, a fact which is remarkably constant all over the Western world. The American ideology of equal opportunity holds that equal qualifications and hours worked should bring equal rewards. But it does not apply to women.

Why women's work is less well paid is a complex question; probably the most crucial factor is the social definition of childrearing as women's responsibility. A woman is kept off the ladder for high prestige jobs because she might leave to get married or have a baby. After some years at home with her children, her skills rusted, she is easily outranked by males of the same age who have supposedly accumulated valuable occupational experience while she has been scrubbing crud from the kitchen floor and running the PTA. Only women can have babies, but the fact that women are also expected to rear them is a man-made decision. At the heart of the women's movement is a wish to share the delights and joys of motherhood. But the idea that they might be expected to partake of such joys and actually rear children—not just "help" their wives occasionally—scares many men nearly out of their wits. We should expect men in the most highly rewarded occupations, professionals and managers, to show the most hostility to change because they have the most to lose. The idea that American society is structured so that women encounter severe occupational discrimination brings forth reactions from male sociologists that are not theoretically disappointing. Let us examine a brief typology.

Although male sociologists have been sensitized to the social and psychological correlates of prejudice, their response to the idea that child care is a parental and societal responsibility to enable women to compete freely in the occupational world parallels the response of certain nonblack blue-collar workers who are afraid that they will suffer economically if discrimination against blacks should end. The full force of male hostility will be more apparent here if the reader substitutes the word "black" for the word "women."

Simple denial occurs when a man claims that he hasn't seen any unhappy women so why stir things up. At the departmental level, he insists that sexism is not now and never has been a factor in the hiring and promotion policies of his department because no one in it is prejudiced against women. The reason more women are not hired, of course, is that they simply couldn't find a qualified woman.

Simple paranoia occurs when a man is convinced that any woman, however stupid, is getting a good job at the expense of a competent male who has a wife and kiddies to support. This assertion is made without a shred of evidence.

Classic liberalism is the response of the man who assures everyone that he never objected one bit to his own wife's working and he is sure that most men don't mind having their wives work. His wife has always felt perfectly free to work. She is usually a secretary or a school teacher who edits his copy after she has put the children to bed.

The *laissez-faire individualist* opposes day care centers because the care of children is not society's responsibility. It is a family obligation. And the day when the family does not shoulder its obligations will be a sorry day for America. By this he means that the father is obliged to pay for Kleenex and music lessons and the mother is obliged to wipe the children's noses and see that they practice.

The *jokester* is full of lighthearted pleasantries such as, "And how are the libbies today?" Fortunately, he has enough sense not to go to the director of black studies and say lightheartedly, "And how are the blackies today?"

The *pseudo-radical* is very serious and sincere. He is more than ready for the total transformation of society as long as it doesn't interfere with his own domestic arrangements. He becomes nervous and defensive if anyone compares women with blacks. He likes to tell women professionals that they should be ashamed of themselves for seeking their own occupational advancement in a society where so many people are so much worse off.

The *kindly humanitarian* is filled with sympathy for women. He admits that women are exploited and he is sorry, but he knows that he doesn't want to have to cope with baby's bowel movement himself. If someone isn't socialized to do the job of child-rearing, the nuclear family might wither away. The human race might even die out. So what else can you do?

The research published in this issue of the *AJS* begins to expose these legitimations for the rationalizations they are. While the situation will not be resolved in the near future, the data reported here about what is happening to women indicate that pressure for institutional adjustments will probably persist. That men will joyously accept the task of rearing children seems unlikely. Widespread day care services for young children will be the great leveler of sexual inequality. The ideology of equal opportunity is ill served when half our citizens are either kept on the sidelines or are allowed to play only part of the time.

Maid of All Work or Departmental Sister-in-Law? The Faculty Wife Employed on Campus

Helen MacGill Hughes
Cambridge, Massachusetts

I

The account given here of 17 years' service on the *American Journal of Sociology*, anomalous as my role was and antedating, as it did, consciousness-raising and the repudiation of nepotism rules, aims at something more significant than personal reminiscence. While the current lively discussion of women in campus jobs focuses mainly on the incumbent and the built-in disabilities under which they suffer,[1] this microcosmic case study interprets a small-scale constitutional change in terms of working standards and practices, on one hand, and the relationships between role players, on the other, ascribing the change to a situation which today is called sexist.

In August 1944, the *Journal*'s editor, Herbert Blumer, asked me to be an editorial assistant, replacing a graduate student in sociology who was leaving on very short notice. There were two editorial assistants then: a typist who was not a sociologist and the student assistant, who got out the *Journal* between classes and on Saturday forenoons, at token pay. The student was usually a woman, for this was one of the few jobs open to the then rare female graduate students; male students had real jobs for real money in the city in, for example, the parole system or Chicago's public parks.

But there was no student available for the vacancy on the *Journal*. Our youngest child was in nursery school, and I was very glad to accept the offer. I had my Ph.D. (Chicago), and the job was one fitted to the circumstances of a graduate student who would work in spare, time for a modest emolument. At that time, however, consciousness-raising was not sparking the spirit of the faculty wife in a campus job. For me this was the beginning of 17 gratifying, underpaid years.

The September issue was already at the Press. But in the editorial assistant's desk was a clutch of papers accepted for future issues. In several, although the readers had occasionally corrected grammar or spelling, the writing was so bad as to defy parsing and comprehension, and the

---

[1] In the spate of reports on the position of academic women, slightly relevant are *The Status of Women in the Profession* of the American Sociological Association (in press) and similar reports of the American Historical Association (1971) and the American Political Science Association (1969–71). However, I know of no study specifically of the faculty wife employed on campus.

Helen MacGill Hughes

pieces cried out for thorough blue-penciling. Contrary to the *Journal's* practice, Blumer gave me permission to make them more presentable. To the authors we gave as the excuse the very real wartime shortage of paper. Behind this face-saving, not entirely accurate explanation, the articles were, of course, being not merely condensed but edited, sometimes brutally. We always wrote the author that he (occasionally she) was at liberty to restore any deleted material that he/she considered indispensable, but it was soon evident that, while we might discard pounds of excess baggage, not even the most ego-threatened author would salvage more than a few ounces. Some authors even wrote letters of thanks!

Now this arduous and time-consuming editorial service is undertaken routinely on behalf of authors, who are fully aware that they can count on being rescued from their wordy morass. Indeed, the present managing editor of the *American Journal of Sociology* reports that she virtually rewrites about half of the articles accepted. The corresponding fraction on the *American Sociological Review*, according to its current editor, is between one quarter and one third.

Without conscious design, I was in reality beginning to build up that job normally intended for a graduate student. Blumer went on leave to Pittsburgh to arbitrate "Big Steel." Of the associate editors, Samuel Stouffer was in Washington finding out for the army what the GIs wanted; Everett Hughes and Lloyd Warner were conducting field studies in Chicago factories of man-, woman-, and Negro-power; Ernest Burgess, Will Ogburn, and Louis Wirth, always concerned citizens, were also caught up in war-connected research. I, meanwhile, kept the editorial office open and busy five forenoons a week, having evolved a conception of my work as getting out on time—a substantial achievement in wartime—a journal more meticulously edited and claiming a minimum of the editors' time and energy.[2]

No one spoke of this shifting of responsibilities as policy; it arose out of the current situation. As, out of necessity, the overwhelmed editors left undone some things they had done before, I picked up what they dropped.[3]

[2] Hughes speaks of the attempts of people who practice an occupation "to revise the conceptions which their various publics have of the occupation and of the people in it" as characteristic behavior in an occupation which seeks to be a "profession," and adds, "In so doing they also attempt to revise their own conception of themselves and of their work" (1958*b*, p. 44).

[3] "The physician . . . has . . . more authority than he can in many cases actually assume. There will probably be in the system, complementary to this position, another of the right-hand-man order; . . . which defers to the first, but which, informally, must often exceed its authority, in order to protect the interests of all concerned. . . . When the doctor isn't there [the nurse] may do some necessary thing which requires his approval—and get the approval when he comes back. . . . Her place in the division of labor is essentially that of doing in a responsible way whatever necessary things are in danger of not being done at all" (Hughes 1958*a*, p. 74).

6

And perhaps the shift occurred, too, out of my need to make the job real work.[4] It was as though permission to lay violent hands on articles submitted to the *Journal* was logically parallel to the physician's license to cut the skin or let the blood of another, in that it opened the door to the legitimation of all manner of invasions which otherwise were impertinences.

Thus, I designed and worded the promotion brochures of our special issues and solicited mailing lists—burdens and prerogatives of the University of Chicago Press. (But the Press, too, was suffering from manpower shortages.) I wrote the "News and Notes" section from snippets sent in to us from hither and yon, and if I thought of a likely reviewer for a book, I sent his name up to the book review editor.

More significantly, I wrote the letters dealing with articles, on minimal instructions from the editor. And while I did not decide any article's fate, I often sent a paper out to a reader of my own choosing for a first opinion and then, by sending paper and opinion together to the editor, gave him a head start in forming a judgment. Only to this extent could the editorial office be said to have had some influence on what was published. Sociologists were few in number then; relatively speaking, there were not many departments of sociology. The subject was smaller, too; gerontology, for instance, was just beginning, and there was not much opinion sampling. (But there *was* ecology. The first course in "Human Ecology" had been given by Robert Park in spring 1926.) If an article came in, say, on the assimilation of Jewish immigrants, Louis Wirth was the logical reader, as were Ernest Burgess and Edwin Sutherland on crime. American sociologists knew each other, and it was not impossible to be more or less at home in the various fields of the discipline.

All these changes in the job called for the adding of routines to the work of the other editorial assistant. In time she did all the proofreading in addition to her clerical office duties. To fill her position had been difficult while the war lasted, but in the late forties, the splendid generation of returned veterans who came to the department on their GI money brought their wives, who provided us for several years with a succession of mature, responsible candidates for the job. But if turnover had been bad before, it was heartbreaking now: the wives were always pregnant! Eventually the position was filled by a competent secretary and stenographer who stayed on year after year, just as I did. Our jobs were part time but no longer temporary.

A more thorough description than this one would perforce take into account the part played by the University of Chicago Press, which, in

[4] Hughes observes of "the occupations and institutions which do things for people": "those who seek to raise standards of practice (and their own status) . . . would do well to study in every case what changes in the other positions and roles in the system will be wrought by changes in their own" (1958a, p. 77).

setting our publication schedule, exerted considerable remote control over the editorial office. The Press could always tell the good guys from the bad: the good ones met the publication deadlines. We did. And when we first began to send edited manuscripts—never galleys—to authors, the Press, at first timorous, watched with delight, for it cost nothing to make changes on manuscript. Basking as we did in the sun of the Press's favor made life easier for our editors.

II

To anticipate the objection that all of this is unrepresentative of the position of the faculty wife employed in a campus job: certainly it was not the situation now being brought to light in some of even the most respected universities, in which an exploited woman is given remuneration which is not competitive, and consigned to the residual work of the department and to such unpopular tasks as teaching unchallenging classes or classes at awkward hours. Yet it was typical insofar as the salary was unrealistic and the position was a blind alley. An editorial assistant who was replaced every two or three years and who took over the work while preparing for more honored eventual status could hardly complain. But salary and position could become the source of complaint when the work was professionalized and a single incumbent filled the place year after year. In any case, 17 years' experience led to nothing further on campus. (Nor, as it turned out, anywhere else, not even to a place on any of the by-then numerous sociological periodicals. But the experience was probably considered a qualification, five years later, for work under the auspices of the American Sociological Association's project, Sociological Resources for the Social Studies.)

Only very discreetly did the issue of nepotism rear its ugly head. The *Journal*'s editor, whoever he happened to be, and I were not on the same payroll: he was a member of the Department of Sociology, and I, though appointed by the department, was paid by the University of Chicago Press. The *Journal* had grown, and the work was increasingly rewarding, though never in a monetary sense. However, the token salary had been twice raised a little. The first time was at the instigation of Burgess, in appreciation of the extra work occasioned by Blumer's leave of absence. But in 1952, when I was completing my eighth year on the *Journal*, Hughes succeeded Blumer as editor, and neither he nor I even dreamed of his asking the Press to raise my salary. There must be many faculty wives in this dilemma today, and there will continue to be until spouses are dealt with as autonomous professionals.

I was kept happy, however, by rewards other than monetary. In making me assistant editor as my second year began, the editors created a new slot on the *Journal*,[5] which I filled for eight and a half years. Then in 1954 Morton Grodzins, incoming director of the Press, told me he intended to get me "a real salary." But the Press, fearing that its other journals might clamor for a like concession, refused it. So he paid me on the masthead: a letter from Chancellor Kimpton notified me that I was managing editor. I continued with this title until we moved to Brandeis in 1961. But the progression from editorial assistant to assistant editor to managing editor had no effect on the work. Whatever the title, it was not a promotion in the usual sense, but enhancement—a *ruban* or a *rosette*.

III

The editors had put themselves in the position of having to deal with a nonstudent in a student's role. In this anomaly may lie a tentative explanation of the situation of the faculty wife employed, typically part time, on campus. For who were my colleagues? Who set the model for my role?

There were wives on several of the Press-owned journals. Occasionally two or three of us would compare notes, capping one another's complaints about authors, editors, and Press people. But our working lives (by which, as everyone knows, is not meant our more complicated and demanding domestic lives) never converged sufficiently for us to have opinions of each other's performance or any strong sentiment of common interests.

Were the assistant's colleagues, then, the editors themselves? It was clear from the first that I enjoyed more autonomy, in part assigned, in part arrogated, than the student predecessors in the editorial office. But I was a graduate of the department and a fellow student, though junior to them, of three of the editors, Blumer, Wirth, and Hughes; a student of a fourth, Burgess; and as if all that were not enough to upset the customary relationships in the office, the wife of one of them. It was a perfect case of Simmel's *Kreuzung sozialer Kreise* (the interacting of social circles) (1908, chap. 6). Perhaps these compounded contradictions in status inhibited the editors from retaining as full control as had been usual. At least, their instructions sounded like suggestions, and none ever dictated a letter: they asked that one be written. It is possible they were not com-

[5] In the early forties, the *Journal*'s masthead listed the editor; three or four members of the Department of Sociology as associate editors, of whom one might specifically be named book review editor; a dozen advisory editors, who were sociologists in other American and in European universities; and two editorial assistants, sometimes three. In 1952, Hughes, noting that the Constitution of the university included among professorial duties service on the departmental journal, if there was one, listed all 12 members of the department as an editorial board, and 15 off-campus advisory editors. Today the masthead bears the names of the editor, two associate editors, one book review editor, one managing editor, and an editorial assistant, together with an editorial board of the 19 members of the department and the 22 members of the off-campus advisory board.

pletely at ease. Yet I was made to feel sure of their confidence and, on my side, enjoyed a sense of something like colleagueship.

I am suggesting that under specific (in 1972 read "sexist") conditions, the editors, or some of them, might to some extent have abdicated and given me my head. Does, then, the paradox in the employment of faculty wives on campus lie in the fact that they may be working, at least in some of the happier cases, under nominal superiors who, under the circumstances, are reluctant to take control? If they are, the balance of power in the office is changed, with the authority of the seniors reduced, partly with their own connivance, and the autonomy of the subordinate commensurately increased. The subordinate follows the role model set by the editors, who, in turn, behave as though they are dealing with one of themselves. In the process, the office is professionalized.

That this was an outcome of sexism is perfectly clear. The position of editorial assistant of the *American Journal of Sociology* would certainly never have been offered to a male Ph.D., or even to a male doctoral student[6] whose mentor[7] would be watching paternally for an opening in which he could set his disciple's feet on the path to a career like his own. But a female Ph.D., in 1944 and perhaps even in 1972, would find herself in this position, although in 1972 she would probably be better able to negotiate.

REFERENCES

American Historical Association. 1971. *Final Report of the Ad Hoc Committee on the Status of Women in the Profession*. Washington, D.C.
American Political Science Association. 1969–71. *Women in Political Science*. Washington, D.C.
American Sociological Association. In press. *The Status of Women in the Profession*. Washington, D.C.
Epstein, Cynthia. 1970. *Woman's Place: Options and Limits in Professional Careers*. Berkeley: University of California Press.
Hall, Oswald. 1948. "The Stages of a Medical Career." *American Journal of Sociology* 53 (March): 327–36.
Hughes, Everett C. 1958a. "Social Role and the Division of Labor." In *Men and Their Work*. Glencoe, Ill.: Free Press. Reprinted in *The Sociological Eye*. Chicago: Aldine-Atherton, 1971.
———. 1958b. "Work and the Self." In *Men and Their Work*. Glencoe, Ill.: Free Press. Reprinted in *The Sociological Eye*. Chicago: Aldine-Atherton, 1971.
Simmel, Georg. 1908. *Soziologie*. Leipzig: Duncker & Humblot.

[6] After 1942, all editorial assistants were women.

[7] For discussion of sponsorship in professional education, see Hall (1948, pp. 334, 336) and other articles by him. Epstein (1970) has shown how sponsorship works in the case of the female graduate student.

My Four Revolutions: An Autobiographical History of the ASA[1]

Jessie Bernard
Pennsylvania State University

I am undoubtedly the only person, living or dead, who has participated in four revolutions in the American Sociological Association (ASA). The first in the 1920s, the second in the 1930s, the third in the 1950s, and the current, or fourth, in the 1970s.

In the early 1920s, a radical young sociologist at Columbia University by the name of W. F. Ogburn, who had himself, both in government service and in academia, participated in the burgeoning movement to quantify sociological research, had the mind-boggling idea that the annual meetings of the American Sociological Society ought to inject into their programs some papers on empirical research. Not, mind you, at the expense of the high-level papers the giants addressed to one another but as an interesting fillip. He proceeded with his idea and solicited papers based on empirical research. That was how I came to participate in the program in 1925 which I now see as far more revolutionary than it appeared to be then. At his invitation—imagine how barren the field must have been—I presented a paper based on my master's dissertation. I am not at all anxious to advertise it, so let that pass. The important thing was that the idea of papers based on empirical research was introduced and took hold. This revolution did not create the emphasis on empirical research; that had a long history.[2] But that first research program did open the door of the Society to the accelerating thrust of empirical research, give it official sanction, and provide it with a recognized forum. The rest is history. The research programs acquired prestige, proliferated into a veritable jungle, and all but overshadowed the theoretical papers. I leave for the official historians of the ASA the job of assessing the impact of this first revolution on the discipline and tracing its implications.

My second revolution, in the 1930s, marked the emancipation of the Society from the fostering protection of the University of Chicago. Until that time, the University of Chicago had, in effect, owned the Society. It supplied the leadership, published the proceedings, and provided a home for the secretary treasurer. In the early 1930s, a group of rebels—led to a large extent by L. L. Bernard—stole the Society away.[3] The *American*

---

[1] This paper is not to be confused with another with a similar title (see Bernard 1966).

[2] See Bernard and Bernard (1943, pts. 10–12).

[3] Much of the documentary material on this revolution is available in the L. L.

Journal of Sociology was no longer to be its official journal. Again I leave for the official historians of the ASA the task of assessing the impact of this second revolution on the discipline and tracing its implications.

The third revolution, in the early 1950s, consisted of the declaration of independence of a group of rebels who, deploring the refusal of the parent organization to take a stand on any policy issue, established the Society for the Study of Social Problems (SSSP).[4] Our gripes were manifold. We objected to the elitist direction the ASA was following, its lack of interest in social problems and issues, its antiseptic "line" on research, its cronyism, and its complacent acceptance of the increasing trend of putting socio-logical research at the service of business and industry. We were concerned also with protecting academic freedom in the era of McCarthy. The SSSP's objectives were: (1) advancement of the study of social problems; (2) application of social science research to the formulation of social policies; (3) improvement of the opportunities and working conditions of social scientists; (4) protection of freedom of teaching, research, and publication; and (5) interdisciplinary cooperation in social science research.[5] Although some of the stars of the ASA agreed to front for us,[6] the actual leadership was in the hands of Alfred McClung Lee and Arnold Rose, who were not afraid to stand up to the conservative ASA elite. We embarrassed the ASA; it didn't know exactly how to deal with us.[7] For a long time, despite the shining stars—E. W. Burgess was the first president—we scared the elite by threatening to give sociology a bad name by taking positions on issues. But we were clearly in tune with the times. Before too many years had passed we became respectable. More's the pity, perhaps. The most elite members of the ASA not only joined but became active. Became officers, in fact. We were not co-opted but the ASA did

---

Bernard papers in the archives of Pennsylvania State University, in charge of Ronald Fillipelli.

[4] The nucleus for this organization was a group of faculty members of Brooklyn College, esp. Alfred McClung Lee, Elizabeth Bryant Lee, Sylvia Fleis Fava, and Barbara Mintz Mishkin, all of whom invested great blocks of time as well as financial support. In a way, this revolution might be viewed as a corrective to oversuccess of the first.

[5] In the early years there were several meetings with our counterparts in psychology and anthropology, the Society for the Psychological Study of Social Issues, and Applied Anthropology.

[6] The journal, *Social Problems,* flaunted among its advisory editors such luminaries as the older Howard Becker, E. F. Frazier, John P. Gillin, A. Irving Hallowell, Otto Klineberg, Clyde Kluckhohn, Max Lerner, Abraham H. Maslow, Francis E. Merrill, Robert K. Merton, and Robin M. Williams, Jr. Although C. Wright Mills was the ideological patron saint—an award in his honor was later established—he was not actively involved in SSSP.

[7] We demanded representation in the International Sociological Association, for example, and refused to accept second-class status in that body.

take over all the "radical" innovations we had introduced, and you can hardly tell the two apart anymore except that there may be more beards and slightly longer hair in the SSSP.[8] Once more I leave to the official historians of the ASA and the SSSP the chore of assessing the impact of this third revolution on our discipline and tracing its implications.

My fourth—feminist—revolution came as something of a surprise to me. It should not have. For although, like my colleagues, I stand accused of not foretelling the uprisings of the 1960s—still, on the basis of research dealing with the feminine "life calendar," I did note "augurs of change" in my (1964, pp. 62–63) study of academic women. By the end of the decade, academic women in several disciplines were protesting their status in the profession. Led by Alice Rossi, the revolution in sociology surfaced in San Francisco in 1969. I was in London at the International Population Conference, so I did not have the privilege of taking part in the meetings at which the Women's Caucus under Alice Rossi's leadership got an astonishing list of resolutions accepted. But I was present the next year in Washington when the Women's Caucus began the process of transforming itself into Sociologists for Women in Society, and I was one of the midwives at the birth of that organization.[9]

The feminist revolution was a complex event. The tasks envisioned by the participants varied. Some were interested primarily in fighting discrimination in the profession. Some were concerned with fighting discrimination against women in society at large. Some wanted to liberate sociology from its establishmentarian bias to make it an instrument for total revolution.[10] And some sought mainly to counteract the sexist bias in

---

[8] I fear that SSSP has run out of innovativeness. The New University Conference has come to preempt many of SSSP's issues and has shoved them to the left.

[9] For a personal account of that organizational meeting, see my letter in the first issue of the *SWS Newsletter*, 1971.

[10] Marlene Dixon was the leader of this group. Since in her view it was the duty of sociology to put research at the service of the oppressed instead of, as now, their oppressors, women, as among the oppressed, constituted an important area for research. Her success was so limited that, in a paper (1970) on "The Failure of the Sociology Liberation Movement," she washed her hands of sociology as an arm of revolution. Her disillusion was complete. The first public professional statement of the sociology-as-servant-of-the-ruling-class-against-the-oppressed was made by Jack Nicklaus at the Boston, 1968, meetings of the ASA. (It sounded strangely like Alfred McClung Lee's strictures in the SSSP almost 20 years earlier.) Dixon was bitterly disappointed in the sequelae. Clever strategy by power wielders, she concluded, had deflected the thrust of the radicals and turned radical sociology into a form of career hustling or radical profiteering which perpetuated the myth that one could have a career in sociology and still remain radical: "Our experience since the first Sociology Liberation Movement in Boston is clear: if you sleep with dogs you'll pick up fleas." (Like so many of the ephemera of radical writers, this mimeographed paper bears no date. It was distributed at the ASA meetings in 1970.) I must say that, abrasive as I find Dixon's style to be, I regret that the fourth revolution will not have the needling her polemics supply.

the discipline. The last of these tasks is my own major concern and is the focus of the discussion here.

I am not attempting to account for any of my four revolutions. In each case, I am sure, "the time had come." This is a cliché that can never be disproved, a tautology; you know the time has come because the revolution occurs. Nor am I trying to explain why this is the time for the feminist revolution in sociology, why this is the time for an attack on sexism in our discipline.[11] Suffice to say that this is the time because the world to which sociology addresses itself has changed so much that a shift is required to take into account the anomalies resulting from "the novelties of fact"[12]—to use Thomas S. Kuhn's phrase—that modern life is introducing into the classic paradigms. Because it is now essential for us to bring our discipline up to date, to fill in the deficiencies its male bias has created. Because if we want sociology to have relevance for the world it is supposed to interpret, it has to look at this world through suitable paradigms. Because, in brief, sociology is in a state of crisis, a word which appears with increasing frequency in sociological discussions. Sociology is in crisis because the old paradigms are overburdened by anomalies and satisfactory new ones are not available. Whatever the reason may be, the fourth revolution is now.

"ASK NOT . . ."

I am concerned, as any fair-minded person must be, with the effects of sexism on the position of women in our profession and in our society; but I am also concerned, as any dedicated sociologist must be, with its effects on our discipline as well. Important as are the costs to women of the male bias in sociology, on which a considerable literature exists (Roby 1972; Rossi 1972), I am concerned here not with them but rather with the costs of this bias to the discipline itself. I am not, therefore, asking what sociology can do for women—for example, by filling in the gaps in our knowledge about them, itself a significant contribution[13]—but rather what women (and sympathetic male colleagues) can do for sociology. How they can correct some of its defects by overcoming deficiencies, broadening its perspective, opening up new areas, asking new questions, offering new paradigms; how, in brief, they can make sociology a better instrument for understanding, explaining, and interpreting the way modern societies

[11] See Ferriss (1971, pp. 1–2) for possible reasons.

[12] Some of the anomalies have to do with the changing sexual allocation of functions in our society (Bernard 1971b, passim).

[13] Merely clearing up stereotypes about women is a major research contribution. Among the sources of the feminist movement that Ferris (1971) specifies are the studies of women made during the 1960s. They supplied polemic tracts with factual support.

operate.[14] Though I despair of my ability to do justice to the problem—a thoroughgoing attack would require a series of monographs—I can at least nibble at it here.

I have selected for comment (1) some of the antecedents of the fourth revolution; (2) critiques by women of such major concepts and paradigms as Parsonian functionalism, interactionism, socialization, and exchange theory; and (3) the attempt to expand sociology into a genuine science of society by including women as well as men.

ANTECEDENTS AND PRECURSORS

Even before the fourth revolution hit sociology, there was already a remarkable corpus of critical-polemical writing by women of the Women's Liberation Movement who came from a wide variety of backgrounds, from Maoist to Christian,[15] on a wide variety of sociological phenomena—functionalism, socialization, interaction, power, exploitation, oppression—which sought to show how the social sciences, especially sociology and psychology, had been used to bolster the power of men and justify discrimination and oppression. The Women's Liberation Movement had been nurtured in the New Left, a disproportionate number of whose members were sociology students, if not professional sociologists. It retained this New Left sociological stamp even when it seceded from the male matrix.

Thus in their written work these early leaders applied to women the same arguments and logic as those applied to the underclasses by their male prototypes. As the Sociology Liberation Movement had accused sociologists of cultivating a power-oriented sociology, creating not a science of society but a science of just one segment of society, honed to help it exploit the other segments, so, in a similar vein, these women charged that sociology was not a science of society but rather a science of male society and that it did not necessarily have great relevance for women. Just as the Sociology Liberation Movement charged that sociological research was on the side of the power structure, these women charged that it had been on the side of men.

These early leaders were almost certainly familiar with C. Wright Mills. Whether or not they had read *The Sociological Imagination,* they followed the tenets it laid down (1959, p. 196). Mills's (1959, pp. 225–26) last imperative—to reveal the human meaning of public issues by relating them to personal troubles—was especially salient in the process that came to be known as consciousness raising. Women who had always been blamed

[14] Women psychologists also look for a similar revolution in their discipline (see Carlson 1972).

[15] For a brief overview of the Women's Liberation Movement, see Bernard (1971b, pt. 5).

Jessie Bernard

for their miseries, rebuked for mentioning them, and told that something was wrong with them were liberated when they came to see that they were not defective individuals but victims of oppressive institutions. Their method, like that of their male counterparts, has since been given the name of ethnomethodolgy (Garfinkel 1967). Young (1971, p. 279) defines it as a special type of conflict methodology which requires one to poke, probe, provoke, and puncture the social system in order to reveal its character-istics.[16] By such techniques, the writings of these early feminists led readers suddenly to become aware of a wide gamut of phenomena which they had always taken for granted. Their consciousness was raised.

THE FEMALE CRITIQUE: THEORY

The work of the present cohort of women critics of sociology has been largely normal science in nature, modifying, correcting, sharpening, or refining the classic paradigms and analyses of traditional sociology, often with the effect of exposing their male bias.

The criticism of *Parsonian functionalism* by women followed essentially the same logic as that of its male critics, namely, that, by implication if not by intention,[17] it had the effect of justifying the sexual status quo, as though a functionalist explanation of it supplied a scientific basis for it.[18] They pointed out that it is one thing to analyze the way social structures operate—including the way they allocate functions—but quite another to

[16] Young (1971, p. 279) illustrates its use in teaching students the invisible, taken-for-granted aspects of trust, for example, by challenging it in some relationship. Pioneer activists in the Women's Liberation Movement, similarly, challenged the invisible, taken-for-granted aspects of the relations between the sexes by violating them. They parodied some of them by outdoing men in the use of obscenities, in aggressive, nonsupportive responses. They refused to play according to the prescribed male script. Thus when David Susskind and Dick Cavett insisted that their women guests talk about the book they wanted them to talk about, women refused. They had become alerted to the conventionalized traps used to control them. The men were nonplussed because the women were not responding according to their design. The men were accustomed to prettily yielding women or prettily protesting women—equally flattering in either case. A woman's eyewitness description of the conventional scenario for relations even between professional sociologists is presented by Geraldine Mintz, pseud. (1967, pp. 158–59).

[17] The intention may be quite hidden in the original assumptions and premises which make only the intended implications logical. Thus Parsons's (1959, pp. 262 ff.) analysis of the integration of the family and occupational systems rests on certain basic assumptions about the primary allegiance of men and women to their respective worlds, assumptions which lead logically to his conclusion that integration of the two world calls for role segregation. Coser and Rokoff (1971, p. 552) explore the possi-bilities which can occur if the basic assumption about the primary allegiances of the sexes is not granted. Their results are not the same as Parsons's.

[18] Friedan (1963, p. 127) set the pattern for this critique of functionalism. For recent examples, see the August and October 1971 issues of *Journal of Marriage and the Family* and the November-December 1970 issue of *Trans-Action*.

accept the sexual allocation of functions in any given system as intrinsic to social systems. As a result of this critique, few sociologists are likely to continue to justify the sexual status quo through functional analysis. This does not mean that they will all necessarily accept changes in the status quo; they will simply find other justifications for it.[19]

The work of women critics has also contributed to overcoming one of the weaknesses of *interactionism* as specified by Rose (1962, p. x), namely, neglect of power relationships.[20] Their analyses of the ways men exert power over women in everyday interaction as well as in sexual relationships has been one of their most important contributions (see Jones 1970; Mainardi 1970).

The explanatory value of both functionalism and interactionism in the form of role theory rests heavily on the paradigm of *socialization,* which the female critique has not only accepted but also greatly expanded. Socialization has, in fact, been an all-but-overwhelming preoccupation of the women critics.[21] They have alerted us to aspects of it not previously recognized by male researchers, highlighting especially the processes by which women are socialized for weakness, dependency, fear of success (Horner 1969), and even mild mental illness (Broverman, Broverman, Charlson, Rosenkrantz, and Vogel 1970), and thus shaped for marriage (Bernard 1971a, pp. 94–95; 1972, chap. 3). The "adjustment" that brings stability of the status quo—which functionalism reports—by means of the techniques—which interactionism describes—becomes a dirty word.

Despite the fact that the whole *exchange* paradigm cries out for a feminist critique, no such analysis has yet been made.[22] Thus far exchange theory in the area of the relations between the sexes has been applied almost exclusively to mate selection or to the exchange of sex favors (see Blau 1964; or Elder 1969). The other kinds of relations between the

[19] Not all, though. In a brilliant tour de force, Grønseth (1971) showed point for point how the present sexual status quo is dysfunctional for society as a whole.

[20] Caroline Rose makes the following comment here: "I don't think Arnold's criticism of interactionism as neglecting power applies to the example you give; interactionism would certainly handle power and conflict relations between or among groups" (personal letter, June 30, 1972).

[21] Hanisch (1971, p. 2) rejects this preoccupation with roles and socialization. She views it as a diversionary tactic, distracting attention from the real—power—basis for the position of women. She finds that male social scientists can cheerfully accept the socialization interpretation of the status of women because they gain greatly in substituting the socialization paradigm for a power paradigm. She specifies in detail the male gain from this substitution.

[22] In their work on Blau's statement on exchange theory, Marie Osmond and Patricia Martin demonstrate the sexist bias in it by the use of simulation and, incidentally, show that "sexist behavior, regardless of social psychological attitudes, is a response to the structure of the game (social system) and the rules (norms) of play (interaction); and that a change in game structure and rules results in a change in game-behavior."

sexes have not been encompassed in it.[23] The female critique has high-lighted the asymmetry in most of these relations, noting that in almost every intersex exchange, "the woman pays," that she is on the losing side, and that she is even expected to accept the situation without complaint.[24] Free exchange under the conditions specified by Adam Smith leaves both parties better off, both having exchanged something they value less for something they value more. But game theory has taught us that both parties can lose; or that one can win and the other lose. The women critics note that in our society the loser is most likely to be the woman. Losing, in fact, is written into her role script; she has a stroke deficit: "Women . . . are enjoined to give out more strokes than they receive by the dictates of their roles as women. The instruction to give more strokes than they receive and to be willing to settle for this disparity are essentially aspects of women's life scripts" (Wyckoff 1971); see also Bernard 1971*b*). In this "stroke economy," women may win an occasional battle, particularly when they are young and especially desirable, but they lose the wars. The presidential address of George Homans, a leading exponent of exchange theory, before the ASA was dedicated to "bringing men back in" to sociology. The feminist revolution calls for bringing women in too.

Women increasingly fault history also for its neglect of women, so that what history we have is almost exclusively a history of men. Male biases determine not only what is selected for study but also how it is interpreted. Turner's theory of the effect of the frontier on American character, for example, deals only with males (Chmaj 1971, p. 65). "Descriptions of the experiences of women servants, slaves, immigrants, pioneers, and factory workers remain buried in court records, journals, letters, travelogs, and newspapers," as yet unexploited for the knowledge they can make available about our society (Greenwald 1971, p. 152). Women also criticize the condescending and patronizing manner what history of women there is has been dealt with.

Much of the female critique to date is remedial, a patching up, merely a first installment of the potential contribution women can make. Still, I challenge any sociologist to read it thoughtfully and nondefensively and not find that a re-thinking of sociological paradigms is indeed in order. But that is not all. In addition to this theoretical critique, there is also a critique of the substantive questions raised by sociology and of the research methods used to answer them.

---

[23] For a discussion of such relations, see Bernard (1968, passim).

[24] Note, for example, the complacency of Parsons's (1949, p. 223) that "it is quite clear that in the adult feminine role there is quite sufficient strain and insecurity so that widespread manifestations are to be expected in the form of neurotic behavior." Or his statement that "absolute equality of opportunity is clearly incompatible with any positive solidarity of the family" (Parsons 1949, p. 174).

CAN SOCIOLOGY TRANSCEND SEX?

I once asked, "Can science transcend culture?" and gave an affirmative reply. Yes, I said, it could if the canons of scientific method were scrupulously observed (Bernard 1950). I am not so sure today.[25] But let that pass. What the fourth revolution asks today is, Can one particular science—sociology—transcend sex? With respect to both contents and methods? Can it become a science of society rather than a science of male society? Or than a male science of society?

To the charge leveled by the fourth revolution that the male bias of sociology to date has interfered with our knowledge-based understanding of the way our society operates, a plea of guilty is in order. There are questions about the functioning of our society that have not been raised or, if raised, not adequately attended to. As a result, we have a lopsided conceptualization of it. Hochschild (1970, p. 14) has reminded us how much our discipline suffers from the absence of the contribution of women. She specifies two kinds of costs, factual and paradigmatic, the first requiring that we figure out what is missing in our discipline, and the second that we get our heads straight.[26]

Sociology as a science of male society.—We can begin to figure out what is missing by looking at the kinds of questions the researcher asks, for, as we are becoming increasingly aware, they reveal his value as well as his acumen.[27] And so far men, of course have asked the questions.[28]

In a book on the future of marriage (Bernard 1972) I had occasion to summarize the large research literature on the so-called discrepant re-

[25] Many of the paradigms developed in the West have not proved successful in the Third World (Bernard 1973, chap. 9).

[26] Among the factual issues mentioned by her are knowledge of the undervalued role of fathers, the social origins of misogyny, female social mobility, the structured strain for women built into our society, the power relationships behind ordinary customs and personality traits, the change in sex differences in the several stages of the life cycle.

[27] For example, white social scientists have asked the questions about blacks that concerned them: the female-headed family, out-of-wedlock births, sexual mores, control. Black men have asked questions about powerlessness, race pride, genocide. Do the data dredged up by the two lines of questioning constitute the same science in both cases? What if one asks how white people can maintain their power over blacks (Blalock 1967, pp. 153–54) and the other how black people can achieve power over whites? Will the same technique fit both questions? Will they arrive at the same kinds of generalizations?

[28] Sociology is not alone in the male bias of its questions. Bart (1972) specifies areas in other disciplines dominated by a male perspective: research on contraception is overwhelmingly oriented to techniques which assign responsibility to women; the management of childbirth and breast-feeding; the psychoanalytic theory of depression; and field-independence–field-dependence research in psychology which assumes that field-independence, more characteristic of males, is superior to field-dependence in perception.

sponses husbands and wives give to identical questions; they tend to agree on a few items such as number of children, but discrepancies occur on almost everything else. Some of the discrepancy can be attributed to selective perception. But, in addition, the "realities" of marriage—the complex institutional web of law, religion, custom, mores that constitute marriage—really are different for husbands and wives. As, indeed, are the "realities" of other institutions. Not only do men and women view a common world from different perspectives, they view different worlds as well. The fourth revolution demands that we include the world women inhabit.

The idea that men and women inhabit different worlds is an old one.[29] I have found it useful to characterize them in terms of the nature of the bonds between and among people, one a status world in which the bonds are on a love/duty basis and the other, one in which they are based on a cash nexus characterized by monetary exchange.[30] By and large, women have lived in a status world and men in a cash-nexus world.[31] Practically all sociology to date has been a sociology of the male world.[32] The topics

[29] Kraditor (1968) has assembled some delineations of "women's sphere" in the 19th century; even today the idea of a "women's world" dominates the thinking of Madison Avenue. Sometimes the two worlds are delineated in terms of home or family and work (Henderson and Parsons 1947, sometimes in terms of subcultures (LeMasters 1957; Ann Battle-Sister 1971), and sometimes in terms of "place" (Epstein 1970).

[30] Only by definition do interactions in a status world constitute exchanges. We speak glibly of the give-and-take of marriage, but research shows that women make more adjustments than men. Interesting to note is the superiority, according to Richard Titmuss, of the blood gathered and distributed on a love/duty basis as in England over blood in this country where it is bought and sold on an exchange basis.

[31] A status world tends to be characterized by the first component of the five Parsonian variables: ascription, diffuseness, particularism, collectivity orientation, and affectivity; the cash-nexus world by their counterparts: achievement, specificity, universalism, self-orientation, and emotional neutrality (Bernard 1971b, pp. 24–25). In the cash-nexus world competition is the preferred way to allocate rewards, and the best man wins; in the status world everyone's needs are taken care of to the extent possible.

[32] Thus, for example, in a—deservedly—award-winning treatise on the American occupational structure, the two-fifths of the labor force constituted of women are excluded. Women appear only as contributors to husbands' careers (Blau and Duncan 1967, chap. 10. See also résumé of current research on the same topic by Mary Salpukas). A glance at the Parsons-Shils source book on sociological theories also shows how pervasive this one-sided orientation has been in sociology From precursors like Hobbes, Locke, Rousseau, and even Adam Smith to recent times, one gets a picture of society as constituted entirely of men. "Man" does this; "men" believe that. Half of the human species is invisible. Men are furiously interacting with one another, but one catches hardly a glimpse of any woman. The economists have been more candid and forthright. They state at the outset that they deal only with the cash-nexus world. This permits them to exclude the enormous contribution that housewives make, not because these services are dispensable for the operation of the economy—they would have to be supplied by industry if housewives did not perform them—but because they are not monetized. Sociologists have not specified that most of their paradigms also fit only that cash-nexus world. Kenneth Boulding (in press) helps to fill in the gap with what he calls the "grants economy." Like all good economists he

that have preoccupied sociologists have been the topics that preoccupy men: power, work, climbing the occupational ladder, conflict, and sex— but not women—or women only as adjuncts to men. When women have been dealt with in this sociology of male society, it has usually been in a chapter or a footnote on "the status of women," thrown in as an extra, almost beside the point, rather than as an intrinsic component of a total society. Very little sociology deals with the nature, structure, and functioning of a female status world. When it is dealt with at all, it is analyzed at its point of intersection with the cash-nexus or work world, as in the instance of the conflicting roles of working wives and mothers. Even here, the results of the work done by men and by women differ markedly.[33]

There is also another way to look at the sexist bias in sociology; it has to do not with a status world but with women as a collective entity, as much a component of our society as other conceptual entities, such as for example, "labor," "ethnic groups," youth, and all the others which are stock-in-trade for sociological analysts and hence worthy of attention. The women now seen by our discipline are almost exclusively viewed in their relations to men as daughters, wives, and mothers or, simply, as sexual partners. There may have been a time when such a limited perspective was justified. If so, it is no longer. Women have become a collective entity and can no longer be viewed exclusively as separate adjuncts to men, the lesser member of a pair. They need instead to be seen as an entity, not, to be sure, in terms of mindless stereotypical generalizations like "women

---

had always recognized that market economics was extremely limited; but unlike them he undertook to analyze the nonmarket or "grants economy," with interesting results: he re-discovered sociology. "The key to a theoretical approach to the grants economy . . . must lie . . . in the theory of the integrative structure of society. Grants fall into place as a perfectly normal, reasonable element of social life, once we realize that they give us a first-approximation measure of the structure of integrative relationships in society. We are familiar with the concept of 'an economy,' which is that part of the total social system that is organized by exchanges. We are less familiar with the concept of an 'integry,' which is that part of the total social system which deals with such concepts and relationships as status, identity, community, legitimacy, loyalty, love, trust, and so on. Nevertheless, this is a distinct segment of the social system with a dynamics of its own, and strong interactions with other elements of the social system" (Boulding 1969, p. 4). It is this "grants economy" which women for the most part inhabit and which has been neglected by male sociologists. Boulding develops the concept of the "sacrifice trap," showing how objects become sacred because they are sacrificed to rather than the other way round. All sacrifices are not grants, but all grants are sacrifices.

[33] For example, when Parsons (1959, pp. 262 ff.) tackles the problem of how the two systems are integrated, he concludes that, because they are governed by such different norms, integration occurs only if just one member in a marriage participates in the work world. Coser and Rokoff (1971, p. 552) call instead for a redefinition of life goals. They conclude (as I have done also) that shared roles in marriage are not only possible but eufunctional and may actually increase family cohesion. Papanek's (1971) analysis of purdah in Pakistan is almost a model of viewing the status and the cash-nexus worlds as parts of a total society.

are such and such" or "women do so and so" but as a collectivity with common bonds and interests, as the entity which the concept of "sisterhood" has taught so many of them to see, a collectivity different to be sure from others but no less indispensable to any analysis of a modern society.

Is it so unreasonable to look forward to a time when introductory texts begin with the fundamental sociological datum that all societies include two collectivities, one in which the members are characteristically smaller, slower, less physically powerful, etc., the other in which members are characteristically less tolerant of sexual deprivation, etc., but both of which must live together in a common locale? What structural outcomes can then be predicted under given technological and other related circumstances? What form will the social processes within and between these collectivities take? If we started coldly, without tittering, to ask how the sexual nature of the bond between members of the two collectivities resembled, or differed from, other kinds of bonds between members of other collectivities, taking nothing for granted, we might see many things more clearly. I am not, of course, seriously proposing that we begin with this datum, but I would be happy if the idea produced even a minuscule shift in at least one person's perspective.

Sociology as a male science of society.—No attempt is made here to explain the male bias in the subject matter sociologists deal with except to note that it is not wholly due to selective perception or limited perspective. It seems to be related also to methodological and technical predilections, for, as we have been reminded so often, we tend to choose our problems on the basis of available techniques rather than on the basis of intrinsic importance. In sociology, as in psychology, a masculine bias has been embedded in the structure of inquiry; the most prestigious methods have tended to be those that yielded "hard" data. And thereby hangs a most interesting tale, a tale of the part played by what might well be called a *machismo* factor in research.

Carlson (1971), a psychologist, has found that the classification of research approaches proposed by Bakan (1972) into "agency" and "communion" can be validated on the basis of several studies she has made. Agency tends to see variables,[34] communion to see human beings. Agentic research tends to see sex as a variable, communal research to see women as people.[35] Agency has to do with separation, repression, conquest, and

---

[34] Bakan (1972, p. 28) refers to the variable approach as a fact-module approach which views human behavior "in terms of specific variables, each of which could be studied separately, yet which, in conjunction, would ultimately 'explain' man and predict his behavior. With statistical tests of significance, one presumably could identify the relationships among variables, factoring out the noise of other uncontrolled variables. It was believed that when psychologists identified all possible relationships, of course, all such noise would be eliminated."

[35] Even as a variable, sex is usually seen in connection with variables that interest

contract; communion with fusion, expression, acceptance, noncontractual cooperation. Agency operates by way of mastery and control; communion with naturalistic observation, sensitivity to qualitative patterning, and greater personal participation by the investigator (Carlson 1972). Nothing in this polarity is fundamentally new. For almost 50 years I have watched one or another version of it in sociology.[36]

What is new and illuminating, however, is the recognition of a *machismo* element in research. The specific processes involved in agentic research are typically male preoccupations; agency is identified with a masculine principle, the Protestant ethic, a Faustian pursuit of knowledge—as with all forces toward mastery, separation, and ego enhancement (Carlson 1972). The scientist using this approach creates his own controlled reality. He can manipulate it. He is master. He has power. He can add or subtract or combine variables. He can play with a simulated reality like an Olympian god. He can remain at a distance, safely invisible behind his shield, uninvolved. The communal approach is much humbler. It disavows control, for control spoils the results. Its value rests precisely on the absence of controls. Jane van Lawick-Goodall (1971), observing primates in their natural habitat, imposed no controls on their life-style. She dealt with a quite different reality from that of H. P. Harlow in his laboratory.

In psychology, the research topics for which the agentic approach is most suitable have been such characteristically male variables as ego strength, reality orientation, objectivity, and delay of gratification. Carlson found corroboration of this observation in a study comparing work by men and by women psychologists: men preferred the agentic, women the communal approach. These findings and insights help to explain why, for reasons no one has yet formally explicated but which, I believe, most of us intuit, the agentic approach which yields "hard" data tends to have more prestige than the communal, which yields "soft" data. Apart from the double entendre in "hard" and "soft" data, one reason is that, as in all societies, what men do is valued more highly than what women do. Problems for which the agentic approach is appropriate attract males and hence have higher status than those for which the communal approach is

---

men more than women, such as aggression, achievement, and others having to do with power or control. There are far more studies on aggression and achievement than on love and tenderness. Females have thus been forced into inappropriate categories so that they have turned out to be merely non-men, and "different" has been read as "deficient." Psychological inquiry has therefore been "constricted and manipulative" and precluded from studying individuals except as "carriers" of variables of immediate interest to the—usually male—experimenter (Carlson 1972).

[36] For example: statistical vs. case method, quantitative vs. qualitative, knowledge vs. understanding or *verstehen,* tough-minded vs. tender-minded, and so on. These poles as related to methods have been paralleled by such conceptual polarities as *Gemeinschaft* and *Gesellschaft,* expressive and instrumental, status and cash nexus, and so on.

suitable. Until recently, in fact, many have argued that the agentic approach was the only scientific approach.[37]

There has been no analysis of sociological research comparable to Carlsons' in psychology.[38] But in a paper on "The Methods of Sociology," Coleman (1969, pp. 109–10) is quite optimistic about such agentic research techniques as quantitative measures and indices, improved techniques, social indicators, and laboratory experiments. Unhappily, he is skeptical about the future of such communal techniques as observation of social behavior in situ. Like Carlson, Coleman (1969, p. 86) speaks of "missing research methods that truncate sociology, and cause some important problems of the discipline and other problems important to society, to languish relatively unexplored." He finds sociologists inhibited

[37] The small coterie with expertise in quantitative and, especially, in mathematical agentic techniques have been able to exert disproportionate influence on the direction of the social- and behavioral-science disciplines. Proponents of the communal approach tend to be on the defensive. Once the *machismo* factor in research was called to my attention, a host of illustrations of how it operates to intimidate others crowded my memory. For example, the social scientist reduced to a pulp at a committee meeting evaluating grant proposals, when he argued in favor of a "soft" project. His willingness to defend it was used to denigrate him by techniques which only a master of communal research like Erving Goffman could do justice to. Or the faculty member who voted to accept a "soft" dissertation made to feel, as he put it, utterly incompetent. Or the editor, intimidated by his agentic referee, who rejected a manuscript because the analysis was not "hard" enough—no multiple regression equations, for example. He was more afraid of the disapproval of his agentic than of his communal constituencies. A standard criticism of the communal approach is that the data it yields are less replicable because they depend so much on the unique personality of the researcher. Isn't it, the criticism continues, more like art, idiosyncratic, a unique "vision" more than a testable scientific observation? The initial "vision" or "insight" is, indeed, as in most scientific innovations, much like that of the artist. But beyond that the communal method is not uniquely different from established procedures. The freshman looking through the microscope can rarely see what his professor tells him he should see. The laboratory manual is not replicable. For all he can tell, the professor could be making it all up. It takes some learning— even consciousness raising—to be able to see what the professor wants him to see. Who, for example, was able to see "lurk-lines," "body gloss," "interaction synchrony," "loller's tuck" (my favorite), before Erving Goffman (1971), like the professor in the laboratory, taught us to see them. With these "sensitizing concepts," even the most dyed-in-the-wool practitioner of agentic techniques can learn to observe them. The analogy with research on women is clear. Until women made clear a score of behavioral patterns that were visible to them but not to men, it was impossible for men to research them. Once attention had been called to them, the evidence of "oppression" —the fact that avant garde women had to use such a pejorative concept is a good example of the inadequacy of our conceptual tool kit—could be made visible to everyone. And I do not doubt that the agentic approach will, in the not-too-distant future, be invoked to study it. Opening up this enormous area in interpersonal relations is one of the major contributions the fourth revolution can make to our discipline.

[38] Except, perhaps, in the study of community power structure, in which the part played by research methods has been reported to be related to kinds of communities selected for study and hence to the results obtained (Bernard 1973, chap. 5).

from asking themselves fundamental questions about what problems are important ones to sociology, their vision narrowly restricted, their horizons limited" (Coleman 1969, p. 113).[39]

The relevance of these comments lies in the fact that, since the agentic approach has more prestige, a disproportionately large amount of research has been invested in the sociology of sex as a variable and a correspondingly smaller amount in the sociology of women as a collectivity, or as simply people. A great deal of research focuses on men with no reference at all to women; but when research is focused on women, it is almost always with reference to men. If comparisons are not made with men, the research is viewed as incomplete. Research on women in their own right, without reference to a male standard, is not viewed as worthy of male attention. Notice how uniformly journals assign books about women to female reviewers.

I close this truncated discussion of the way research mode affects choice of topics and findings with a personal example of the moral it points. In my book on academic women, "controlling" as many variables as I could, I was unable, by the agentic method (which is peculiarly inappropriate for research on the subtleties of interaction between the sexes), to document discrimination against women (Bernard 1964, chap. 3). Later researchers, going beyond one of my major "controls"—proportion of women in the qualified pool—explained by way of the communal approach why there were, relatively, so few women in it in terms of all the hurdles women had to overcome to arrive at the qualified pool.[40]

The implications of these comments is not that only women can study female reality. Or even that all women can, for women have been so trained to accept the male definition of almost every situation, to accept the reality constructed by men, that it takes a considerable amount of consciousness raising to get them to construct their own, even to believe in it. And even when the "conversion" takes place, it requires reinforcement to maintain the new consciousness. For the present, only sociologists whose consciousness has been raised will be able to deal adequately with the realities so urgently demanding study. Among them there will doubtless be some men, especially among those who have been so assiduously study-

---

[39] Coleman (1969, pp. 105–6) illustrates what he calls "research lacunae" with such examples as changes in the relation of youth to adult society and the increasing age segregation of the age. But he has not a word about women. This oversight by a master research sociologist is thought provoking.

[40] Much of this research is summarized in Roby (1972) and Rossi (1972). I hasten to save face by noting that I did recognize the importance of what I called the "stag effect" in accounting for scientific productivity (Bernard 1964, pp. 157, 302). I should add that my interest in that book was more in the sociology of knowledge than in the status of women in academia.

ing how to "become"—reality constructionists, marijuana users, world savers, nudists, and deviants. It should be no harder for men to "become" feminists than for them to "become" deviant in other ways.

In the meanwhile, I agree with Carlson who concludes that "by achieving liberation from the constraints of 'agentic' modes of inquiry and developing the 'communal' aspects of content and method, women [and their male confreres] may succeed in bringing forth those new research paradigms needed for the scientific revolution" (Carlson 1972) which will make sociology a genuine science of society.

ENVOI

All four of my revolutions have been important, necessary, and, I believe, have had a benign effect on our discipline. In the case of the first three, the evidence is in. It was essential for sociology in the 1920s that the ASS give official recognition to the importance of empirical research along with the grand conceptualizing of the early giants. It was essential that sociology be emancipated from the control, however benign, of one university, that the American Sociological Society achieve independence from the University of Chicago, great as that university was and great as its role as alma mater had been. It was essential that the neglect of social problems and policy be corrected, that the uncritical placing of sociological research know-how at the disposal of industry be criticized, that sociologists be protected against McCarthyism in the 1950s, that the Society for the Study of Social Problems shake its fist at the American Sociological Association. The American Sociological Association is a better organization and sociology itself a more adequate discipline as a result of these three revolutions.

Returns on the success of the fourth revolution are not yet all in. So far as the activist phase in the profession is concerned, it has been remarkably successful. The Rossi resolutions were favorably received; a Committee on the Status of Women was appointed; a section on the sociology of sex roles was established which will provide the matrix for important contributions to the needed expansion of our discipline. Much of this knowledge will be useful in helping to free women in society from the handicaps of discrimination. Now the question is, Will the harder phase—that of reorienting the paradigms to take account of women—be equally successful?

The reaction of sociologists, male and female, to the theoretical and methodological challenge of the fourth revolution will test the validity of its critique. Will they slough off the challenges as trivial, a passing fad, unworthy of serious professional attention? Will they impose a male test, namely, What will meeting the challenges add to our knowledge or potential for control and power? If not, why bother?

I would hope for at least some "conversions"; for a bemused "How about that?" or a friendly "They've got something there." And even if some reject the challenges, the fourth revolution will have achieved at least a modicum of success if it leads them to ask themselves if their writing would be any different if it included women; if, for example, instead of the generic "mankind," they had to say "humankind?" If, instead of the generic "man," they had to say "human being"?[41] If every generalization they made about the way societies operate had to include the ways the female component fit in?

Or if, on a more practical level, they remembered that the brilliant young women they talked to at meetings knew as much sociology as they did, if not more, so that they did not patronize them and, above all, did not try to co-opt them by flattery or put them down by ignoring them.

REFERENCES

Bakan, David. 1972. "Psychology Can Now Kick the Science Habit." *Psychology Today* 5 (March): 26, 28, 86–88.
Bart, Pauline. 1972. "Why Women's Studies?" In *Female Studies IV,* edited by Ray Siporin. Pittsburgh: KNOW.
Battle-Sister, Ann. 1971. "Conjectures on the Female Culture Question." *Journal of Marriage and the Family* 33 (August): 411–20.
Bernard, Jessie. 1950. "Can Science Transcend Culture?" *Scientific Monthly* 71 (October): 268–73.
———. 1964. *Academic Women.* University Park: Pennsylvania State University Press. Reprint. New York: Meridian Press, 1966.
———. 1966. "The Fourth Revolution." *Journal of Social Issues* 23 (April): 76–87.
———. 1968. *The Sex Game.* Englewood Heights, N.J.: Prentice-Hall. Reprint. New York: Atheneum Press, 1972.
———. 1971a. "The Parodox of the Happy Marriage." In *Women in Sexist Society,* edited by Vivian Gornick and Barbara Moran. New York: Basic Books.
———. 1971b. *Women and the Public Interest: An Essay on Policy and Protest.* Chicago: Aldine-Atherton.
———. 1972. *The Future of Marriage.* New York: World.
———. 1973. *The Sociology of Community.* Glenview, Ill.: Scott, Foresman.
Bernard, L. L., and Jessie Bernard. 1943. *Origins of American Sociology.* New York: Crowell. Reprint. New York: Russell & Russell, 1965.
Blalock, Hubert M., Jr. 1967. *Toward a Theory of Minority-Group Relations.* New York: Wiley.
Blau, Peter. 1964. *Exchange and Power in Social Life.* New York: Wiley.
Blau, Peter M., and Otis Dudley Duncan. 1967. *The American Occupational Structure.* New York: Wiley.
Boulding, Kenneth E. 1969. "The Grants Economy." *Michigan Academician* 1 (Winter): 4, 5.
———. In press. *The Economy of Love and Fear: A Preface to Grants Economics.* Belmont, Calif.: Wadsworth Publishing Company.

[41] Or "men and women," as Mills (1959, p. 225) did in the passage noted above.

Jessie Bernard

Broverman, Inge K., Donald M. Broverman, Frank E. Charlson, Paul S. Rosenkrantz, and Susan R. Vogel. 1970. "Sex-Role Stereotypes and Clinical Judgments of Mental Health." *Journal of Consulting and Clinical Psychology* 34 (February): 1–7.

Carlson, Rae. 1971. "Sex Differences in Ego Functioning: Exploratory Studies of Agency and Communion." *Journal of Consulting and Clinical Psychology* 37 (April): 267–77.

————. 1972. "Understanding Women: Implications for Personality Theory and Research." *Journal of Social Issues* 28(2).

Chmaj, Betty E. 1971. *American Women and American Studies*. Pittsburgh: KNOW.

Coleman, James S. 1969. "The Methods of Sociology. In *A Design for Sociology: Scope, Objectives, and Methods,* edited by Robert Bierstedt. Monograph no. 9, American Academy Political and Social Science. Philadelphia: American Academy of Political and Social Science.

Coser, Rose, and Gerald Rokoff. 1971. "Women in the Occupational World: Social Disruption and Conflict." *Social Problems* 18 (Spring): 535–54.

Dixon, Marlene. 1970. "The Failure of the Sociology Liberation Movement." Mimeographed.

Elder, Glen H., Jr. 1969. "Appearance and Education in Marriage Mobility." *American Sociological Review* 34 (August): 519–32.

Epstein, Cynthia. 1970. *Man's World Woman's Place*. Berkeley: University of California Press.

Ferriss, Abbott L. 1971. *Indicators of Trends in the Status of American Women*. New York: Russell Sage.

Friedan, Betty. 1963. *The Feminine Mystique*. New York: Norton.

Garfinkel, Harold. 1967. *Studies in Ethnomethodology*. Englewood Cliffs, N.J.: Prentice-Hall.

Goffman, Erving. 1971. *Relations in Public: Microstudies of the Public Order*. New York: Basic.

Greenwald, Maurine. 1971. "On Teaching Women's History." In *American Women and American Studies,* edited by Betty E. Camaj. Pittsburgh: KNOW.

Grønseth, Eric. 1971. "The Dysfunctionality of the Husband Provider Role in Industrialized Societies." Paper prepared for International Sociological Association, Varna.

Hanisch, Carol. 1971. "Male Psychology: A Myth to Keep Women in Their Place." *Women's World* 1 (July–August): 2.

Henderson, A. M., and Talcott Parsons, trans. 1947. "Introduction." In *The Theory of Social and Economic Organization,* by Max Weber. New York: Free Press.

Hochschild, Arlie. 1970. "The American Woman: Another Idol of Social Science." *Trans-Action* 8 (November–December): 13–14.

Horner, Matina. 1969. "Fail: Bright Women." *Psychology Today* 3 (November): 36, 38, 69.

Jones, Beverley. 1970. "The Dynamics of Marriage and Motherhood." In *Sisterhood Is Powerful,* edited by Robin Morgan. New York: Vintage.

Kraditor, Aileen. 1968. *Up from the Pedestal*. Chicago: Quadrangle.

LeMasters, E. E. 1957. *Modern Courtship and Marriage*. New York: Macmillan.

Mainardi, Pat. 1970. "The Politics of Housework." In *Sisterhood Is Powerful,* edited by Robin Morgan. New York: Vintage.

Mills, C. Wright. 1959. *The Sociological Imagination*. New York: Oxford.

Mintz, Geraldine (pseud.). 1967. "Some Observations on the Function of Women Sociologists at Sociology Conventions." *American Sociologist* 2 (August): 158–59.

Osmond, Marie, and Patricia Martin. "From Closed to Open Systems: Game Simulation of Sex Role Behavior." Unpublished manuscript.

Papanek, Hanna. 1971. "Purdah in Pakistan: Seclusion and Modern Occupations for Women." *Journal of Marriage and Family* 33 (August): 517–30.

Parsons, Talcott. 1949. "Age and Sex in the Social Structure of the United States." In *Essays in Sociological Theory*. New York: Free Press.

————. 1959. "The Social Structure of the Family." In *The Family: Its Function and Destiny,* edited by Ruth Nanda Anshen. New York: Harper.

Roby, Pamela. 1972. "Institutional and Internalized Barriers to Women in Higher Education." In *Toward a Sociology of Women,* edited by Constantina Safilios-Rothschild. Lexington, Mass.: Xerox College Publishing.

Rose, Arnold, ed. 1962. "Preface." In *Human Behavior and Social Processes.* Boston: Houghton-Mifflin.

Rossi, Alice, ed. 1972. *Academic Women on the Move.* New York: Russell Sage.

Salpukas, Mary. 1972. "The Man Who Gets Ahead: Being Married Really Helps." *New York Times,* July 24.

van Lawick-Goodall, Jane. 1971. *In the Shadow of Man.* Boston: Houghton-Mifflin.

Wyckoff, Hogie. 1971. "The Stroke Economy in Women's Scripts." *Journal of Transactional Analysis* 1 (July): 3.

Young, T. R. 1971. "The Politics of Sociology: Gouldner, Goffman, and Garfinkel." *American Sociologist* 6 (November): 276–81.

The Origins of the Women's Liberation Movement[1]

Jo Freeman

University of Chicago

The emergence in the last few years of a feminist movement caught most thoughtful observers by surprise. Women had "come a long way," had they not? What could they want to be liberated from? The new movement generated much speculation about the sources of female discontent and why it was articulated at this particular time. But these speculators usually asked the wrong questions. Most attempts to analyze the sources of social strain have had to conclude with Ferriss (1971, p. 1) that, "from the close perspective of 1970, events of the past decade provide evidence of no compelling cause of the rise of the new feminist movement." His examination of time-series data over the previous 20 years did not reveal any significant changes in socioeconomic variables which could account for the emergence of a women's movement at the time it was created. From such strain indicators, one could surmise that any time in the last two decades was as conducive as any other to movement formation.

I

The sociological literature is not of much help: the study of social movements "has been a neglected area of sociology" (Killian 1964, p. 426), and, within that field, virtually no theorists have dealt with movement origins. The *causes* of social movements have been analyzed (Gurr 1970; Davies 1962), and the *motivations* of participants have been investigated (Toch 1965; Cantril 1941; Hoffer 1951; Adorno et al. 1950; but the mechanisms of "how" a movement is constructed have received scant attention.[2] As Dahrendorf (1959, p. 64) commented, "The sociologist is generally interested not so much in the origin of social phenomena as in their spread and rise to wider significance." This interest is derived from an emphasis on cultural processes rather than on people as the major dynamic of social change (Killian 1964, p. 426). Consequently, even the "natural history" theorists have delineated the stages of development in a way that is too vague to tell us much about how movements actually start (Dawson and Gettys 1929, pp. 787–803; Lowi 1971, p. 39; Blumer 1951;

---

[1] I would like to thank Richard Albares and Florence Levinsohn for having read and criticized earlier versions of this paper.

[2] "A consciously directed and organized movement cannot be explained merely in terms of the psychological disposition or motivation of people, or in terms of a diffusion of an ideology. Explanations of this sort have a deceptive plausibility, but overlook the fact that *a movement has to be constructed* and has to carve out a career in what is practically always an opposed, resistant or at least indifferent world" (Blumer 1957, p. 147; italics mine).

King 1956), and a theory as comprehensive as Smelser's (1963) is postulated on too abstract a level to be of microsociological value (for a good critique, see Currie and Skolnick [1970]).

Part of the problem results from extreme confusion about what a social movement really is. Movements are rarely studied as distinct social phenomena but are usually subsumed under one of two theoretical traditions: that of "collective behavior" (see, especially, Smelser 1963; Lang and Lang 1961; Turner and Killian 1957) and that of interest-group and party formation (Heberle 1951; King 1956; Lowi 1971). The former emphasizes the spontaneous aspects of a movement; and the latter, the structured ones. Yet movements are neither fully collective behavior nor incipient interest groups except in the broadest sense of these terms. Rather, they contain essential elements of both. It is "the dual imperative of spontaneity and organization [that] . . . sets them apart from pressure groups and other types of voluntary associations, which lack their spontaneity, and from mass behavior, which is altogether devoid of even the rudiments of organization" (Lang and Lang 1961, p. 497).

Recognizing with Heberle (1951, p. 8) that "movements *as such* are not organized groups," it is still the structured aspects which are more amenable to study, if not always the most salient. Turner and Killian (1957, p. 307) have argued that it is when "members of a public who share a common position concerning the issue at hand supplement their informal person-to-person discussion with some organization to promote their convictions more effectively and insure more sustained activity, a social movement is incipient" (see also Killian 1964, p. 426). Such organization(s) and other core groups of a movement not only determine much of its conscious policy but serve as foci for its values and activities. Just as it has been argued that society as a whole has a cultural and structural "center" about which most members of the society are more or less "peripheral" (Shils 1970), so, too, can a social movement be conceived of as having a center and a periphery. An investigation into a movement's origins must be concerned with the microstructural preconditions for the emergence of such a movement center. From where do the people come who make up the initial, organizing cadre of a movement? How do they come together, and how do they come to share a similar view of the world in circumstances which compel them to political action? In what ways does the nature of the original center affect the future development of the movement?

II

Most movements have very inconspicuous beginnings. The significant elements of their origins are usually forgotten or distorted by the time a

Jo Freeman

trained observer seeks to trace them out, making retroactive analyses difficult. Thus, a detailed investigation of a single movement at the time it is forming can add much to what little is known about movement origins. Such an examination cannot uncover all of the conditions and ingredients of movement formation, but it can aptly illustrate both weaknesses in the theoretical literature and new directions for research. During the formative period of the women's liberation movement, I had many opportunities to observe, log, and interview most of the principals involved in the early movement.[3] The descriptive material in Section III is based on that data. This analysis, supplemented by five other origin studies made by me, would support the following three propositions:

Proposition 1: The need for a preexisting communications network or infrastructure within the social base of a movement is a primary prerequisite for "spontaneous" activity. Masses alone don't form movements, however discontented they may be. Groups of previously unorganized individuals may spontaneously form into small local associations—usually along the lines of informal social networks—in response to a specific strain or crisis, but, if they are not linked in some manner, the protest does not become generalized: it remains a local irritant or dissolves completely. If a movement is to spread rapidly, the communications network must already exist. If only the rudiments of one exist, movement formation requires a high input of "organizing" activity.

Proposition 2: Not just any communications network will do. It must be a network that is *co-optable* to the new ideas of the incipient movement.[4] To be co-optable, it must be composed of like-minded people whose background, experiences, or location in the social structure make them receptive to the ideas of a specific new movement.

Proposition 3: Given the existence of a co-optable communications network, or at least the rudimentary development of a potential one, and a situation of strain, one or more precipitants are required. Here, two distinct patterns emerge that often overlap. In one, a crisis galvanizes the network into spontaneous action in a new direction. In the other, one or more

[3] As a founder and participant in the younger branch of the Chicago women's liberation movement from 1967 through 1969 and editor of the first (at that time, only) national newsletter, I was able, through extensive correspondence and interviews, to keep a record of how each group around the country first started, where the organizers got the idea from, who they had talked to, what conferences were held and who attended, the political affiliations (or lack of them) of the first members, etc. Although I was a member of Chicago NOW, information on the origins of it and the other older branch organizations comes entirely through ex post facto interviews of the principals and examination of early papers in preparation for my dissertation on the women's liberation movement. Most of my informants requested that their contribution remain confidential.

[4] The only use of this significant word appears rather incidentally in Turner (1964, p. 123).

persons begin organizing a new organization or disseminating a new idea. For spontaneous action to occur, the communications network must be well formed or the initial protest will not survive the incipient stage. If it is not well formed, organizing efforts must occur; that is, one or more persons must specifically attempt to construct a movement. To be successful, organizers must be skilled and must have a fertile field in which to work. If no communications network already exists, there must at least be emerging spontaneous groups which are acutely atuned to the issue, albeit uncoordinated. To sum up, if a co-optable communications network is already established, a crisis is all that is necessary to galvanize it. If it is rudimentary, an organizing cadre of one or more persons is necessary. Such a cadre is superfluous if the former conditions fully exist, but it is essential if they do not.

Before examining these propositions in detail, let us look at the structure and origins of the women's liberation movement.

III

The women's liberation movement manifests itself in an almost infinite variety of groups, styles, and organizations. Yet, this diversity has sprung from only two distinct origins whose numerous offspring remain clustered largely around these two sources. The two branches are often called "reform" and "radical," or, as the sole authoritative book on the movement describes them, "women's rights" and "women's liberation" (Hole and Levine 1971). Unfortunately, these terms actually tell us very little, since feminists do not fit into the traditional Left/Right spectrum. In fact, if an ideological typography were possible, it would show minimal consistency with any other characteristic. Structure and style rather than ideology more accurately differentiate the two branches, and, even here, there has been much borrowing on both sides.

I prefer simpler designations: the first of the branches will be referred to as the older branch of the movement, partly because it began first and partly because the median age of its activists is higher. It contains numerous organizations, including the lobbyist group (Women's Equity Action League), a legal foundation (Human Rights for Women), over 20 caucuses in professional organizations, and separate organizations of women in the professions and other occupations. Its most prominent "core group" is the National Organization for Women (NOW), which was also the first to be formed.

While the written programs and aims of the older branch span a wide spectrum, their activities tend to be concentrated on legal and economic problems. These groups are primarily made up of women—and men—who work, and they are substantially concerned with the problems of working women. The style of organization of the older branch tends to be traditionally formal, with elected officers, boards of directors, bylaws, and the other trappings of democratic procedure. All started as top-down national organizations, lacking in a mass base. Some have subsequently developed a mass base, some have not yet done so, and others do not want to.

Conversely, the younger branch consists of innumerable small groups—engaged in a variety of activities—whose contact with each other is, at best, tenuous. Contrary to popular myth, it did not begin on the campus nor was it started by the Students for a Democratic Society (SDS). However, its activators were, to be trite, on the other side of the generation gap. While few were students, all were "under 30" and had received their political education as participants or concerned observers of the social action projects of the last decade. Many came direct from New Left and civil rights organizations. Others had attended various courses on women in the multitude of free universities springing up around the country during those years.

The expansion of these groups has appeared more amoebic than organized, because the younger branch of the movement prides itself on its lack of organization. From its radical roots, it inherited the idea that structures were always conservative and confining, and leaders, isolated and elitist. Thus, eschewing structure and damning the idea of leadership, it has carried the concept of "everyone doing her own thing" to the point where communication is haphazard and coordination is almost nonexistent. The thousands of sister chapters around the country are virtually independent of each other, linked only by numerous underground papers, journals, newsletters, and cross-country travelers. A national conference was held over Thanksgiving in 1968 but, although considered successful, has not yet been repeated. Before the 1968 conference, the movement did not have the sense of national unity which emerged after the conference. Since then, young feminists have made no attempt to call another national conference. There have been a few regional conferences, but no permanent consequences resulted. At most, some cities have a coordinating committee which attempts to maintain communication among local groups and to channel newcomers into appropriate ones, but these committees have no power over any group's activities, let alone its ideas. Even local activists do not know how big the movement is in their own city. While it cannot be said to have no organization at all, this branch of the movement has informally adopted a general policy of "structurelessness."

Despite a lack of a formal policy encouraging it, there is a great deal of homogeneity within the younger branch of the movement. Like the older branch, it tends to be predominantly white, middle class, and college educated. But it is much more homogenous and, unlike the older branch, has been unable to diversify. This is largely because most small groups tend to form among friendship networks. Most groups have no requirements for membership (other than female sex), no dues, no written and agreed-upon structure, and no elected leaders. Because of this lack of structure, it is often easier for an individual to form a new group than to find and join an older one. This encourages group formation but discourages individual diversification. Even contacts among groups tend to be along friendship lines.

In general, the different style and organization of the two branches was largely derived from the different kind of political education and experiences of each group of women. Women of the older branch were trained in and had used the traditional forms of political action, while the younger branch has inherited the loose, flexible, person-oriented attitude of the youth and student movements. The different structures that have evolved from these two distinctly different kinds of experience have, in turn, largely determined the strategy of the two branches, irrespective of any conscious intentions of their participants. These different structures and strategies have each posed different problems and possibilities. Intra-movement differences are often perceived by the participants as conflicting, but it is their essential complementarity which has been one of the strengths of the movement.

Despite the multitude of differences, there are very strong similarities in the way the two branches came into being. These similarities serve to illuminate some of the microsociological factors involved in movement formation. The forces which led to NOW's formation were first set in motion in 1961 when President Kennedy established the President's Commission on the Status of Women at the behest of Esther Petersen,[5] to be chaired by Eleanor Roosevelt. Operating under a broad mandate, its 1963 report (*American Women*) and subsequent committee publications documented just how thoroughly women are still denied many rights and opportunities. The·most concrete response to the activity of the president's commission was the eventual establishment of 50 state commissions to do similar research on a state level. These commissions were often urged by politically active women and were composed primarily of women. Nonetheless, many believe the main stimulus behind their formation was the alleged view of the governors that the commissions were excellent opportunities to pay political debts without giving women more influential positions.

The activity of the federal and state commissions laid the groundwork for the future movement in three significant ways: (1) it brought together many knowledgeable, politically active women who otherwise would not

[5] Then director of the Women's Bureau.

have worked together around matters of direct concern to women; (2) the investigations unearthed ample evidence of women's unequal status, especially their legal and economic difficulties, in the process convincing many previously uninterested women that something should be done; (3) the reports created a climate of expectations that something would be done. The women of the federal and state commissions who were exposed to these influences exchanged visits, correspondence, and staff and met with each other at an annual commission convention. Thus, they were in a position to share and mutually reinforce their growing awareness and concern over women's issues. These commissions thus created an embryonic communications network among people with similar concerns.

During this time, two other events of significance occurred. The first was the publication of Betty Friedan's (1963) book, *The Feminine Mystique*. An immediate best seller, it stimulated many women to question the status quo and some to suggest to Friedan that a new organization be formed to attack their problems. The second event was the addition of "sex" to Title VII of the 1964 Civil Rights Act. Many men thought the "sex" provision was a joke (Bird 1968, chap. 1). The Equal Employment Opportunity Commission (EEOC) certainly treated it as one and refused to adequately enforce it. The first EEOC executive director even stated publicly that the provision was a "fluke" that was "conceived out of wedlock" (Edelsberg 1965). But, within the EEOC, there was a "pro-woman" coterie which argued that "sex" would be taken more seriously if there were "some sort of NAACP for women" to put pressure on the government. As government employees, they couldn't organize such a group, but they spoke privately with those whom they thought might be able to do so. One who shared their views was Rep. Martha Griffiths of Michigan. She blasted the EEOC's attitude in a June 20, 1966 speech on the House floor (Griffiths 1966) declaring that the agency had "started out by casting disrespect and ridicule on the law" but that their "wholly negative attitude had changed—for the worse."

On June 30, 1966, these three strands of incipient feminism were knotted together to form NOW. The occasion was the last day of the Third National Conference of Commissions on the Status of Women, ironically titled "Targets for Action." The participants had all received copies of Rep. Griffith's remarks. The opportunity came with a refusal by conference officials to bring to the floor a proposed resolution that urged the EEOC to give equal enforcement to the sex provision of Title VII as was given to the race provision. Despite the fact that these state commissions were not federal agencies, officials replied that one government agency could not be allowed to pressure another. The small group of women who had desired the resolution had met the night before in

Friedan's hotel room to discuss the possibility of a civil rights organization for women. Not convinced of its need, they chose instead to propose the resolution. When the resolution was vetoed, the women held a whispered conversation over lunch and agreed to form an action organization "to bring women into full participation in the mainstream of American society now, assuming all the privileges and responsibilities thereof in truly equal partnership with men." The name NOW was coined by Friedan, who was at the conference researching her second book. Before the day was over, 28 women paid $5.00 each to join (Friedan 1967).

By the time the organizing conference was held the following October 29–30, over 300 men and women had become charter members. It is impossible to do a breakdown on the composition of the charter membership, but one of the first officers and board is possible. Such a breakdown accurately reflected NOW's origins. Friedan was president, two former EEOC commissioners were vice-presidents, a representative of the United Auto Workers Women's Committee was secretary-treasurer, and there were seven past and present members of the State Commissions on the Status of Women on the 20-member board. Of the charter members, 126 were Wisconsin residents—and Wisconsin had the most active state commission. Occupationally, the board and officers were primarily from the professions, labor, government, and the communications industry. Of these, only those from labor had any experience in organizing, and they resigned a year later in a dispute over support of the Equal Rights Amendment. Instead of organizational expertise, what the early NOW members had was media experience, and it was here that their early efforts were aimed.

As a result, NOW often gave the impression of being larger than it was. It was highly successful in getting publicity, much less so in bringing about concrete changes or organizing itself. Thus, it was not until 1969, when several national news media simultaneously decided to do major stories on the women's liberation movement, that NOW's membership increased significantly. Even today, there are only 8,000 members, and the chapters are still in an incipient stage of development.

In the meantime, unaware of and unknown to NOW, the EEOC, or to the state commissions, younger women began forming their own movement. Here, too, the groundwork had been laid some years before. Social action projects of recent years had attracted many women, who were quickly shunted into traditional roles and faced with the self-evident contradiction of working in a "freedom movement" without being very free. No single "youth movement" activity or organization is responsible for the younger branch of the women's liberation movement; together they created a "radical community" in which like-minded people continually interacted with each other. This community consisted largely of those who had participated in one or more of the many protest activities of the sixties and had established its own ethos and its own institutions. Thus, the women in it thought of themselves as "movement people" and had incorporated the adjective "radical" into their personal identities. The values of their radical identity and the style to which they had been trained by their movement participation directed them to approach most problems as political ones which could be solved by organizing. What remained was to translate their individual feelings of "unfreedom" into a collective consciousness. Thus, the radical community provided not only the necessary network of communication; its radical ideas formed the framework of analysis which "explained" the dismal situation in which radical women found themselves.

Papers had been circulated on women,[6] and temporary women's caususes had been held as early as 1964, when Stokely Carmichael made his infamous remark that "the only position for women in SNCC is prone." But it was not until late 1967 and 1968 that the groups developed a determined, if cautious, continuity and began to consciously expand themselves. At least five groups in five different cities (Chicago, Toronto, Detroit, Seattle, and Gainesville, Florida) formed spontaneously, independent of each other. They came at a very auspicious movement. The year 1967 was the one in which the blacks kicked the whites out of the civil rights movement, student power had been discredited by SDS, and the organized New Left was on the wane. Only draft-resistance activities were on the increase, and this movement more than any other exemplified the social inequities of the sexes. Men could resist the draft; women could only counsel resistance.

What was significant about this point in time was that there was a lack of available opportunities for political work. Some women fit well into the "secondary role" of draft counseling. Many did not. For years, their complaints of unfair treatment had been ignored by movement men with the dictum that those things could wait until after the revolution. Now these movement women found time on their hands, but the men would still not listen.

A typical example was the event which precipitated the formation of the Chicago group, the first independent group in this country. At the August 1967 National Conference for New Politics convention, a women's caucus met for days but was told its resolution wasn't significant enough to merit a floor discussion. By threatening to tie up the convention with procedural motions, the women succeeded in having their statement tacked to the end of the agenda. It was never discussed. The chair refused to

---

[6] "A Kind of Memo," by Hayden and King (1966, p. 35) circulated in the fall of 1965 (and eventually published), was the first such paper.

recognize any of the many women standing by the microphone, their hands straining upward. When he instead called on someone to speak on "the forgotten American, the American Indian," five women rushed the podium to demand an explanation. But the chairman just patted one of them on the head (literally) and told her, "Cool down little girl. We have more important things to talk about than women's problems."

The "little girl" was Shulamith Firestone, future author of *The Dialectic of Sex* (1971), and she didn't cool down. Instead, she joined with another Chicago woman, who had been trying to organize a women's group that summer, to call a meeting of those women who had half-heartedly attended the summer meetings. Telling their stories to those women, they stimulated sufficient rage to carry the group for three months, and by that time it was a permanent institution.

Another somewhat similar event occurred in Seattle the following winter. At the University of Washington, an SDS organizer was explaining to a large meeting how white college youth established rapport with the poor whites with whom they were working. "He noted that sometimes after analyzing societal ills, the men shared leisure time by 'balling a chick together.' He pointed out that such activities did much to enhance the political consciousness of the poor white youth. A woman in the audience asked, 'And what did it do for the consciousness of the chick?'" (Hole and Levine 1971, p. 120). After the meeting, a handful of enraged women formed Seattle's first group.

Groups subsequent to the initial five were largely organized rather than emerging spontaneously out of recent events. In particular, the Chicago group was responsible for the creation of many new groups in that city and elsewhere and started the first national newsletter. The 1968 conference was organized by the Washington D.C. group from resources provided by the Center for Policy Studies (CPS), a radical research organization. Using CPS facilities, this group subsequently became a main literature-distribution center. Although New York groups organized early and were featured in the 1969–70 media blitz, New York was not a source of early organizers.[7]

Unlike NOW, the women in the first groups had had years of experience as local-level organizers. They did not have the resources, or the desire, to form a national organization, but they knew how to utilize the infrastructure of the radical community, the underground press, and the

---

[7] The movement in New York has been more diverse than other cities and has made many major ideological contributions, but, contrary to popular belief, it did not begin in New York. In putting together their stories, the news media, concentrated as they are in New York, rarely looked past the Hudson for their information. This eastern bias is exemplified by the fact that, although the younger branch of the movement has no national organization and abjures leadership, all but one of those women designated by the press as movement leaders live in New York.

free universities to disseminate ideas on women's liberation. Chicago, as a center of New Left activity, had the largest number of politically conscious organizers. Many traveled widely to Left conferences and demonstrations, and most used the opportunity to talk with other women about the new movement. In spite of public derision by radical men, or perhaps because of it, young women steadily formed new groups around the country.

Initially, the new movement found it hard to organize on the campus, but, as a major congregating area of women and, in particular, of women with political awareness, campus women's liberation groups eventually became ubiquitous. While the younger branch of the movement never formed any organization larger or more extensive than a city-wide coordinating committee, it would be fair to say that it has a larger "participationship" than NOW and the other older branch organizations. While the members of the older branch knew how to use the media and how to form national structures, the women of the younger branch were skilled in local community organizing.

IV

From this description, there appear to be four essential elements contributing to the emergence of the women's liberation movement in the mid-sixties: (1) the growth of a preexisting communications network which was (2) co-optable to the ideas of the new movement; (3) a series of crises that galvanized into action people involved in this network, and/or (4) subsequent organizing effort to weld the spontaneous groups together into a movement. To further understand these factors, let us examine them in detail with reference to other relevant studies.

1. Both the Commissions on the Status of Women and the "radical community" created a communications network through which those women initially interested in creating an organization could easily reach others. Such a network had not previously existed among women. Historically tied to the family and isolated from their own kind, women are perhaps the most organizationally underdeveloped social category in Western civilization. By 1950, the 19th-century organizations which had been the basis of the suffrage movement—the Women's Trade Union League, the General Federation of Women's Clubs, the Women's Christian Temperance Union, the National American Women's Suffrage Association—were all either dead or a pale shadow of their former selves. The closest exception was the National Women's Party (NWP), which has remained dedicated to feminist concerns since its inception in 1916. However, since 1923, it has been essentially a lobbying group for the Equal Rights Amendment. The NWP, having always believed that a small group

of women concentrating their efforts in the right places was more effective than a mass appeal, was not appalled that, as late as 1969, even the majority of avowed feminists in this country had never heard of the NWP or the ERA.

References to the salience of a preexisting communications network appear frequently in the case studies of social movements, but it has been given little attention in the theoretical literature. It is essentially contrary to the mass-society theory which "for many . . . is . . . the most pertinent and comprehensive statement of the genesis of modern mass movements" (Pinard 1968, p. 682). This theory hypothesizes that those most likely to join a mass movement are those who are atomized and isolated from "a structure of groups intermediate between the family and the nation" (Kornhauser 1959, p. 93). However, the lack of such intermediate structures among women has proved more of a hindrance than a help in movement formation. Even today, it is those women who are most atomized, the housewives, who are least likely to join a feminist group.

The most serious attack on mass-society theory was made by Pinard (1971) in his study of the Social Credit Party of Quebec. He concluded that intermediate structures exerted *mobilizing* as well as restraining effects on individuals' participation in social movements because they formed communications networks that assisted in the rapid spread of new ideas. "When strains are severe and widespread," he contended, "a new movement is more likely to meet its early success among the more strongly integrated citizens" (Pinard 1971, p. 192).

Other evidence also attests to the role of previously organized networks in the rise and spread of a social movement. According to Buck (1920, pp. 43–44), the Grange established a degree of organization among American farmers in the 19th century which greatly facilitated the spread of future farmers' protests. In Saskatchewan, Lipset (1959) has asserted, "The rapid acceptance of new ideas and movements . . . can be attributed mainly to the high degree of organization. . . . The role of the social structure of the western wheat belt in facilitating the rise of new movements has never been sufficiently appreciated by historians and sociologists. Repeated challenges and crises forced the western farmers to create many more community institutions . . . than are necessary in a more stable area. These groups in turn provided a structural basis for immediate action in critical situations. [Therefore] though it was a new radical party, the C.C.F. did not have to build up an organization from scratch." More recently, the civil rights movement was built upon the infrastructure of the Southern black church (King 1958), and early SDS organizers made ready use of the National Student Association (Kissinger and Ross 1968, p. 16).

Indirect evidence of the essential role of formal and informal communications networks is found in diffusion theory, which emphasizes the importance of personal interaction rather than impersonal media communication in the spread of ideas (Rogers 1962; Lionberger 1960), and in Coleman's (1957) investigations of prior organizations in the initial development of conflict.

Such preexisting communications networks appear to be not merely valuable but prerequisites, as one study on "The Failure of an Incipient Social Movement" (Jackson, Peterson, Bull, Monsen, and Richmond 1960) made quite clear. In 1957, a potential tax-protest movement in Los Angeles generated considerable interest and public notice for a little over a month but was dead within a year. According to the authors, its failure to sustain itself beyond initial spontaneous protest was largely due to "the lack of a pre-existing network of communications linking those groups of citizens most likely to support the movement" (Jackson et al. 1960, p. 40). They said (p. 37) that "if a movement is to grow rapidly, it cannot rely upon its own network of communication, but must capitalize on networks already in existence."

The development of the women's liberation movement highlights the salience of such a network precisely because the conditions for a movement existed *before* a network came into being, but the movement didn't exist until afterward. Socioeconomic strain did not change for women significantly during a 20-year period. It was as great in 1955 as in 1965. What changed was the organizational situation. It was not until a communications network developed among like-minded people beyond local boundaries that the movement could emerge and develop past the point of occasional, spontaneous uprising.

2. However, not just any network would do; it had to be one which was co-optable by the incipient movement because it linked like-minded people likely to be predisposed to the new ideas of the movement. The 180,000-member Federation of Business and Professional Women's (BPW) Clubs would appear to be a likely base for a new feminist movement but in fact was unable to assume this role. It had steadily lobbied for legislation of importance to women, yet as late as "1966 BPW rejected a number of suggestions that it redefine . . . goals and tactics and become a kind of 'NAACP for women' . . . out of fear of being labeled 'feminist' " (Hole and Levine 1971, p. 81). While its membership has become a recruiting ground for feminism, it could not initially overcome the ideological barrier to a new type of political action.

On the other hand, the women of the President's and State Commissions on the Status of Women and the feminist coterie of the EEOC were co-optable, largely because their immersion into the facts of female status and the details of sex-discrimination cases made them very conscious of the need for change. Likewise, the young women of the "radical community" lived in an atmosphere of questioning, confrontation, and change. They absorbed an ideology of "freedom" and "liberation" far more potent than any latent "antifeminism" might have been. The repeated contradictions between these ideas and the actions of their male colleagues created a compulsion for action which only required an opportunity to erupt. This was provided by the "vacuum of political activity" of 1967–68.

The nature of co-optability is much more difficult to elucidate. Heretofore, it has been dealt with only tangentially. Pinard (1971, p. 186) noted the necessity for groups to *"possess* or *develop* an ideology or simply subjective interests congruent with that of a new movement" for them to "act as mobilizing rather than restraining agents toward that movement" but did not further explore what affected the "primary group climate." More illumination is provided by the diffusion of innovation studies which point out the necessity for new ideas to fit in with already-established norms for changes to happen easily. Furthermore, a social system which has as a value "innovativeness" itself (as the radical community did) will more rapidly adopt ideas than one which looks upon the habitual performance of traditional practices as the ideal (as most organized women's groups did in the fifties). Usually, as Lionberger (1960, p. 91) points out, "people act in terms of past experience and knowledge." People who have had similar experiences are likely to share similar perceptions of a situation and to mutually reinforce those perceptions as well as their subsequent interpretation.

A co-optable network, therefore, is one whose members have had common experiences which predispose them to be receptive to the particular new ideas of the incipient movement and who are not faced with structural or ideological barriers to action. If the new movement as an "innovation" can interpret these experiences and perceptions in ways that point out channels for social action, then participation in social movement becomes the logical thing to do.

3. As our examples have illustrated, these similar perceptions must be translated into action. This is the role of the "crisis." For women of the older branch of the movement, the impetus to organize was the refusal of the EEOC to enforce the sex provision of Title VII, precipitated by the concomitant refusal of federal officials at the conference to allow a supportive resolution. For younger women, there were a series of minor crises. Such precipitating events are common to most movements. They serve to crystallize and focus discontent. From their own experiences, directly and concretely, people feel the need for change in a situation that allows for an exchange of feelings with others, mutual validation, and a subsequent reinforcement of innovative interpretation. Perception of an immediate need for change is a major factor in predisposing people to

accept new ideas (Rogers 1962, p. 280). Nothing makes desire for change more acute than a crisis. If the strain is great enough, such a crisis need not be a major one; it need only embody symbolically collective discontent.

4. However, a crisis will only catalyze a well-formed communications network. If such networks are only embryonically developed or only partially co-optable, the potentially active individuals in them must be linked together by someone. As Jackson et al. (1960, p. 37) stated, "Some protest may persist where the source of trouble is constantly present. But interest ordinarily cannot be maintained unless there is a welding of spontaneous groups into some stable organization." In other words, people must be organized. Social movements do not simply occur.

The role of the organizer in movement formation is another neglected aspect of the theoretical literature. There has been great concern with leadership, but the two roles are distinct and not always performed by the same individual. In the early stages of a movement, it is the organizer much more than any "leader" who is important, and such an individual or cadre must often operate behind the scenes.[8] Certainly, the "organizing cadre" that young women in the radical community came to be was key to the growth of that branch of the women's liberation movement, despite the fact that no "leaders" were produced (and were actively discouraged). The existence of many leaders but no organizers in the older branch of the women's liberation movement and its subsequent slow development would tend to substantiate this hypothesis.

The crucial function of the organizer has been explored indirectly in other areas of sociology. Rogers (1962) devotes many pages to the "change agent" who, while he does not necessarily weld a group together or "construct" a movement, does do many of the same things for agricultural innovation that an organizer does for political change. Mass-society theory makes reference to the "agitator" but fails to do so in any kind of truly informative way. A study of farmer's movements indicates that many core organizations were organized by a single individual before the spontaneous aspects of the movement predominated. Further, many other core groups were subsidized by older organizations, federal and state governments, and even by local businessmen (Salisbury 1969, p. 13). These organizations often served as training centers for organizers and sources of material support to aid in the formation of new interest groups and movements.

Similarly, the civil rights movement provided the training for many another movement's organizers, including the young women of the women's

---

[8] The nature and function of these two roles was most clearly evident in the Townsend old-age movement of the thirties. Townsend was the "charismatic" leader, but the movement was organized by his partner, real estate promoter Robert Clements. Townsend himself acknowledges that, without Clement's help, the movement would never have gone beyond the idea stage (see Holzman 1963).

liberation movement. It would appear that the art of "constructing" a social movement is something that requires considerable skill and experience. Even in the supposedly spontaneous social movement, the professional is more valuable than the amateur.

V

The ultimate results of such "construction" are not independent of their origins. In fact, the attitudes and styles of a movement's initiators often have an effect which lasts longer than they do. Those women and men who formed NOW, and its subsequent sister organizations, created a national structure prepared to use the legal, political, and media institutions of our country. This it has done. The EEOC has changed many of its prejudicial attitudes toward women in its recent rulings. Numerous lawsuits have been filed under the sex provision of Title VII of the Civil Rights Act. The Equal Rights Amendment has passed Congress. Complaints have been filed against over 400 colleges and universities, as well as many businesses, charging violation of Executive Order 11246 amended by 11375, which prohibits sex discrimination by all holders of federal contracts. Articles on feminism have appeared in virtually every national news medium, and women's liberation has become a household word.

These groups have and continue to function primarily as pressure groups within the limits of traditional political activity. Consequently, their actual membership remains small. Diversification of the older branch of the movement has been largely along occupational lines and primarily within the professions. Activity has stressed using the tools for change provided by the system, however limited these may be. Short-range goals are emphasized, and no attempt has been made to place them within a broader ideological framework.

Initially, this structure hampered the development, of older branch organizations. NOW suffered three splits between 1967 and 1968. As the only action organization concerned with women's rights, it had attracted many different kinds of people with many different views on what and how to proceed. With only a national structure and, at that point, no local base, it was difficult for individuals to pursue their particular concern on a local level; they had to persuade the whole organization to support them. Given NOW's top-down structure and limited resources, this placed severe limits on diversity and, in turn, severe strains on the organization. Additional difficulties for local chapters were created by a lack of organizers to develop new chapters and the lack of a program into which they could fit. NOW's initiators were very high-powered women who lacked the time or patience for the slow, unglamorous, and tedious work of putting together a mass organization. Chapter development had to wait for the national media to attract women to the organization or the considerable physical mobility of contemporary women to bring proponents into new territory. Locally, women had to find some common concern around which to organize. Unlike that of New York, which had easy access to the national media and many people skilled at using it, the other chapters had difficulty developing programs not dependent on the media. Since the national program consisted almost exclusively of support of legal cases or federal lobbying, the regional chapters could not easily fit into that either. Eventually, connections were made; and, in the last year, national task forces have begun to correlate with local efforts so that individual projects can combine a national thrust with instrumentation on the local level. After initial difficulties, NOW and the other older branch organizations are thriving at this point because they are able to effectively use the institutional tools which our society provides for social and political change. Yet, these groups are also limited by these tools to the rather narrow arenas within which they are designed to operate. The nature of these arenas and the particular skills they require for participation already limit both the kind of women who can effectively work in older branch groups and the activities they can undertake. When their scope is exhausted, it remains to be seen whether organizations such as NOW will wither, institutionalize themselves as traditional pressure groups, or show the imagination to develop new lines for action.

The younger branch has had an entirely different history and faces different prospects. It was able to expand rapidly in the beginning because it could capitalize on the infrastructure of organizations and media of the New Left and because its initiators were skilled in local community organizing. Since the prime unit was the small group and no need for national cooperation was perceived, multitudinous splits increased its strength rather than drained its resources. Such fission was often "friendly" in nature and, even when not, served to bring ever-increasing numbers of women under the movement's umbrella.

Unfortunately, these masses of new women lacked the organizing skills of the initiators, and, because the idea of "leadership" and "organization" were in disrepute, they made no attempt to acquire them. They did not want to deal with traditional political institutions and abjured all traditional political skills. Consequently, the growth of the movement institutions did not go beyond the local level, and they were often inadequate to handle the accelerating influx of new people into the movement. Although these small groups were diverse in kind and responsible to no one for their focus, their nature determined both the structure and the strategy of the movement. One result has been a very broad-based creative movement to which individuals can relate pretty much as they desire with no concern for orthodoxy or doctrine. This branch has been the major source of new feminist ideas and activities. It has developed several ideological perspectives, much of the terminology of the movement, an amazing number of publications and "counter-institutions," numerous new issues, and even new techniques for social change. The emphasis of this branch has been on personal change as a means to understand the kind of political change desired. The primary instrument has been the consciousness-raising rap group which has sought to change women's very identities as well as their attitudes.

Nonetheless, this loose structure is flexible only within certain limits, and the movement has not yet shown the propensity to transcend them. While rap groups have been excellent techniques for changing individual attitudes, they have not been very successful in dealing with social institutions. Their loose, informal structure encourages participation in discussion, and their supportive atmosphere elicits personal insight; but neither is very efficient in handling specific tasks. While they have been of fundamental value to the development of the movement, they also lead to a certain kind of political impotency. It is virtually impossible to coordinate a national action, or even a local one, assuming there could be any agreement on issues around which to coordinate one.

Individual rap groups tend to flounder when their numbers have exhausted the virtues of consciousness raising and decide they want to do something more concrete. The problem is that most groups are unwilling to change their structure when they change their tasks. They have accepted the ideology of "structurelessness" without realizing its limitations.

The resurgence of feminism tapped a major source of female energy, but the younger branch has not yet been able to channel it. Some women are able to create their own local-action projects, such as study groups, abortion counseling centers, bookstores, etc. Most are not, and the movement provides no coordinated or structured means of fitting into existing projects. Instead, such women either are recruited into NOW and other national organizations or drop out. New groups form and dissolve at an accelerating rate, creating a good deal of consciousness and very little action. The result is that most of the movement is proliferating underground. It often seems mired in introspection, but it is in fact creating a vast reservoir of conscious feminist sentiment which only awaits an appropriate opportunity for action.

In sum, the current status of the women's movement can be said to be structurally very much like it was in its incipient stages. That section which I have called the older branch remains attached to using the tools the system provides, while the younger branch simply proliferates horizontally, without creating new structures to handle new tasks.

Jo Freeman

REFERENCES

Adorno, L. W., et al. 1950. *The Authoritatian Personality*. New York: Harper.
Bird, Caroline. 1968. *Born Female: The High Cost of Keeping Women Down*. New York: David, McKay.
Blumer, Herbert. 1951. "Social Movements." In *New Outline of the Principles of Sociology*, edited by A. M. Lee. New York: Barnes & Noble.
———. 1957. "Collective Behavior." *Review of Sociology: Analysis of a Decade*, edited by Joseph B. Gittler. New York: Wiley.
Buck, Solon J. *The Agrarian Crusade*. 1920. New Haven, Conn.: Yale University Press.
Cantril, Hadley. 1941. *The Psychology of Social Movements*. New York: Wiley.
Coleman, James. 1957. *Community Conflict*. Glencoe, Ill.: Free Press.
Currie, Elliott, and Jerome H. Skolnick. 1970. "A Critical Note on Conceptions of Collective Behavior." *Annals of the American Academy of Political and Social Science* 391 (September): 34–45.
Dahrendorf, Ralf. 1959. *Class and Class Conflict in Industrial Society*. Palo Alto, Calif.: Stanford University Press.
Davies, James C. 1962. "Toward A Theory of Revolution." *American Sociological Review* 27 (1): 5–19.
Dawson, C. A., and W. E. Gettys. 1929. *An Introduction to Sociology*. New York: Ronald.
Edelsberg, Herman. 1965. N.Y.U. 18th Conference on Labor." *Labor Relations Reporter* 61 (August): 253–55.
Ferriss, Abbott L. 1971. *Indicators of Trends in the Status of American Women*. New York: Russell Sage.
Firestone, Shulamith. 1971. *Dialectics of Sex*. New York: Morrow.
Friedan, Betty. 1963. *The Feminine Mystique*. New York: Dell.
———. 1967. "N.O.W.: How It Began." *Women Speaking* (April).
Griffiths, Martha. 1966. Speech of June 20, *Congressional Record*.
Gurr, Ted. 1970. *Why Men Rebel*. Princeton, N.J.: Princeton University Press.
Hayden, Casey, and Mary King. 1966. "A Kind of Memo." *Liberation* (April).
Heberle, Rudolph. 1951. *Social Movements*. New York: Appleton-Century-Crofts.
Hoffer, Eric. 1951. *The True Believer*. New York: Harper.
Hole, Judith, and Ellen Levine. 1971. *Rebirth of Feminism*. New York: Quadrangle.
Holzman, Abraham. 1963. *The Townsend Movement: A Political Study*. New York: Bookman.
Jackson, Maurice, Eleanora Petersen, James Bull, Sverre Monsen, and Patricia Richmond. "The Failure of an Incipient Social Movement." *Pacific Sociological Review* 3, no. 1 (Spring): 40.
Killian, Lewis M. 1964. "Social Movements." In *Handbook of Modern Sociology*, edited by R. E. L. Faris. Chicago: Rand McNally.
King, C. Wendell, 1956. *Social Movements in the United States*. New York: Random House.
King, Martin Luther, Jr. 1958. *Stride toward Freedom*. New York: Harper.
Kissinger, C. Clark, and Bob Ross. 1968. "Starting in '60: Or From SLID to Resistance." *New Left Notes,* June 10.
Kornhauser, William. 1959. *The Politics of Mass Society*. Glencoe, Ill.: Free Press.
Lang, Kurt, and Gladys Engle Lang. 1961. *Collective Dynamics*. New York: Cromwell.
Lionberger, Herbert F. 1960. *Adoption of New Ideas and Practices*. Ames: Iowa State University Press.
Lipset, Seymour M. *Agrarian Socialism*. Berkeley: University of California Press, 1959.
Lowi, Theodore J. 1971. *The Politics of Disorder*. New York: Basic.
Pinard, Maurice. 1968. "Mass Society and Political Movements: A New Formulation." *American Journal of Sociology* 73, no. 6 (May): 682–90.

————. 1971. *The Rise of a Third Party: A Study in Crisis Politics*. Englewood Cliffs, N.J.: Prentice-Hall.

Rogers, Everett M. 1962. *Diffusion of Innovations*. New York: Free Press.

Salisbury, Robert H. 1969. "An Exchange Theory of Interest Groups." *Midwest Journal of Political Science,* vol. 13, no. 1 (February).

Shils, Edward. 1970. "Center and Periphery." In *Selected Essays*. Center for Social Organization Studies. Department of Sociology, University of Chicago.

Smelser, Neil J. 1963. *Theory of Collective Behavior*. Glencoe, Ill.: Free Press.

Toch, Hans. 1965. *The Social Psychology of Social Movements*. Indianapolis: Bobbs-Merrill.

Turner, Ralph H. 1964. "Collective Behavior and Conflict: New Theoretical Frameworks." *Sociological Quarterly*.

Turner, Ralph H., and Lewis M. Killian. 1957. *Collective Behavior*. Englewood Cliffs, N.J.: Prentice-Hall.

Adult Sex Roles and Mental Illness[1]

Walter R. Gove
Vanderbilt University

Jeannette F. Tudor
Central Michigan University

Mental illness has been the focus of innumerable studies, many of which have looked at the relationship between sociological variables and psychiatric disorders. It has, by now, been established that there is an inverse relationship between social class and mental illness (e.g., Hollingshead and Redlich 1958; Dohrenwend and Dohrenwend 1969; Rushing 1969), although the cause of this relationship is still debated. However, the relationships between mental illness and most other sociological variables remain unclear.

This paper will explore the relationship between adult sex roles and mental illness. Previous attempts to clarify this relationship have produced inconsistent and contradictory results (see, e.g., Dohrenwend and Dohrenwend 1965, 1969; Manis 1968). We believe that a major reason that these results occur in studies dealing with persons in psychiatric treatment is that mental illness has frequently been treated as a residual category in which diverse and unrelated disorders have been grouped (Scheff 1966). In this paper, mental illness will be treated as a fairly specific phenomenon —a disorder which involves personal discomfort (as indicated by distress, anxiety, etc) and/or mental disorganization (as indicated by confusion, thought blockage, motor retardation, and, in the more extreme cases, by hallucinations and delusions) that is not caused by an organic or toxic condition. Two major diagnostic categories which fit our definition are the neurotic disorders and the functional psychoses. The chief characteristic of the neurotic disorders is anxiety in the absence of psychotic disorganization. The functional psychoses (schizophrenia, involutional psychotic reaction, manic depressive reaction, psychotic depressive reaction, and paranoid reaction) are psychotic disorders with no (known) organic cause (American Psychiatric Association 1968).

The two other major diagnostic psychiatric categories, the personality

[1] A condensed version of this paper was presented at the September 1971 meeting of the American Sociological Association. We would like to thank S. Frank Miyamoto for encouraging the pursuit of some suggestive relationships discovered in work done under his very helpful supervision (see Gove 1967), and Antonina Gove, William Rushing, James Thompson, Bruce Dohrenwend, and Mayer Zald for their comments on an earlier draft of this paper. The research for this paper was supported by the Vanderbilt University Research Council.

disorders and the acute and chronic brain disorders, do not conform to our conception of mental illness. Persons with a personality disorder do not experience personal discomfort, being neither anxious nor distressed, nor are they suffering from any form of psychotic disorganization. They are viewed as mentally ill because they do not conform to social norms and are typically forced into treatment because their behavior is disruptive to others. These persons are characterized by aggressive, impulsive, goal-directed behavior which is either antisocial or asocial in nature (American Psychiatric Association 1968; Rowe 1970; Klein and Davis 1969). Not only are the symptoms associated with the personality disorders different from those associated with mental illness (as we are defining it), but the forms of therapy effective in the treatment of mental illness are typically not effective in the treatment of the personality disorders. In fact, it is only recently that the personality disorders have come to be considered within the domain of psychiatry (e.g., Robbins 1966, p. 15). The brain disorders (the acute and chronic brain syndromes) are caused by a physical condition, either brain damage or toxins, and are not a functional disorder. Since personality and brain disorders do not conform to our conception of mental illness, in this paper neither of these disorders will be treated as mental illness.[2]

Almost all psychiatric patients are classified under the diagnostic categories already discussed. Three of the remaining categories, "mental deficiency," "without mental disorder," and "undiagnosed," are largely self-explanatory, infrequently used, and are not relevant to the present paper. The remaining two categories may be of interest. The transient situational (personality) disorder is an acute symptom response to an overwhelming situation where there is no underlying personality disturbance.[3] When the situational stress diminishes, so do the symptoms. This diagnostic

[2] We would emphasize that in our view there are a number of advantages to limiting the category mental illness to the neuroses and the functional psychoses. Most important, we believe that with mental illness delineated in this manner, it is possible to develop a general theory of mental illness. Some work has already been done along these lines (Gove 1968, 1970a). For instance, it has been shown how acute distress may lead to the development of psychotic disorganization in the mentally ill. We recognize that not all readers will agree with our definition of mental illness. Regarding this, we would note that one of the most critical problems in the development of a viable theory is the delimitation of the phenomenon to be explained. As we know from the history of science, attempts at such delimitation are controversial, even when they lead to a synthesis previously lacking (Kuhn 1970). If, using our conception of mental illness, we are able to discover patterns of mental illness that appear to be theoretically meaningful (as we think we do in the latter part of the paper), it is up to the critics of our definition to support their criticism by a systematic marshaling of contrary evidence.

[3] Up until 1968, when the *Diagnostic and Statistical Manual on Mental Disorders* was revised (see American Psychiatric Association 1968), the transient situational disorders were referred to as the transient situational personality disorders.

category is applied mainly to children and adolescents, but it is also occasionally used with adults. Perhaps a person so diagnosed should be included in our conception of mental illness, but it is not absolutely clear. The other category is comprised of the psychophysiologic disorders which are characterized by somatic symptoms that appear to be the consequence of emotional tension although the person is frequently unaware of emotional stress.

We will now turn to a discussion of the characteristics of adult sex roles which we believe are related to mental illness. Implicit in our analysis is the assumption that stress may lead to mental illness. We would like to emphasize that our discussion will be limited to the modern industrial nations of the West, particularly the United States. After looking at the relationship between adult sex roles and mental illness (as indicated by neurosis and the functional psychoses), we will briefly look at other disorders where there is almost undeniably a high degree of distress or anxiety, namely, the transient situational disorders, the psychophysiologic disorders, and suicide.

SEX ROLES

In Western society, as elsewhere, sex acts as a master status, channeling one into particular roles and determining the quality of one's interaction with others (Hughes 1945; Angrist 1969). There are several reasons to assume that, because of the roles they typically occupy, women are more likely than men to have emotional problems. First, most women are restricted to a single major societal role—housewife, whereas most men occupy two such roles, household head and worker. Thus, a man has two major sources of gratification, his family and his work, while a woman has only one, her family. If a male finds one of his roles unsatisfactory, he can frequently focus his interest and concern on the other role. In contrast, if a woman finds her family role unsatisfactory, she typically has no major alternative source of gratification (Bernard 1971, pp. 157–63; also see Lopata 1971, p. 171; Langner and Michael 1963).

Second, it seems reasonable to assume that a large number of women find their major instrumental activities—raising children and keeping house—frustrating. Being a housewife does not require a great deal of skill, for virtually all women, whether educated or not, seem to be capable of being at least moderately competent housewives. Furthermore, it is a position of low prestige.[4] Because the occupancy of such a low-status,

---

[4] Most authors routinely assume that the role of housewife has little prestige (e.g., Harrison 1964; Rossi 1964; Friedan 1963; Parsons 1942; Bardwick 1971; Bernard 1971); however, we have been unable to locate any systematic evaluation of this assumption.

technically undemanding position is not consonant with the educational and intellectual attainment of a large number of women in our society, we might expect such women to be unhappy with the role.

Third, the role of housewife is relatively unstructured and invisible. It is possible for the housewife to put things off, to let things slide, in sum, to perform poorly. The lack of structure and visibility allows her to brood over her troubles, and her distress may thus feed upon itself. In contrast, the job holder must consistently and satisfactorily meet demands that constantly force him to be involved with his environment. Having to meet these structured demands should draw his attention from his troubles and help prevent him from becoming obsessed with his worries.[5]

Fourth, even when a married woman works, she is typically in a less satisfactory position than the married male. There has been a persistent decline in the relative status of women since 1940 as measured by occupation, income, and even education (Knudsen 1969). Women are discriminated against in the job market, and they frequently hold positions that are not commensurate with their educational backgrounds (Harrison 1964; Knudsen 1969; Epstein 1970; Kreps 1971). Furthermore, working wives are typically viewed by themselves and by others as primarily supplementing the family income, which makes their career involvement fairly tenuous (Harrison 1964, p. 79; Epstein 1970, pp. 3–4; Hartley 1959–60). Perhaps more important, working wives appear to be under a greater strain than their husbands. In addition to their job, they apparently typically perform most of the household chores, which means that they work considerably more hours per day than their husbands.[6]

Fifth, several observers have noted that the expectations confronting women are unclear and diffuse (Goode 1960; Parsons 1942; Angrist 1969; Rose 1951; Epstein 1970); many have argued that this lack of specificity creates problems for women[7] (see esp. Rose 1951; Parsons 1942; and Cottrell 1942). Rose (1951), Angrist (1969), Epstein (1970), and Bardwick (1971) note that the feminine role is characterized by the adjusting to and preparing for contingencies. Rose (1951), for example, found that women tend to perceive their career in terms of what men will do, whereas men perceive their career in terms of their own needs. At

---

[5] Although this analysis is somewhat speculative, evidence consistent with it is provided by Langner and Michael (1963, pp. 301–57), Phillips and Segal (1969), Gove (1967), and especially Bradburn and Caplovitz (1965, pp. 95–127).

[6] The evidence indicates this is the case in Europe (Haavio-Manila 1967; Prudenski and Kolpakov 1962; Dahlström and Liljeström 1971), and it appears to be the case in the United States (Hartley 1959–60).

[7] Some investigators (e.g., Mead 1949; Komarovsky 1946; Friedan 1963; Steinmann and Fox 1966; Bardwick 1971) have suggested that the expectations confronting women are not merely diffuse but are in fact contradictory and that women are placed in a serious double bind.

best, it is likely that many women find the uncertainty and lack of control over their future frustrating.

Many authors (Komarovsky 1950; McKee and Sherriffs 1959; Friedan 1963; Mead 1949; Gavron 1966; Rossi 1964; Hartley 1970) have viewed the difficulties confronting women as being a result of recent changes in the woman's role in industrial societies. According to this argument, women previously had a more meaningful role. Families were large, and during most of their adult life women were responsible for the care of children. Without the conveniences of modern industrial society, housework required more time and skill and was highly valued. Since the family's economic support was frequently provided by a family enterprise, the wife played a role in supporting the family. With the development of industrialization and the small nuclear family, the woman's child-rearing years were shortened, her domestic skills were largely replaced by modern conveniences, and she was no longer part of a family enterprise supporting the family. During this time, both sexes were receiving more education; for the male, education produced occupational advancement and diversity; for the female, education was accompanied by a role shrinking in importance. These changes in women's roles were accompanied by changes in the legal and ideological structure, which held that the same standards should apply to men and women. However, instead of being treated as equals, women remained in their old institutionalized positions. If this analysis is correct, much of the presumed stress on women is a relatively recent phenomenon.

To summarize, there are ample grounds for assuming that women find their position in society to be more frustrating and less rewarding than do men and that this may be a relatively recent development. Let us, then, at this point postulate that, because of the difficulties associated with the feminine role in modern Western societies, more women than men become mentally ill. Our analysis of roles has focused primarily, but not exclusively, on the roles of married men and women, and it is within this group that we might expect to find the greatest difference in the rates of mental illness of men and women. Unfortunately, most existing data are presented by sex and not by sex and marital status.

Before we turn to an analysis of the data on mental illness, we might note two types of evidence that appear to support our framework. First, there is considerable evidence that women have a more negative image of themselves than men have of themselves (McKee and Sherriffs 1957, 1959; Sheriffs and McKee 1957; Gurin, Veroff, and Feld 1960, p. 70; Rosenkrantz, Vogel, Bee, Broverman, and Broverman 1968). Second, the available evidence on depression uniformly indicates that women are more likely to become depressed than men (e.g., Silverman 1968).

RATES OF MENTAL ILLNESS FOR ADULT MALES AND FEMALES

To evaluate rates of mental illness for males and females we will look at community surveys, first admissions to mental hospitals, psychiatric admissions to general hospitals, psychiatric care in outpatient clinics, private outpatient psychiatric care, and the prevalence of mental illness in the practices of general physicians. The National Institute of Mental Health (NIMH) provides data for the United States on first admissions to mental hospitals, psychiatric admissions to general hospitals, and psychiatric care in outpatient clinics. Because these data are much more comprehensive than any provided by individual investigators, our discussion of such treatment will be limited to these data. For community surveys and private outpatient care, we will, of course, have to depend upon the outcomes of individual studies (and our ability to locate them).

Community surveys.—In keeping with our concern with sex roles in modern industrial societies, we will discuss only community studies conducted after World War II.[8] We were able to locate 21 community studies done within the time period which dealt with the relationship between sex and mental illness. Three of these studies investigated a population which we felt was probably not relevant for our purposes,[9] and a fourth study provided only very limited information,[10] leaving 17 relevant and usable

[8] There are a number of reasons for taking the period around World War II as a cutoff point. We are concerned with adults, and much of their frame of reference will have been determined by the type of world they grew up in. Women received the vote in 1920, and persons born at this time were only 25 years old at the end of World War II. Furthermore, the major impact of industrialization did not really start until around World War I. Thus, persons much older than 25 at the end of World War II were raised in a situation where the roles and expectations were quite different than they are now. Perhaps one of the best indicators of the change in the woman's role is the proportion of married women who hold jobs, and it wasn't until World War II that a significant proportion of married women held jobs.

[9] The studies were those of Eaton and Weil (1955) who investigated mental illness in the Hutterites, Bellin and Hardt (1958) who investigated mental illness in the aged, and Helgason (1964) who investigated mental illness in all persons born in Iceland between 1895 and 1897. All of these studies, incidentally, found women to have higher rates of mental illness than men.

[10] The reports of the Midtown study (Srole, Langner, Michael, Opler, and Rennie 1962; Langner and Michael 1963) present no statistical breakdown by sex. Of the community studies of mental illness that do not break mental illness down into diagnostic categories, this is the only one whose authors include the personality disorders within their operational definition of mental illness. Thus, their conception of mental illness does not correspond to ours. Using their measure of mental illness, they report they found no significant sex differences at four age levels. Women, however, did report more psychoneurotic and psychophysiological symptoms than men (Langner and Michael 1963, p. 77). As most persons with a personality disorder are men, it would appear (although we cannot be sure) that there were more men with a personality disorder and more women with a psychoneurotic disorder and that they tended to balance each other out.

studies. These studies range from prevalence at a particular point of time (cf. Essen-Möller 1956), to incidence over a specified proportion of time (cf. Hagnell 1966), to an attempt to identify an incident of mental illness at any time in the respondent's lifetime up to the time of the study (Leighton, Leighton, Hardin, Macklin, and MacMillan 1963). Most of the studies focus primarily, although not exclusively, on prevalence at the time of the study. In all the studies that do not provide a diagnostic breakdown, the measures of mental illness relate very well to our conception of mental illness. The results of these studies are presented in table 1. In each case more women than men were found to be mentally ill.

First admissions to psychiatric hospitals.—There are three types of psychiatric hospitals in the United States—public mental hospitals (state and county), private mental hospitals, and VA psychiatric hospitals. The NIMH reports yearly on first admissions to public and private mental hospitals. According to their definition, first admissions include only persons with no prior inpatient psychiatric experience. Their definition thus not only excludes persons who have previously been in a mental hospital but also those who have received inpatient psychiatric treatment in a general hospital (NIMH 1967a, p. 16). Using these reports (NIMH 1967a, 1967b), we have calculated the rates of admissions to public and private mental hospitals in the United States by diagnosis for persons 18 and over.[11] These rates are based on the estimates for 1967 of the number of persons in the civilian[12] resident population who are 18 and over and have been age adjusted (standardized).[13] The only relevant information available on the VA psychiatric hospitals is the total number of psychiatric admissions (first admissions and readmissions) with no diagnostic breakdown (Administrator of Veterans' Affairs 1967, p. 207). We have therefore had to estimate the number of first admissions to the VA hospitals. Because VA patients are predominantly male, and we have predicted that more women than men would be mentally ill, we have made estimates which we are virtually certain are too large to avoid favorably biasing our results.[14]

[11] The reports on the hospitals are not entirely complete, with 9.1% of public hospitals and 11.1% of private hospitals not reporting. In computing the rates we have corrected for these hospitals by assuming that their rates were equal to the overall hospital average.

[12] By taking the civilian population we are slightly inflating the male rate which from our point of view unfavorably biases the results. It should be noted that the military population has received a psychiatric screening which leaves a disproportionate number of mentally ill persons in the civilian population.

[13] The age-specific rates were calculated using the U.S. Bureau of the Census (1970) estimates of the 1967 population. These rates were then standardized on the 1966 population (U.S., Bureau of the Census 1966).

[14] The specific procedures used in making these estimates as well as our rationale

TABLE 1

PERCENTAGE OF MEN AND WOMEN FOUND TO BE MENTALLY ILL IN
COMMUNITY SURVEYS

Source	Male	Female	Sample Size
A. Rates Based Solely on Responses to Structured Interview			
Martin, Brotherston, and Chave (1957, p. 200) ..	25	Over 40	750
Phillips and Segal (1969, p. 61)	21.2	35.5	278
Phillips (1966)	21	34	600
Bradburn and Caplovitz (1965, p. 30)	31	54	2,006
Tauss (1967, p. 122)	18.4	38.0	707
Taylor and Chave (1964, p. 50)	22	43	422
Gurin et al. (1960, p. 189)*	22	40	2,460
Haberman (1969):			
Washington Heights	18.2	25.3	1,865
New York City	14.9	33.3	706
Hare and Shaw (1965, p. 25):			
New Adam	15.6	22.9	1,015
Old Bute	13.1	26.3	924
Public Health Service (1970, p. 27)†	14.9	34.2	6,672
Bradburn (1969, p. 119)‡	20.3	38.9	2,379
Melle and Haese (1969, p. 239)	...	§	5,498
B. Rates Based on Clinical Evaluation (Psychosis and Neurosis)			
Pasamanick et al. (1959, p. 188)	4.2	7.1	809
Primrose (1962, pp. 18–24)‖	4.7	14.7	1,701
Essen-Möller (1956, pp. 148–49)	1.7	3.7	2,550
Hagnell (1966, pp. 99–103)‖,#	6.0	15.6	2,550
C. Rates Based on Several Sources** (Psychosis and Neurosis)			
Leighton et al. (1963, pp. 265–67)	45	66	1,010

* Gurin et al. (1960) present their data along four symptom factors—psychological anxiety, physical health, immobilization, and physical anxiety. The figures presented refer to a score of 5 or more on the psychological anxiety factor. Women also scored higher than men on the other three factors.
† Rate indicates persons with three or more symptoms.
‡ Rates of persons high on symptoms of anxiety.
§ 2.5 times male rate.
‖ Study involved the complete survey of an entire community and excludes psychosis due to organic disorder.
Rates for neurosis calculated by authors from data on pp. 99–102. (Child neurosis was not considered when calculating the rates.)
** Rates combine psychosis and neurosis and are based on interviews, observations of interviewer, hospital and other institutional records, impressions of physicians in contact with respondent, and impressions of community informants.

The data on first admissions to mental hospitals are presented in table 2. Because we have overestimated VA admissions, the true rate falls somewhere between the combined rate for public and private hospitals and

for them are available from the authors upon request. We would simply note here that data presented by Pollack, Radick, Brown, Wurster, and Gorwitz (1964, p. 511) for Louisiana and Maryland indicate that our estimates for VA admissions are between two and four times too large.

TABLE 2

First Admissions to Mental Hospitals in the United States
(Persons per 100,000)

	State and County	Private	Combined	Ratio F/M	VA Hospitals Over-estimate	All Hospitals	Ratio F/M
Functional psychosis:							
Male	293	89	382 ⎫		61	443 ⎫	
			⎬	1.27		⎬	1.10
Female	322	162	484 ⎭		2	486 ⎭	
Neurosis:							
Male	107	99	206 ⎫		22	238 ⎫	
			⎬	1.68		⎬	1.46
Female	165	182	347 ⎭		1	348 ⎭	
Total:							
Male	400	188	588 ⎫		83	671 ⎫	
			⎬	1.41		⎬	1.24
Female	487	344	831 ⎭		3	834 ⎭	

the rate presented for all hospitals. Even looking at the all-hospital rate, which inflates the rate for males, it is obvious that there are more mentally ill women admitted to mental hospitals.

Psychiatric care in general hospitals.—About as many persons receive inpatient psychiatric treatment in general hospitals as are cared for in mental hospitals. Such treatment is generally quite brief with most of the persons returning to the community, although a few go on to become patients in mental hospitals. The NIMH reports yearly on the number and characteristics of the psychiatric discharges from general hospitals with inpatient psychiatric services. This report does not cover general hospitals under federal control. Using the NIMH (1967d) report, we have calculated the discharge rates for 1967 by diagnosis for persons 18 and over in the United States.[15] As before, these rates are based on estimates of the civilian population 18 and over (U.S., Bureau of the Census 1970) and have been age standardized. Because of the rapid patient turnover in general hospitals, the psychiatric admission rates (first admissions and readmissions combined) and discharge rates should be virtually equivalent. For the VA general hospitals we have the total

[15] The reports on the general hospitals with psychiatric inpatient services are not complete, with 31.4% of the hospitals not reporting. In computing the rates we have corrected for these hospitals by assuming that their discharge rates were equivalent to the average of the other hospitals.

number of psychiatric admissions but lack additional information (Administrator of Veterans' Affairs 1967, p. 207). In calculating these rates, we, therefore, have had to make estimates for two parameters.[16] From the Public Health Service (1967) we have discharge data on all public health general hospitals by sex and diagnosis. In the same manner as before we have used these data to calculate age-standardized rates. More mentally ill women are treated in general hospitals, with the discrepancy between men and women being even greater than in the mental hospitals (table 3).

TABLE 3

PSYCHIATRIC CARE IN GENERAL HOSPITALS IN THE UNITED STATES
(PERSONS PER 100,000)

	Nonfederal Hospitals*	VA General Hospitals†	Public Health Hospitals*	All General Hospitals	Ratio F/M
Functional psychosis:					
Male	816	109	6	931	1.44
Female	1,334	3	0	1,337	
Neurosis:					
Male	959	128	11	1,098	1.89
Female	2,068	4	4	2,076	
Total:					
Male	1,775	237	17	2,029	1.68
Female	3,402	7	4	3,413	

* Rates based on discharges.
† Rates based on admissions.

Psychiatric out-patient care (excluding private practice).—The NIMH (1967e) also conducts a yearly survey of outpatient psychiatric facilities. In their yearly report, they present information on terminations by age, sex, and diagnosis. We have, as before, used this information to compute age-standardized rates based on the civilian population for persons 18 and over for 1967.[17]

[16] To estimate the proportion of men and women who were discharged we used the proportion of men and women who were psychiatric residents in the VA hospitals in 1967 (NIMH 1967c). To estimate the diagnostic distribution of admissions to the VA hospitals we used the diagnostic distribution of men and women discharged from the nonfederal general hospitals.

[17] The reports on the outpatient clinics not associated with the VA are not complete, with 27.2% of such clinics not reporting. In computing the rates we have corrected for these clinics by assuming that the termination of the nonreporting clinics were

Walter R. Gove and Jeannette F. Tudor

The rates for men and women are quite similar to those which dealt with psychiatric hospitalization, with more mentally ill women than men treated in these clinics (table 4). It should be noted that the NIMH report does not include facilities where a mental health professional other than a psychiatrist directs the mental health program and assumes responsibility for the patients. However, a study by Zolik and Marches (1968) indicates that the proportions of men and women who are treated as mentally ill in such facilities are very similar to the proportions presented here.

TABLE 4

CARE IN PSYCHIATRIC CLINICS IN THE UNITED STATES (PERSONS PER 100,000)
RATES BASED ON TERMINATIONS

	All Outpatient Clinics (Except VA)	VA Out-patient Clinics	All Clinics	Ratio F/M
Functional psychosis:				
Male	573	114	687	
Female	832	2	834	1.21
Neurosis:				
Male	433	122	555	
Female	956	3	959	1.73
Total:				
Male	1,006	236	1,242	
Female	1,788	5	1,793	1.44

Private outpatient psychiatric care.—To discover the relative proportions of mentally ill men and women in private outpatient psychiatric care we again must turn to studies conducted by various investigators. Unfortunately, we have only been able to locate a few studies which indicate the sex distribution of the practices of psychiatrists. As indicated in table 5, these studies all found that more women than men are seen by psychiatrists. The magnitude of this relationship may be somewhat obscured by the fact that all of these studies include disturbances such as the personality disorders.

Most persons who receive treatment for mental illness are treated by physicians in the community who lack special psychiatric training. These

---

equivalent to the average of the reporting clinics. The rates for the VA clinics are based on estimates made by the NIMH for *all* VA clinic terminations.

TABLE 5

CONTACT WITH A PSYCHIATRIST—ALL TYPES OF MENTAL DISORDERS

Source	Men (%)	Women (%)	Patients (N)
Private office practice:			
Gordon and Gordon (1958, p. 544):			
Bergen County	41	59	(746)
Ulster County	34	66	(264)
Cattaraugus County	37	63	(239)
Bahn, Gardner, Alltop, Knatterud, and			
Solomon (1966, p. 2046)	...	*	(270)
Referred to psychiatrist:			
Watts, Caute, and Kuenssberg (1964, p. 1355)			
Referrals	39	61	(4,452)†
Innes and Sharp (1962, p. 449)			
Referred from general population in given			
year	0.5	0.6	(2,003)
Outpatients:‡			
Hagnell (1966, p. 46)	2.9	7.6	(2,550)

* Rates higher for females.
† Based on a study of 261 general practices.
‡ Persons from the general population who saw a psychiatrist as outpatients over a 10-year period.

physicians also play a major role in channeling persons into more specialized psychiatric care (see Susser 1968; p. 246). Most of the mentally ill persons treated by general physicians are suffering from a psychoneurotic disorder. In table 6 we have presented some of the findings regarding the proportion of men and women that are treated for mental illness by general practitioners.[18] All of the studies that have looked at this relationship have found that more women receive such treatment. The finding by Shepherd, Cooper, Brown, and Kalton (1964, p. 1361) that psychiatric disorders ranked third among presenting conditions for women and seventh among men suggests that this relationship cannot be explained by assuming that women simply go to physicians more frequently than men.

In summary, *all* of the information on persons in psychiatric treatment indicates that more women are mentally ill. This information exactly parallels the data from the community studies and is thus consistent with our formulation that the adult woman in modern industrial society is more likely to experience mental illness.

Other relevant psychiatric disorders.—Earlier, while discussing the relationship between the various diagnostic categories and mental illness (as

[18] Table 6 does not present all the relevant studies, being limited to those that are relatively recent and readily available. For a discussion of the earlier and less easily located studies, see Ryle (1960) and Watts (1962).

Walter R. Gove and Jeannette F. Tudor

TABLE 6

TREATMENT OF MEN AND WOMEN FOR MENTAL ILLNESS BY GENERAL PRACTITIONERS

Source	Men (%)	Women (%)	Patients (N)	Practices Studied (N)
	A. Percentage in Specified Population Being Treated			
Hare and Staw (1965, p. 26):				
New Adam	3.0	7.5	(990)	...
Old Bute	3.4	7.4	(875)	...
Taylor and Chave (1964, p. 118)	5.5	9.4	(2,826)	...
	B. Percentage of Mentally Ill Patients in Practice			
Fry (1960, p. 86)	7.1	16.3	(5,471)	(1)
Ryle (1960, p. 324)	1.4	7.1	(2,400)	(1)
Logan and Cushion (1958, pp. 69–70) ...	3.0	6.4	(114,294)	(106)
Kessel (1960, p. 18)	11.1	15.8	(670)	(1)
Martin et al. (1957, p. 199)	3.5	7.5	...	...
Shepherd et al. (1964, p. 1361)	5.9	12.6	(14,697)	(40)
Cooper (1966, p. 9)	17.4	27.2	(7,454)	...
Cooper, Brown, and Kalton (1962)	6.9	15.6	(743)	...
	C. Sex Distribution of Patients Receiving Treatment for Mental Illness			
Watts et al. (1964, p. 1355)	32.0	68.0	(6,123)	...
Mazer (1967)	31.8	68.2	(154)	...

we have identified it), we noted that there were two relatively infrequently used categories—the transient situational personality disorders, and the psychophysiologic disorders—which appear to reflect a high degree of anxiety or distress.

As noted, the transient situational personality disorders are characterized by an acute symptom response to an overwhelming situation which is followed by the disappearance of the symptoms when the stress is withdrawn. Using the same sources and techniques as before, we calculated the rates in the United States for the transient disorders for persons 18 and over by (1) first admissions to mental hospitals, (2) psychiatric treatment in general hospitals, and (3) terminations from outpatient clinics. There are many more women treated for transient disorders in general hospitals and outpatient clinics (table 7). Only a very few persons with transient disorders are admitted to mental hospitals, and here the rates for males and females are roughly equal. These data, taken together, indicate that considerably more women experience a transient situational personality disorder.

The psychophysiologic disorders are characterized by a somatic disorder that appears to result from emotional tension. Some authors have

TABLE 7

PSYCHIATRIC TREATMENT OF THE TRANSIENT SITUATIONAL DISORDERS IN
THE UNITED STATES (PERSONS PER 100,000)

Type of Hospital	Male	Female
	First Admissions to Mental Hospitals	
State and county	26	23
Private	5	6
VA (high estimate)	5	0
Total	36	29
	Psychiatric Care in General Hospitals	
Nonfederal*	65	120
VA†	9	0
Public health*	...	...
Total	74	120
	Care in Psychiatric Outpatient Clinics‡	
All except VA	166	271
VA	0	0
Total	166	271

* Rates based on discharges.
† Rates based on admissions.
‡ Rates based on terminations.

speculated (e.g., Hagnell 1966, p. 155) that men tend to react to stress by developing a psychophysiologic disorder, while women may in comparable situations become mentally ill, and that this may explain the higher rate of psychiatric morbidity in women. In the same manner as before, we have calculated the rates in the United States for the psychophysiologic disorders for persons 18 and over by (1) first admission to mental hospitals, (2) psychiatric treatment in general hospitals, and (3) terminations from outpatient clinics (table 8). A few of the community surveys and three of the studies of the practices of general physicians present the proportion of men and women with a psychophysiologic disorder. The data on psychiatric treatment,[19] the practices of general physicians, and the results of the community surveys all indicate that more women than men have a psychophysiologic disorder (table 8). The data on the transient and the psychophysiologic disorders thus supplement the earlier finding that women are more likely than men to be mentally ill.

[19] It is only in the general hospital that many persons receive psychiatric treatment for psychophysiologic disorders, and it is only here that there is a difference between male and female rates.

TABLE 8

Psychophysiologic and Psychosomatic Disorders
A. Psychiatric Treatment of Psychophysiologic Disorders in the United States
(Persons per 100,000)

Type of Hospital	Male	Female
	First Admissions to Mental Hospitals	
State and county	2	2
Private	2	2
VA (high estimate)	0	0
Total	4	4
	Psychiatric Care in General Hospitals	
Nonfederal*	70	137
VA general†	9	0
Public Health	2	0
Total	81	137
	Care in Psychiatric Outpatient Clinics‡	
All except VA	20	27
VA	6	0
Total	26	27

B. Community Surveys

Source	Male (%)	Female (%)	Sample Size
Pasamanick, Roberts, Lemkau, and Kreuger (1959, p. 188)	18.9	52.4	809
Essen-Möller (1956, pp. 148–49)§	18.2	30.7	2,550
Llewellyn-Thomas (1960, p. 201)	31.0	59.0	274
Leighton et al. (1963, p. 264)	65.0	71.0	1,010

C. Studies of Practices of General Physicians

Source	Male (%)	Female (%)	Sample Size	Practices Studied (N)
Shepherd et al. (1964, p. 1361)‖	2.5	3.5	14,697	(46)
Mazur (1967)#	41.6	58.4	89**	(5)
Watts (1962, p. 40)††	...	‡‡	114,294	(106)

* Rates based on discharges.
† Rates based on all admissions.
‡ Rates based on terminations.
§ Persons age 15 and over.
‖ Proportion of persons over age 15 with psychosomatic disorders.
Sex distribution of patients with psychophysiologic disorders.
** Patients with disorder.
†† Sex distribution of patients with psychosomatic disorders.
‡‡ 3 women to 2 men.

Suicide.—Although not a form of mental illness, suicide reflects a high degree of distress. More men than women commit suicide (Farberow and Schneidman 1965; Stengel 1969; Maris 1969), which might be taken as suggesting that more men are distressed. However, "the number of suicidal attempts is six to ten times that of the suicides, at least in urban communities" (Stengel 1969, p. 89), and women are much more likely to attempt suicide (Stengel 1969; Farberow and Schneidman 1965). Thus, if we look at suicide attempts (including those that were successful), we would conclude that women are more distressed than men. In short, a simple comparison of the suicidal behavior of men and women gives ambiguous results and makes any generalization rather tenuous. However, as shown elsewhere (Gove 1972*a*), a more detailed analysis does seem to support our role framework. To cite simply one example, in England and Wales (Stengel 1969, p. 26) and in the United States (Maris 1969, p. 7) the rates of suicide among women have greatly increased in recent years whereas they have not among men, which, of course, is consistent with the discussed changes in the woman's role in Western society.

All the data on mental illness (as we have defined it) indicate that more women than men are mentally ill. It is especially important to note that this finding is not dependent on who is doing the selection. For example, if we look at admissions to mental hospitals, where the societal response would appear to be of prime importance, women have higher rates; if we look at treatment by general physicians, where self-selection would appear to be of prime importance, women have higher rates; and if we look at community surveys, where the attempt is to eliminate selective processes, women have higher rates.

Before we evaluate other explanations for the sex difference in the rate of mental illness, we will briefly discuss some data that suggest that this difference results from the characteristics of male and female roles in modern society.

EVIDENCE FOR THE ROLE EXPLANATION

If the reader reviews our argument regarding why women are more likely to be mentally ill then men, he will note that we focused primarily on the roles of married women and men, which we indicated were quite different. In contrast, the roles of unmarried men and women appear to be more similar. Thus, our role analysis suggests that the major difference in rates of mental illness between men and women is found among married men and women.

Elsewhere, Gove (1972*b*) has reviewed the studies in the modern industrial nations conducted after World War II that present the relationship between marital status and mental disorder. Unfortunately, these studies use quite varying definitions of mental disorder. However, all these studies indicate that married women are more likely to have a mental disorder than married men. The results were quite different for unmarried persons. When never-married men were compared with never-married women, divorced men with divorced women, and widowed men with widowed women, it was found that within each of these statuses some studies indicated that men had higher rates and others that women had higher rates. Furthermore, if there was a pattern within these categories, it was that men were more likely than women to be mentally ill, for within each of the unmarried statuses more studies found men to have the higher rates of mental illness.

Because woman's position in our society has undergone major changes in the relatively recent past, we might expect some changes over time in the ratio of men to women that were mentally ill. There is, in fact, some evidence that there was a change in this ratio some time around World War II. It appears, for example, that prior to World War II more men than women with psychotic disorders were admitted to mental hospitals (Landis and Page 1938, p. 40; Goldhamer and Marshall 1953, p. 65; U.S., Bureau of the Census 1930, 1941). Furthermore, the community studies cited by Dohrenwend and Dohrenwend, which they feel indicate that there is no sex difference in rates of mental illness, also suggest a shift toward relatively higher rates of mental illness in women. Of the studies they cite, which were conducted in Western Europe or North America following World War II, 12 showed higher rates for women, while none showed higher rates for men. However, of the pre–World War II studies conducted in these areas, three show higher rates for women and eight show higher rates for men (Dohrenwend and Dohrenwend 1969, p. 15).

Further evidence that the disproportionately large number of mentally ill women is a product of the social system is provided by the community study by Leighton et al. (1963, pp. 322–53). As in other community surveys, they found that in general more women than men were mentally ill. More important, they discovered two types of communities that had con- trasting results, namely a set of three communities that were undergoing a severe economic depression, and an Acadian French village which was extremely well integrated. As one might expect, the depressed communities had a higher than average rate of mental illness. What is interesting is that in these communities men had somewhat higher rates of mental illness than women. This makes sense considering that an extremely poor employ- ment situation probably has more impact on men. The integrated French Acadian community had very low rates of mental illness, with women being noticeably lower than men. This community was an extremely close- knit, traditional, family-oriented village, culturally isolated from the larger society. It is likely that in this community the woman's role corresponded rather closely to that of a preindustrial Western society.

ALTERNATIVE PERSPECTIVES

The societal reaction perspective.—During the past decade the societal reaction perspective has been one of the most pervasive and influential sociological approaches to deviance (e.g., Becker 1963; Erikson 1964; Scheff 1966; Schur 1969). Scheff (1966), in particular, has used this approach to explain stabilized mental illness. According to this perspective, a person comes to occupy the role of the mentally ill primarily because of the actions of others. It is Scheff's (1966) formulation that: (1) virtually everyone at some time commits acts that correspond to the public stereotype of mental illness; (2) if these acts should become public knowledge, the individual may, depending upon various contingencies, be referred to the appropriate officials; and (3) the person will then be routinely processed as mentally ill and placed in a mental institution. In short, a person becomes mentally ill primarily because others perceive him as mentally ill and act accordingly.

There is fairly strong evidence that if both men and women perform acts indicative of mental illness, men are much more likely to be perceived and reacted to as mentally ill. For example, Phillips (1964), using hypothetical case descriptions of mental illness, consistently found that men were rejected more strongly than women even though the behavior in each case was the same. The discrepancy between the sexes was the greatest in the case of the simple schizophrenic characterized primarily by the non-performance of instrumental roles. Fairly similar findings have been presented by Larson (1970) and Fletcher (1969). Furthermore, the evidence from these case descriptions appears to reflect real processes. For example, psychotic males are hospitalized at an earlier age than psychotic women (e.g., Gove 1972c), and an important finding by Raskin and Golob (1966) indicates that the males' earlier hospitalization is not due to an earlier manifestation of symptoms but to a quicker response by society to their psychotic symptoms.

If the rates of manifest distress and disorganization were equal for males and females, the fact that such symptoms are more inconsistent with the masculine role would lead people to perceive and respond to males as mentally ill more frequently than to females. Thus, the societal reaction perspective leads (at least in its pure form) to the prediction that more males than females would be treated as mentally ill.[20] As we have seen,

[20] This prediction is obvious in the area of psychiatric hospitalization, where societal reaction typically plays a major role in effecting entrance into treatment. Societal

this prediction is incorrect, for women appear, on all indicators, to have higher rates of mental illness. Furthermore, we do not feel that the societal reaction perspective could be used to explain the patterned variations discussed in the previous section. We therefore conclude that the societal reaction perspective does not provide a satisfactory explanation for the data presented in this paper. This finding complements other evidence (Gove 1970b), which indicates that the societal reaction perspective does not provide a valid general theory of mental illness.

Women are expressive.—Phillips and Segal (1969) recently noted that community studies of mental illness which are based on self-reported symptoms find that women have a higher rate of psychiatric disturbance than men. They believe, however, that this is due not to "real sex differences in frequency of disturbance but rather to man's greater reluctance to admit certain unpleasurable feelings and sensation," since men believe such behavior is not masculine (Phillips and Segal 1969, p. 69). In other words, it is "more culturally appropriate and acceptable for women to be more expressive about their difficulties" (Phillips and Segal 1969, p. 59). However, they apparently do not feel that the simple willingness to express symptoms would lead persons to seek professional help, for they note that when other relevant variables are controlled the expression of such symptoms is not related to seeking medical help, and they feel that "respondents themselves probably do not often interpret these psychiatric symptoms as indicators of illness—physical or psychological—that could profit from professional attention" (Phillips and Segal 1969, p. 65).

The Phillips-Segal explanation is based on the different cultural roles of men and women. Because space does not permit us to systematically evaluate all the possible elaborations of this type of explanation, we will simply point to some areas which suggest that this approach will not serve as a general explanation of the differences in the rates of mental illness of men and women. First, unmarried men have as high, if not higher, rates of mental illness as unmarried women. Second, the fact that the rates for men appear to have been higher prior to World War II would appear to contradict the "women are expressive" explanation. Third, we do not see how the expressive explanation can account for women having higher rates of admissions to mental hospitals, for typically hospitalization is initiated by someone else. Fourth, all the community studies based on a *clinical* evaluation, which (presumably) are not affected by the expressiveness of women, found women to have higher rates of mental illness.

---

reaction theorists generally have not dealt with the issue of voluntary self-referrals. However, we (perhaps debatably) reason that males would be more likely than females to perceive the manifestation of psychiatric symptoms as indicating they were mentally ill, for such symptoms are more out of tune with the masculine than the feminine stereotype.

Although we feel the expressiveness explanation does not account for the main thrust of the data presented in this paper, we do tentatively accept the hypothesis that women are more expressive than men, and we would like some solid data on how this trait interacts (if at all) with the various ways of identifying mental illness.

SUMMARY

We have argued that the woman's role in modern industrial societies has a number of characteristics that may promote mental illness and have explored the possibility that in such societies women have higher rates of mental illness than men. In our analysis we have utilized a fairly precise definition of mental illness, limiting it to functional disorders characterized by anxiety (neurosis) and/or mental disorganization (psychosis). The information on first admissions to mental hospitals, psychiatric treatment in general hospitals, psychiatric outpatient clinics, private outpatient psychiatric care, the practices of general physicians, and community surveys all indicate that more women than men are mentally ill. A survey of the information on two other diagnostic categories which may reflect mental illness (as we have defined it)—the transient situation disorders and the psychophysiologic disorders—also revealed that women are more likely to have these disorders. Patterned variations in the rates of mental illness among men and women have been described suggesting that the ordering of these rates is a reflection of the position of men and women in society. However, we would like to emphasize that we need to know much more about how the woman's role produces high rates of mental illness, and without more research we can only speculate, as we have done, on what the important factors might be.

REFERENCES

Administrator of Veterans' Affairs. 1967. *Annual Report 1967.* Washington, D.C.: Government Printing Office.

American Psychiatric Association. 1968. *Diagnostic and Statistical Manual on Mental Disorders.* Washington, D.C.: American Psychiatric Association.

Angrist, Shirley. 1969. "The Study of Sex Roles." *Journal of Social Issues* 25 (January): 215–32.

Bahn, Anita, Elmer Gardner, Lacoe Alltop, Genell Knatterud, and Murray Solomon. 1966. "Admission and Prevalence Rates for Psychiatric Facilities in Four Register Areas." *American Journal of Public Health* 56 (December): 2033–51.

Bardwick, Judith. 1971. *The Psychology of Women: A Study of Bio-Cultural Conflicts.* New York: Harper & Row.

Becker, Howard. 1963. *Outsiders: Studies in the Sociology of Deviance.* New York: Free Press.

Bellin, Seymour, and Robert Hardt. 1958. "Marital Status and Mental Disorders among the Aged." *American Sociological Review* 23 (April): 155–62.

Bernard, Jessie. 1971. *Women and the Public Interest.* Chicago: Aldine-Atherton.

Walter R. Gove and Jeannette F. Tudor

Bradburn, Norman. 1969. *The Structure of Psychological Well-being.* Chicago: Aldine.
Bradburn, Norman, and David Caplovitz. 1965. *Reports on Happiness.* Chicago: Aldine.
Cooper, Brian. 1966. "Psychiatric Disorder in Hospital and General Practice." *Social Psychiatry* 1(1): 7–10.
Cooper, B., A. C. Brown, and G. G. W. Kalton. 1962. "A Pilot Study of Psychiatric Morbidity in General Practice." *Journal of the College of General Practitioners* 5 (November): 590–602.
Cottrell, Leonard. 1942. "The Adjustment of the Individual to His Age and Sex Roles." *American Sociological Review* 7 (October): 617–20.
Dahlström, Edmund, and Rita Liljeström. 1971. "The Family and Married Women at Work." In *The Changing Roles of Men and Women,* edited by Edmund Dahlström. Boston: Beacon.
Dohrenwend, Bruce, and Barbara S. Dohrenwend. 1965. "The Problem of Validity in Field Studies of Psychological Disorder." *Journal of Abnormal Psychology* 70(4): 52–69.
———. 1969. *Social Status and Psychological Disorder.* New York: Wiley.
Eaton, Joseph, and Robert Weil. 1955. *Culture and Mental Disorders.* Glencoe, Ill.: Free Press.
Epstein, Cynthia. 1970. *Woman's Place.* Berkeley: University of California Press.
Erikson, Kai. 1964. "Notes on the Sociology of Deviance." In *The Other Side,* edited by Howard Becker. New York: Free Press.
Essen-Möller, Erik. 1956. "Individual Traits and Morbidity in a Swedish Rural Population." *Acta Psychiatrica et Neurologica Scandinavica,* Supplementum 100: 1–160.
Farberow, Norman, and Edwin Schneidman. 1965. *The Cry for Help.* New York: McGraw-Hill.
Fletcher, Richard. 1969. "Measuring Community Mental Health Attitudes by Means of Hypothetical Case Descriptions." *Social Psychiatry* 4(4): 152–56.
Friedan, Betty. 1963. *The Feminine Mystique.* New York: Norton.
Fry, John. 1960. "What Happens to Our Neurotic Patients?" *Practitioner* 185 (July): 85–89.
Gavron, Hannah. 1966. *The Captive Wife: Conflicts of Housebound Mothers.* London: Routledge & Kegan Paul.
Goldhamer, Herbert, and Andrew Marshall. 1953. *Psychosis and Civilization: Two Studies in the Frequency of Mental Disease.* Glencoe, Ill.: Free Press.
Goode, William. 1960. "Norm Commitment and Conformity to Role Status Obligations." *American Journal of Sociology* 66 (November): 246–58.
Gordon, Richard, and Katherine Gordon. 1958. "Psychiatric Problems of a Rapidly Growing Suburb." *A.M.A. Archives of Neurology and Psychiatry* 79 (May): 543–48.
Gove, Walter. 1967. "Types of Psychiatric Patients." Master's thesis, University of Washington, Seattle.
———. 1968. "A Theory of Mental Illness: An Analysis of the Relationship between Symptoms, Personal Attributes and Social Situations." Ph.D. dissertation, University of Washington, Seattle.
———. 1970a. "Sleep Deprivation: A Cause of Psychotic Disorganization." *American Journal of Sociology* 75 (March): 782–99.
———. 1970b. "Societal Reaction as an Explanation of Mental Illness: An Evaluation." *American Sociological Review* 35 (October): 873–84.
———. 1972a. "Sex Roles, Marital Status and Suicide." *Journal of Health and Social Behavior* 13 (June): 204–13.
———. 1972b. "The Relationship between Sex Roles, Mental Illness and Marital Status." *Social Forces,* vol. 51 (September).
———. 1972c. "The Interaction of Sex Roles and Mental Illness as a Factor Determining Time of Entrance into Treatment and the Development of Chronicity." Unpublished manuscript.

Gurin, Gerald, Joseph Veroff, and Sheila Feld. 1960. *Americans View Their Mental Health*. New York: Basic.

Haavio-Mannila, Elina. 1967. "Sex Differentiation in Role Expectations and Performance." *Journal of Marriage and the Family* 29 (August): 368–78.

Haberman, Paul. 1969. "Cross-Survey Analysis of Psychiatric Symptomology: A Corroborative Report on Subgroup Differences." Paper read at annual meeting of the American Sociological Association, San Francisco.

Hagnell, Olle. 1966. *A Prospective Study of the Incidence of Mental Disorder*. Sweden: Berlingska Boktryckeriet.

Hare, E. H., and G. K. Shaw. 1965. *Mental Health on a New Housing Estate*. London: Oxford University Press.

Harrison, Evelyn. 1964. "The Working Women: Barriers in Employment." *Public Administration Review* 24 (June): 78–85.

Hartley, Ruth. 1959–60. "Some Implications of Current Changes in Sex Role Patterns." *Merrill-Palmer Quarterly of Behavior and Development* 6 (April): 153–64b.

———. 1970. "American Core Culture: Changes and Continuities." In *Sex Roles in a Changing Society,* edited by Georgene Seward and Robert C. Williamson. New York: Random House.

Helgason, Thomas. 1964. "Epidemiology of Mental Disorders in Iceland." *Acta Psychiatrica Scandinavica,* Supplementum 173:1–258.

Hollingshead, August, and Fredrick Redlich. 1958. *Social Class and Mental Illness*. New York: Wiley.

Hughes, Everett. 1945. "Dilemmas and Contradictions of Status." *American Journal of Sociology* 50 (March): 353–59.

Innes, George, and Geoffrey Sharp. 1962. "A Study of Psychiatric Patients in North-East Scotland." *Journal of Mental Science* 108 (July): 447–56.

Kessel, W. I. N. 1960. "Psychiatric Morbidity in a London General Practice." *British Journal of Preventive Social Medicine* 14 (January): 16–22.

Klein, Donald, and John Davis. 1969. *Diagnosis and Drug Treatment of Psychiatric Disorders*. Baltimore: Williams & Wilkins.

Knudsen, Dean. 1969. "The Declining Status of Women: Popular Myths and the Failure of Functionalist Thought." *Social Forces* 48 (December): 183–93.

Komarovsky, Mirra. 1946. "Cultural Contradiction and Sex Roles." *American Journal of Sociology* 52 (November): 184–89.

———. 1950. "Functional Analysis of Sex Roles." *American Sociological Review* 15 (August): 508–16.

Kreps, Juanita. 1971. *Sex in the Market Place: American Women at Work*. Baltimore: Johns Hopkins Press.

Kuhn, Thomas. 1970. *The Structure of Scientific Revolutions*. Chicago: University of Chicago Press.

Landis, Carney, and James Page. 1938. *Modern Society and Mental Disease*. New York: Farrar & Rinehart.

Langner, Thomas, and Stanley Michael. 1963. *Life Stress and Mental Health*. New York: Free Press.

Larson, Richard. 1970. "The Influence of Sex Roles and Symptoms on Clergymen's Perceptions of Mental Illness." *Pacific Sociological Review* 13 (Winter): 53–61.

Leighton, Dorothea, Alexander Leighton, John Hardin, David Macklin, and Allister MacMillan. 1963. *The Character of Danger*. New York: Basic.

Llewellyn-Thomas, Edward. 1960. "The Prevalence of Psychiatric Symptoms within an Island Community." *Canadian Medical Association Journal* 83 (July): 197–204.

Logan, W. P. D., and A. A. Cushion. 1958. *Morbidity Statistics from General Practice*. Vol. 1. Studies on Medical Population Subjects no. 14. London: Her Majesty's Stationery Office.

Lopata, Helena. 1971. *Occupation Housewife*. New York: Oxford University Press.

McKee, John, and Alex Sheriffs. 1957. "The Differential Evaluation of Males and Females." *Journal of Personality* 25 (March): 356–71.

Walter R. Gove and Jeannette F. Tudor

———. 1959. "Men's and Women's Beliefs, Ideals and Self-Concepts." *American Journal of Sociology* 64 (January): 356–63.

Manis, Jerome. 1968. "The Sociology of Knowledge and Community Mental Health Research." *Social Problems* 15 (Spring): 488–501.

Maris, Ronald. 1969. *Social Forces in Urban Suicide*. Homewood, Ill.: Dorsey.

Martin, F. M., J. H. F. Brotherston, and S. P. W. Chave. 1957. "Incidence of Neurosis in a New Housing Estate." *British Journal of Preventive Social Medicine* 11 (October): 196–202.

Mazer, Milton. 1967. "Psychiatric Disorders in General Practice: The Experience of an Island Community." *American Journal of Psychiatry* 124 (November): 609–15.

Mead, Margaret. 1949. *Male and Female*. New York: Morrow.

Meile, Richard, and Philip Haese. 1969. "Social Status, Status Incongruence and Symptoms of Stress." *Journal of Health and Social Behavior* 10 (September): 237–44.

National Institute of Mental Health. 1967a. *Patients in State and County Mental Hospitals 1967*. Washington, D.C.: Government Printing Office.

———. 1967b. *Patient Characteristics Private Mental Hospitals 1967*. Washington, D.C.: Government Printing Office.

———. 1967c. *Veterans with Mental Disorders 1963–1967*. Washington, D.C.: Government Printing Office.

———. 1967d. *General Hospital Inpatient Psychiatric Service 1967*. Washington, D.C.: Government Printing Office.

———. 1967e. *Outpatient Psychiatric Services 1967*. Washington, D.C.: Government Printing Office.

Parsons, Talcott. 1942. "Age and Sex in the Social Structure of the United States." *American Sociological Review* 7 (October): 604–16.

Pasamanick, Benjamin, Dean Roberts, Paul Lemkau, and Dean Krueger. 1959. "A Survey of Mental Disease in an Urban Population: Prevalence by Race and Income." In *Epidemiology of Mental Disorder,* edited by Benjamin Pasamanick. Washington, D.C.: American Association for the Advancement of Science.

Phillips, Derek. 1964. "Rejection of the Mentally Ill: The Influence of Behavior and Sex." *American Sociological Review* 29 (October): 679–87.

———. 1966. "The 'True Prevalence' of Mental Illness in a New England State Community." *Mental Health Journal* 2 (Spring): 35–40.

Phillips, Derek, and Bernard Segal. 1969. "Sexual Status and Psychiatric Symptoms." *American Sociological Review* 34 (February): 58–72.

Pollack, Earl, Richard Redick, Vivian Brown, Cecil Wurster, and Kurt Gorwitz. 1964. "Socioeconomic and Family Characteristics of Patients Admitted to Psychiatric Services." *American Journal of Public Health* 54 (March): 506–18.

Primrose, E. J. R. 1962. *Psychological Illness*. Springfield, Ill.: Charles C Thomas.

Prudenski, G., and B. Kolpakov. 1962. "Questions concerning the Calculations of Non-working Time in Budget Statistics." *Problems of Economics* 6 (April): 12–31.

Public Health Service. 1967. *Division of Direct Health Service Annual Statistical Summary Fiscal Year 1967. Part II. Diagnostic and Demographic Data*. Washington, D.C.: Government Printing Office.

———. 1970. *Selected Symptoms of Psychological Distress*. Public Health Service Publication no. 1000, ser. 11, no. 37. Washington, D.C.: Government Printing Office.

Raskin, Allen, and Risa Golob. 1966. "Occurence of Sex and Social Class Differences in Premorbid Competence, Symptom and Outcome Measures in Acute Schizophrenia." *Psychological Reports* 18 (February): 11–22.

Robbins, Lewis. 1966. "A Historical Review of the Classification of Behavior Disorders and Once Current Perspective." In *The Classification of Behavior Disorders,* edited by Leonard Eron. Chicago: Aldine.

Rose, Arnold. 1951. "The Adequacy of Women's Expectations for Adult Roles." *Social Forces* 30 (October): 69–77.

Rosenkrantz, Paul, Susan Vogel, Helen Bee, Inge Broverman, and Donald Broverman.

1968. "Sex Role Stereotypes and Self-Conceptions in College Students." *Journal of Consulting Psychology* 32 (3): 287–95.

Rossi, Alice. 1964. "Equality between Sexes: An Immodest Proposal." *Daedalus* 93 (Spring): 607–52.

Rowe, Clarence. 1970. *An Outline of Psychiatry.* Dubuque, Iowa: Brown.

Rushing, William. 1969. "Two Patterns in the Relationship between Social Class and Mental Hospitalization." *American Sociological Review* 34 (August): 533–41.

Ryle, A. 1960. "The Neuroses in a General Practice." *Journal of the College of General Practitioners* 3 (August): 313–28.

Scheff, Thomas. 1966. *Being Mentally Ill: A Sociological Theory.* Chicago: Aldine.

Schur, Edwin. 1969. "Reactions to Deviance: A Critical Assessment." *American Journal of Sociology* 75 (November): 309–22.

Shepherd, Michael, Brian Cooper, A. C. Brown, and G. W. Kalton. 1964. "Minor Mental Illness in London: Some Aspects of a General Practice Survey." *British Medical Journal* 2 (November): 1359–63.

Sherriffs, Alex, and John McKee. 1957. "Qualitative Aspects of Beliefs about Men and Women." *Journal of Personality* 25 (June): 450–64.

Silverman, Charlotte. 1968. *The Epidemiology of Depression.* Baltimore: Johns Hopkins Press.

Srole, Leo, Thomas Langner, Stanley Michael, Marvin Opler, and Thomas Rennie. 1962. *Mental Health in the Metropolis.* New York: McGraw-Hill.

Steinmann, Anne, and David Fox. 1966. "Male-Female Perceptions of the Female Role in the United States." *Journal of Psychology* 64 (November): 265–79.

Stengel, Erwin. 1969. *Suicide and Attempted Suicide.* Baltimore: Penguin.

Susser, Mervyn. 1968. *Community Psychiatry: Epidemologic and Social Themes.* New York: Random House.

Tauss, W. 1967. "A Note on the Prevalence of Mental Disturbance." *Australian Journal of Psychology* 19 (August): 121–23.

Taylor, Lord, and Sidney Chave. 1964. *Mental Health and Environment.* London: Longman's Green.

U.S., Bureau of the Census. 1930. *Mental Patients in State Hospitals 1926 and 1927.* Washington, D.C.: Government Printing Office.

———. 1941. *Patients in Mental Institutions 1938.* Washington, D.C.: Government Printing Office.

———. 1966. "Estimates of the Population of the United States by Age, Color, Sex: July 1, 1966." Current Population Reports Series P-25, no. 352. Washington, D.C.: Government Printing Office.

———. 1970. "Estimates of the Population of the United States by Age, Race, and Sex: July 1, 1967 to July 1, 1969." Current Population Reports Series P-25, no. 441. Washington, D.C.: Government Printing Office.

Watts, C. A. H. 1962. "Psychiatric Disorders." In *Morbidity Statistics from General Practice.* Vol. 3. Studies on Medical Population Subjects no. 14. London: Her Majesty's Stationery Office.

Watts, C. A. H., E. C. Caute, and E. U. Kuenssberg. 1964. "Survey of Mental Illness in General Practice." *British Medical Journal* 2 (November): 1351–59

Zolik, Edwin, and Joseph Marches. 1968. "Mental Health Morbidity in a Suburban Community." *Journal of Clinical Psychology* 24 (January): 103–108.

73

Salon, Foyer, Bureau: Women and the Professions in France[1]

Catherine Bodard Silver
Brooklyn College, The City University of New York

During the great revolution of 1789—rhetorically dedicated to abstract equality—the women of France rioted, demonstrated, and struggled in the cause. However, apart from references to *citoyennes*—the female version of the new, universal social rank, *citoyen*—women received no substantive benefits from the redistribution of rights after the destruction of the monarchy and aristocracy (see Duhet 1971).[2] Such a pattern has long characterized the situation of women in France—not least those women who seek to enter the most skilled and prestigious occupational positions, the professions. France has long been characterized by abstract commitments to equality—but also by strong familistic traditions stressing women's subordinate and domestic role. Since 1900, higher education has been available to women in proportions that compare favorably with other European societies; yet today they are minimally represented at the highest professional levels. At the same time, French women have wider access to professional careers than do their counterparts in many other Western societies.

Thus, French women are very far indeed from that "equality" proclaimed in the Republic's motto, but simplistic images of "repression" or "discrimination" are insufficient for an adequate sociological understanding of the professional aspirations, frustrations, and achievements of women in France. The situation of professional women in France reveals some of the complex interactions among economy, polity, and culture defining "women's place," illuminating by comparison and contrast the more familiar situation in English-speaking societies.

THE CLASS AND OCCUPATIONAL SETTING

Some distinctive characteristics of French social and occupational structure must be understood as a prologue to analysis. Professional occupations in

[1] I wish to acknowledge the help of Elinor Barber and Allan Silver in the preparation of this paper.

[2] The Constitution of 1791 treated women as *passif* rather than *actif* citizens; the legislative committee of the Convention in 1793 excluded women—together with minors, the mad, and the criminal—from political rights; shortly after, they were prohibited from attending any political assembly (Duhet 1971, pp. 165–66). The Revolution's unprecedented provision for divorce, however, formally conferred equal rights on both spouses.

France cannot be taken as the direct equivalents of American ones. They include, of course, the classic "liberal professions"—law, medicine, the professoriat; but in France, *professeurs* are found not only in universities but at the educational level just below, the *lycées*. High government administrators—*cadres supérieurs*—are more highly professionalized in France, both in occupational style and educational requirements (roughly equivalent to American graduate studies short of the doctoral dissertation). For this reason, as well as the traditional dignity and prestige of the higher public administration in France, government administration is appropriately regarded as a profession.

Other occupations, too, are more readily accorded professional status in France. This is true of some in which women are numerous, such as teachers below the *lycée* level (*instituteurs*), and middle-level administrators; such strata comprise the *cadres moyens*. Both *cadres supérieurs* and *cadres moyens* are classifications used by the French census, but they are also terms of daily speech used to describe social distinctions in French society.

These distinctions suggest how inapplicable to France is the American notion of a broad middle class which—however heterogeneous in occupational, educational, and ethnic terms—nonetheless shares core social values which widely serve as models for other strata. The term *bourgeoisie,* often translated misleadingly as "middle class," refers to about 26% of the French population (in 1962), a group sharply distinguished both from manual workers (*ouvriers*) and white-collar personnel (*employés*). Within the *bourgeoisie* must be distinguished the 4% or 5% of the population forming the *grande bourgeoisie*—*cadre supérieurs,* the liberal professions, and the most wealthy property owners, employers, investors, and businessmen. The *grande bourgeoisie* differs significantly not only in wealth and status but also in values and style of life from the *petite bourgeoisie* (10% of the population) and the *bourgeoisie moyenne* (12%) (who include the *cadres moyens,* i.e., *instituteurs,* nurses, administrators, and smaller businessmen and property owners). As we shall see, distinctions between the values of the *grande bourgeoisie* and other strata are important in understanding the position and opportunities of professional women.[3]

PROFESSIONAL WOMEN IN THE OCCUPATIONAL STRUCTURE

Compared with other Western nations, the proportion of women employed in nonagricultural occupations in France ranks among the highest—36%

---

[3] The status and life styles of professions and the *bourgeoisie* in France are also affected by the continuing presence of very large proportions of rural and manual workers. Of the labor force, 15% (a proportion applying to both sexes) are in the agricultural sector—three times that of Britain, and almost twice that of the United States. Fully 39% of the total labor force are manual workers, *ouvriers*; of working women, 22%

(Organisation Internationale du Travail 1967).[4] However, the extent of women's participation in the labor force is an ambiguous indicator of equality between the sexes; a high rate may denote women's large-scale relegation to low-paying, unskilled, and dead-end positions, whose major social function is to supplement low family incomes or to support families without male heads of households. The nature of women's participation in professional occupations partakes of analogous ambiguities. In the non-agricultural labor force, the proportion of each sex who are professionals (the liberal professions, *cadres supérieurs, cadres moyens*) is essentially identical—17% for women, 17.8% for men. But distinguishing within professional occupations, only 18% of professional women are in the higher-status positions (liberal professions, *cadres supérieurs*) compared with 42% of the men. The absolute number of French professional women is about half that of men—in 1968 there were 1,002,940 such women, compared with 2,003,960 men.

Although French women enjoy considerable access to the professions, they tend to cluster in the middle ranks. Yet this state of affairs is in some ways not so unsatisfactory as the comparable one in the United States. The relatively high status of middle-level professionals in France, and some distinctive characteristics of professional occupations like teaching and public administration—in which women are heavily concentrated—work to modify somewhat what would otherwise be a position of very marked inferiority in professional life.

The most important case in point is that of *lycée professeurs,* of whom 55% were women in the school year 1968–69. In all, 46,307 were *lycée professeurs,* constituting one-quarter of all women in the *cadre supérieur* and liberal professions. *Lycées,* although the stage before university studies, are hardly the same as American high schools. Academically, their last two years are comparable with the first two in superior American colleges. The selection of teachers is rigorous, and requirements are intellectually strenuous. Candidates receive specialized educations in the Ecoles Normales Supérieures, at academic levels higher than that provided in university faculties attended by students of the same age. Both *lycée* and university *professeurs* usually pass a difficult competitive examination, the *agrégation,* requiring several years of preparation and testing general culture as well as specialized knowledge. Teaching staffs in *lycées* are organized in a hierarchy of ranks, and high rank is achieved both by seniority and by indications of professional achievement. These schools are understood to be vehicles of high culture, and successful completion of such a school

---

are *ouvrières.* (All descriptive statistics not otherwise attributed have been drawn from 5% samples of census data; these figures are drawn from the 1968 census.)

[4] Other "leaders" in this respect are Finland (42% in 1960), Denmark (38% in 1967), and the United States (36% in 1967).

provides an automatic entitlement to university admission. Thus, *lycée* teaching is clearly assimilated to university education rather than lower education; it represents an arduous and prestigious achievement. *Lycée professeurs* are widely regarded as representatives of science and culture in a society where official values accord high status to these domains. That half of these *professeurs* are women meets an abstract criterion of equality without devaluating the profession by "overfeminizing" it, in a society in which women are not admitted on equal terms to the highest occupational ranks. In both qualitative and quantitative senses, then, *lycée* teaching represents a most significant professional area available to women, one essentially lacking in American society.[5]

Similar considerations apply to *instituteurs*. In 1962, 72% of these were women (Ministère de l'Education National 1968–69)—certainly a high proportion but lower than the comparable figure for primary school teachers in the United States, which is more than 90% (Institut National de la Statistique et des Etudes Economiques [INSEE]). As representatives of culture in a society which officially holds its culture to be a national treasure, their prestige benefits; also, their professional preparation is clearly superior to that of their American counterparts.[6] Thus, at all levels of state-supported teaching below the university, but particularly in *lycées*, teaching careers open to women are significantly more professionalized than their American counterparts.

There remain the universities. As is well known, the distinction between academic ranks is far sharper than in the United States, with the professoriat constituting by far a smaller fraction of the total teaching staff, and exercising distinctive kinds of authority.[7] In these ranks, women are indeed few—less than 2% in the faculties of law and medicine, 4.5% in the *facultés des lettres* (teaching literature, philosophy, and social science), and 6% in the science faculties. However, below the professorial rank—at instructional levels which in rights and relative compensation rank below associate and assistant professors in the American system—the proportion of women jumps to 25% (reaching 35% in the *facultés des lettres*)

---

[5] Conditions of employment and compensation have been equal for men and women in *lycée* teaching since 1927. It is important to add, however, that positions of higher administrative authority within *lycées* are dominated by men. *Lycées* are sexually segregated, both as to students and teaching staff—a circumstance that has offered women "built-in" *entrée* to this important profession.

[6] Equality of working conditions among *instituteurs* of both sexes was achieved in 1882. We may note that women staffing the *écoles maternelles*—caring for children between the ages of three and six years—must have achieved essentially the same educational qualifications as *instituteurs* and have often begun advanced studies (Berger 1952).

[7] The rank of university professor usually requires the completion of the *thèse d'Etat*—a degree more strenuous than the American Ph.D that normally requires 10 years for completion.

(Dumas 1965). In the United States in 1961, 9% of university full professors were women, and 16% of the associate professors (Fogarty et al. 1971). Once again, a characteristic pattern emerges—a tiny participation of women at the very highest professional levels but a very considerable presence at the middle levels, one comparing favorably indeed with other Western societies.

Given the significance of academic intellectuals in defining and interpreting the nature of social problems, it is curious that this discrepancy between women's participation at high and low levels of instructional authority within the university has not produced in France an ideological focus upon the special problems of academic women, as it has in the United States. Data are lacking to show how long this sort of discrepancy has characterized French university faculties, but, in any case, the general problems of French universities—overcrowding, concentration of authority in the professorial "mandarinate," restricted opportunities for nonprofessorial staff, and others—have overshadowed concern with the problems of women. None of the major competing interpretations of the universities' difficulties—financial, administrative, Marxist, *gauchiste,* or other—stresses discrimination against women, as compared with such issues as class inequality, generational conflict, disputes about intellectual authority, or insufficient resources.

Apart from teaching, public administration is the other large-scale set of professional opportunities sponsored by the state. Its significance is very great, given the long tradition in France of centralized state administration, the high qualifications required for it, and the prestige surrounding it. Women were first admitted into the civil service at the end of the last century, but it was the First World War which significantly widened their opportunities in the state sector and led to a formal equality of treatment and conditions in most respects. Only after the Second World War, however, were the highest administrative positions made accessible to women, who were admitted to the Ecole Nationale d'Administration, the intellectually rigorous and key point of entry into these posts. As of 1962, 11.2% of the highest administrative positions—finance inspectors, members of the Conseil d'Etat, and others—were women. In the United States as of 1961, the proportion of women in the highest grades of the civil service was 4.4% (Fogarty et al. 1971). Nonetheless, whole ministries—Justice, Foreign Affairs, Finance—have very few women in higher positions, and admission to some administrative careers remains formally closed.[8] Women

[8] Women are excluded from the Ecole des Mines, Ecole du Génie Rural, and the Ecole des Eaux et Forets. On the other hand, although data are lacking, their presence at responsible levels in the Ministries of Education, of Labor, and of Health appears to be significant.

are still formally barred from the office of *préfet*—the extremely important representatives of central government in the *départements* into which France is administratively divided. Indeed, the very law which established equal rights for women in the public service provided also for exceptions due to the "physical unfitness" of women and "psychological difficulties which the presence of women might provoke" (Michèl and Texier 1964).[9] Nonetheless, public administration clearly represents an important professional opportunity for women. Among women in positions of high administrative responsibility, three-quarters are in the public service (*Avenir* 1965). Furthermore, the rate at which the number of women administrators among the *cadres supérieurs* is increasing is the highest of any profession; and this rate is double that of the increase among males (OCDE 1970).[10] As of 1962, 21,000 women were at administrative ranks corresponding to the *cadres supérieurs* compared with 172,740 men. The major significance of public administration as a profession for women lies in the *cadres moyens,* where in 1962 there were 79,060 women (and 168,700 men).

We have already observed that the high qualifications and prestige of public administration in France lend it both the aura and the substance of a professional career.[11] But this rather high participation of women professionals in public administration occurs in the context of their low participation in the liberal professions. Law and medicine remain heavily masculine (15% of French physicians are women); and engineering even more so (3% of the latter are women).[12] The achievement of professional women in France is thus very much weighted on the side of public employment, especially in teaching and government administration, at the expense of accomplishment in entrepreneurial and private professions.

Given the "statist" tradition of France—in which, historically, public administration and education have played central roles as stabilizing and conservatizing forces—this means that professional women are largely engaged in the least dynamic and change-oriented aspects of French life. As we shall see below, when analyzing aspects of French culture, this is but one way in which French professional women are particularly affected by the most conservative tendencies in French society. At this point, it is sufficient to point out that in the context of France, professional achievements by women do not necessarily contribute to accelerated social change.

[9] "L'inaptitude physique," "les difficultés psychologiques que pourraient soulever une présence féminine" (Michel and Texier 1964).

[10] The rate is even higher in the private sector, where the absolute number of women is smaller.

[11] The substantive benefits are described by Vimont (1965, pp. 23–55).

[12] One percent of architects are women.

Catherine Bodard Silver

ACCESS TO HIGHER EDUCATION IN PROFESSIONAL CAREER LINES

Higher education being an indispensable prerequisite for entry to professional occupations, it is necessary to consider women's access to universities. In these terms, France emerges as among the most egalitarian of European nations: in 1963, 43% of university students were women, compared with 32% in Britain, 35% in Denmark, 24% in Germany, and 22% in Norway (OCDE 1970).[13] And the significant proportion of women among French university students has not been a recent development: from 2.5% in 1900, it grew to 12.5% in 1920, 26% in 1930, and fully 34% at the start of the Second World War. The postwar period saw a slowing of the growth of female representation as the total university population began to expand considerably; from 38% in 1959 it moved to 43% in 1963, where it has roughly remained (UNESCO 1968).

France has thus made higher education available to women on a larger scale, and over a longer period, than has been the case in many other, if not all, Western European countries. However, access of women to higher education in France is largely a function of class inequality. The *grande bourgeoisie* in 1962 represented 4% of the population but 29% of the university students; the *cadres moyens* amounted to 7.8% of the population but 18% of the students (OCDE 1965). Among women university students, the proportion of *bourgeois* origin is higher than among men. Thus, higher education in France consolidates the class position of the *bourgeoisie* more often among women than among men (Bourdieu and Passeron 1964). The daughters of the *bourgeoisie* are more likely to go to universities than the sons of nonmanual occupational strata, let alone of *ouvriers*. Women in France are by no means denied access to professions because they are blocked off from university education. There is a marked discrepancy between their educational opportunities and the extent of their professional achievement. This situation, now developing on a large scale in the United States and some other nations for the first time, has existed in France for decades. Yet women in France have displayed less overt discontent on this account or indeed on any other account that involves woman's place. Tellingly, Simone de Beauvoir's subtle and powerful *De deuxième sexe*, published in 1949, was the first notable occasion on which the problem of women's role was comprehensively raised; by no means restricted to France, it analyzes those aspects of French society which women of Beauvoir's stamp find particularly irksome. In France today, this book can still be regarded as ahead of its time— its impact having been limited to some intellectual and ideological circles—while, in translation, it has been widely read in the English-speaking societies, where

[13] Comparisons with the United States are more difficult, given the far greater heterogeneity of post–high school educational institutions in America than in Western Europe.

the problem was raised decades earlier in both intellectual and agitational terms. To understand why feminist formulations and movements have been so slow to develop in France, we may begin with a discussion of some cultural factors particularly distinctive to French society.

CULTURAL DEFINITIONS OF WOMEN

If it is true that everywhere images of women's nature play a large role in defining and reinforcing "appropriate" roles for them, in no Western society is this more palpably obvious than in France. Surely no other Western culture has developed more elaborated and intricate ideas about women and more closely interwoven them with the "high culture" and the style of life of whole social classes. The two centuries that produced the classical culture of France, the 17th and 18th, also produced a series of women eminent as both sponsors and creators of high culture. Beside such names as la duchesse de Rambouillet, la marquise de Sevigné, Madame de Lafayette, Madame de Maintenon, Mademoiselle de Lespinasse, and Madame de Staël, corresponding figures in Anglo-American culture (Jane Austen and Emily Dickinson, for example) are comparatively pale and late. Women helped shape the core values and the very language that are crucial to the substance of French culture. Such women, of course, were few and highly privileged, flourishing in the setting of an aristocratic social order. The rise of commercial society in the 19th century demoted women from the highest reaches of cultural creativity and participation as key sponsors of culture. Balzac and Flaubert, among others, described the emergence of a new type of woman—a highly elaborated aesthetic object, the property of men, and seeking expression as wife or mistress. "The destiny of woman and her sole glory," writes Balzac in his *Physiologie du mariage,* "is to excite the hearts of men. Woman is a property acquired by contract; she is disposable property, . . . in short, woman properly speaking is only an annex of man" (cited by Beauvoir 1949). Older themes portraying woman as an idealized erotic object, finding fulfillment and power over men in love, certainly persisted; but more significant by far was the new dominance of the domestic ideal, associated above all with the most prosperous *bourgeoisie.* The focus of emotional life became the *foyer*—an idea for which "home" is a weaker equivalent; as an arena for women, the *foyer* was far more restricted and passive than the aristocratic milieu.[14]

It would be anachronistic to regard this development solely as a decrease of *bourgeois* women's power. On the contrary, their enhanced role within

[14] A succinct contrast of *bourgeois* and aristocratic notions of women and family life is found in Barber (1955, pp. 78–81). For more extended statements, see the essays by Xavier Lannes and Jean Maitron on the 18th and first half of the 19th centuries, respectively, in Prigent (1954). A large historical view is offered by Ariès (1962, esp. pt. 3).

the family—the expectation of being loved, some responsibility for the rearing and education of children—represented a significant improvement. Until about the middle of the 18th century, *bourgeois* and aristocratic women had little or nothing to do in these terms. On the whole, they neither reared children nor administered households; these tasks were discharged by servants, nurses, and tutors under the ultimate direction of husbands. Ironically, in view of later developments, among the first conquests and achievements of higher-status women in France was the role of *maîtresse de maison* (see Sullerot 1968). (The very phrase, the counterpart of *maître de maison,* differs from the English "housewife" [*ménagère*]; it implies an important and distinct role in the administration of the home as a social and moral entity.) We shall see that the impact of this "achievement" is still meaningful among *bourgeois* women in contemporary France. To appreciate this, we must understand the historical and cultural aspects of prevalent ideology about the family and women's place in it as they evolved in France.

After the Bourbon Restoration of 1815, conservative ideologists elaborated a social philosophy which defined the domestic, nuclear family as a major element of social stability. This represented a shift in the alleged basis of social stability from earlier emphases upon the extended aristocratic lineage, public ties of dependence and obligation based upon locality, the "corporations" of artisans and merchants, the parish, and other groupings—all of them larger than the domestic family and, of course, excluding women from significant power. The influential conservative Bonald, for example, worked out such a theory, comparing domestic authority with fundamental social and political authority, and assigning to women a subordinate but vital place in the newly significant domestic scheme.[15]

Such values, however, were very far from the exclusive property of the Catholic reaction. Rousseau, seminal both for Romanticism and the Enlightenment, called for domesticated, loving motherhood, even to the point of having mothers nurse their own children—a suggestion ridiculed in the aristocratic *salons* as an expression of "les vanités de la mamelle."[16] The

[15] "L'homme est à la femme ce que la femme est à l'enfant; ou le pouvoir [sovereign authority] est au ministre, ce que le ministre est au sujet" (cited by Beauvoir 1949, p. 186). As we have observed it was a *gain* for women to be regarded as "ministers" in Bonald's sense. (This did not prevent Bonald from describing the adultery of men as a cause only of personal unhappiness to wives, while that of wives represented the destruction of the family—a widespread French perspective.) On the distinctive contribution of the domestic family to social order in Bonald's thought, see his "Du divorce consideré au XIXᵉ siècle relativement à l'état domestique et à l'état public de la société" (in Bonald 1864, esp. chaps. 2, 3, 4). At more popular levels, comparable images of the family and women's role were promulgated during the Restoration with unprecedented scope and intensity. See Deniel (1965).

[16] Awkwardly translated, at best, as "the conceit of breasts" (Sullerot 1968, p. 80).

apostle of rational progress, Comte, saw women as inferior by reason of their "biological childishness" (*infantilisme biologique*). He rather vaguely sentimentalized them as morally superior to men, but saw men as stronger "not only in body, but also in intellect [*esprit*] and character. . . . We must above all act and think, struggling against the difficulties of our real destiny; thus, men must command, despite their lesser morality" (Comte 1848, p. 204). Comte, like Rousseau and Bonald, saw woman's chief role and contribution as lying in the *foyer*, in the education of children and the refinement of emotional impulses. Like Rousseau's, his definition of women's role was not seen as reactionary and retrograde but was linked to a vision of progress. "In order to assure [woman's] emotional destiny," Comte wrote, man must make woman's life "more and more domestic," and "above all detach her from all outside work. . . . *The man must feed the woman*: this is the natural law of our species" (Comte 1848, pp. 242–43). To grasp how such a vision could possibly be understood as expressing a kind of liberating progress, the briefest excursion into Comtean thinking is necessary. For him, the domestication of women was a phase of progress in emotional life—part of the grand Comtean vision—in which society would pass from family arrangements, like those of aristocracy, linking it to the past; move on to the new type of voluntary, conjugal, and domestic arrangement linking it to the present and the living; and finally arrive at "paternal" impulses expressing a "universal sociability" linking humanity to the future (Comte 1848, p. 91). Such perspectives may seem obscure, muddled, or quaint; but only by grasping them do we understand how the domesticizing of higher-status women in France was understood as a form of progress rather than a regressive and reactionary development.

Perhaps the most indigenously French founder of the European Left, Proudhon, was a fervent mysogynist. Woman was fit only to choose between being "mistress or housewife" (*courtisane ou ménagère*).[17] Her inferiority was intrinsic, not conditioned; in the family—as much the cell of social stability, in Proudhon's thought, as in the reactionary Bonald's—her task was to educate children in moral duty, but "under paternal sanction," since she was only a "living reflection, her mission [being] to embody, simplify and transmit to young minds the father's thought."

Even Emile Durkheim, later in the century, explained some sex differences in suicide rates as a function of women's less complex and sensitive

---

Rousseau's family doctrine is found chiefly in his didactic novels, *Emile* and *La nouvelle Héloise* and included, it must be noted, a parallel domestication of men.

[17] Proudhon did not regard the woman question lightly. In his *De la justice dans la Révolution et dans l'Eglise* (1858) he devoted 300 pages to "Amour et mariage"; just before his death, he wrote another 270 pages replying to female critics, under the title *La pornocratie; ou les femmes dans les temps modernes* (see Maitron 1954).

emotional character, requiring lessened dependence upon social control.[18]

Neither a radical thinker like Fourier nor, more important, writers in the mainstream of French Marxism or socialism subscribed to these perspectives. Attacking the *bourgeois* family, they included women's subjection among the evils of capitalist society. But French Marxism has always interpreted the subjection of women in a context of class conflict. The powerful emphasis on class themes in French social protest has operated to discourage specifically "feminist" diagnoses of women's situation such as those characteristic of England and America. As we have seen, such advantages as higher-status women do enjoy in France—in state employment and access to higher education—are indeed strongly linked to the political and social status quo. The problems of lower-status women have characteristically been assimilated to a class- rather than a women-centered definition of the situation.

We see that important representatives of widely diverse and opposed French thought—Catholic conservatives, Romantic individualists, scientific progressivists, antibourgeois polemicists—have all agreed, in different tones and in different perspectives, on the value or necessity of women's domestic and subordinate mission. There was no French counterpart to the role played by a John Stuart Mill in the struggle for women's rights in the 19th century. The dominant conservative impulses found wide echo, and still do. "She is to charm, console, understand. Her role is that of a helpful, available assistant, but without initiative. She exists essentially in relation to others; her place in the scheme of things is not in the outside world of action, but in the privacy of the home, where she arranges and prepares the times of relaxation" (Chombart de Lauwe 1963, p. 120). Thus does a sociologist, summing up contemporary research findings, describe the modal image of women in France.

To assess this image only as passive and self-effacing is to underestimate its strength and appeal. It also provides a positive role for woman, interpreting her familial functions as crucial rather than ornamental, dignified rather than subordinate. Thus, the woman becomes the agent of high culture within the domestic circle—not only in substantive terms that provide a function for women's education—but also as teacher and exemplar of *la politesse* to children—a concept of far greater social scope and cultural resonance than its American analogues, 'politeness" or "good manners." This value complex is strongest in the *bourgeoisie*. Thus, we will

---

[18] "Her sensibility is rudimentary rather than highly developed. As she lives outside of community existence more than man, she is less penetrated by it; society is less necessary to her because she is less impregnated by sociability. With a few devotional practises and some animals to care for, the old unmarried women's life is full. . . . Man, on the contrary, is hard beset in this respect. . . . Because he is a more complex social being, he can maintain his equilibrium only by finding more points of support outside himself" (Durkheim 1951, pp. 215–16).

see below, familistic definitions of woman's role are strongest precisely in that stratum which, in Anglo-American societies, is among the least familistic.

Such values were, until very recently, strongly reflected in French laws. The Napoleonic Code, drawing often on Roman models, found both precedent and conceptual imagery for reaffirming the domestic hegemony of the *pater*, and conceiving of women only in a domestic context. Until 1938, women could not work, attend universities, or participate in decisions about childrens' education, without their husbands' permission; husbands were administrators of their wives' property and wealth; women were defined, with the criminal, the insane, and children, as legally "unfit." The Napoleonic Code defined the obedience of wives to husbands as a legal obligation. After 1938, only a successful request for a special form of marriage contract could prevent husbands from being invested with total ownership of family property, including that owned by women before marriage; in recent years, about three-quarters of French women have been married without making such requests. Husbands are still legally defined as the *chef de la communauté* and *chef de famille*—both much more extensive notions than "head of the family." In France, it has been secular law, not religious ritual, that proclaimed the wife's duty to "obey the man." As *chef de la communauté* he was entitled to make major financial, educational, and other decisions without consulting the wife. Until 1965, when some reforms were introduced, wives needed the formal consent of husbands to work outside the home or to buy on credit; even those reforms left many of the husbands' privileges untouched.[19]

Thus, married women in France have long suffered from legal disabilities. Yet French values assign far higher social esteem to the married than the unmarried woman; the single state is regarded as deeply anomalous for women, and nowhere except in deviant subcultures is it identified with notions of freedom and self-determination. These values are not peculiar to France, of course, but are especially deep there. A forceful indicator of their strength is found in a recently enacted law providing that all women

[19] A good summary of these aspects of French law is given in Michael and Texier (1964, pp. 71–106). They led, in the words of these authorities, to a situation in which "a sane wife is never the [legal] equal of a mad husband" (p. 73). The concept of the *foyer* and of women's place in it is clearly expressed in an aspect of French marriage law which provided that adultery by husbands was punishable only by light sanctions, unless the offense was actually committed in his home, in which case it was cause for divorce. Adultery by wives anywhere was cause for divorce and sometimes imprisonment. The backwardness of French law on women is hardly restricted to family life. Women did not receive the right to vote until 1945, when their participation in the Resistance was frequently cited as justification for enfranchising them. They thus received, after the Second World War, what American and British women received after the First World War without having had to become heroines or martyrs to do so.

over the age of 25 are entitled to be addressed as *Madame*, even if unmarried; and that an unmarried woman above that age who is persistently addressed as *Mademoiselle* may bring legal action for slander.[20] Thus, single women in France have traditionally been subject to social deprivations, and married women, to legal ones. Expressive of these attitudes were debates that occurred in the French Assembly after World War I, on the subject of enfranchising women: it was argued, in opposition, that the vote should be given to unmarried but not to married women, on the grounds that married women could not be "political individuals" with wills other than those of their husbands. This reverses the view, conventional in England and America, that the married are in general more "mature" or "responsible" than the unmarried.[21]

To call these perspectives "traditional" would suggest an unbroken continuity that, as we have seen, distorts history. In fact, they are linked above all to a class which only developed in the 19th century, the *bourgeoisie*; and this historical association is strongly manifested in contemporary data on the distribution of family values and behavior in French society. Repeatedly, the *bourgeoisie* emerges as *more* "traditional" in these areas than the *classe moyenne* or the working class. Thus, *the very class whose cultural, economic, and social advantages are such as to render many of its women qualified candidates for professional careers is that least disposed to approve and provide for women's work outside the home.*

The data are striking indeed—perhaps especially to American readers who are likely to think of higher social status and education as implying greater approval for the equality of women. In France, the percentage of women who play significant roles in decisions about the family budget is 15% among the *bourgeoisie*, 53% for the *classe moyenne*, and 78% in the working class. The lower the social class, the more likely men are to help in domestic tasks. The higher the class, the more women's working outside the home is perceived as incompatible with the obligations of family life (Chombart de Lauwe 1963, p. 158).

In professional strata, the strength of the *femme au foyer* image remains very strong. Among professional women with at least one child, two-thirds think it wise to remain at home while children are small (Andrieux 1962, pp. 351 ff.). It is not unduly speculative to imagine the psychic cost to those professional women who, accepting this ideology, continue careers through this stage of the life cycle. The great majority of these women

[20] These provisions contrast sharply with the emergence of "Ms." as a form of address that ignores marital status, in the United States, or the general use of "Miss" as a way to gain the attention of receptionists, sales personnel, and waitresses.

[21] In Britain the vote was, in fact, extended during the 1920s to women in two stages, beginning with those above the age of 28, with no attention paid to marital status. Thus, in Britain it was considered anomalous for *younger* women, and in France, for *married* women, to vote.

regard their family roles as requiring a full-time commitment. Not only familistic but "women-of-cultivated-leisure" imagery is very strong: 59% of professional women express the desire to cease work in order to pursue cultural interests after children have left the home (Andrieux 1962, pp. 351 ff.). Thus, professional commitments among French women are accompanied both by familistic commitments and the attractions of a consummatory attitude to culture as a substitute for a professional career.

That this "traditionalism" is apparently especially strong among the *bourgeoisie* means that there is a greater tendency for women professionals to come from the *classe moyenne,* who are more disposed to utilize higher education as a means of social mobility and comparatively less inhibited by such values (Chombart de Lauwe 1963, pp. 197–205). Thus, the greatest opportunities for professional advances have been made available to those women whose class and family styles are least likely to encourage serious professional commitments. Indeed, among the few women who have achieved the highest positions in the professional civil service, the proportion of unmarried ones is extremely high—50% (Vimont 1965, pp. 23–52). In France, the claims of family and profession are incompatible for women to a degree extraordinary in a modern society. Each is treated as sovereign, making the kind of claims upon life and being that do not easily tolerate the coexistence of the other.

CONCLUSIONS

Characterized by strong commitments to abstract equality and universalism, France has long evolved a richly wrought set of conservatively defined roles and values governing the social existence of women. These values have continuing and compelling influence.[22] Their fulfillment is conceived as rewarding, not merely as restrictive and constraining, by many French women. The role of the women in the *foyer,* especially in the more advantaged classes likely to furnish higher proportions of professionals, is charged with satisfying content, psychologically and culturally. Even among those who choose professional life, the competing tug of the *femme au foyer* remains strong.

But French women have also achieved considerable professional success and have long enjoyed access—within the limits of overarching class inequalities—to free higher education. As we have seen, many of their successes are within the context of state-sponsored activity. Indeed, there is a sense in which the state has created the professional women in France.

[22] The continuing social conservatism of French women can be shown by their disproportionate electoral support for the parties of order and hierarchy in postwar France, regardless of age or social class. The number of women in elective office at all levels has, in fact, declined considerably since a high point after the Liberation (see Duhamel 1971).

Thus, the extent and nature of women's professional activities reflects the characteristic French cleavage between the society's modal social values, on the one hand, and those of the French state, on the other—a difference that has led some to describe France as an "administered" rather than a "governed" society. In these respects, the professional successes of French women run against the grain of the culture, in much the same way as the universalism of the French government has often ignored or overridden the localism, Catholicism, and individualism of the French people.

This sort of state-sponsored success for women's professional aspirations involves considerable costs. It fails, of course, to eliminate the tensions and limits imposed by the continuing cultural conservatism of French society with respect to women's place and role. Indeed, given the great gap in France between those values suffusing government and public administration and those of the society, the professional aspirations of many women can be seen as diverted into insulated and conservative sectors of French life.

We saw earlier that French women made a large advance into the professional labor market after the First World War, but that there were signs of a decline or stagnation in the situation after the Second World War. Rapid defeat and occupation meant that France did not experience prolonged mobilization of the domestic economy, unlike other Western nations during 1939–45. The French economy since 1945 has grown at a rate that has not compelled a major "talent hunt" among women for scarce aptitudes required in newly emerging specialties. Men have only slowly, if at all, "abandoned" the less dynamic professional careers to women, as might happen to a greater extent in a more rapidly growing economy (we have seen a few signs of this in the sex patterns of professional employment in government and the private sector).

Despite the holding of an "Estates-General" of Women at Versailles in the fall of 1970—an event which surprised many by the vigor and clarity of the complaints and demands that the delegates and leaders manifested—there is little sign of the emergence of a modern women's movement in search of expanded opportunities. Forces of the Left—above all, the Communist party—are slow to deal with the question of women's rights, least of all those of women professionals. Themes of protest center on the rigidities of administration in government and institutions; the insufficiency of resources for education, housing, and transport; inflation and the slow rate of economic growth; and the maldistribution of wealth and income in a society that has not become significantly less socially hierarchical in the postwar period. The few groups—among them, weak and scattered *gauchistes*—who raise the issue of women's role as such, often in accents borrowed from contemporary American polemic, are barely heard and widely ignored.

In such a setting, the prospects for an expansion of professional opportunities for women are not encouraging. Whether one defines the situation as depressing or moderately promising is a matter of personal style and social ideology. But, in any event, it seems unlikely that the weight of French tradition in the matter of women will be rapidly lightened in the decades to come. The limited and deeply ambiguous "success" of French professional women is likely to endure for some time.

REFERENCES

Andrieux, Cécile. 1962. "Ideologies traditionelle et moderne dans les attitudes sociales feminines." Thèse de troisième cycle, Université de Paris.

Ariès, Phillipe. 1962. *Centuries of Childhood*. London: Cape.

Avenir. "Les carrières feminines" (April–May 1965).

Barber, Elinor. 1955. *The French Bourgeoisie in the Eighteenth Century*. Princeton, N.J.: Princeton University Press.

Beauvoir, Simone de. 1949. *Le deuxième sexe*. Paris: Gallimard.

Berger, Ida. 1952. *Les maternelles*. Paris: Centre d'Etudes Sociologiques.

Bonald, Louis de. 1864. "Du divorce considéré au XIXe siècle relativement à l'état domestique et à l'état public de société." In *Oeuvres complètes*. Vol. 2. Paris: Migne.

Bourdieu, Pierre, and J. C. Passeron. 1964. *Les héritiers*. Paris: Editions de Minuit.

Chombart de Lauwe, Paul-Henry. 1963. *La femme dans la société: Son image dans différents milieux*. Paris: Centre Nationale de la Recherche Scientifique.

Comte, Auguste. 1848. *Discours sur l'ensemble du positivisme*. Paris: Mathias.

Deniel, Raymond. 1965. *Une image de la famille et de la société sous la Restauration (1815–1830)*. Paris: Editions Ouvrières.

Duhamel, Alain. 1971. "Les femmes et la politique." *Monde* (March 10).

Duhet, Paul-Marie. 1971. *Les femmes et la Révolution*. Paris: Juillard.

Dumas, Francine. 1965. "La femme dans la vie sociale." In *Femmes du XXe siècle*. Paris: Presses Universitaires de France.

Durkheim, Emile. (1897) 1951. *Suicide*. Trans. John Spaulding and George Simpson. Glencoe, Ill.: Free Press.

Fogarty, Michael, et al. 1971. *Sex, Career and Family*. Beverly Hills, Calif.: Sage.

Institut National de la Statistique et des Etudes Economiques (INSEE). 1970. *Annuaire statistique de la France*. Paris.

Maitron, Jean. 1954. "Les penseurs sociaux et la famille dans la première moitié du XXe siècle." In *Renouveau des idées sur la famille,* edited by Robert Prigent. Paris: Presses Universitaires de France.

Michèl, Andrée, and Geneviève Texier. 1964. *La condition de la française aujourd'hui*. Paris: Gauthier.

Ministère de l'Education Nationale. 1968–69. *Le personnel de l'enseignement public. Statistique des enseignants.* No. 3 (1). Paris.

Organisation de la Coopération et du Dévelopment Economique. 1965. *Origines sociales des professeurs et instituteurs*. Paris: Direction des Affaires Scientifiques.

———. 1968. *Enseignement primaire et secondaire*. Paris: Direction des Affaires Scientifiques.

———. 1970. *L'emploi des femmes*. Paris: Seminaire Syndicale Regional.

Organisation Internationale du Travail. 1967. *Annuaire statistique du travail*. Paris.

Prigent, Robert, ed. 1954. *Renouveau des idées sur la famille*. Paris: Presses Universitaires de France.

Sullerot, Evelyne. 1968. *Histoire et sociologie du travail feminin*. Paris: Presses Universitaires de France.

UNESCO. 1968. *World Survey of Education*. Paris: UNESCO.

Vimont, Claude. 1965. "Un enquête sur les femmes fonctionnaires." *Population* (January-February), pp. 22–55.

Men, Women, and Work: Reflections on the Two-Person Career[1]

Hanna Papanek
University of Indonesia

Our viewpoints as social scientists, no less than as novelists and poets, are developed through what we are, where we have come from, and where we have been. Our choice of research problems reflects concerns which often underlie our own lives, and even our accidentally chosen problems come to define our later work. Other points of view become foreclosed through the cumulative effect of specialized knowledge and of concepts which we have found congenial. Much of American sociology, for example, reflects the world of men, most often the world of white men in industrial society. But even where the concerns of women are considered, the focus is often exclusively on the American middle class. Such a restricted perspective not not only damages our collection of relevant data but also constrains the analysis of what we find. From my specific viewpoint, as a woman born in Europe, most of whose professional work has been done in Muslim South Asia where women are secluded or segregated, much current sociological analysis suffers from the neglect of relevant comparisons with other societies. More subtly also, the life experiences of American women— including professionals married to fellow professionals—have been left out of systematic consideration in much of the analysis of our own society.

In this paper, I discuss some of the aspects of American women's "vicarious achievement" (Press and Whitney 1971; Lipman-Blumen 1972) through their husbands' jobs in a special combination of roles which I call the "two-person single career." This combination of formal and informal institutional demands which is placed on both members of a married couple of whom only the man is employed by the institution is particularly prevalent in middle-class occupations in the United States but is not restricted to them, or indeed to the United States. The pattern plays a particularly significant role, however, where an explicit ideology of educational equality between the sexes conflicts with an implicit (and now often illegal) inequality of occupational access. This particular American dilemma is resolved in a very American style—by providing a social control mechanism which serves to derail the occupational aspirations of educated women into the noncompetitive "two-person career" without openly injuring the concept of equality of educational opportunity for both sexes. The

[1] I am grateful to Everett C. Hughes, Gustav F. Papanek, and Sylvia Vatuk for their comments and criticisms. An earlier version of this paper was presented at the South Asia Seminar, University of Chicago, in May 1972.

social control mechanism comes into full force after the educational process is completed, although it is of course anticipated by many years in which children learn conformity to sex roles and sex-role stereotypes. The "two-person career" pattern is fully congruent with the stereotype of the wife as supporter, comforter, backstage manager, home maintainer, and main rearer of children. The timing and nature of this particular resolution of the dilemma in which educated American women are placed is illuminated more clearly through comparisons with other societies in which sex segregation is more consistent, more open, and more pervasive.

Incidentally, the concept of the "two-person single career" should not be confused with that of the "two-career family" (Holmstrom 1972), although elements of the "two-person career" pattern clearly present major problems for the family in which both husband and wife follow independent careers. In fact, women often find the demands of their husbands' jobs to be a major factor in their own reluctance or inability to develop independent careers at levels for which their education has prepared them, and move instead into patterns which may be highly productive and innovative and in which the demands of the husband's job are incorporated into the wife's own work in a career.

The deliberate focus in this discussion on the role played by women in the orbit of men's occupations raises several sets of questions. It should by now be obvious that the sociological and anthropological study of women is not very advanced, even in societies where women are accessible to researchers and not isolated by *purdah* (seclusion) as they are in much of South Asia. It is clear that data about the life of women are generally insufficient, especially if compared with what is known in the same society about the life of men. This insufficiency reflects a lack of interest on the part of predominantly male social scientists, but also speaks to the problems of access and empathy with people who are felt to be very different from oneself. Of course, the challenge of learning about a very different culture, to penetrate into very different worlds, is often a major element in the underlying motivation of sociologists and anthropologists, who have made a professional virtue out of what is otherwise considered a vice— intense curiosity about other people. But for some reason, the challenge of learning about another sex is less clearly part of our professional motivations and is hedged in by so many external social restraints and internal psychological complications that it tends to play only a small role in the published literature. Its role in the less formal pattern of interaction between professionals and co-workers is, of course, another story.

In the case of studies of women, there is also the additional problem that public written materials, such as historical records, literary works, and codes of law, usually do not directly reflect the life experiences of women. Knowledge about women's lives in societies to which one is a stranger, either in space or in time, is too often derived from what men have written —and perhaps we do not fully understand some of the problems which this entails. What role do male fantasies play in what is written about women, both in novels and in legal codes? What kinds of women do men feel free to discuss among themselves? There have certainly been times and places where men have only spoken about women outside their own families, or women who were somehow in the public domain. At the same time, there has been a dearth of women writers, as Virginia Woolf (1929) and Tillie Olsen (1965) among many others have pointed out. What women might have written about women's lives must be found in oral materials, unpublished diaries, stories, and direct observation. Again, this is particularly important if one studies societies, or segments of societies, to which one is an outsider.

At another level, the insufficiency of data about women's lives also contributes to an inaccurate understanding of societies where little is known about half the population, its women. Studies often report on "the people" of an area, without necessarily specifying whether women have been included, and whether their customs and manners differ in any way from those of the men. Such differences are most likely to occur in societies which are highly sex segregated, and where access to women is particularly difficult for male researchers; but such societies may also be particularly instructive about the operation of sex distinctions.

One moves to another point in the argument if it is suggested that knowledge about the lives of men, and the transactions between them, does after all include most of the significant truths about a society. From much of sociological theory one could, indeed, gain this impression, since there is a very definite focus on public acts and public actors—in political systems, bureaucracies, religious institutions, the economy. In some societies more than in others, women do participate to significant degrees in some of these sectors, as, for example, the market women of West Africa participate in the economy; but these public spheres of action tend to be male dominated in many societies. The consumers of the products of public action and the persons with whom interaction occurs on other levels are often excluded from the sociological domain.

In a very general way, the distinction between public and private worlds corresponds to the differences which have long been established in sociology through such concepts as primary and secondary groups, or *Gemeinschaft* and *Gesellschaft* types of association. But the study of sex segregation in South Asian societies suggests that some very specific factors may be involved in such systems, and that the public-private distinction may be particularly useful in an exploration of women's roles.

While societies differ sharply from each other in the extent to which women are restricted in their access to the world outside the home, this is the defining characteristic of sex segregation in much of South Asia. There are differences between Muslims and Hindus in the actual operation of seclusion practices, and these are consistent with the value systems associated with the two religions (Papanek 1971, 1973). Both reflect a preoccupation with the dimension of sexual and reproductive behavior, especially as it affects women. Sexuality, and its implications for reproductive behavior, purity of descent, contacts between males and females, child rearing, economic behavior, and so on, must be obvious elements in any study of sex segregation. And the family group, however it is defined, tends to be the focus for much sexual and reproductive behavior, particularly its systematic and sanctioned aspects. This point makes it important to develop a valid system of analysis which takes account of the special nature of sexuality, and the relationships based upon it, in a study of women's lives.

It is probably useful to begin with this assumption, rather than to use analogies to other forms of association, such as caste. While the concept of "women as a caste" may have obvious advantages in calling attention to the many inequities of sex discrimination, it is not useful in the development of social theory as it affects women. If sexual relationships and reproductive behavior are used as points of departure for analyzing the place of women in most societies, relevant concepts must include distinctions between social groups within which it does or does not occur in systematic, sanctioned ways. There are obvious problems connected with using a public-private distinction based on this point, of course. Large areas of sexual behavior are indeed private but occur outside the family setting. They constitute very important areas of social behavior which have been studied far too little by sociologists (see Marcus 1966; Humphreys 1970). Homosexual relationships—that is, sexual relationships not connected with reproductive behavior—also require integration into an analytical system.

The specific topic of this discussion—"vicarious achievement" in the two-person single career—is concerned with transactions which occur at the boundary between public and private spheres. They involve a three-way relationship, between employer and two partners in a marriage, in which two sets of relationships are of the "secondary" type and one is of the "primary." Usually, the wife of the employee is inducted into the orbit of her husband's employing institution not because of her own, or the institution's, specific choice but because she is related to her husband through sexual, economic, and emotional bonds. The relationship between the wife and the employer also tends to be maintained and expressed through dimensions which are somewhat different from those used in the relationship with the employee. While terms such as instrumental and expressive relationships have been very useful in some studies, they are not the most appropriate terms for the two-person career, since elements of both are involved in the relationships.

The induction of the wife into the husband's work orbit may take the form of adding new types of work to her activities as a housekeeper or mother, or as someone with a career of her own. Or it may take the form of modifying only slightly the activities which she already carries on as part of her complex of roles, such as influencing her life style, adding to her role as a hostess, and so on. This makes it difficult to distinguish specifically which activities result from her involvement with her husband's work, except through reference to the goals of the work or the group of people whom it concerns. In general, it is also true that the institution which employs the husband proceeds on the assumption that the alternative uses of the wife's time are neither important nor productive, in the economic sense of the term, and that her "opportunity costs" are therefore low. This is, of course, consistent with the general view of housework and women's work, in general, as a low-status nonproductive activity. Oddly enough, few suggestions have been made for getting along without it.

"VICARIOUS ACHIEVEMENT" IN THE TWO-PERSON SINGLE CAREER

"Vicarious" is defined by Webster as "experienced or realized through imaginative or sympathetic participation in the experience of another . . . acting for a principal . . . having the function of a substitute . . . taking the place of something primary or original." Its use in current research on women tends to be asymmetrical, being applied only to women who fulfill "their achievement needs either completely or predominantly through the accomplishments of their husbands" (Lipman-Blumen 1972, p. 36). Presumably, the concept would also lend itself to application in the sense of men being "vicarious homemakers," or bringing up their children "vicariously" through their wives' activities in these spheres. Interestingly enough, the distinctions which have been made tend to follow other lines. Tresemer and Pleck (1972) in their study of men's reactions to women of achievement point out that American men "are simultaneously living through their wives' emotionality [while the] women live vicariously through their husbands' achievement." The complementarity indicated in this study between expressive and instrumental relationships of men and women must be considered in light of the fact that, at least in some instances, instrumental activities tend to be more highly valued in American society than expressive ones. The terms are so closely attached to behavioral and gender stereotypes that they should be used with caution.

"Vicarious achievement" is probably most typical of the American middle class, since the employing institutions which foster it and the educational preparation which makes it possible function mainly at this level. There appear to be class distinctions in the extent to which the occupational worlds of men affect the lives of women. Rainwater, Coleman, and Handel (1962) point out that working-class wives are much less involved with their husbands' occupational roles than are the wives of middle-class men in their study. There are probably also differences between ethnic and racial groups. In any case, the type of participation in "two-person careers" described in this paper differs in many important respects from the situations where wives must also hold jobs to support the family, or those in which they are working partners, as on small farms, in small businesses, mama and papa stores, and other joint enterprises. In the middle-class two-person career pattern, the wife is neither formally employed nor remunerated in any direct sense.

But there are sharp differences between middle-class occupations in the extent to which the participation of wives is elicited; in Rose Coser's terms, some institutions are more "greedy" than others (Rose Coser and Rokoff 1971). At the same time, the vicarious achievement pattern is structurally a part of the middle-class wife's role, rather than being a matter of choice, accident, or conflict. Some parallels can be drawn with the ways in which ambivalence has been found to be structurally inherent in some occupational roles. Some of the ambivalent aspects of the physician's role, for example, were seen as "conflicting normative expectations socially defined for a particular social role associated with a single social status" (Merton and Elinor Barber 1963, p. 96). Similarly, conflicting normative expectations are part of the middle-class married woman's role; and structured ambivalence is associated with her participation in the two-person career on the part of all three participants—the wife, the husband, and the employing institution.

Some indications of the relative importance of two-person careers is given in Helena Lopata's study of Chicago-area housewives in 1956 and 1962 (Lopata 1965, 1971), which clarifies some of the varieties of role orientations of women in different income levels, backgrounds, and places of residence. Among the group of "husband-oriented wives" in her classification, she singles out the "more highly educated woman who has herself worked in complex organizations" as the one most likely to be "interested in her husband's job, its problems and social relations" (1971, p. 104). This is the relatively small group which is most likely to be involved in the two-person career. Lopata concluded that, in her sample, "few women expressed an interest in what the man does when he is outside the home" (1965, p. 121); but the specific wording of her questionnaire may have contributed to this view. Possibly, the question "Does a wife have a great deal of influence on her husband's job? Why? How?" may contradict the prevailing ideology that women should not do so. Perhaps, if women had been asked about the kinds of modifications in their lives which had been brought about through the man's career demands, the proportions might have been different. In any case, Lopata's study does indicate that husband-oriented women were most likely to occur among women with "successful husbands," with professional degrees or Ph.D.'s and comparatively high incomes (1971, p. 65). This group also includes those women, such as a group of Air Force officers' wives, who had "a strong dependence upon their husband's job" (1965, p. 123), and whose husband-orientation could be the result of the man's external commitments.

Many of the examples of two-person careers described in this paper fit the Lopata categories, although the focus of the analysis is somewhat different.

The best-known two-person career pattern is that of the corporate executive's wife described by Whyte (1952, 1956) and many others. Of course, the pattern is not confined to business executives but occurs particularly often in the case of large, complex institutions employing highly educated men. Colleges and universities, large private foundations, the U.S. government (particularly the armed forces and the foreign service), and similar institutions all develop their own version of the two-person career pattern among their employees. They all communicate certain expectations to the wives of their employees. These expectations serve the dual function of reinforcing the husband's commitment to the institution and of demanding certain types of role performance from the wife which benefit the institution in a number of ways. A pattern of pressures is generated for both members of the couple which is closely related to social mobility, mobility within the employing institution, loyalty, and interpersonal rivalry.

While this pattern is typical of the United States, it probably exists in many other industrial societies to some degree. In some societies, such as Japan (Vogel 1967), the pattern of lifetime commitment by the employee to the employing institution may accentuate some elements of the pattern, such as involvement in social activities with colleagues, and possibly diminish some others involving specific contributions by the wife. Similarly, in the bureaucracies of some former British colonies, as for example the Civil Service of Pakistan and the Indian Administrative Service, wives are deeply involved in the rank distinctions of their husbands; and in the social life they share almost exclusively with fellow civil servants but they may be barred from more specific helpmeet activities by the social customs which segregate men and women.

The wife's involvement with her husband's career frequently begins before the career itself, during the stage when he is undergoing the advanced training so typical of these middle-class careers, while she is working in a temporary job to support them both, having abandoned or interrupted her own studies. The process of induction into the two-person career pattern proper begins when the husband is interviewed for a job or considered for a fellowship. It is called "finding out whether the wife is suitable." The most important aspect of this suitability is related to social mobility, that is, whether the wife is able to maintain a certain kind of life style and to change it along with her husband's changes in rank, but no faster or slower.

The most general characteristics, in fact, of the two-person career pattern focus on the status and rank aspects of the man's job. Wives are enlisted in the institutional pressures connected with mobility in the organization and with the hazing of low-ranking members. It is the wives who are most closely involved with the institutionalized perquisites of rank outside the office—housing, level of consumption, friendship circles, clothes, sociability, manners, club memberships, and so on. It is no accident, of course, that the most clear-cut application of these pressures occurs in situations where the employing institution operates in a social enclave, as in overseas diplomatic missions, army posts, college towns, and company towns. A recent State Department directive, reported in the *New York Times* (January 26, 1972), illustrates both the rank and hazing aspects. It was stated that "the wife of a Foreign Service employee who has accompanied her husband to a foreign post is a 'private person' and 'not a Government employee.'" She could no longer be required to perform services, including menial work, for the wives of her husband's superiors. It is, of course, clear that such services had previously been required, and that many of them are likely to continue to be customary. For example, volunteer work, participation in the entertainment of guests, holding children's parties, and so on are all nominally optional activities, but participation is strongly expected. A wife who does not participate risks injuring her husband's career, in much the same way that it is likely to be injured by a wife who drinks too much, talks too much, or has strong independent aspirations. Wives of overseas personnel of the U.S. government are also expected to participate in formal courses of training before going overseas.

Pointing up the contrast between the role of such training in the participation of men and women in direct and vicarious achievement is the practice of many institutions of barring wives from the "serious" training programs developed for men. It has been the practice, for example, at the Harvard Business School's advanced management training programs to stipulate that the wives of participants may not live on campus (and preferably not in Cambridge) during the intensive course, since it is felt that their presence would distract the men from their immersion in course work and contacts with other executives.

The fact that the women's activities are labeled as being outside the men's work orbit, while being within their ranking system, reinforces the ambivalence which characterizes most aspects of the two-person career.

This ambivalence is particularly destructive to the self-esteem of many participants, since it often emphasizes activities which women personally reject but are expected by their husband's colleagues to perform (see Evelyn Riesman 1958). This is consistent with the low valuation which employing institutions normally place on the time as well as the work performance of wives. This low "opportunity cost" placed by institutions on the time of wives assumes that they have no alternative earning opportunities, but is clearly destructive of developing such alternatives. The lowest opportunity costs are often assumed to exist in those institutions which are most prestigious and competitive for men, as is indicated to some extent by the dearth of equal-level careers among the wives of high-status academics.

The high degree of ambivalence which accompanies the induction of women into the institutional orbits of their husbands is based on the need to enlist the women's participation and loyalty without letting their actual contributions decrease the importance which the institution places on the husband's work. This is very similar to the ambivalent valuation placed on the work of women in the male-female complementary pairs which are so typical of many Western societies but absent in sex-segregated societies (Papanek 1971). These pairs include doctor and nurse, executive and secretary, principal and teacher, editor and research assistant, among many others. In each, the division of labor stresses the indispensability of the woman along with the man's higher status and higher salary. In each of these pairs, there are also obvious incongruities between expected and recognized areas of responsibility, as the woman's potential responsibility in her complementary job is tacitly recognized by all concerned to be very large, while neither her status nor her salary recognizes this potential in formal terms. For instance, nurses are tacitly expected to take over several important medical functions in cases of emergency, as is also the case in the roles of many secretaries, assistants, and teachers. There is usually very little reciprocity, however, as well as a greater tendency to replace the female member of the pair with a substitute female.

Other types of involvement by women in two-person single careers concern other elements of the man's job in addition to its status dimensions. Many activities are aimed at increasing the husband's competitive advantage in the actual work situation. These helpmeet activities are usually not specifically required by the institution, although they are rarely rejected when performed. They include typing and editing manuscripts, collaborating in the laboratory, taking notes in classes and meetings, and participating in fieldwork. Judging from the frequency of authors' acknowledgements to their wives—"without whom I would not have been able to work with the women in X community"—there exists a large group of paraprofessional sociologists and anthropologists in the United States. They do not publish independently and are not usually co-authors, and their professional recognition tends to be informal and vicarious.

There is often a high degree of tension surrounding the contributions made by wives to the work of their husbands, and there are many possible alternatives. In an older generation of academics, for example, one can find many wives who worked productively for many years as their husbands' private or acknowledged research assistants. They may have exerted considerable influence on their husbands' work, which was acknowledged both by the husband and his closer colleagues but rarely by the profession at large. In other cases, academic wives combined their unofficial colleagueship with professional activities, such as editing a professional journal. As Helen Hughes (1973) points out, some of these jobs lent themselves to considerable expansion in terms of professional influence when they were occupied by faculty wives for a long period rather than a succession of graduate students.

On the other hand, many of these older wives suppressed or diverted their own professional ambitions and chose occupations which would not bring them into their husbands' professional orbits, such as real estate agents in college towns or teachers in local private or public schools. Such women sometimes report that they would have liked to work more closely with their husbands, as official or unofficial colleagues, but that this would not have been acceptable or would have created too many tensions. The alternative jobs which they chose may not have been helpmeet activities in the sense of this discussion, therefore; but their choices do illustrate some of the factors involved in accepting or rejecting a vicarious achievement role.

Some of the tensions inherent in the vicarious achievement role are dramatically illustrated in the life of Zelda Fitzgerald (Milford 1970). In her case, rejection of the vicarious role demanded by her husband created serious conflicts between them both as artists and as husband and wife. Her biography indicates many of the profound questions which a discussion of women as vicarious achievers cannot even begin to answer. For example, the complex emotional and intellectual exchanges which may occur in a marriage or any similar kind of long-range relationship make obvious contributions to the work of both members of the couple. Usually, however, the institutional pressures which help to define the job of the husband tend to emphasize a more public presentation of ideas and skills than is usually the case for the wife. Prevailing social stereotypes tend to require her to be satisfied with knowing the extent of her contribution to her husband's work and to the growth and development of her children. And who, indeed, should measure published output in books and journals against such tangibles as children? In fact, men who are under heavy pressures from their employing institutions often express overt or covert jealousy toward women who face different sets of pressures, while attempting to maintain their intellectual and emotional development at high levels. This jealousy—usually expressed in such terms as "be glad you don't *have* to be in the rat race"—is often a factor in the development of independent careers for women and should be distinguished from the exploitative attitudes which often are expressed in similar terms.

Once the discussion of wives' contributions to their husbands' work goes beyond the obvious and simple levels of direct assistance of the kind which could also be performed by a substitute, such as a laboratory assistant, research assistant, secretary, and so on, it is clear that many complicated problems arise. Leaving these aside for the moment, it is probably correct to say that openly acknowledged collaboration, in the context of a two-person career, is not very frequent. This ambivalence surrounding the wife's contribution suggests that many institutions, again particularly in the academic world, recognize the fragility of male self-esteem in American society and have adopted a number of ways of safeguarding it. Acknowledged collaboration can more often be expressed in the case of a team of professionals who are also married, but even in these cases both institutional and personal problems are considerable. It is, of course, clear that employing institutions, run mainly by men in these cases, usually recognize the problems of male colleagues more clearly, and that safeguards built into career patterns, hiring practices, and reward systems are geared to men rather than women, whether wives or potential female colleagues.

A third type of two-person career emphasizes the man's public image. These jobs include some where the wife's participation is almost, but not quite, formally institutionalized—the ambassador's wife, the mayor's wife, the wife of a large foundation representative abroad, the wife of a company president, the First Lady, and so on. All of these women are expected to give acknowledged public performances, as are also the wives of political candidates (McCarthy 1972). The rejection of such public roles by the wife requires considerable effort and is generally seen as injuring the husband's work performance. On the other hand, some wives may be used as overt or covert excuses to reject a male candidate, as personnel reports and newspaper stories often indicate. The limits to acceptable participation by the wife in the husband's public image are illustrated by those cases where the wives become public personalities themselves and no longer operate only in the context of the husband's role. The key expression which indicates that these stereotyped limits have been exceeded is the statement "she is a . . . in her own right," indicating that an exceptional achievement has occurred. This expression is not used in the case of husbands of exceptional women, even where there are stereotyped expressions of disdain, as in the case of actresses' husbands who may be referred to as "Mr. her-name." Women who develop their own public image, starting from their base as the wives of prominent personalities, usually evoke fierce attacks and loyalties which are partly based on their having violated stereotyped standards of proper behavior in the vicarious achievement role. The complex career of Eleanor Roosevelt illustrates the development of this pattern especially well, particularly the process of rejecting the shadow role (Lash 1971, 1972). In her case, it is perhaps possible to speculate that her husband's disabling illness made it first possible for her to develop a more activist role in the public eye and to be accepted in such a role, at least at the beginning, by those who later became detractors. It must also be noted that, until recently, the widows of public figures have had a much better chance of independent election than other women in the United States (see Dreifus 1972).

The kinds of contributions which wives in these careers make to their husbands' work thus include status maintenance, intellectual contributions, and public performance. All of them are informally required by the man's employing organization, but their acceptance is accompanied by very high degrees of ambivalence by the employer, the husband, and the wife. In all cases, the induction of the wife into the orbit of the husband's employing institution is intended to increase the couple's commitment to the employer, to raise the husband's motivation to achieve in order to maintain a high level of consumption, and to increase his competitive advantage.

Needless to say, the wife's contribution is usually not directly acknowledged, nor is it directly remunerated. For example, the entertainment allowances given by some firms for the home entertainment of business guests do not include the wife's labor as an expense, while that of a hired maid can usually be reimbursed. Travel costs incurred by wives attending their husbands' business meetings, unless specifically required by the organization, are considered part of the husband's taxable income if they are paid for by the employer. This ruling transforms the wife's participation in her husband's business convention into a fringe benefit for him. It is instructive to examine the rulings and court cases which have been concerned with the application of this concept, despite their vagaries, for they illustrate many of the prevailing notions connected with the two-person career.

Wives who participate in two-person careers, therefore, can expect to be paid for their work only vicariously through the husband's income. Their reward, as is clearly implied by their involvement in rank distinctions, comes through raises in salary and perquisites granted to the husband. In another sense, the wife can consider that her activities enable the husband to devote additional time and energy to his institutional employer. The concept which might be applicable here is that she is "gainfully unemployed"—that is, not considered "employed" in the economists' or census-takers' sense but nevertheless "gainfully" occupied in the context of a two-person career. At the same time, of course, the wife's participation in a two-person career can cost the couple considerable money, if she is thereby prevented from developing an independent, and independently remunerated, career. It is only if the wife's opportunity costs are in fact as low as the husband's employer considers them to be that the couple benefits financially from her participation in the two-person career.

Tax rulings concerning the tax-deductibility of "substitute" child care and housekeeping expenses indicate that the prevailing conception of very low opportunity costs for wives characterizes the entire pattern of women's access to equal opportunities in employment. While the stereotypes affecting these rulings are derived from the middle-class conceptions of judges, tax lawyers, and government bureaucrats, they affect all women, most harshly those who are heads of households or who are in the labor market because they help to support their families. In this sense, the derailing pattern which the two-person career represents for middle-class women has serious consequences for women outside the middle class in its widespread effects on general conceptions of how women should be employed.

Finally, a small semantic point should be made which is relevant to the entire pattern of women's employment. It is still customary, even among writers who profess to be sympathetic to the needed changes in women's lives, to differentiate between "women who work" and "women who do not work." It should be obvious that if any such distinctions must be made, they should be made between "women who work in the home," "women who work outside the home," and perhaps for a small category, "women who do not work." This would eliminate some of the invidious comparisons which continue to be made between different groups of women. It might also advance, by a very small amount, the accurate understanding of women's roles in American society.

TRAINING FOR WOMEN'S WORK

The two-person career has been described as a derailment solution of an American women's dilemma, produced by the ideology of equal educational opportunity for both sexes, which is often in conflict with continuing inequalities of opportunity in employment. There are many aspects to the educational component of this dilemma, some of which can be clarified by comparisons with the upbringing and education of women in a highly sex-segregated society of South Asia (India, Pakistan, and Bangladesh).

In the United States, the preparation of women for participation in the middle-class two-person career remains the barely latent function of many colleges. It is an important aspect of the role of colleges in American social mobility and consists not only of providing the great meeting grounds for the American middle class but also of perpetuating an existing sex-role ideology through formal and informal practices. Training suitable wives for important men is a function which is only now beginning to be challenged—not only by students but also by some women's colleges and coeducational institutions themselves.

The crucial aspect of the role of the college in the development of two-person careers is that it combines two otherwise separate functions. First, in its narrowly defined educational role, it serves to channel the educational aspirations of women students through available course offerings, possible role models, and career counseling. These often modify existing egalitarian commitments and serve to channel women students into fields which are conventionally regarded as more suitable for them. Second, the American college has been notable among universities throughout the world for its specific social mobility functions. More than is usual in many other countries, the American college experience tends to define the class and occupation into which students intend to move, rather than those from which they come. Friends and acquaintances at college tend to remain crucial in the later personal and occupational orbits of many students, especially among men, and particularly in elite colleges and in those large state institutions whose constituency comes from within the state and remains within it later. The importance of meeting one's future marriage partner at college is affected to some degree by all of these functions of the American college. The choice of college often serves to express certain intentions and ambitions, and a shared college experience may express some degree of shared expectation, which affects the importance of making marriage choices in college. A similar concern with shared life styles is evident also in the criteria used by parents arranging their children's marriages in the Pakistani middle class.

The importance of secondary and advanced education for women, moreover, is one of the keys to the prevalence of the two-person career, since it brings women into the potential recruitment patterns of many professions and middle-class occupations. Not only do women become possible entrants into many fields on the basis of their training, but the same training also means that they become available to assist their husbands in the various ways that have been mentioned for two-person careers. The contrast with more highly sex-segregated societies is very striking in this regard. While secondary and advanced education is available to women in South Asia, and they are participating in it in increasing numbers, special occupations for women have developed (particularly in Pakistan) for female clienteles. The importance of these specialized occupations and the prestige which they gain for women deeply affect the career choices made by educated women. The values of a purdah society also keep women from participating in two-person careers with their husbands to a very large extent. With a few exceptions, women participate little in the public image of their husbands, and social contacts between business or professional colleagues most often exclude or downgrade the participation of wives. Since the complementary occupations which are usually filled by women in industrialized countries (secretaries, nurses, assistants, etc.) are usually filled by men in sex-segregated societies, wives also tend to participate less in formal or informal helpmeet activities with their husbands. The South Asian situation is very different from the American one in the sense that a few definite career opportunities are open for educated women, and these lead to high prestige and high accomplishment. The two most prevalent special women's occupations are medicine and teaching, although it should be made clear that "lady doctors" are acceptable while female nurses generally are not, because of the menial connotations of their work and their contact with male patients. Sex segregation similarly excludes many other occupations from consideration by women, although the system operates far more stringently in Pakistan and Bangladesh than in India. The lack of advanced education—or indeed any education—for most Muslim women in South Asia until quite recently has also meant that very few adult women are available to help their husbands in those ways for which formal education is necessary.

At the same time, there are outstanding women with unusual careers in South Asia; in some instances, their participation is either actually greater, or perceived more frequently, than is the case in the United States. Women in politics, in careers in the communications media (particularly radio), and in the civil service (in the case of India) are some specific examples. It is likely that such women, having overcome many social pressures in the process of attaining their education and training, move freely into available careers without being derailed by considerations of possible two-person careers. Both their own guilt feelings and public opposition to them may be less than would be the case in the United States.

Despite the important role played by sex-role stereotypes in the United States, comparison with the highly sex-segregated societies of South Asia does clarify some of the points about women's education in the United States which have led me to characterize it as at least ideologically equal for male and female students. In Pakistan and Bangladesh, for instance, most of the education of girls takes place in segregated institutions, especially between the ages of 11 and 18. The overall values of the purdah system result in a sharp separation between the worlds of men and women, even for those who do not observe seclusion in their own families (Papanek 1973). Competence is learned and achieved within the separate world of each sex, usually from a teacher of the same sex. There is relatively little competition between the sexes, since the ideals to be achieved by men and women are seen as very different from each other. Complementarity between the sexes is seen as very important, and the highly specific allocation of labor between the sexes produces a high degree of dependency between them, especially for services defined as strictly men's or women's work. Independence and self-reliance are not seen as virtues in the sense that they are understood in the United States. Continued reliance on parental guidance is considered appropriate long after the age at which it would be considered acceptable in North America. The most obvious example is the prevalence of the arranged marriage in South Asia, but other examples can also be seen in occupational choice, educational goals, business decisions, and so on.

Illustrating this process even in a highly unusual situation, a young Bengali university teacher with an American Ph.D. described how her father had deliberately turned his three daughters away from feminine pursuits toward masculine occupational goals and achievement standards. She recalled that "when he once found us playing with dolls, at a dolls' wedding, he snatched away a doll and tore it up, and when we wore bangles on our arms, he made us take them off. My elder sister was told she would be a teacher, and I was to become a doctor until my father decided this was not a good idea when a cousin started to talk about the difficult anatomy courses he was taking at the medical college. . . . We read a lot of books in my house and talked about all these things too, of course."

Training for women's work is a key underlying factor in the development of the vicarious achievement pattern, as has already been noted; but two different kinds of education are really involved in this distinction—education in a formal setting and training for women's work in the home. In the South Asian case, both ascriptive group membership and traditional learning "at the mother's knee" tend to be very important, even for the educated urban middle class. Other kinswomen are teachers, models, and critics, while men are consumers of the work products but are not generally skilled in the same processes. In the American setting, the traditional feminine activities of cooking, sewing, and housekeeping are much more likely to become incorporated into the school curriculum and into the activities of nonfamily agencies, such as Girl Scouts, church groups, 4-H clubs. Of course, similar clubs also exist in South Asia, especially in the cities, and domestic science is an important part of the curriculum of women's educational institutions; but the balance of the emphasis seems to be somewhat different.

In South Asia, the pattern of family training for women's work is reinforced further by the separateness of the women's world and by the central role of food in the society. Food preparation in both Muslim and Hindu society is surrounded by many sets of rules. Both raw materials and modes of preparation make food the medium through which regional, linguistic, caste, religious, and status differences are often expressed. Food exchanges between men play a crucial role in the ranking aspects of the caste system (Marriott 1968). While women do not necessarily play central roles in these transactions—although they are likely to be the preparers of food, and it would be interesting to find out if it plays a role in their ranking—food remains part of a very important complex of emotions and practices for women. In the American setting, the analogies which come to mind would include the Jewish example, in which a long tradition of orthodox concern with food purity combined with a long history of persecution and food anxieties to produce a pattern in which food becomes a central symbol in the woman's relationship with her family. The preparation of food is learned in the context of the woman's family in South Asia—that is, in the private sphere—while in American middle-class society some impersonal agencies in the public domain may also be involved. In addition to the ones already noted, there are cookbooks, advice columns in newspapers and magazines, friends, "gourmet clubs," and other sources from which a woman can learn to overcome her family and ethnic heritage, if she chooses.

One of the consequences of these differences in the learning process is that changes in the definition of women's work and in the allocation of labor between the sexes is easier in the United States. Family size is also a factor in this regard. Large extended families are usually the ideal, if not always the practice, in many parts of South Asia, and changes in women's work may be quite difficult in such a setting. In Indonesia, on the other hand, family groups tend to be nuclear, with only limited relationships to bilateral kin (Hildred Geertz 1961). Outside influences and other languages may be easier to introduce in such a situation, possibly including modifications in the pattern of women's work. It may be only through comparisons with many other societies, however, that these differences can be clarified and the very large possibilities for change in the American woman's role can become apparent.

Early marriages are customary in South Asia, although this is changing as a result of legislation, education, and other factors. As a result, learning in the context of family life is likely to occur quite early in the girl's life. Once a woman has learned her basic skills, there is little occasion for much further learning, especially if her life circumstances and basic diet remain unchanged. The learning process becomes associated with youth and low status in a society where age is honored, especially in the case of women's learning. There is little occasion to emphasize continuing education throughout life, although change-oriented outside agencies in fields like family planning and adult education are beginning to emphasize these new ideas. The family-based mode of learning is, in effect, at the heart of what we consider "tradition"—customs embedded in a complex pattern of relationships, not readily detached from them or changed. In this sense, there are also beliefs in the "immutability" of persons and their work skills;

such beliefs are often referred to in the large literature dealing with the difficulties of changing people's food, health, and work habits.

In the case of women, there are apparently some situations in which this "immutability" is particularly important. For instance, Saghir Ahmad (1967) has noted that in a Punjabi Muslim village members of the cultivators' group tended to marry outside their occupational grouping (*quom*) more readily than members of artisan groups (p. 88). In this area, it is not customary for women to work in the fields, although they do assist men with specific tasks, such as the drying of crops, in the home. The wives of artisans generally have customary tasks which supplement their husbands' performance. This is an example of joint work, carried out within the limits of the purdah system. Zekiye Eglar, writing about another Punjabi Muslim village (1960), probably provides an explanation for this difference in marriage patterns in her comment that the village barber must marry a woman brought up in a barber family, so that she can perform the important work of a barber's wife (p. 34). Otherwise, he cannot be a satisfactory village barber and must leave the village. It seemed to be assumed that these specific skills could not be learned by some other woman—as indeed they could not, if they were customarily taught only to a growing girl in her own family.

It is also in this context that the congruence between natal and affinal family life styles is examined very closely in South Asia when marriage arrangements are made. This emphasis is based not only on the importance of congeniality in a situation where love is expected to develop after the wedding, not before, but also on the unspoken assumption that early family learning is crucial and that there is no substitute for it.

These differences parallel the distinctions made by Hall (1959) among formal, informal, and technical learning. "Formal activities are taught by precept and admonition. . . . [It] is a two-way process [which] tends to be suffused with emotion. Informal learning is largely a matter of the learner picking others as models . . . most commonly it occurs out-of-awareness. . . . Technical learning, in its pure form, is close to being a one-way street. . . . The knowledge rests with the teacher [and] is usually transmitted in explicit terms" (pp. 93–95).

In these terms, what girls practice in the setting of their family to prepare them for "women's work," in the South Asian case is both formal and informal learning. Very little of it is technical. Technical learning occurs in the formal educational institution, and more boys than girls go to school in South Asia. The boys are more likely to experience technical learning, which they later elaborate in formal and informal ways in the social system of their work with colleagues. It is possible that lack of experience with technical learning in an impersonal environment is of major importance in the generally assumed tendency of women to be "more traditional" than men. It is the lack not only of what educational institutions teach but also of the way in which it is taught that may affect the future possibilities of changing women's lives in societies similar to those in South Asia. In the United States, on the other hand, both boys and girls have access to technical learning, in Hall's sense; the significant differences between the sexes are likely to occur on the level of formal and informal learning. It is at this level that appropriate sex-role behavior is taught. The later choices made by American women of vicarious achievement roles, or of failure (see Horner 1970), are likely to be nominally voluntary; in the South Asian case, there is much less room for personal choice.

All of these factors make it very unlikely that women's training in South Asian society would prepare them for roles of vicarious achievement through their husband's work if this entailed any kind of active participation. The men's work orbit remains largely male, especially in Pakistan—as is made graphically clear by the usual index: a total absence of toilets for women in most employment premises. But changes are occurring very rapidly in all South Asian countries, as the result of changes in both employment and education. The future of women's employment, and women's lives more generally, is likely to take very different directions in Bangladesh, Pakistan, and India. As these changes occur, new social control patterns will also develop, most probably in connection with educational systems and problems of unemployment.

Changes in the American pattern, on the other hand, are most likely to occur at those points where divergences are greatest between legally granted equality of access to educational opportunities by both sexes and the actual denial of equal access through the informal control mechanisms, which include the vicarious achievement pattern and its related sex-role ideology. For one of the results of the ideology of equality is that women have become motivated to achieve and perform in the same spheres and with the same skills as men. The elements in the two-person career pattern which have been discussed in this paper indicate some aspects of ideology, conflict, and change. The combination of achievement motivation and education in the skills through which men satisfy their achievement needs in American society is one of the powerful forces illustrated in the two-person career. The addition to these forces of continuing ambivalences, ambiguities, and derailment practices indicates a series of underlying stresses which many women have long experienced and which some are now making more visible. It is in this context of making things visible that it becomes useful to reflect on personal experiences, informal observations carried on over many years, and to speculate on past and future developments.

REFERENCES

Ahmad, Saghir. 1967. "Class and Power in the Punjabi Village." Ph.D. dissertation, Michigan State University, East Lansing.

Coser, Rose L., and Gerald Rokoff. 1971. "Women in the Occupational World: Social Disruption and Conflict." Mimeographed. Presented at the annual meeting of the Eastern Sociological Society, New York.

Dreifus, Claudia. 1972. "Women in Politics: An Interview with Edith Green." *Social Policy* 2 (January-February): 16–22.

Eglar, Zekiye. 1960. *A Punjabi Village in Pakistan*. New York: Columbia University Press.

Geertz, Hildred. 1961. *The Javanese Family*. Glencoe, Ill.: Free Press.

Hall, Edward T. 1959. *The Silent Language*. New York: Doubleday.

Holmstrom, Lynda Lytle. 1972. *The Two-Career Family*. Cambridge, Mass.: Shenkman.

Horner, Matina S. 1970. "Femininity and Successful Achievement: A Basic Inconsistency." In *Feminine Personality and Conflict*, by Judith M. Bardwick, Elizabeth Douvan, Matina S. Horner, and David Gutman. Belmont, Calif.: Brooks/Cole.

Hughes, Helen M. 1973. "Maid of All Work or Departmental Sister-in-Law." *American Journal of Sociology* 78 (January): 767–72.

Humphreys, Laud. 1970. *Tearoom Trade: Impersonal Sex in Public Places*. Chicago: Aldine.

Lash, Joseph P. 1971. *Eleanor and Franklin*. New York: Norton.

————. 1972. *Eleanor: The Years Alone*. New York: Norton.

Lipman-Blumen, Jean. 1972. "How Ideology Shapes Women's Lives." *Scientific American* 226 (1): 34–42.

Lopata, Helena Z. 1965. "The Secondary Features of a Primary Relationship." *Human Organization* 24 (2): 116–23.

————. 1971. *Occupation: Housewife*. New York: Oxford University Press.

McCarthy, Abigail. 1972. *Private Faces—Public Places*. Garden City, N.Y.: Doubleday.

Marcus, Steven. 1966. *The Other Victorians: A Study of Sexuality and Pornography in Mid-nineteenth Century England*. New York: Basic.

Marriott, McKim. 1968. "Caste Ranking and Food Transactions: A Matrix Analysis." In *Structure and Change in Indian Society*, edited by Milton Singer and Bernard S. Cohn. Chicago: Aldine.

Merton, Robert, and Elinor Barber, 1963. "Sociological Ambivalence." In *Sociological Theory, Values and Sociocultural Change*, edited by E. A. Tiryakian. Glencoe, Ill.: Free Press.

Milford, Nancy. 1970. *Zelda*. New York: Harper & Row.

Olsen, Tillie. 1965. "Silences: When Writers Don't Write." *Harper's Magazine* (October), pp. 153–61.

Papanek, Hanna. 1971. "Purdah in Pakistan: Seclusion and Modern Occupations for Women." *Journal of Marriage and the Family* 33 (3): 517–30.

————. 1973. "Purdah: Separate Worlds and Symbolic Shelter." *Comparative Studies in Society and History*, in press.

Press, M. Jean, and Fraine Whitney. 1971. "Achievement Syndromes in Women: Vicarious or Conflict Ridden." Mimeographed. Presented at the annual meeting of the Eastern Sociological Society, New York.

Rainwater, Lee, R. P. Coleman, and Gerald Handel. 1962. *Workingman's Wife*. New York: McFadden-Bartell.

Riesman, Evelyn T. 1958. "Pouring Tea." *Southwest Review* 43 (3): 222–31.

Tresemer, David, and Joseph H. Pleck. 1972. "Maintaining and Changing Sex Role Boundaries in Men (and Women)." Paper presented at the Radcliffe Institute Conference on "Women: Resource for a Changing World," Cambridge, Mass.

Vogel, Ezra F. 1967. *Japan's New Middle Class: The Salary Man and His Family in a Tokyo Suburb*. Berkeley: University of California Press.

Whyte, William H. "The Wife Problem." *Life,* January 7, 1952. Reprinted in *The Other Half,* edited by Cynthia F. Epstein and W. J. Goode. Englewood Cliffs, N.J.: Prentice-Hall, 1971.
———. 1956. *The Organization Man.* New York: Simon & Schuster.
Woolf, Virginia. 1929. *A Room of One's Own.* New York: Harcourt Brace.

Cultural Contradictions and Sex Roles: The Masculine Case[1]

Mirra Komarovsky

Barnard College, Columbia University

In a rapidly changing society, normative malintegration is commonly assumed to lead to an experience of strain. Earlier research (Komarovsky 1946) on cultural contradictions and the feminine sex role showed that women at an eastern college suffered uncertainty and insecurity because the norms for occupational and academic success conflicted with norms for the traditional feminine role. A replication (Wallin 1950) at a western university reported agreement in the questionnaire data, but the interview material led the investigator to conclude that the problem was less important to the women than the earlier study had suggested. However, Wallin pointed out that, in his replication, the respondents were oriented to marriage, while the Komarovsky study had included an appreciable number of women oriented to careers. This finding tended to support the view that women who were satisfied with the traditional female role would show less strain when confronted with contrary expectations than women who hoped to have both a rewarding career and a rewarding marriage.

Men are also confronted with contradictory expectations. For example, the traditional norm of male intellectual superiority conflicts with a newer norm of intellectual companionship between the sexes. This research investigated the extent of masculine strain experienced by 62 college males randomly selected from the senior class of an Ivy League male college. The study included a variety of status relationships, but the results reported here deal with intellectual relationships with female friends and attitudes toward working wives.

METHODS

Each of the 62 respondents contributed a minimum of three two-hour interviews and also completed a set of five schedules and two psychological tests, the California Personality Inventory and the Gough Adjective Check List. The psychological tests were interpreted by a clinical psychologist. The 13-page interview guide probed for data on actual role performance, ideal role expectations and limits of tolerance, personal preferences, per-

[1] This research is supported by NIMH grant MH 14618. Associated with the author in the interviewing were Mr. Wesley Fisher, Mrs. Susanne Riveles, and Dr. Edith Sanders. Mrs. Ana Silbert analyzed the scored psychological tests and prepared the 62 psychological profiles. The field work was done in 1969–70.

ception of role partner's ideal expectations, and relevant attitudes of significant others. Direct questions on strains came only at the end of this sequence. Extensive use was made of quasi-projective tests in the form of brief episodes. The total response rate of the original sample ($N = 79$) was 78%.

INTELLECTUAL RELATIONSHIPS WITH FEMALE FRIENDS

When fewer women attended college, the norm of male intellectual superiority might have had some validation in experience. But today college women are more rigorously selected than men in terms of high school academic performance (*Princeton Alumni Weekly* 1971). Nevertheless, social norms internalized in early childhood are resistant to change. The first question for this research was, How many men would show insecurity or strain in their intellectual relationships with women when confronted with both bright women and the traditional norm of male superiority?

The Troubled Third

Of the 53 men for whom the data were available (six did not date, three could not be classified reliably), 30% reported that intellectual insecurity or strain with dates was a past or current problem. This number included men who, having experienced stress, sought to avoid it by finding dates who posed no intellectual threat. The following excerpts from interviews illustrate the views of this troubled third:

> I enjoy talking to more intelligent girls, but I have no desire for a deep relationship with them. I guess I still believe that the man should be more intelligent.
>
> *   *   *
>
> I may be a little frightened of a man who is superior to me in some field of knowledge, but if a girl knows more than I do, I resent her.
>
> *   *   *
>
> Once I was seeing a philosophy major, and we got along quite well. We shared a similar outlook on life, and while we had some divergent opinions, I seemed better able to document my position. One day, by chance, I heard her discussing with another girl an aspect of Kant that just the night before she described to me as obscure and confusing. But now she was explaining it to a girl so clearly and matter-of-factly that I felt sort of hurt and foolish. Perhaps it was immature of me to react this way.

The mode of strain exemplified by these men might be termed "a socially structured scarcity of resources for role fulfillment." Apart from the ever-present problem of lack of time and energy, some social roles are intrinsically more difficult to fulfill, given the state of technical skills, the inherent risks, or other scarcities of facilities. The strain of a doctor called upon to treat a disease for which modern medicine has no cure is another case in point.

Selective dating and avoidance of superior women solved the problem for some troubled youths, but this offered no solution for six respondents who yearned for intellectual companionship with women but dreaded the risk of invidious comparisons. The newly emerging norm of intellectual companionship with women creates a mode of strain akin to one Merton and Barber (1963) termed "sociological ambivalence." Universalistic values tend to replace sex-linked desiderata among some male undergraduates who now value originality and intelligence in female as well as in male associates. The conflict arises when, at the same time, the norm of masculine intellectual superiority has not been relinquished, as exemplified in the following case: "I am beginning to feel," remarked one senior about his current girl friend, "that she is not bright enough. She never says anything that would make me sit up and say, 'Ah, that's interesting!' I want a girl who has some defined crystal of her own personality and does not merely echo my thoughts." He recently met a girl who fascinated him with her quick and perceptive intelligence but this new girl made him feel "nervous and humble."

The problem of this youth is to seek the rewards of valued attributes in a woman without arousing in himself feelings of inferiority. It may be argued that in a competitive society this conflict tends to characterize encounters with males as well. Nonetheless, if similar problems exist between two males, the utility curve is shaped distinctively by the norm of male intellectual superiority because mere equality with a woman may be defined as a defeat or a violation of a role prescription.

The Adjusted Majority

The 37 students who said that intellectual relationships with dates were not a problem represented a variety of types. Eleven men felt superior to their female friends. In two or three cases, the relationships were judged equalitarian with strong emphasis on the rewards of intellectual companionship. In contrast, several men—and their dates—had little interest in intellectual concerns. In a few instances the severity of other problems overwhelmed this one. Finally, some eight men were happily adjusted despite the acknowledged intellectual superiority of their women friends. What makes for accommodation to this still deviant pattern?

In seven of the eight cases, the female friend had some weakness which offset her intellectual competence, such as emotional dependence, instability, or a plain appearance, giving the man a compensating advantage. A bright, studious, but relatively unattractive girl may be acceptable to a man who is not as certain of his ability to win a sexually desirable female as he is of his mental ability. In only one of the eight cases the respondent admitted that his steady girl was "more independent and less emotional, actually a little smarter than I. But she doesn't make me feel like a dunce." Her superiority was tolerable because she provided a supportive relationship which he needed and could accept with only mild, if any, emotional discomfort.

Another factor which may account for the finding that 70% of the sample reported no strain is the fact that intellectual qualities are no longer considered unfeminine and that the imperative of male superiority is giving way to the ideal of companionship between equals. This interpretation is supported by responses to two standard questions and by the qualitative materials of the interviews. A schedule testing beliefs on 16 psychological sex differences asked whether the reasoning ability of men is greater than that of women. Only 34% of the respondents "agreed" or "agreed somewhat," while 20% were "uncertain"; almost half "disagreed" or "disagreed somewhat."

Another question was put to all 62 respondents: what are for you personally the three or four most desirable characteristics in a woman (man) who is to be close to you? Of all the traits men desired in a woman, 33% were in the "intellectual" cluster, in contrast with 44% of such traits if the friend were male. The fact that the sex difference was not larger seems significant. The major difference in traits desired in male and female intimates (apart from sexual attractiveness and love) was the relative importance of "social amenities and appearance" for women.

The qualitative data amply document the fact that the majority of the respondents ideally hoped to share their intellectual interests with their female as well as their male friends. To be sure, what men occasionally meant by intellectual rapport with women was having an appreciative listener: "I wouldn't go out," declared one senior, "with any girl who wasn't sharp and perceptive enough to catch an intellectual subtlety." But for the majority a "meaningful relationship" with a woman included also a true intellectual interchange and sharing. As one senior put it, "A guy leaving a movie with his date expects her to make a stimulating comment of her own and not merely echo his ideas." Another man wanted a date with whom he could "discuss things that guys talk about," and still a third man exclaimed: "What I love about this girl is that she is on my level, that I can never speak over her head."

It is this ideal of intellectual companionship with women, we suggest, that may explain the relative adjustment of the men in this sphere. As long as the expectation of male superiority persisted, anything near equality on the part of the woman carried the threatening message to the men: "I am not the intellectually *superior* male I am expected to be." But when the ideal of intellectual companionship between equals replaces the expectation of male superiority, the pressure upon the man eases and changes. Now he need only reassure himself that he is not inferior to his date, rather than that he is markedly superior to her. Once the expectation of clear superiority is relinquished, varieties of relationships may be accommodated. Given a generally similar intellectual level, comparative evaluations are blurred by different interests, by complementary strengths and weaknesses, and occasionally by rationalizations ("she studies harder") and other devices.

One final explanation remains to be considered. May the intellectual self-confidence of the majority be attributed in part to women's readiness to play down their intellectual abilities? That such behavior occurs is attested by a number of studies (Komarovsky 1946; Wallin 1950).

When respondents were asked to comment upon a projective story about a girl "playing dumb" on dates, the great majority expressed indignation at such "dishonest," "condescending" behavior. But some three or four found the behavior praiseworthy. As one senior put it, "Her intentions were good; she wanted to make the guy feel important."

Although we did not interview the female friends of our respondents, a few studies indicate that such playing down of intellectual ability by women is less common today than in the 1940s. Questionnaires filled out in 1970 and 1971 by 87 members of two undergraduate classes in sociology at an eastern women's college duplicated earlier studies by Wallin (1950) and Komarovsky (1946). The 1970 class was a course on the family, and the 1971 class probably recruited a relatively high proportion of feminists. Table 1 indicates that the occasional muting of intellectual competence by women may have played some role in the adjustment of the men, but it would appear to be a minor and decreasing role.

The hypothesis that the emerging ideal of intellectual companionship serves as a buffer against male strain needs a test which includes (as our study did not) some index of intellectual ability as well as indices of norms and of strain. Of the 27 men who disagreed with the proposition that the reasoning ability of men is greater than that of women, only five reported intellectual insecurity with women, whereas of the 34 men who believed in masculine superiority or were uncertain, nine experienced strain. Most troubled were the 12 men who were "uncertain"; four of them were insecure with women. Case analyses suggest that the interplay between a man's experience, personality, and beliefs is complex. For example, one traditional man, having confessed feelings of intellectual insecurity on dates, clung all the more tenaciously to the belief in superior male reasoning ability.

Some men took the "liberal" position on sex differences as a matter of principle. Of the nine black students, eight rejected the belief in male

Mirra Komarovsky

TABLE 1

READINESS OF WOMEN TO PLAY DOWN INTELLECTUAL ABILITIES (%)

	Wallin 1950 (N = 163)	Sociology Class 1970* (N = 33)	Advanced Sociology Class 1971* (N = 55)
When on dates how often have you pretended to be intellectually inferior to the man?			
Very often, often, or several times.	32	21	15
Once or twice.	26	36	30
Never	42	43	55
In general, do you have any hesitation about revealing your equality or superiority to men in intellectual competence?			
Have considerable or some hesitation.	35	21	13
Very little hesitation.	39	33	32
None at all.	26	46	55

* Mirra Komarovsky, unpublished study.

superiority, perhaps because they opposed group comparisons in intelligence. Again, in some cases, the direction of the causal relation was the reverse of the one we posited: men who felt in fact intellectually superior were hospitable to the "liberal" ideology. In view of these complexities, our suggestive results as to the positive association between egalitarian norms and the absence of strain remain to be tested in larger samples.

ATTITUDES TOWARD FUTURE WIVES' OCCUPATIONAL ROLES

The ethos on the campus of this study clearly demanded that men pay at least lip service to liberal attitudes toward working wives. If the initial responses to structured questions were accepted as final, the majority would have been described as quite feminist in ideology. But further probing revealed qualifications which occasionally almost negated the original response. For example, an affirmative answer to a proposition, "It is appropriate for a mother of a preschool child to take a fulltime job," was, upon further questioning, conditioned by such restrictions as "provided, of course, that the home was run smoothly, the children did not suffer, and the wife's job did not interfere with her husband's career." The interview provided an opportunity to get an assessment of normative expectations, ideal and operative, as well as of actual preferences. The classification of attitudes to be presented in this report is based on the total interview. Preferences reported here assume that a wife's paycheck will not be an economic necessity. The overwhelming majority were confident that their own earnings would be adequate to support the family.

116

Throughout the discussion of working, only two or three men mentioned the temptation of a second paycheck.

Four types of response to the question of wives' working may be identified. The "traditionalists," 24% of the men, said outright that they intended to marry women who would find sufficient fulfillment in domestic, civic, and cultural pursuits without ever seeking outside jobs. "Pseudo-feminists," 16% of the men, favored having their wives work, at least when the question was at a high level of abstraction, but their approval was hedged with qualifications that no woman could meet.

The third and dominant response included almost half (48%) of the respondents. These men took a "modified traditionalist" position which favored a sequential pattern: work, withdrawal from work for child rearing, and eventual return to work. They varied as to the timing of these stages and as to the aid they were prepared to give their wives with domestic and child-rearing functions. The majority saw no substitute for the mother during her child's preschool years. Even the mother of school-age children, were she to work, should preferably be at home when the children return from school. Though they were willing to aid their wives in varying degrees, they frequently excluded specific tasks, for instance, "not the laundry," "not the cleaning," "not the diapers," and so on. Many hoped that they would be "able to assist" their wives by hiring maids. The greater the importance of the wife's work, the more willing they were to help her. (One senior, however, would help only if his wife's work were "peripheral," that is, not as important to her as her home.)

The last, the "feminist" type, was the smallest, only 7% of the total. These men were willing to modify their own roles significantly to facilitate their future wives' careers. Some recommended a symmetrical allocation of tasks—"as long as it is not a complete reversal of roles." In the remaining 5% of the cases, marriage was so remote that the respondents were reluctant to venture any views on this matter.

The foregoing summary of types of male attitudes toward working wives fails to reveal the tangled web of contradictory values and sentiments associated with these attitudes. We shall presently illustrate a variety of inconsistencies. But underlying them is one basic problem. The ideological support for the belief in sharp sex role differentiation in marriage has weakened, but the belief itself has not been relinquished. Increasing skepticism about the innate character of psychological sex differences and some convergence in the ideas of masculinity and femininity (see McKee and Sheriffs 1957, 1959) have created a strain toward consistency. The more similar the perceptions of male and female personalities (see Kammeyer 1964), the more universalistic must be the principles of evaluation applied to both sexes. "If you could make three changes in the personality of the girl friend who is currently closest to you, what would they be?"

we asked the seniors. Universalistic values were reflected in the following, as in many other responses: "I would like her to be able to set a goal for herself and strive to achieve it. I don't like to see people slacking off." Earlier cross-sex association in childhood and early adolescence (see Udry 1966) has raised male expectation of enjoying an emotional and intellectual companionship with women. These expectations, however, coexist with the deeply rooted norm that the husband should be the superior achiever in the occupational world and the wife, the primary child rearer. One manifestation of this basic dilemma is the familiar conflict between a value and a preference. "It is only fair," declared one senior, "to let a woman do her own thing, if she wants a career. Personally, though, I would want my wife at home."

More interesting are the ambivalent attitudes manifested toward both the full-time homemaker and the career wife. The image of each contained both attractive and repellent traits. Deprecating remarks about housewifery were not uncommon, even among men with traditional views of women's roles. A conservative senior declared, "A woman who works is more interesting than a housewife." "If I were a woman," remarked another senior, "I would want a career. It must be boring sitting around the house doing the same thing day in, day out. I don't have much respect for the type of woman whom I see doing the detergent commercials on TV."

But the low esteem attached by some of the men to full-time homemaking coexisted with other sentiments and convictions which required just such a pattern for one's wife. For example, asked about the disadvantages of being a woman, one senior replied, "Life ends at 40. The woman raised her children and all that remains is garden clubs and that sort of thing—unless, of course, she has a profession." In another part of the interview, this young man explained that he enjoyed shyness in a girl and detested aggressive and ambitious women. He could never be attracted to a career woman. It is no exaggeration to conclude that this man could not countenance in a woman who was to be his wife the qualities that he himself felt were necessary for a fulfilling middle age.

A similar mode of contradiction, incidentally, was also disclosed by some seniors with regard to women's majors in college. "There are no 'unfeminine' majors," declared one senior: "I admire a girl who is premed or prelaw." But the universalistic yardstick which led this senior to sanction and admire professional goals for women did not extend to the means for their attainment, as he unwittingly revealed in another part of the interview. Questioned about examples of "unfeminine" behavior, this senior answered: "Excessive grade consciousness." If a premed man, anxious about admission to a good medical school, should go to see a professor about a C in chemistry, this senior would understand although he would disapprove of such preoccupation with grades. But in a woman premed he would find such behavior "positively obnoxious."

If the image of the full-time homemaker contained some alienating features, the main threat of a career wife was that of occupational rivalry, as illustrated in the following excerpt from the interviews. A senior speaks:

> I believe that it is good for mothers to return to fulltime work when the children are grown, provided the work is important and worthwhile. Otherwise, housewives get hung up with tranquilizers, because they have no outlet for their abilities. . . . Of course, it may be difficult if a wife becomes successful in her own right. A woman should want her husband's success more than he should want hers. Her work shouldn't interfere with or hurt his career in any way. He should not sacrifice his career to hers. For example, if he is transferred, his wife should follow—and not vice versa.

In sum, work for married women with grown children is approved by this young man, provided that the occupation is of some importance. But such an occupation is precisely one which carries a threat to the husband's pride.

The expectation that the husband should be the superior achiever appears still to be deeply rooted. Even equality in achievement of husband and wife is interpreted as a defeat for the man. The prospect of occupational rivalry with one's wife seems intolerable to contemplate. "My girl friend often beats me in tennis," explained one senior. "Now, losing the game doesn't worry me. It in no way reduces my manhood. But being in a lower position than a woman in a job would hurt my self-esteem."

Another student, having declared his full support for equal opportunities for women in the occupational world, added a qualification: "A woman should not be in a position of firing an employee. It is an unpleasant thing to do. Besides, it is unfair to the man who is to be fired. He may be a very poor employee, but he is still a human being and it may be just compounding his unhappiness to be fired by a woman."

In sum, the right of an able woman to a career of her choice, the admiration for women who measure up in terms of the dominant values of our society, the lure but also the threat that such women present, the low status attached to housewifery but the conviction that there is no substitute for the mother's care of young children, the deeply internalized norm of male occupational superiority pitted against the principle of equal opportunity irrespective of sex—these are some of the revealed inconsistencies.

Such ambivalences on the part of college men are bound to exacerbate role conflicts in women. The latter must sense that even the men who pay lip service to the creativity of child rearing and domesticity reserve their admiration (if occasionally tinged with ambivalence) for women achievers who measure up in terms of the dominant values of our society. It is becoming increasingly difficult to maintain a system of values for women only (Komarovsky 1953).

Nevertheless, to infer from this account of male inconsistencies that this is an area of great stress for them would be a mistake. It is not. By and large, the respondents assumed that the women's "career and marriage" issue was solved by the sequential pattern of withdrawal and return to work. If this doomed women to second-class citizenship in the occupational world, the outcome was consistent with the conviction that the husband should be the superior achiever.

Men who momentarily worried about the fate of able women found moral anchorage in their conviction that today no satisfactory alternative to the mother's care of young children can be found. Many respondents expressed their willingness to help with child care and household duties. Similarly, many hoped to spend more time with their own children than their fathers had spent with them. But such domestic participation was defined as assistance to the wife who was to carry the major responsibility. Only two or three of the men approved a symmetrical, rather than a complementary, allocation of domestic and occupational roles. An articulate senior sums up the dominant view:

> I would not want to marry a woman whose only goal is to become a housewife. This type of women would not have enough bounce and zest in her. I don't think a girl has much imagination if she just wants to settle down and raise a family from the very beginning. Moreover, I want an independent girl, one who has her own interests and does not always have to depend on me for stimulation and diversion. However, when we both agree to have children, my wife must be the one to raise them. She'll have to forfeit her freedom for the children. I believe that, when a woman wants a child, she must also accept the full responsibility of child care.

When he was asked why it was necessarily the woman who had to be fully responsible for the children, he replied:

> Biology makes equality impossible. Besides, the person I'll marry will want the child and will want to care for the child. Ideally, I would hope I'm not forcing her to assume responsibility for raising the children. I would hope that this is her desire and that it is the happiest thing she can do. After we have children, it will be her career that will end, while mine will support us. I believe that women should have equal opportunities in business and the professions, but I still insist that a woman who is a mother should devote herself entirely to her children.

The low emotional salience of the issue of working wives may also be attributed to another factor. The female partners of our respondents, at this particular stage of life, did not, with a few exceptions, force the men to confront their inconsistencies. Apparently enough women will freely make the traditional-for-women adjustments—whether scaling down their own ambitions or in other ways acknowledging the prior claims of the man's career. This judgment is supported by the results of two studies of female undergraduates done on the same campus in 1943 and 1971 (table 2). The big shift in postcollege preferences since 1943 was in the decline of

TABLE 2

COLLEGE WOMEN'S ATTITUDES TOWARD WORK AND FAMILY PATTERNS (%)

	Random Sample of Sophomore Class at Women's Liberal Arts College 1943 ($N = 78$)	Class in Introductory Sociology, Same College 1971 ($N = 44$)
Assume that you will marry and that your husband will make enough money so that you will not have to work unless you want to. Under these circumstances, would you prefer:		
1. Not to work at all, or stop after childbirth and decide later whether to go back.	50	18
2. To quit working after the birth of a child but definitely to go back to work.	30	62
3. To continue working with a minimum of interruption for childbearing.	20	20

SOURCE.—Mirra Komarovsky, unpublished studies.

women undergraduates who opted for full-time homemaking and volunteer activities. In 1971, the majority chose the sequential pattern, involving withdrawal from employment for child rearing. The proportion of committed career women who hope to return to work soon after childbirth has remained constant among freshmen and sophomores.

If women's attitudes have not changed more radically in the past 30 years, it is no doubt because society has failed to provide effective supports for the woman who wishes to integrate family life, parenthood, and work on much the same terms as men. Such an option will not become available as long as the care of young children is regarded as the responsibility solely of the mother. In the absence of adequate child care centers, an acceptance of a symmetrical division of domestic and work responsibilities, or other facilitating social arrangements, the attitudes of the majority of undergraduates reflect their decision to make some kind of workable adjustment to the status quo, if not a heroic struggle to change it.

SUMMARY

Role conflicts in women have been amply documented in numerous studies. The problem underlying this study was to ascertain whether recent social changes and consequent malintegration with regard to sex roles have created stressful repercussions for men as well as for women. In a randomly selected sample of 62 male seniors in an eastern Ivy League college, nearly one-third experienced some anxiety over their perceived failure to live up to the norm of masculine intellectual superiority. This stressful minority suffered from two modes of role strain: scarcity of resources for role performance and ambivalence. The absence of strain in the majority may be explained by a changed role definition. Specifically, the normative expectation of male intellectual superiority appears to be giving way on the campus of our study to the ideal of intellectual companionship between equals. Attitudes toward working wives abounded in ambivalences and inconsistencies. The ideological supports for the traditional sex role differentiation in marriage are weakening, but the emotional allegiance to the modified traditional pattern is still strong. These inconsistencies did not generate a high degree of stress, partly, no doubt, because future roles do not require an immediate realistic confrontation. In addition, there is no gainsaying the conclusion that human beings can tolerate a high degree of inconsistency as long as it does not conflict with their self-interest.

REFERENCES

Kammeyer, Kenneth. 1964. "The Feminine Role: An Analysis of Attitude Consistency." *Journal of Marriage and the Family* 26 (August): 295–305.

Komarovsky, Mirra. 1946. "Cultural Contradictions and Sex Roles." *American Journal of Sociology* 52 (November): 182–89.

———. 1953. *Women in the Modern World, Their Education and Their Dilemmas.* Boston: Little, Brown.

McKee, John P., and Alex C. Sherriffs. 1957. "The Differential Evaluation of Males and Females." *Journal of Personality* 25 (March): 356–63.

———. 1959. "Men's and Women's Beliefs, Ideals, and Self-Concepts." *American Journal of Sociology* 64 (4): 356–63.

Merton, Robert K., and Elinor Barber. 1963. "Sociological Ambivalence." In *Sociological Theory, Values and Socio-cultural Change,* edited by E. A. Tiryakian. Glencoe, Ill.: Free Press.

Princeton Alumni Weekly, February 23, 1971, p. 7.

Udry, J. Richard. 1966. *The Social Context of Marriage.* Philadelphia: Lippincott.

Wallin, Paul. 1950. "Cultural Contradictions and Sex Roles: A Repeat Study." *American Sociological Review* 15 (April): 288–93.

Swinging: A Study of Decision Making in Marriage[1]

Anne-Marie Henshel
York University

One very important aspect of the life of married couples, sex, has been generally omitted in studies of decision-making patterns among married couples. Swinging, defined as the pursuit of sexual activities with extra-marital partners by both spouses at the same time and usually in the same place (Walshok 1971), can, because of its nonspontaneous character, lend itself to research from the decision-making perspective. While studies of marital decision-making patterns became prevalent more than a decade ago, only in the late 1960s did researchers direct their attention to swinging as a social phenomenon. This new research trend partakes of a more general cultural impetus leading to experimentation with alternate life styles and follows the windfall of the "sexual revolution" of the past decades, a revolution characterized by a diminution of the double standard (Reiss 1967), a wider acceptance of premarital coitus among women, the pill, and a growing interest in sex as a form of leisure and of achievement (Gagnon and Simon 1970).

Measurements of marital decision-making patterns have traditionally involved the eight areas included in Blood and Wolfe's now classic study (1960, p. 19): the choice of husband's job, car, life insurance, vacation, housing, wife's working, physician, and food budget. Other researchers have added items regarding child rearing (Smith 1969), family planning (Dyer and Urban 1958), relations with relatives, and choice of friends (Safilios-Rothschild 1969). Most studies on middle-class couples point to a certain equalization of decision making (e.g., Kandel and Lesser 1972; Smith 1969; Blood and Wolfe 1960). However, certain researchers have questioned these conclusions. The possible advantage the male retains in this process is being reviewed in light of various structural factors (Gillespie 1971). In addition, methodological shortcomings have been pinpointed in the reappraisal of past studies. Most important for our purposes is the criticism that, in the overall decision-making score, all decisions are given equal weight regardless of their importance for the entire family. It is also pointed out that since some decisions are made less frequently than others, they may alter the absolute power of either spouse. Depending on which decisions a researcher chooses to include, "one could get a completely

---

[1] Paper read at the annual meeting of the Canadian Sociological Association, Montreal, June 1972. I am grateful to Frederick Elkin for his most helpful comments on an earlier draft of this article.

different picture of the over-all power structure" (Safilios-Rothschild 1969, pp. 297–98).

Swinging has been described as "an outgrowth of the dramatic changes that have taken place in this century in the position of women in American society and, more crucially, changes that have taken place in the conception of female sexuality and female sexual rights" (Denfeld and Gordon 1970, p. 89). Bell (1972) points out that "swinging represents a single standard of sex—that what is right for the man is also right for the woman." Swinging is also seen as benefiting wives as much as and, in certain respects, more than their husbands (Bartell 1971; Smith and Smith 1970). Yet, in spite of these equalitarian trends, researchers note passim that husbands are the usual instigators in the initial involvement in swinging (Palson and Palson 1972; Bell 1972, 1971; Bartell 1971; Smith and Smith 1970). However, a systematic decision-making approach has yet to be applied; the present article is a modest attempt in this direction.

THREE QUESTIONS

Three questions related to the preinvolvement stage of swinging are explored in this pilot study, with the ultimate aim of relating swinging to a more general discussion of marital power. (1) Which of the two spouses first becomes aware of swinging as an activity engaged in by people similar to them? (2) Which of the two spouses first suggests swinging as a likely alternative? (3) Who makes the final decision to swing? In each instance, there are three possible outcomes: the husband, the wife, or the two jointly.

The inclusion of the first question deserves additional explanation. It is very important that swinging be perceived by either or both spouses as an activity accessible to them rather than as an activity restricted to a particular, perhaps deviant, group. The first question, like the second and third, pertains to the relative position of the spouses in society. The spouse who has more access to certain information may have a double advantage; not only will he or she be able to act as the informant to the other and thereby acquire a measure of power but also, in the context of swinging, he or she may distort the information to induce the other into this activity or to avoid involvement.

METHOD AND SAMPLE

This research was designed as a pilot study to explore the attitudes and decision-making behavior of women who swing, using a nonstructured, open-end questionnaire. The sample was purposely limited to women. While husband-wife response discrepancies have occurred whenever both spouses have been studied regarding decision making (Safilios-Rothschild

1970, 1969), the answers the women in this sample gave are largely validated by other researchers' work on swinging where both partners had been interviewed and/or observed (Palson and Palson 1972; Bell 1971; Smith and Smith 1970).

The first contact was made through a personal referral; additional names were solicited from each interviewee. Thirty-two names were gathered; three could not be reached and four refused. The final sample of 25 is not random, and, at this point, it is difficult to imagine how randomness could be achieved with swingers. A preset sampling condition was that all the women had to be currently living with the husband they were swinging with. Two exceptions occurred: one couple had ceased swinging two months earlier; and another woman was swinging as a single, with married couples but as the extra female, while the husband was unaware of her activities.

All the women lived in the Toronto metropolitan area. The median and average age was 30, with a range from 23 to 40. Fifteen were full-time housekeepers, nine were employed—four of these part-time only—and one was a student. Occupations included nursing, teaching, and secretarial work. Five had attended only high school, eight had additional training such as nursing, another five had some college, and seven had a baccalaureate. Five couples had no children; the median number for the others was two (average 2.2). The husbands were close to their wives in age, had more education (10 had graduate training), and tended to be semiprofessionals, professionals, and executives.

I made initial contact when I arrived at the homes of respondents unannounced. I immediately told them how I had obtained their names and emphasized the confidentiality of the study. I saw the women alone; the usual length of the interview was 2–2.5 hours. While some subjects' answers were probably influenced by their perception of the interview situation, there is ample evidence that the women confided in me as frankly as possible. For instance, while social conventions usually preclude such admissions (Laws 1971, p. 485), most discussed their marital problems. Then, all volunteered unsolicited information, and practically all said that they had enjoyed the interview. Finally at least half switched roles with me at some point during the encounter.

RESULTS

The responses to the three questions are summarized in table 1. The husband is shown to have a definite advantage over his wife by being the first to become aware of swinging as an accessible activity. This advantage is structural; occupational circumstances were the main source of their information. As we proceed through the decision-making process, the wife

TABLE 1

INITIATING AGENT(S) TOWARD INVOLVEMENT IN SWINGING:
INCIDENCE BY STAGE

Initiating Agent(s)	First to Learn of Swinging (1)	First Suggested It (2)	Reached Final Decision (3)	Total
Husband	11	17	16*	44
Wife	4	3	2	9
Both spouses together	9	5	7	21
No data	1	0	0	1
Total	25	25	25	75

* One of these 15 cases is not clear-cut. Although the scale seemed tipped in favor of the husband, the spouses could have actually reached the decision jointly.

as the sole or joint initiator plays an ever lesser role. Only three women, including the "lone" swinger, were the first to suggest swinging as a possibility, and five others went through this process jointly with their husbands.[2] Seventeen husbands (68%) made the initial suggestion. Finally, only two women, again including the "lone" swinger, reported having been the one who had made the decision that led to involvement, and seven other wives reported a joint decision. The husbands alone therefore made 59% of *all* the initial decisions, 28% were joint decisions, while only 12% were made by the women.[3]

It appears that there was a lapse between the time the couples learned of swinging and the time when they considered it seriously. More time elapsed before the final decision was reached, indicating that decision making as discussed here is multiphasic (Safilios-Rothschild 1970). A third lapse occurred between the decision to swing and the involvement. Unfortunately, while the respondents could recall the threefold decision-making process, they could not recall well enough the duration of various time spans involved. It would be interesting to know whether the process proceeds more quickly when the husband initiates the idea and makes the final decision as, for instance, Goode found for the decision to divorce (1965, p. 145).

[2] A joint suggestion means that the matter was discussed jointly even though, in terms of seconds, one of the two spouses may have said it first. This is in contrast to the other cases when one spouse leaps ahead, brings up the suggestion, and there is an obvious psychological discrepancy between the two partners at that time.

[3] As the spouses' relative resources have been a topic of importance in discussions on decision making (e.g., Rodman 1967; Heer 1963; Blood and Wolfe 1960), the wife's employment status was taken into consideration and found to be unrelated to the phenomenon under study.

DISCUSSION

That husbands have an advantage in decisions about swinging is usually mentioned only casually by researchers; rather, there is a tendency to emphasize that women tend to adapt better to the new sexual freedom than their husbands, that they may obtain more sexual gratification than their husbands, and that swinging may be a more important channel of socialization toward true sexual freedom for them. These advantages are not shrugged off here but are viewed within the implicit and probably unconscious value context in which they were presented. For instance, if sexual freedom and equality is seen as an improvement over the double standard, one may be tempted to conclude that it is "good"; and, if it is such a great improvement for women that it offsets their decision-making disadvantage, we may thereby have an indication that the sexual freedom advantage may be more highly valued than the possible advantage the women could have were they the decision makers (jointly or singly).

Unlike studies of swinging, studies of marital decision making have tended to emphasize who made the decision rather than the comparative advantages to either spouse once the decision had been implemented. For example, if the husband decides to buy a car, the subsequent advantages arising from this decision for the wife are not discussed. It is pertinent that we adopt the same approach here for comparative purposes. Nevertheless, it should be added that, in this study, when the advantages the wives reported having gained from swinging were compared to the disadvantages similarly reported, the latter outweighed the former in 11 cases.[4]

Our data, as well as those mentioned by other researchers, seem to indicate that when we can obtain a measure of decision making with regard to nonspontaneous sex—and sex in general is an important correlate of marital happiness (Burgess and Wallin 1953; Locke 1951)— the egalitarian model does not hold in its entirety.

In spite of expectations of change in the sex structure, males still have a higher status than females; by the same token, they are the ones to confer status on women, both professionally and globally, the latter through marriage.[5] There are also indications that marriage is more important for women's happiness than for men's in our society (Bernard 1971, p. 87).

[4] The interviewees were asked (1) what they thought swinging had added to their lives and to their marital relationships, (2) to evaluate the problems involved, and (3) to weigh the advantages against the disadvantages.

[5] In another study, 30% of 113 Toronto students agreed with the statement that they tended to take unmarried women above 35 less seriously than unmarried men of the same age. This finding surfaced in spite of the fact that many students had tried to adopt a "liberal" attitude. Subsequent classroom discussions more than amply validated the trend.

Anne-Marie Henshel

Therefore, applying principles of lesser commitment (e.g., Blau 1964) or of least interest (Waller and Hill 1951, p. 191) for the males, it is not surprising that wives tend to do more of the adjusting in marriage (Blood and Wolfe 1960, p. 23; Rainwater and Weinstein 1960, pp. 68–69; Burgess and Wallin 1953, p. 618). Our data support these related points. In terms of exchange, the wife usually has less power (and decision making is one indicator of power) for she has fewer alternatives outside marriage;[6] she has fewer "commodities" of high *social* value to offer, and she has a higher need for the husband's *social* commodities than he has for hers. Her contributions to the marital relationship are of lower social value (Pitts 1964), thereby requiring that she increase them even if there already was imbalance (Blau 1964). Again, our data substantiate this perspective. In the context of decision making, swinging can be viewed as a male institution, and confirmations of the advent of a "sexual revolution" and of the abolition of the double standard should be reconsidered.

REFERENCES

Bartell, Gilbert D. 1971. *Group Sex.* New York: Wyden.
Bell, Robert R. 1971. *Social Deviance.* Homewood, Ill.: Dorsey.
———. 1972. Review of *Group Sex,* by Gilbert D. Bartell. *Journal of Marriage and the Family* 34 (February): 193–94.
Bernard, Jessie. 1971. "The Paradox of the Happy Marriage." In *Woman in Sexist Society,* edited by Vivian Gornick and Barbara K. Moran. New York: Basic.
Blau, Peter M. 1964. *Exchange and Power in Social Life.* New York: Wiley.
Blood, Robert O., Jr., and Donald M. Wolfe. 1960. *Husbands and Wives: The Dynamics of Married Living.* New York: Free Press.
Burgess, Ernest W., and Paul Wallin. 1953. *Engagement and Marriage.* Philadelphia: Lippincott.
Denfeld, Duane, and Michael Gordon. 1970. "The Sociology of Mate Swapping: Or the Family That Swings Together Clings Together." *Journal of Sex Research* 6 (May): 85–100.
Dyer, William G., and Dick Urban. 1958. "The Institutionalization of Equalitarian Family Norms." *Marriage and Family Living* 20 (February): 53–58.
Gagnon, John H., and William Simon, eds. 1970. *The Sexual Scene.* Chicago: Transaction.
Gillespie, Dair L. 1971. "Who Has the Power? The Marital Struggle." *Journal of Marriage and the Family* 33 (August): 445–58.
Goode, William J. 1965. *Women in Divorce.* New York: Free Press.
Heer, David M. 1963. "The Measurement and Bases of Family Power: An Overview." *Journal of Marriage and the Family* 25 (May): 133–39.
Kandel, Denise B., and Gerald S. Lesser. 1972. "Marital Decision-Making in American and Danish Urban Families: A Research Note." *Journal of Marriage and the Family* 34 (February): 134–38.
Laws, Judith Long. 1971. "A Feminist Review of Marital Adjustment Literature: The Rape of the Locke." *Journal of Marriage and the Family* 33 (August): 483–516.
Locke, Harvey J. 1951. *Predicting Adjustment in Marriage: A Comparison of a Divorced and a Happily Married Group.* New York: Holt.

[6] Thibaut and Kelley's (1959) treatment of power in the dyad is highly relevant here.

Palson, Charles, and Rebecca Palson. 1972. "Swinging in Wedlock." *Society* 9 (February): 28–37.

Pitts, Jesse R. 1964. "The Structural-Functional Approach." In *Handbook of Marriage and the Family,* edited by Harold T. Christensen. Chicago: Rand McNally.

Rainwater, Lee, and Karol K. Weinstein. 1960. *And the Poor Get Children.* Chicago: Quadrangle.

Reiss, Ira L. 1967. *The Social Context of Premarital Sexual Permissiveness.* New York: Holt, Rinehart & Winston.

Rodman, Hyman. 1967. "Marital Power in France, Greece, Yugoslavia and the United States." *Journal of Marriage and the Family* 29 (May): 320–24.

Safilios-Rothschild, Constantina. 1969. "Family Sociology or Wives' Family Sociology? A Cross-Cultural Examination of Decision Making." *Journal of Marriage and the Family* 31 (May): 290–301.

———. 1970. "The Study of Family Power Structure: A Review 1960–1969." *Journal of Marriage and the Family* 32 (May): 539–52.

Smith, Herbert L. 1969. "Husband-Wife Task Performance and Decision-Making Patterns." In *Perspectives in Marriage and the Family,* edited by J. Ross Eshleman. Boston: Allyn & Bacon.

Smith, James R., and Lynn G. Smith. 1970. "Co-Marital Sex and the Sexual Freedom Movement." *Journal of Sex Research* 6 (May): 131–42.

Thibaut, John W., and Harold H. Kelley. 1959. *The Social Psychology of Groups.* New York: Wiley.

Waller, W. W., and R. Hill. 1951. *Family.* Rev. ed. New York: Holt, Rinehart & Winston.

Walshok, Mary Lindenstein. 1971. "The Emergence of Middle-Class Deviant Subcultures: The Case of Swingers." *Social Problems* 18 (Spring): 488–95.

The Changing Role of Women in the Armed Forces[1]

Nancy Goldman
University of Chicago

The position of women in the armed forces—the epitome of a male-dominated establishment—offers a striking and limiting case of the changing role of women in occupational and bureaucratic structures. In his analysis of the American military, Charles Moskos has spoken of "the military as a vestige of male sanctity" (1970, p. 64). Traditionally, in the United States military, women are excluded from direct combat roles and from significant assignments in administration. In fact, since the end of World War II, the armed forces have not even filled the 2% authorized quota for women. In the U.S. forces they are entirely volunteers, although the basic military structure for manpower has rested on a draft system.

However, during the second half of the 1960s the number of uniformed women in the armed forces increased, and there is evidence of a trend toward a very gradual expansion of their roles. While the concentration of these women will remain limited, the armed forces anticipate, in the decade of the 1970s, an increase in their number and percentage from less than 2% to approximately 4%.

The encountered and projected increase of women in the armed forces reflects, first, external social change in the United States and the conscious effort of the military to recognize and incorporate such change. Second, because of the relatively low status of the profession, the traditional anti-military attitudes in the society, and the negative impact generated by the war in Vietnam, the movement to an all-volunteer force requires the military to intensify its search for sufficient personnel. The armed forces have traditionally recruited some from the margins of American society; they have recruited heavily from the rural areas, particularly the South; and more recently, personnel have been sought in the black community (Janowitz 1971, pp. 79–101; Moskos 1970, pp. 108–18). Women are also a potential source of labor, especially since they are already recruited on a volunteer basis. Third, the changing character of the military establishment, together with its great emphasis on administration, logistics, and the like, plus its increasing emphasis on deterrence (Kissinger 1965), alter the organizational milieu of the armed forces and potentially broaden sex roles in a direction favorable to women.

This paper will examine the profound organizational resistances and role strains associated with increasing the concentration of women in

[1] I wish to acknowledge the helpful comments of Beth Coye, Otis Bryan, Morris Janowitz, Charles Moskos, William Zierdt, and the support of the Inter-University Seminar on Armed Forces and Society.

the armed forces. However, it is necessary to examine more specifically the symbolism and ideology found in an institution which manages violence, since changes in the position of women tend to be limited in such organizations. (Similar problems exist in the role definition of women in the police force.) Two basic issues are offered as points of departure. First, the movement toward "occupational and professional equality" for women in the military establishment occurs without their involvement in jobs similar to those held by men, that is, without systematic incorporation into "operations" and other key military assignments. What form and degree of strain will result from such a process of organizational adaptation? One hypothesis is based on the notion of relative deprivation. If there is no possibility of effective equality for women in the military, increasing the number and roles of women in the armed forces will produce greater women's militancy. An alternative hypothesis, which seems to be supported by the limited available evidence, is that selective recruitment will limit the strain.[2] This hypothesis assumes that those women who voluntarily select the military profession would be likely to accept its existing authority structure and its internal values.

The recruitment pattern of women into the military is not expected to produce cadres who are committed to militant demands for "complete equality," but groups who are, instead, mainly concerned with extending the roles of women into a wide range of assignments, including those associated with the deterrence functions. Therefore, the analysis of the roles of women in the military offers a locus for the analysis of the trend toward equality without similarity of task—or "functional equality" versus "functional similarity."

Second, with the introduction of an all-volunteer force, new mechanisms of integration of the armed forces into civilian society will be required to maintain civilian supremacy and to prevent the social isolation of the military profession. At the end of the draft in 1973, even with a marked reduction in the overall size of the armed forces to 2 million or less, the military establishment will be a large-scale organization capable of developing and maintaining its own internal subculture. Thus, in the years ahead it will be necessary to ascertain the impact—if any—of more women on the organizational climate of the military as it becomes less of an all-male organization.

A wide range of official documentary sources, reports, and statistical data on manpower were reviewed in the preparation of this paper. In conjunction with the trend toward an all-volunteer force, the armed forces have conducted personnel studies such as *The American Soldier in the 70's*

---

2 Although black women in the military have already demonstrated the strongest degree of militant demands and behavior, their response should be seen more as a reflection of the black community in the military than of the women's group.

(1971) in which data have been assembled on women. A study project by Lt. Comdr. Beth F. Coye (1971) based on survey interviews with 34 women naval line officers produced relevant data on their attitudes and conceptions of professionalism. In addition, I interviewed 30 military officials and personnel officers, both active duty and retired, both on and off military bases, in each case the subject being aware that the material was being collected for university-based research. In addition, strikingly candid contents and reports contained in newspapers published commercially for military personnel provided useful material.

TRENDS IN THE UTILIZATION OF WOMEN

Until World War II, women in the United States who served as military personnel did so as nurses. The only exception was the "Yeomanettes" who, during World War I, were organized as a woman's naval auxiliary to free men for sea duty. However, this service was dissolved in 1919 after the Armistice. Civilian women first served as military nurses in 1854, when Florence Nightingale was asked to organize a group of nurses to care for the wounded in the Crimea (Woodham Smith 1950). In the United States, women served similarly during the Civil War. However, the history of women as uniformed personnel in the armed forces began in 1902 during the Spanish-American War, when the Army Nurse Corps was formed. In 1908 the Navy Nurse Corps was established. It was not, however, until after World War I that nurses were granted military rank. During World War II one-fourth of all American professional nurses volunteered for service. Following the format of the nursing profession in civilian life, the military nurse became rapidly institutionalized and distinct from the women's military corps (Jamieson, Sewall, and Suhrie 1966).

At this time, each of the armed services also established a women's auxiliary unit which has gradually become more and more a permanent and integral part of the service. The navy spelled out its initial, temporary intentions when in 1942 it labeled its women personnel WAVES, namely, Women Accepted for Volunteer Emergency Service. The army established the Women's Army Auxiliary Corps (WAAC) in 1942, and a year later redesignated it the Women's Army Corps (WAC), indicating the trend from an auxiliary service to a regularized component. With the establishment of an independent air force in 1947, Women in the Air Force (WAF) automatically came into being (from 1943 to 1947 they were called Air WACS). Both the marines and the Coast Guard (SPARS) created women's auxiliaries in 1942, although the SPAR corps was dissolved after World War II, except for a small group of reserves. These wartime measures were designed to mobilize effective manpower and to be a symbolic device representing the inclusion of women in the national war effort.

Although the introduction of women into the military during World War II was seen as a short-term wartime measure, even the most male-oriented officers were satisfied with the ability of the forces to use female personnel. However, after the Korean conflict in the late 1950s the position of women in the armed forces remained doubtful, with the prospect that they might become a vestigial element. In the late 1960s, changes in the civilian social structure and the advent of the all-volunteer force made reevaluations by the military necessary and resulted in a limited trend toward the revitalization of the women's element.

Historically, the increase in number and the expansion of women's assignments in the United States armed forces created resistances comparable with those found in other professions such as law, medicine, and university teaching. The oft-quoted assertion by General Lewis Hershey perhaps overstated the issue but reflected, in more picturesque language, the organizational realities. "There is no question but that women could do a lot of the things in the military services. So could men in wheelchairs. But you couldn't except the services to want a whole company of people in wheelchairs." In his study of *The Professional Soldier,* completed in 1960, Morris Janowitz did not find it necessary to deal in any depth with women personnel because of their derivative role and lack of impact on the organizational climate of the profession (Janowitz 1971, pp. 417–30). While Janowitz foresaw the end of the mass army and the movement toward a more contractual system, he did not anticipate an increased emphasis on the recruitment of women into the military. Charles Moskos, a decade later, still had to point out that the position of women in military organizations is almost completely unresearched (Moskos 1971*b*, p. 286).

The trend in the use of women in the armed forces has been examined in this study for the period from 1945 to spring 1972. In 1945, the military reached a high point of over 12 million active officers and enlisted persons, with 265,006 women. As part of a process of "total" mobilization, the percentage of 2.18 women in the armed forces was the high point in their utilization. By 1950, the total number of women in service had declined to 22,069 or 1.51% of the forces. During the Korean War, the number of uniformed women rose to 35,191 in 1955 (1.27%). From 1960 to 1966, the number of women in the forces remained fairly constant, approximately 30,000, and the percentage decreased slightly (from 1.27 to 1.05) because of a limited increase in total personnel.

In 1967, under the impact of Vietnam hostilities, recruitment was intensified and the number of women increased slowly from 35,173 to 42,814 in 1971, with the percentage moving steadily up toward the 2% level. On November 8, 1967, Public Law 90-130, in anticipation of a

TABLE 1

Military Personnel on Active Duty, 1960–Spring 1972, by Service and by Sex

	Army	%	Navy	%	Air Force	%	Marines	%	Total	%
1960:										
Men	860,536	98.6	609,913	98.7	805,426	98.9	169,010	99.1	2,444,885	98.7
Women	12,542	1.4	8,071	1.3	9,326	1.1	1,611	0.9	31,540	1.3
Total	873,078	100.0	617,984	100.0	814,752	100.0	170,621	100.0	2,476,425	100.0
1965:										
Men	955,987	98.7	663,156	98.8	814,792	98.9	188,606	99.2	2,622,546	98.8
Women	12,326	1.3	7,862	1.2	8,841	1.1	1,581	0.8	30,610	1.2
Total	968,313	100.0	671,018	100.0	823,633	100.0	190,187	100.0	2,653,156	100.0
1970:										
Men	1,305,135	98.7	684,199	98.7	778,346	98.3	257,893	99.2	3,025,573	98.7
Women	16,724	1.3	8,683	1.3	13,654	1.7	2,418	0.8	41,479	1.3
Total	1,321,859	100.0	692,882	100.0	792,000	100.0	260,311	100.0	3,067,052	100.0
1971:										
Men	1,200,513	98.6	635,442	98.6	738,469	98.1	222,927	98.9	2,797,351	98.5
Women	16,865	1.4	8,801	1.4	14,850	1.9	2,298	1.1	42,814	1.5
Total	1,217,378	100.0	644,243	100.0	753,319	100.0	225,225	100.0	2,840,165	100.0
1972 (Spring):										
Men	868,965	98.1	586,200	98.5	731,774	97.8	193,807	98.8	2,380,746	98.2
Women	16,814	1.9	8,993	1.5	16,225	2.2	2,273	1.2	44,305	1.8
Total	885,779	100.0	595,193	100.0	747,999	100.0	196,080	100.0	2,425,051	100.0

SOURCE.—*Statistical Abstract of the United States.* Table published by Department of Defense, Comptroller: "Women Military Personnel on Active Duty, May 31, 1945 to Date."

demand for more female personnel, removed the 2% quota, but the expansion in the numbers of women has been very gradual.

Table 1 shows that for the past decade the army has employed the largest number of women. However, on a percentage basis the air force had the highest concentration. An indication of continued trends can be seen in a comparison of 1970, 1971, and 1972. Although the number of men was markedly reduced through demobilization, the total number of women was not. In fact, in 1970 there were 41,479 women on active duty and the number rose to 44,305 in 1972; thus, as of 1972, the overall percentage of women on active duty was 1.8, with corresponding increases over 1970 in all four services.

Despite the very low ratio of women to men in the military it is interesting to note that the ratio of officers to enlisted personnel is about twice as high for women as for men. Among male active-duty personnel in 1970, 13% were officers compared with 36% of the women. Of course, these women officers had a strong concentration of specialists, particularly nurses. Nevertheless, within the military, with its manifest rank system, the high proportion of female officers has the effect of giving greater visibility to women than they would have were the concentration of officers the same as among male personnel.

A comparison of the percentage of women officers in the armed forces, regardless of specialists, with women in other professions reveals that the practices of the military do not vary widely from those of the major professional groups. (Officers are the appropriate group for comparison with other professions.) As of 1970, 3.8% of the army's officers were women, while the air force had 3.6% and the navy, 4.0%. The most recent available data for civilian professions are for 1960, and they do not reflect changes over the last five years. In 1960, the percentage for engineers was 0.8, dentists, 2.1, lawyers, 3.5, while for doctors it was 6.8, and scientists, 9.9. These percentages are rising, as they are in the military, although women officers are not found in these particular specialties.

Because Great Britain has had an all-volunteer force for the past 10 years it is relevant to compare the percentage of women on active duty in the United States with that in Great Britain. Since service became fully volunteer, Great Britain has expanded the concentration of women to meet its personnel requirements. In 1970, it had 14,000 women out of 372,500 in the services (3.8%) (see table 2), or twice as many as in the United States. This difference cannot be accounted for by any difference in age structure.

With the advent of the all-volunteer force scheduled for the summer of 1973, the concentration of women is likely to increase at a modest but steady rate. As already mentioned, the armed forces are more capable of

Nancy Goldman

TABLE 2

PERSONNEL ON ACTIVE DUTY, UNITED STATES AND GREAT BRITAIN, 1970

	United States	%	Great Britain	%
Women	41,000	1.3	14,000	3.8
Men	3,025,000	98.7	358,500	96.2
Total	3,066,000	100.0	372,500	100.0

SOURCE.—*Britain 1971: An Official Handbook.*

meeting volunteer quotas of women than of men since women have always been recruited on a volunteer basis. The air force alone has, for example, a goal of 15,000 women by 1975. To meet these labor needs, the forces have instituted study groups on required organizational and professional changes and have instituted new recruiting programs. The air force has moved toward including women in its ROTC units. Both symbolically and in terms of professional roles, the incorporation of women into the military establishment will result in pressure for women graduates from the military academies. In the fall of 1971, Senator Jacob Javits and Congressman Jack McDonald each sought to have a young woman appointed to the United States Naval Academy from their states.

In September of 1971, the army undertook a staff study, in connection with the advent of the volunteer armed forces, that called for the permanent elimination of the ceiling of 2% on female personnel, a ceiling which was labeled "unrealistic and debilitating" (U.S. Army Combat Developments Command 1971, p. 93). The study showed that between 20% and 35% of army positions could be filled by women, and it also emphasized the necessity of training women in army ROTC units. An advisory commission of 50 civilian women first established in 1951 to investigate the position of women in the military (called the Defense Advisory Commission on Women in the Armed Forces, and during most of its existence relatively inactive) has in recent years been more involved in the debate on the role of women in the armed services.

Interview data with both male and female officers, especially with officers responsible for personnel planning, as well as the findings of the naval survey (Coye 1971, p. 33) indicated that the further increase of women and the expansion of their roles are resisted by some top women officers. One reason is that they see a change in opportunities for women in the military as a threat to their well-being and to their elite positions. Further, their age places them at some distance from the younger women.

Some male officers, because of traditional beliefs, oppose the increase of women and their greater roles; however, since the numerical goals are limited, there is actually very little ideological opposition. In fact, many traditional male officers are more likely to change their opinion about this issue than about many other issues associated with a volunteer force, such as modifications in military justice. There are, indeed, considerable diffuse and positive sentiments toward women. Many traditionalists feel that women entering the service will fit in, since they will make the military more like civilian organizations and will be an asset in the recruitment of young men, and many traditionalists are not adverse to having more "attractive young women" around military headquarters.

Concern about high personnel turnover because of marriage and pregnancy was expressed by military personnel officers. However, a period of three to five years of active duty service is more and more seen as meeting the cost of training and assignment. Also, special arrangements are being slowly developed for married women personnel. Since court cases on issues of pregnant military personnel are underway it is likely that maternity leaves will be instituted. Military women who have children may request to remain in the service once arrangements are made for the child's care (AR 635-200 and AR 635-120 [enlisted personnel separations and officer personnel separations]). Unwanted pregnancies are not a major problem and are infrequent; the effective dissemination of birth control information is probably more extensive in the military than in comparable civilian groups because of the high quality of medical services available. In fact, in 1970 the military medical services took steps to offer expanded abortion service to their personnel and dependents. However, President Richard Nixon issued a presidential order on April 1, 1971 requiring the services to follow local state law, but field observations indicate that military doctors tend to give a "liberal" interpretation to existing law and administration regulations.

Organizational living quarters constitute the greatest area of opposition to an increase in the number of women, since the idea of mixed barracks is strongly resisted by top-ranking female officers. In the air force, bachelor barracks were made coeducational but enlisted personnel still have sex-segregated living quarters.

ROLES OF WOMEN IN THE MILITARY

At the root of the changing roles of women in the armed forces are the special problems of "arming" women. The historical record during the last century in industrial societies indicates only a few cases of institutionalized arming of women, even in nations under the gravest national security threat. Russia, under Kerensky in 1917 during the "Great War," did form a women's battalion which went to the front to fight. This was a desperate attempt to stimulate patriotism and increase manpower. The results, however, were hardly successful. In addition to many losses, the women as a battalion were resented and ridiculed by the men (Beard 1946).

During World War I, England, with a shortage of personnel, organized women's auxiliary groups to a much greater extent than other nations— the Women's Army Auxiliary Corps (WAAC), Women's Royal Air Force (WRAF), and Women's Royal Naval Service (WRNS). Previously, as in the United States, women had served only as nurses (Haldane 1923). Although these auxiliary groups constituted a uniformed women's corps they were not given full military status: that is, they did not "enlist," they "enrolled," and were regarded as civilians.

During World War II, the democratic nations mobilized women both in uniform and in civilian war production far more than did the Axis powers, particularly Nazi Germany. About the possibility of employing German women to reduce the labor shortage during World War II, Speer reports, "Sauckel laid great weight on the danger that factory work might inflict moral harm upon German womanhood; not only might their 'psychic and emotional life' be affected but also their ability to bear" (1970, pp. 220–21). In Great Britain, in addition to inducting women into uniformed auxiliary services, the army employed females in the Auxiliary Territorial Army in air control and as radar operators, and they manned antiaircraft weapons—roles which involved defensive combat (Essame 1970). The Soviet Union trained and gave extensive publicity to a very limited number of women pilots in order to dramatize the need for wartime mobilization and commitment. The Soviet approach can be called "tokenism" rather than an institutionalized use of women in the armed forces. Women have also been used as parachutists behind enemy lines. In Communist China, throughout the whole guerrilla war of national liberation, women were not armed but were used as auxiliaries. Occasionally women have been armed as a result of accident or happenstance and they have been found in small detached guerrilla forces, but there is little evidence that they have been deployed as a significant part of mainline guerrilla forces. Che Guevara in his diary gives his view on the masculinity of the guerrilla status: "This type of fight gives us the opportunity of becoming revolutionaries, the highest level of human species, and it also permits us to graduate as men" (1968, p. xiii).

The case of Israel is particularly noteworthy. In Israel, the large and highly respected women's corps is given training in arms, namely with rifles and submachine guns. However, they are not regularly deployed with arms or mobilized as an armed formation during war (Rolbant 1970, p. 136). They are attached to combat units in training and in the reserves as educational officers (Bar-On 1964).

In the United States during World War II, women in uniform generally filled nursing, administrative, and clerical jobs, although a small minority held more varied posts, especially in naval intelligence and communications. After that conflict their assignments narrowed, and in all of the services women were employed mainly as clerks, secretaries, and in routine types of communications. Continuously since 1945, the U.S. military operated on the notion that women would be excluded from "armed combat," and this concept is applied to military planning for the future. Even the most innovative proposals and staff plans maintain this formal assertion (U.S. Army Combat Development Command 1971, p. 95). However, the changing nature of the military organization weakens the sharp distinction between male and female type of assignments. The military establishment has seen a long-term growth in the proportion and importance of both men and women assigned to logistics and communications and thereby a decline in the segregation of men and women. In fact, the range of functions which women perform has widened. The linkages of women with military missions can be seen in their recent or renewed entrance into intelligence, essential communications functions, and more complex aspects of logistics and maintenance administration.[3] It is also striking to note that selected occupations which are typed as "female" in civilian life have a higher concentration of males in the military, for instance, nurses and social workers, blurring sexual differentiation.

However, the root of the issue of sex-typed positions rests in the changing definitions of military roles. With the development of nuclear weapons and the emergence of deterrence as the central goal of the military, the significance of traditional combat roles is also altered. Women penetrate into the support and administration of deterrence tasks, decreasing the differences in the importance of tasks assigned to men and women (Moskos 1971a, p. 24). In other words, because of the importance of deterrence, many of the tasks of logistics, intelligence, communications and control, and command mean that while the distinction between combat and roles concerned with the mechanics and administration of deterrence is still operative, it becomes attenuated. The effect of deterrence is to expand the number and variety of sedentary noncombat tasks in which the "fighter spirit" is irrelevant. Potentially, women could perform many deterrence tasks such as surveillance by radar equipment, but they are still restricted. In this connection it is important to note that as of Spring 1972, the air force, which has the smallest number of traditional combat roles, had the highest concentration of women personnel. New definitions of sex-

[3] The wider range of assignments for females in the armed forces has very slowly increased the situations in which they supervise males. For a long period, female nurses had responsibilities which required them to be in charge of male personnel. Women officers are supervisors of enlisted personnel, both male and female, in selected administrative and logistics settings, but these are rare cases because of the limitations in the number of women military officers and the procedures for assigning personnel.

based roles and assignments nevertheless remain to be established and formalized. In Great Britain, naval experiments with women aboard ship were terminated, partly because the added manpower advantages seemed trivial and outweighed the personal inconveniences. In 1970 the U.S. navy, aside from their use of nurses, assigned one woman to an operational ship, and it was not a successful experiment.

CHANGING ATTITUDES OF WOMEN

The changing assignments of women in the military must be examined in the light of the demands by women both in civilian society and in the military. The movement for women's equality has a long tradition in the United States, but the current phase encompasses not only traditional goals of equality in economic, occupational, and public life, but also, in the name of women's liberation, includes a psychological and cultural dimension as well as a critique of the moral values of contemporary society. In particular, the militant dimension of women's liberation is linked to the opposition to the war in Vietnam and indifference, at least, about the position of women in the armed forces. However, it is my impression from conversations with militant advocates of the women's liberation movement that when they consider the issues of women in the armed forces, they hold the ideological belief that women should be armed just like men.

In contrast, women recruited into the military, or who are planning to enter, reveal that they are not attached to the militant women's liberation movement. Special effort was made to observe the attitudes of recently recruited women in order to infer any impact of the women's rights movement. The new and younger females entering the military are more self-assertive than the older and earlier recruited personnel. However, the pattern of self-recruitment is such that "militancy" is very low or effectively absent. Selecting the military as a place of employment goes hand in hand with a rejection or indifference to the militant women's liberation movement.

The new recruits—both officers and enlisted personnel—think of themselves as entering a service which has a strong emphasis on equal opportunities, made more emphatic by the fixed and uniform pay rates. Likewise, realistically or unrealistically, they assume that women in the military have better job security than in civilian employment. Sources of dissatisfaction are mainly with living quarters, irritation over administrative detail, and the quality of specific supervisors. "Relative deprivation," always difficult to assess, seems to be limited, not only by selective recruitment but also because resignation rather than opposition is the typical response to frustration and dissatisfaction. Thus, for example, of the 34 naval women officers interviewed, only three expressed dissatisfaction when questioned (Coye 1971, p. 32).

As a result, most of these women accept the existing rate of organization change. But there is an equivalent of a "subdued" women's movement whose manifestations and tactics are very restrained. As a response to the changing context of the military service, there have been continual rounds of official staff discussions, preparation of special internal staff papers plus pressure to change administrative regulations, and even individual court suits, as in the cases of women who have become pregnant and are faced with dismissal.

Outwardly, the demands of the women in the military are pragmatic, specific, and generally negotiable. Occupationally and professionally, the goal is to press for a broader range of assignments, often under the category of line- or unrestricted line-officers' duties. The formulation is that—potentially—women should be able to serve in the broadest range of assignments, depending on the requirements of the service and of the task to be performed. Married women personnel concerned with change are interested in administrative arrangements which would facilitate the utilization, retention, and careers of married women. In this regard, the key demands center around the issues of pregnancy and the right of female military personnel to have children and pursue their careers. The change in procedures desired by women officers and enlisted personnel are documented in considerable detail in the specialized "trade" publications, such as the *Army Times* and the *Air Force Times,* which circulate among military personnel. All these demands are tempered by the general belief—of those who wish to pursue a military career—that such a career imposes some limitations on personal freedom. With respect to child rearing, the demands of new arrangements are grounded in a highly matter-of-fact assertion, offered by both males and females and incorporated into planning documents, that effective birth control is available and, therefore, there is a real alternative to the disruptions associated with childbearing.

Underlying these specific issues and orientations, especially for women officers, is a set of diffuse attitudes which agree with concepts of military affairs and with changes in the structure and outlook of the male military professionals. In Coye's study, on the basis of informal interviews and a partial survey of the attitudes of 34 women naval officers, the range of opinions can be preliminarily identified (Coye 1971, pp. 27–32).

One essential source of data is the response elicited by the probe, "What do you think are the navy's reasons for maintaining women officers today?" The traditionalist's viewpoint rested on the "nucleus" notion—that active duty women (officers and enlisted) provide a trained nucleus in the event of mobilization. According to this view, the role of the women line officers is essentially the administration of women personnel. This concept of women's role in the military is based on a concept of military organization which antedates the introduction of nuclear weapons and the threat of mass destruction.

Second, closely related but less traditionalist, is the outlook that women, as a significant part of the labor force, are a resource base and should therefore be used. Moreover, they have proved their worth and competence and are available elements of the naval organization as it currently operates. Those with this point of view believe that women officers can be just as competent as men, but believe that before this is accepted (by the male officers) the image of women in the country must be changed. These less traditional women have a strong element of equalitarianism in their thinking, but they are resigned to accepting the system, and they anticipate that changes will come from the outside; they are in effect the gradualists.

The third group appears to be not only the most change oriented, with respect both to the status of women and to the naval organization, but they also appear to be the most aware that mobilization concepts are only partially valid, or in a "state of limbo," since the relevance of the naval force is mainly as a force in being. These women are thinking about greater equality through functional equivalences. This point of view was expressed in interviews by the following attitudes: "The navy wants women for their general and special talents, and at the same time, offers young women the opportunity to serve their country." "The quality of women officers has been steadily improving; women have proven themselves useful and have become an integral part of the navy." By inference, for these women, administration and being a generalist in administration are a partial equivalent to sea duty.

A scattered few held a "tough minded" point of view, namely that women were in the military because the armed forces were "stuck with them by law." All of these groups, as witnessed by their continued naval service, accepted the system in varying degrees. However, three out of a sample of 34 were outspokenly negative. For them, women in the navy did essentially secretarial and paperwork duties. Their responses included opinions such as "We are high-paid office managers doing the navy's paperwork. . . . We still get scruffy billets that the men don't want. . . . We are performing well, but are kept down in how we perform. . . . We are restricted."

INSTITUTIONAL MECHANISMS FOR CONTROLLING SEX ROLES

As in any organization, personal attitudes and role relations in the military are contained and controlled by a series of institutional mechanisms; but the military has special features which impinge directly on these attitudes and relations. The overall number of women in the armed forces is set by formal allocations or quotas. Once a decision has been made to increase the number or percentage, the institutional mechanisms of control reveal many of the requisites for integrating women into the formal structure. In fact, there are institutional mechanisms of control which facilitate the integration of women into the civilian professional and occupational structure found in the armed forces. To identify these mechanisms is not to overlook the crucial issue of sex typing of professional and occupational roles, especially as they are linked to the ideology and reality of combat. The military is exclusively in the public sector and under a civil service format. Women in occupations and professions generally fare better in the public sectors, as has been demonstrated in a variety of studies. The civil service concept, with all of its limitations, at least requires equal pay for equal work and emphasizes more explicit criteria for promotion.

Moreover, while the protégé system and collegial relations are dominated by men in the military, they operate mostly at the very top. Throughout the military there are powerful pressures for the development of elaborated and explicit standards of promotion, which serve to penalize the most gifted and creative of both sexes. Likewise, women in the uniformed services have never developed sex-segregated occupational associations believed by some sociologists to be devices for deflecting the integration of women in the larger organizational settings. Moreover, women officers have had access to officers' clubs although their role in these clubs has been marginal.

However, at the higher levels, despite the trend toward managerial authority, the military is a crisis-prone organization in which innovation is in the hands of charismatic leaders or under centralized control, devices which serve to hamper the extension of women into positions of authority.

Defined standards of performance assist in the integration of women. The military constantly emphasizes a skill structure of specialists. However, the idea of the generalist—the operations officer—is very powerful, and it is noteworthy that, while there is a strong concentration of women in specialist assignments, the woman contingent has developed a functional equivalent of the generalist in operations, namely, the generalist in administration.

Career length and professional relations, or, more specifically, a system of ranking, are another positive factor (Epstein 1970, pp. 979–81). In the military this variable is operative to a considerable extent because of the system of formal grades. The rank system in the armed forces serves to separate, to some extent, the office from the person, with special relevance for the position of women. Nevertheless, there is some evidence that the rate of promotion for women officers is at least in some cases different from that of men. Until recently there were no authorizations for female general rank officers, and women officers in the navy are at times assigned to "billets" which are rated below their military rank. In April 1971, 22% of the captains, 27% of the commanders, and 17% of the lieutenant commanders had such assignments (Coye 1971, p. 10). However, comparable data on the underutilization of men are not available.

Finally, the ability to perform formal professional roles and to shift rapidly into the informal role requirements of a woman is a positive factor in integrating women into an occupational structure. In the military environment, especially at the officer level, there is considerable emphasis on appropriate manners and protocol. However, for the military, which is a communal institution—a setting in which work and residential roles strongly overlap and where the elements of sexual symbols are linked to the imagery of the fighting man—it is necessary to examine the sex symbolism of professional roles in somewhat deeper categories.

SEX AND SEXUAL SYMBOLISM

The literature on military institutions reveals a relative neglect of the study of sexual relations and of sexual symbolism in the military community. One sociological issue is that of family relations in the military community; another is the imagery and life circumstances of female military personnel. Charles Moskos's study of the American enlisted man focuses on the sexual behavior of military personnel while they are stationed abroad during the period 1945–70, when over one-third were on overseas assignments (Moskos 1970, pp. 78–107). He presents the conclusion that "indeed, from the viewpoint of many bachelor soldiers, it is the widespread opportunity for sexual promiscuity that most distinguishes overseas from stateside assignments" (1970, p. 91). In Vietnam, under the impact of actual hostilities and in the setting of extensive local corruption, catering to the sexual desires of American servicemen becomes a major and openly tolerated enterprise. An article with the headline "U.S. Viet Bases Welcome Shady Ladies" states that "the army is permitting ladies of the evening to be signed onto central Vietnam bases officially to meet U.S. troops in their barracks. . . . [Officers] maintain that the risks are worthwhile in the interest of keeping the peace in an increasingly disgruntled and demoralized army" (Chicago *Sun-Times*, January 24, 1972, p. 4).

The issue at hand is that of sexual values as an aspect of the social personality of the military, if that construct has relevance and validity. The social personality of the military profession—officer or enlisted man— is a matter more of impressionistic observation and literary reference than of systematic research. Nevertheless, for career personnel, and especially for those in highly specialized volunteer units, selection and self-selection in terms of social personality do operate (Janowitz 1965, pp. 50–76).

Even in the absence of extensive documentation and without probing underlying personality dynamics, two themes characterize, in ideal typical terms, the conventional military establishment. On the one hand, it has been noted by Little (1971, p. 249) that the military establishment has a strong familistic culture. The cult of manliness which emphasizes sexual virility and sexual exploits is the alternate theme which, although contradictory in one sense, may not necessarily be antithetical to the maintenance of family ties, if these relationships are adequately institutionalized.

Both ideologically and in reality family life and the importance of family ties are dominant in the military (Janowitz 1971; Little 1971, pp. 247–71). Careful research by Williams on the air force notes the lower divorce rate as a reflection of the culture of the military family (Williams 1971). One is struck by the relative absence of unmarried male officers, the few divorced personnel, and the very few childless families.

The family is a device for accommodation to the strains of military life, and family instability is linked to the exodus of those who do not fit in. Traditionally, in the peacetime armed force an officer, or—increasingly —a top noncommissioned officer, does not move easily into the overlap between occupational and social obligations without a family (Little 1971, p. 253); the officer's wife is seen as an active ingredient of the military community and antedated the corporation wife. There is, as well, a widespread assumption (not necessarily based on fact) that promotions into the higher ranks and responsible assignments go to the family man. For example, in the air force, particularly in the Strategic Air Command with its responsibility for nuclear weapons, married men are thought of as being more safe and sane and having a sense of responsibility. In air force imagery, fighter pilots can well be single men but they are considered to be less appropriate members of a strategic deterrence bomber crew (Williams 1971).

Before World War II the social position of the military wife was relatively fixed. In addition to her family role, she participated in the elaborate social protocol of the military base and had definite although limited obligations in voluntary associations and in the military's system of mutual self-help. However, with the vast expansion of the military establishment, the extensive rotations of assignments, and the weakening of military protocol, the old system has been drastically undermined (Lang 1964, pp. 77–80). Therefore, the military has organized itself to assist family life, and elaborate programs involving professionals and volunteers have become necessary (Little 1971, p. 248).

Despite its strains, military life is a form of communal living; most military activities are carried out on the base, which is as well the locus of much of military family life (although housing shortages require that an important percentage of the military live elsewhere). Consequently, the unmarried female military personnel occupy an ambiguous position in the social life of the base. Women officers are, to some degree, incorporated into its formal social life and thereby come into contact with the wives of officers; but the gulf between enlisted women and the wives of noncommissioned officers is much wider.

The theme of the cult of masculinity, on the other hand, implies that the good fighter is the man of sexual power and exploits. In imagery, as much as in reality, this aggressive sexual symbolism is based on the assumption that an effective officer cannot be a sissy or a virgin. The more combat oriented the locus or setting, the more pronounced the sexual symbolism and mythology. The heroic officer is an active type of man; in the past, he engaged in horseback riding and even polo, while in the contemporary scene his activities are survival training, parachuting, and the like, plus a range of hard-driving sports. Drinking is standard, but drunkenness is considered in bad taste. Before World War II, many military bases in the United States assumed that nearby local communities would openly tolerate brothels frequented mainly by their enlisted men and young and unmarried officers. Within the confines of the military community, codes of conduct were well developed, since scandal, if revealed, was highly disruptive of the small, closely knit, and compact military establishment. Mass mobilization during World War II and the continued tensions of the Cold War strained the ability of the military to control and deal with these two themes of the family man and the cult of masculinity. As the number of women increased, both as civilian and as military personnel, the emphasis on appropriate and proper relations continued—but the cult of masculinity found more and more opportunities for expression within the military establishment. In the 1960s the changing mores of the outside world and the disruption of the military community caused by Vietnam only served to sharpen the dilemmas. In addition, the issues of homosexuality—including homosexuality among women—had to be faced in new and more explicit terms.

In the military community as in the civilian society, the role relations and protocol between the sexes are being redefined. The consequences of new trends in socialization cannot be anticipated and may produce strong reactions. However, the hypothesis can be offered that there will be a reduction in overt sexual competition, since the new generation appears to be more prepared for "coeducational" existence in most segments of their daily life. The military will not be able to differentiate itself sharply from civilian society in this respect, except in highly specialized units.

The coeducational format has already been introduced in important aspects of military training, with notable implications. The impact, even if limited to the specific training situation, has been to reduce or at least contain the cult of masculinity and render the organizational climate more pragmatic and less ritualistic. For example, during the period 1966–70, which included expansion of Vietnam hostilities, the officer training school of the air force contained a small but regular percentage of WAFs. In 1968, there were 7% in the class, a percentage large enough to make a direct impact (Wamsley 1972). Wamsley's analysis of this training institution concluded that the presence of women added a "measure of decorum and realism," and generally dampened the zeal and ferocity with which particular activities such as drill, discipline, and even room arrangements were approached. He quotes a training officer: "Some of the Mickey Mouse crap the cadets used to pull is beneath these guys and especially with the girls around. They feel just plain foolish pulling some of those stunts around the WAFs" (unpublished). The impact of the presence of women should not be exaggerated, but, in this case, some coeducational training was compatible with military requirements, as it would appear to be for a force committed to a deterrence philosophy. Likewise, leading educational officers in the Israeli defense forces emphasize that the presence of girls in the army is responsible for a polite atmosphere and the maintenance of more appropriate language and behavior among soldiers. It seems not to affect battle performance and probably contributes to the sense of civility found in the Israeli forces.

Data on the patterns of contacts of women military personnel with civilians in the local communities would be useful; these patterns will change both as the number of women in the military increase and as the military moves more toward a volunteer force. Although it is possible that these contacts may not serve to integrate the military into the civilian social structure, there is reason to believe that they may well work to prevent the social isolation of the military, since women are more likely to maintain their previous civilian contacts and many serve limited tours of duty.

Problems of personal and social adjustment rest more heavily on the unmarried enisted women than on officer personnel. Not only are women officers more readily accepted into the social life of the military base, but they enter with a stronger sense of personal competence and are afforded a more individualized life-style. They have generally been given separate quarters, which contributes to a feeling of esteem. As mentioned earlier, enlisted women are less likely to engage in social contacts with the families of the enlisted ranks and are less interested in doing so. Their social life is oriented to other unmarried personnel—male and female. The services are conscious of their problems of social adjustment. Nevertheless, their housing is most limited and generally in some form of barracks. The new female recruit finds herself in a situation in which there is a strong emphasis on appropriate form and protocol. The services, in fact, conduct seminars on "social maturity" and personal style in the military. But basically social adjustment is based on self-selection since those who find the life confining or unsatisfactory leave.

CONCLUSION

There is no reason to believe that the proportion of women in the armed forces will increase or that the range of their employment and responsibility will expand rapidly or dramatically with the advent of the all-volunteer armed force. However, I believe there is ample reason to expect a gradual increase in numbers and a slow but steady expansion of assignment. Conceptually, the position of women in the armed forces offers a special case for analyzing both the women's liberation movement and the search for occupational equality. The armed forces operate under the federal sanction of equal pay for equal work and in an ethos of institutional change oriented toward equality. However, the context of the armed forces and the nature of the military is such that women in the military present a clear-cut case of the search for equality on the basis of autonomy and functional equivalence without the opportunity for similarity of specialization or task. The greater emphasis on deterrence increases the opportunity for women to become more directly involved in new types of "military" assignments. But women are not likely to be trained and armed for assault or direct combat operations. The institutional need for such deployment is slight; and the larger society has not yet been receptive to the idea that such equality is an essential demonstration of women's equality. The need for the military to adjust to more women who have broader assignments will increase the strains in the establishment, especially in connection with child-rearing requirements and the symbolism connected with sexual relations. However, under an all-volunteer system, the armed forces have an organizational structure to accommodate such strains, especially since, from a social and ideological point of view, they will not be recruiting the most "militant" younger women.

REFERENCES

Bar-On, Moshe. 1964. *Education Process in the Israel Defense Forces.* Jerusalem: Israel Digest.
Beard, Mary R. 1946. *Woman as a Force in History: A Study in Traditions and Realities.* New York: Macmillan.
Coye, Beth F. 1971. "The Woman Line Officer in the U.S. Navy: An Exploratory Study." Paper presented to the September 1971 Inter-University Seminar on Armed Forces and Society, University of Chicago.
Epstein, Cynthia. 1970. "Encountering the Male Establishment: Sex-Status Limits on Women's Careers in the Professions." *American Journal of Sociology* 75 (May): 965–82.
Essame, Hubert. 1970. "The Second World War: The Years of Retreat, 1939–49." In

History of the British Army, edited by Peter Young and J. P. Lawford. London: Barker.

Guevara, Ernesto. 1968. *The Diary of Che in Bolivia, November 7, 1966–October 7, 1967.* Calcutta: National Book Agency.

Haldane, Elizabeth Sanderson. 1923. *The British Nurse in Peace and War.* London: Murray.

Jamieson, Elizabeth Marion, Mary F. Sewall, and Eleanor B. Suhrie. 1966. *Trends in Nursing History: Their Social, International and Ethical Relationships.* Philadelphia: Saunders.

Janowitz, Morris, in collaboration with Roger W. Little. 1965. *Sociology and the Military Establishment.* New York: Russell Sage Foundation.

Janowitz, Morris. 1971. *The Professional Soldier.* New York: Free Press.

Kissinger, Henry. 1965. *Problems of National Strategy: A Book of Readings.* New York: Praeger.

Lang, Kurt. 1964. "The Effects of Succession: A Comparative Study of Military and Business Organization." In *The New Military,* edited by Morris Janowitz. New York: Wiley.

Little, Roger W. 1971. "The Military Family." In *Handbook of Military Institutions,* edited by Roger W. Little. Beverly Hills, Calif.: Sage Publications.

Moskos, Charles C., Jr. 1970. *The American Enlisted Man: The Rank and File in Today's Military.* New York: Russell Sage Foundation.

———. 1971a. "The Emergent Military: Civilianized, Traditional or Pluralistic?" In *Public Opinion and the Military Establishment,* edited by Charles Moskos. Beverly Hills, Calif.: Sage Publications.

———. 1971b. "Minority Groups in Military Organization." In *Handbook of Military Institutions,* edited by Roger Little. Beverly Hills, Calif.: Sage Publications.

Rolbant, Samuel. 1970. *The Israeli Soldier: Profile of an Army.* South Brunswick, N.J.: Barnes.

Speer, Albert. 1970. *Inside the Third Reich.* New York: Macmillan.

United States Army Combat Developments Command. Personnel and Administrative Services Agency, Deputy Chief of Staff for Personnel, U.S. Army. 1971. *The American Soldier in the 70's.* Vol. 1, *The Personnel Offensive (Phase I).*

Wamsley, Gary. 1972. "Contrasting Institutions of Air Force Socialization: Happenstance or Bellwether?" *American Journal of Sociology* 78 (September): 399–417.

Williams, John. 1971. "Divorce and Family Dissolution." Paper presented at American Sociological Association Annual Meeting in Denver, September.

Woodham Smith, Cecil Blanche. 1950. *Florence Nightingale.* London: Constable.

Young, Peter, and J. P. Lawford, eds. 1970. *History of the British Army.* London, Barker.

Positive Effects of the Multiple Negative: Explaining the Success of Black Professional Women[1]

Cynthia Fuchs Epstein
Queens College of the City University of New York and Bureau of Applied Social Research, Columbia University

Despite American society's myth and credo of equality and open mobility, the decision-making elites and elite professions have long remained clublike sanctuaries for those of like kind (Goode 1957; Merton, Reader, and Kendall 1957; Hughes 1962; Hall 1948; Epstein 1970*b*, p. 968).

To be Jewish, black, foreign born, or a woman have all been bases for exclusion from law, medicine, engineering, science, the supergrades of the civil service, architecture, banking, and even journalism. Only a few in the professions find that good can come from being born of the wrong sex, race, religion, or ethnic group. This is a report on a set of these deviants who possess at least two—and often more—statuses deemed to be "wrong." It attempts to analyze why they nevertheless were successful in the occupational world.

In the exchange system of American society, women's sex status and blacks' racial status have typically cost them prestigious and remunerative jobs because society did not evaluate them as being high in either capacity or potential. Those who did succeed had to be brighter, more talented, and more specialized than white males in a comparable labor pool, whom the society ranked higher. Thus, they paid more for the same benefits (or "goods"), if they were permitted to acquire them at all.

Where categories of persons have more than one of these negative statuses, there often tends to be a cumulative negative effect. The costs of having several negatively evaluated statuses are very high and lead to social bankruptcy when people simply cannot muster the resources to pay them. This effect has been elsewhere conceptualized as "cumulative disadvantage" and has explained the poor representation of blacks (among others) in skilled occupations. Black women, for example, because of their

[1] This is publication A-662 of the Bureau of Applied Social Research, Columbia University. It is a revision of a paper presented at the Annual Meeting of the American Sociological Association, 1971, in Denver, Colorado, and was prepared with the support of grants from the Research Foundation of the City University of New York, no. 1079 and grant no. 91-34-68-26 from the Manpower Administration, U.S. Department of Labor. The author is indebted to Diana Polise for help in its preparation and to Florence Levinsohn and Howard Epstein for editorial suggestions. Critical issues were raised by William J. Goode, Gladys G. Handy, Jacqueline J. Jackson, Robert K. Merton, and Lauren Seiler (some resolved, others not).

two negatively evaluated statuses, are situated at the very bottom of the occupational pyramid.

Indeed, the status set which includes being black and being a woman has been one of the most cumulatively limiting.

These ascribed sex (female) and race (black) statuses are dominant;[2] they are visible and immutable and impose severe limits on individuals' capacities to alter the dimensions of their world and the attitudes of others toward them. In the elite professions, blacks and women have been considered inappropriate and undervalued, and as a result they have constituted only a tiny proportion of the prestigious professionals.[3] Not only have they been prevented from working in the elite professions, but the few who do manage to become professionals tend to work in the less remunerative and prestigious subfields (Epstein 1970c, p. 163).

Women typically have jobs which rank lower than men at every class level, and, contrary to some current misconceptions about the existence of a black matriarchy, black women are most typically at the very bottom of the occupational pyramid. They earn less than white women who, in turn, make less than men, white or black.[4] This economic distribution is constant for every category of worker, including professionals, with the sole exception of domestic workers. Although black women earn less, they are also much more apt to work than white women of the same age and education (Bureau of the Census, *Current Population Reports,* P-60, no. 75 [1970], table 50, p. 113).[5]

Yet there are black women who have achieved success in the popular definition of the term, becoming professionals of high prestige and acquiring high incomes as well. For them the effect of status sets with two immutable negatively evaluated statuses—the sex status of female and the race status of black—did not result in negative consequences but formed a positive matrix for a meaningful career.

[2] According to Robert K. Merton, statuses are dominant when they determine the other statuses one is likely to acquire (see Epstein 1970c, p. 92). Part of this analysis (as that in my earlier work [1970b, 1970c]) draws on Robert K. Merton's conceptualization of the dynamics of status sets, part of which is found in *Social Theory and Social Structure* (1957, pp. 368–84), and much of which has been presented in lectures at Columbia University and is as yet unpublished (see footnotes in Epstein 1970b, p. 966).

[3] In 1960, blacks constituted 1.3% of all lawyers, and the proportion of women in law was 3.4%.

[4] Median earnings of full-time, year-round workers were reported as follows for 1967: Negro women—$3,194; white women—$4,279; Negro men—$4,777; white men —$7,396 (U.S. Bureau of Census, *Current Population Reports,* ser. P-60, no. 60, table 7, p. 39). Although figures went up in 1970 the relationship remained the same (U.S. Bureau of Census, *Current Population Reports,* ser. P-60, no. 75, table 45, pp. 97–98).

[5] In 1968, 49% of Negro women were in the work force compared with 40% of white women (Brimmer 1971, p. 550).

Cynthia Fuchs Epstein

This paper is based on interviews with a sample of 31 such women who achieved occupational success in the prestigious male-dominated professions and occupations of law, medicine, dentistry, university teaching, journalism, and public relations.[6]

Studying these successful black professional women we located three major patterns resulting from the interaction between statuses which accounted for their success. They may be outlined as follows:

1. Focusing on one of the negatively valued statuses canceled the negative effect of the other. (That is, raised its "worth." For example, in a white professional milieu, a black woman is viewed as lacking the "womanly" occupational deficiencies of white women—for example, seeking a husband—and the black woman's sex status is given a higher evaluation.)

2. Two statuses in combination create a new status (for example, the hyphenated status of black-woman-lawyer) which may have no established "price" because it is unique. In this situation, the person has a better bargaining position in setting his or her own worth. This pattern may also place the person in the role of a "stranger," outside the normal exchange system and able to exact a higher than usual price.

3. Because the "stranger" is outside the normal opportunity structure, he or she can choose (or may be forced to choose) an alternate life-style. This choice was made by many black women forced to enter the occupational world because of economic need, and, in turn, it created selective barriers which insulated the women from diversions from occupational success and from ghetto culture, thus strengthening ambition and motivation.

In the sections which follow, we will locate black professional women among other professionals to demonstrate their very special position in the social structure and further illustrate the process by which they were able to "make it" in American society.

BLACK WOMEN IN THE PROFESSIONS

Like the pattern for whites over 25, black women currently in the labor force have had more median years of schooling than black men, and more of them have been high school graduates. Furthermore, although black men in college now exceed black women, more black women over 25 are college graduates than are men in this age group (U.S. Department of Commerce,

[6] Because no lists exist of black women in any of these professions, there was no way to systematically sample the universe of black women professionals. Instead, respondents were obtained by referral from friends and colleagues. Because of the extremely small absolute number of black women in these fields, and because the study was limited to the New York area, a great deal of time was spent simply trying to find subjects.

Statistical Abstract 1968 [1968], table 156, p. 110; *Statistical Abstract 1970* [1970], table 157, p. 109; data derived from the *U.S. Census of the Population: 1960,* vol. 1, and *Current Population Reports,* ser. P-20, nos. 169, 194). Their educational advantage accounts partly for their greater access to professional jobs, and a significantly higher proportion of black women than men hold professional jobs—60% of the total numbers of blacks holding such jobs—as reported by the 1960 census (Bureau of the Census, *1960 Subject Reports. Occupational Characteristics,* PC(2) and 7A, table 3, p. 21). Of all employed black women, 7% were professionals, in contrast to 3% of all employed black men (Ginzberg and Hiestand 1966, p. 210).

Like all American college women, black women are often steered into teaching and nursing careers. Black college women generally have taken B.A. degrees in education[7] and found employment in the segregated school systems of the South (Ginzberg and Hiestand 1966, p. 216). Although the census has always counted teachers as professionals, teaching has always ranked low in occupational prestige,[8] and black men, like white men, did not enter teaching in any numbers.[9]

There are no census figures on the total number of graduate and professional degrees earned by black men and women,[10] and seemingly contra-

---

[7] In predominantly Negro colleges and universities, for the years 1963–64, the proportion of women students majoring in elementary education was 24.4% as compared with 6.4% of the men (McGrath 1965, p. 80). The field of education alone accounted for 38% of all bachelor's degrees earned by women in 1967. Education also accounted for 51% of the master's and 29% of the doctor's degrees earned by women in 1967 (*Handbook of Women Workers 1969,* pp. 192–93); 53.5% of black women in the "Professional, Technical & Kindred Workers" category in the U.S. census were elementary (43.1%) and secondary (10.4%) school teachers (Ginsberg and Hiestand 1966, p. 215).

[8] Teaching ranked thirty-sixth in the NORC study of occupational prestige in 1947 and rose to twenty-sixth place in 1963, still placing it far below medicine, law, banking, college teaching, etc.

[9] Black men have gone into teaching to a somewhat greater degree than white men but not nearly to the extent of the women. Of professional men, 11.9% were elementary school teachers and 13.1% were secondary school teachers; the absolute numbers being considerably smaller as well, as the table below indicates:

PERCENTAGE OF NEGRO PROFESSIONAL, TECHNICAL AND KINDRED CENSUS CATEGORY WHO WERE TEACHERS, BY SEX, 1960

| | MEN | | WOMEN | |
TEACHERS	Number	%	Number	%
Elementary	13,451	11.9	75,695	43.1
Secondary	14,823	13.1	18,194	10.4

SOURCE.—Ginsberg and Hiestand 1966, pp. 210, 215.

[10] Statistics on doctorate production of blacks can only be based on the number of graduate degrees produced by the predominantly black colleges and by estimates of

dictory figures appear in the sources available. A study of Negro colleges—where the majority of blacks have earned their graduate degrees (Blake 1971, p. 746)—shows that black women earned 60% of the graduate and professional degrees awarded in 1964–65 (United Negro College Fund 1964–65, appendix I). However, a Ford Foundation study (1970) of all black Ph.D. holders in 1967–68 (p. 3) indicated that of a 50% sample of the total, only 21% were women. Another source covering black colleges for the same period as the UNCF report (1964) lists more women than men earning M.A.'s (799 as compared with 651; probably a majority were education degrees) but more men than women earning Ph.D.'s (five men and two women) (Ploski 1967, p. 527).[11]

If one compares the proportion of black women with black men in those professions higher in prestige than teaching, we find a more traditional picture. More black men than women are editors, doctors, lawyers, scientists, and college teachers (Bureau of the Census, *1960 Subject Reports. Occupational Characteristics,* PC (2)-7A, table 3, p. 21). Furthermore, they consistently have higher median incomes than do the women in these professions (Bureau of the Census, *1960 Subject Reports. Occupational Characteristics,* PC (2)-7A, table 25, p. 296; table 26, p. 316).[12]

But relative to their male colleagues, black career women have done better than their white sisters; they constitute a larger proportion of the black professional community than women in the white professional world. Only 7% of white physicians are women, but 9.6% of black doctors are women; black women make up 8% of black lawyers but white women constitute only 3% of all white lawyers. Black women approach real equality with black men in the social sciences—they are 34% of all blacks in the profession—although the absolute numbers are small (data derived from same Bureau of the Census 1960 as indicated above).

In most professional groups, black women constitute a larger proportion of women than black men do among males in these groups (U.S. Bureau of the Census, *1960 Subject Reports. Occupational Characteristics,* PC (2)-

---

the number of blacks in the integrated colleges. Statistics are unavailable because of fair educational practices laws. The absolute number of black doctorates ever held is small, estimated by Horace Mann Bond (1966) at 2,485 (comprising those awarded 1866–1962) (Ginsberg and Hiestand 1966, p. 564). The Ford Foundation study cited herein found 2,280 current holders of Ph.D. degrees in 1967–68.

11 Although the Ford study included education doctorates, we suppose that the high figure for women graduates in black institutions is probably due to the high proportion of education doctorates awarded by Negro institutions when compared with the range of doctorates awarded by white institutions. This is probably due to perennial fiscal problems and inability to fund programs in the hard sciences until quite recently.

12 If one uses nonwhite categories (which, for the general population, is 92% black) to get figures for blacks in the professions, a misleading impression will result. Certain professions (see n. 15) have almost equal numbers of blacks and other nonwhites, such as Chinese, Japanese, etc.

7A, table 3, p. 21). In terms of earnings they are also far more equal to white women than black men are to white men. In fact, black women accountants, musicians, professional nurses, and social workers exceeded their white female colleagues in earnings, according to the 1960 census (U.S. Bureau of the Census, *1960 Subject Reports. Occupational Characteristics*, PC (2)-7A, table 25, p. 296; table 26, p. 316).

However, one cannot ignore the fact that for all professions the absolute numbers of blacks are small, and the numbers of black women are so tiny that they may go unreported and unanalyzed. In the 1960 census, only 220 black women lawyers and about 370 black women social scientists were counted. No doubt there have been increases in all fields, but this remains conjectural in view of the fact that the proportion of all women in the professions has remained fairly static over the past 40 years (Epstein 1970*b*).

BLACK WOMEN HAVE GREATER ACCESS

It is believed that in some sectors, probably as professionals in white firms, hospitals, and communities, black women have done better than black men. Historically, black women have had more access to white society than black men and have had opportunities to learn the "ropes" of the white world. Because they were desired as house servants, nurse-maids, and sexual partners, black women often became intimates of whites, learnings their values and habits. They could be intimates because as women they were not only powerless but were never regarded as potentially powerful, an attribute which has its analogue in their admission to the male-dominated professions.

Although it is difficult, if not impossible, to document the sense of threat with which white male professionals react to the thought of black men as colleagues, it is clear that black men and women perceive this reaction as a barrier to them. It was a common feeling among the black women in this study that this perceived threat was not as great for them. Being a woman reduced the effect of the racial taboo.

On the other hand, black women are found in professions and occupations known to be difficult for white women to penetrate. Because these women are black they are perhaps not perceived as women; they may be regarded as more "serious" professionals than white women; they may not be viewed as sexual objects nor be seen as out to get a husband. The stereotypes attached to the so-called feminine mind, emotions, or physiology may not seem easily transferable to black women, for whom there seem to be fewer stereotypes in the context of the professionally trained.

We have concentrated on several themes: (1) the special conditions which created for these women an image of self and an achievement value structure, (2) the problems attached to playing out traditional, idealized female dependency roles; and (3) the reinforcing components of the work situation.

WOMAN AS DOER

Although the situation of the black woman is in many ways unique, many of the problems she faces are also experienced by other groups of women with negatively evaluated statuses. The mechanisms she uses to cope with strain are mirrored in their experiences as well. But perhaps more than the others, the black woman has been the subject of myths and misinterpretations often applied to behavior of minority group members (see Hyman 1969; Mack 1971).

The most pernicious of the popular stereotypes about the black woman holds that a black matriarchy exists and is a key factor in the social disorganization of the Negro family and the "irresponsibility" of the male as provider and authority. It is a perfect example of the "damned if you do, damned if you don't" syndrome (Merton 1957, p. 480).

Although a greater proportion of black women than white women work, and a greater proportion are the heads of families, the assumption that these factors have an independent negative effect has been challenged. The great majority of black families are intact families and, although a higher proportion of black wives work than do white wives, the typical pattern of black family life is an equalitarian one rather than one of wife-mother dominance. The strong mother figure is prevalent in the black family, but as Ladner (1971) has recently pointed out, strength is not the same as dominance. There have been many instances of strong mother figures in American history (immigrant mothers and pioneer mothers) who have been idealized as women who made it possible for their families to endure in punishing situations. Somehow, these other women were subjected to a different set of norms in contexts in which work was considered appropriate, in which running the shop, sitting at the cash register, or administering the farm was not viewed as masculine or, worse "castrating" behavior. Sometimes the work was done side by side with the husband, sometimes alone because of his incapacity or unavailability. Only the rich could afford to keep their women unoccupied and unhelpful.[13]

The analogue of the immigrant woman probably fits the black woman's situation best, for she also was aware that the men in her family might

---

[13] The managerial ability of women throughout history has been understated. Although women have always worked in agrarian societies and at the lower strata in all societies, upper-class women have assumed economic roles in a variety of circumstances. Women of rank managed estates in France and England in the absence of male heirs or when men went off to war.

not be able to provide for it entirely. Sharing or assuming work obligations were real expectations, and enough women did so to become models for generations to come. Both this study of black women professionals and my earlier study of women lawyers, many of whom came from immigrant families, showed that these women had in their lives models of mother-provider figures[14]—a mother or grandmother who, as a domestic worker or proprietor of a small store, or as a seamstress and, later, teacher and suffragette, generated a positive image of woman as doer, not as a passive and dependent person. The mother-provider figure appeared not in the absence of a father but often as the figure who worked with a father in a family business or who shared the economic burden by working at another enterprise. In fact, the mother-provider as heroine is a common image in many of these case studies because the activity of these women was so positively experienced and cherished.

The following description of a mother, offered by a woman physician in the study, is typical: "My mother was not the stronger of my parents but she was the more aggressive, always planning and suggesting ideas to improve the family's situation. A dressmaker by trade, she would slip out to do domestic work by the day when times got hard, often not telling my father about it. He was a bricklayer and carpenter but had trouble finding work because he was unable to get union membership."

Most of this sample of black women came from intact families. What was important was that their mothers, forced to work, canceled the "female effect" of motivation and offered an alternative model of adult women to that of the larger white culture. The black women interviewed showed a strong maternal influence; of the 30 interviewed, only four said their mothers had never worked (and one of these "nonworking" mothers had 13 children). Even more unusual was the fact that many of the mothers had been professionals or semiprofessionals. Seven had been teachers, one a college professor, two were nurses, and one a physician. This heritage is unique for any population of women, including professional women, whose mothers are more likely to have worked.

MIDDLE-CLASS VALUES

Most women interviewed in this study came from families which stressed middle-class values, whether or not their incomes permitted middle-class amenities. I have already noted the high proportion of mothers who held

[14] In my sample of women lawyers, nearly all of whom were white, 20% had mothers who were or had been engaged in professional occupations, nine of whom were teachers. Thirty percent never worked (Epstein 1968, p. 96). In Rita Stafford's larger study of women in *Who's Who*, 11.5% of the mothers of lawyers were in a profession and close to 70% were housewives (Epstein 1968, p. 236).

Cynthia Fuchs Epstein

professional jobs, and although far fewer of the fathers' jobs ranked high (five of the 30), the fathers all had occupational talents and skills. Generally the fathers held a variety of jobs which defy ordinary classification because, though not middle-class jobs by white standards (e.g., as truckers and post office employees), they were at the time good opportunities for blacks.

THE SPECIAL CASE OF THE WEST INDIANS

Considering the size of its population in the United States, an unusually large proportion of my sample (one-third) is West Indian, and this helps account for the high level of aspiration found in the sample. It is generally believed that black professionals are of West Indian extraction in far greater proportion than could be expected by chance.[15] The situation of the black women of this group is illustrative of the "positive" effect of holding two or more negative statuses.

The experience of West Indians in the United States is different from that of other blacks because they face double discrimination—from the larger society for being black and from the black community for being

[15] West Indians have contributed disproportionately to the current Negro leadership, including Stokely Carmichael, Lincoln Linch, Roy Inniss, and other accomplished people. Glazer and Moynihan (1963) assert that in the 1930s foreign-born persons were to make up as much as one-third of the Negro professional population, especially physicians, dentists, and lawyers. We can assume these foreign born were predominantly West Indian. This seems to hold true today if one examines the proportion of foreign-born nonwhites in the professions. Almost one-half of the nonwhite male college instructors, presidents, etc., were listed as foreign born in the 1960 census, about 20% of the natural scientists, about 40% of the doctors, but only a tiny percentage, 0.8, of the lawyers. This also holds true for black women with almost 11% of the nonwhite female college faculty being foreign born, 26% of the natural scientists, 60% of the doctors, and no lawyers listed (U.S. Bureau of Census 1963, vol. 2, PC [2]-7A, table 8, pp. 114–15). And the census figures do not include the large numbers of professionals who were born here of West Indian parentage. Although the nonwhite population is 92% black, and the category in the census data is often taken to mean "mostly black," one must be wary of the percentages for certain professions because tiny numbers of blacks are often matched in number by other nonwhites, such as Chinese. This can be seen in the following table:

NUMBER OF NEGRO AND OTHER NONWHITES IN SELECTED OCCUPATIONS, UNITED STATES, 1960

	Negroes	Other Nonwhites
College pres., prof., instruct.	5,910	2,794
Chemists	1,799	1,115
Physicians, surgeons	5,038	5,007
Lawyers, judges	2,440	530

Source.—*U.S. Census of the Population*, vol. 2, *1960 Subject Reports, Occupational Characteristics*, PC (2)-7A, table 3, pp. 21–22.

foreign.[16] West Indian children are often persecuted and taunted as "monkey chasers." Their way of speech identifies them to other blacks as foreigners, and they experience the same kind of ostracism as white immigrants who bear visible negatively valued statuses. But, as a group, West Indians are known to have a sense of pride, to value education, and be characterized by Protestant Ethic strivings. Although the assimilation of second-generation immigrants into the main culture is common, and they may have difficulty maintaining their values in the context of competing views of work and study in the ghetto, being a West Indian black does create a circumscribed set of possibilities and insulation from the larger society, black and white. Marginality to black society (as immigrants) and to white society (as blacks) means an absence of diversion from the group's goals and competing values. Because they are isolated and the young women are segregated by their parents even more than the men,[17] the threat of the street and the illegitimate opportunity structure is cut off. At the same time, West Indian youth receive a heavy dose of achievement input from parents and their extended-kinlike community.[18] Many prominent West Indians referred repeatedly to their British training in thrift and self-esteem, to the importance given by their elders to education, to respect for adults, and at the same time, to the importance of being "spunky."

SELF-CONFIDENCE

Black women seem to have acquired a sense of confidence in their competence and ability. Interviews with these black professional women revealed a strong feeling of self-assurance. Further support comes from Fichter's study of graduates from predominantly black colleges, which indicates that college-educated black women have more confidence in their abilities than

[16] Cruse (1967, p. 121) suggests that native (New York) Negroes frowned on West Indians mainly because the islanders presented a threat of competition for jobs available to blacks. The West Indian influx into New York in the 1920s coincided with the great migration of Negroes from the South. However, he does note the severe antipathy of native blacks to West Indians because of their alleged "uppity" manner.

[17] One women commented: "I was not only protected; I was overprotected. West Indians are real Victorians regarding the behavior of their girls."

[18] The isolation and special character of the black West Indian have probably emphasized a sense of community bolstered by mutual benevolent associations (also known as "meetings" and "hands") which are often church associated. Members have pooled resources to meet mortgage payments on homes, appraised property, and in other ways have acted as pseudokin groups in assisting talented youngsters with college scholarships. Often these groups had a geographic base and were Jamaican, or Trinidadian, etc. Paule Marshall's *Brown Girl, Brownstones* (1959) is a vivid portrait of a Barbadian community in Brooklyn, focusing on a young girl growing up, her hardworking mother, and the influence of a Barbadian community organization in reinforcing work, ownership, and scholarship norms.

Cynthia Fuchs Epstein

a comparable group of white women graduates (1964, p. 12; table 5.17, p. 92).

Asked by Fichter if they thought they had personalities suitable to a career as business executives, 49% of the white women interviewed but 74% of the black women thought they did (1964, table 5.18, p. 93).

This high degree of self-confidence may result from their special condition of having gone to college, a very special event in the black community. Their self-confidence is probably reinforced as they overcome each obstacle on the way to the top.

EDUCATION AND ITS STRUCTURE

It is commonly believed that a greater premium is placed on the higher education of girls than boys in the black community.[19] Until recently the greater numbers of black women college graduates have supported this assumption. This view and the statistics supporting it have their origins in the structure of discrimination; even with college degrees, black men could not penetrate the high-ranking occupations, while black women graduates could always go into schoolteaching. Thus it has been suggested that contrary to the pattern believed to be true of underprivileged white families, in which male children got preference if not all could be sent to college, in the black family the female child would get preference.

However, the number of black men in college has grown steadily in the past decade and by 1963 surpassed the number of black women students. Further, if one measures the proportion of women among blacks in professions other than teaching, it is not true that more girls get professional training than men. Only 9.6% of black doctors are women (again a higher percentage than in the white community, where only 7% of doctors are women). Certainly black families, like many white immigrant families in the past, could not afford sex discrimination when they needed the contribution of any family member who showed promise. As one dentist of West Indian extraction put it: "Girls or boys—whoever had the brains to get education was the one pushed to do it and encouraged."

Although white families support the notion of college education for girls, they are somewhat ambivalent about encouraging them to go beyond the B.A., viewing professional training as a waste, detrimental to marriage chances, or simply inappropriate for a woman (Epstein 1970c, p. 62). Not a single black woman in the study reported opposition from her family

19 See, for example, Silberman's assertion about the black woman: "Her hatred of men reflects itself in the way she brings up her own children; the sons can fend for themselves but the daughters must be prepared so that they will not have to go through what she has gone through" (1964, p. 119). And Cogan's statement: "In the Negro family the oldest girl is most protected and most often encouraged to go on with her education" (1968, p. 11).

160

on the matter of professional training; many referred to their parents' attitudes in the same terms as the dentist quoted above, and with the intensity characterized by a physician: "From the time you could speak you were given to understand that your primary interest in life was to get the best education you could, the best job you could. There was no other way!"

Where the parents could, they paid for the education of their daughters, often at the cost of years of savings and great personal sacrifice. Most of the women interviewed received at least a small amount of financial help from their parents and supplemented the costs of education by working while in school or through scholarship aid.

The black woman's education is considered a real investment in her future. She could not expect, like a white woman, to put her husband through college in order to enjoy a life of leisure on her husband's achievement and income. She knows, too, that a stable marriage is much more problematical as she moves up in educational status.

Of the black women college graduates studied by Noble, 90% said that "preparing for a vocation" was first in a list of reasons for going to college (1956, p. 46, table 16). These responses followed a pattern reported in two earlier studies (Johnson 1938; Cuthbert 1942). And it should be noted that, far more than for the black man, a college education radically improves the income potential of the black woman; her median income is even higher than that of white women with college degrees (*The Social and Economic Status of Negroes in the United States, 1970*, table 102, p. 125, and table 25, p. 34).

In general, black women are more concerned with the economic rewards of work than are white women (Shea, Spitz, and Zeller 1970, p. 215).

Furthermore, the economic necessity expected by black women indicates a canceling of female occupational role stereotypes. The black women interviewed were not bound by conventional stereotypes of the professions deemed suitable "for a woman"; instead, they weighed the real advantages and disadvantages of the occupation. Although my earlier study of white women lawyers found that some of their parents had tried to deter them from that male-dominated occupation, the black women interviewed for this project reported their parents not only encouraged them but a number had suggested they try law or medicine. One woman who wanted to be a nurse was persuaded by her mother to become a physician.

PROFESSIONAL SCHOOLS

Most of the women interviewed were educated at white schools, a number of them having gone to private white elementary schools, to white colleges (79%), and to white professional schools (70%). A little more than half

Cynthia Fuchs Epstein

of the physicians went to white medical schools (and most of these attended the very top schools—Yale and Columbia, for example), and the rest went to predominantly Negro schools.[20] This is extremely unusual because the great majority of black doctors have always been educated in black medical schools.

No figures exist on the proportion of male and female black students admitted to white medical schools, and one can only suppose that black women had as hard a time getting admitted as any women or any blacks. A few of the doctors interviewed, however, felt that they had a slight edge over both groups—again the interaction effect of their two negative statuses; their uniqueness made their admission more likely. None, however, could say exactly why they thought this was true. One commented: "I think that being both black and female may have been an asset, in a peculiar sense, both in getting into medical school and subsequently."

Being black attenuated the effect of feminine roles in the university setting. Dating was difficult because there were so few black men; furthermore, being a specially selected female meant a high commitment to scholarship. The girls who went to all-white schools were good students, and most reported they had virtually no social life.

MARRIAGE

For most women, getting married and becoming a mother are still the most salient decisions in the setting of a life course. These decisions usually follow a fairly certain pattern and serve as limits on the acquisition of other statuses, especially occupational ones. But marriage is not by any means a certainty for black women, and for those who do marry being a wife may not offer the security to replace a career.

The factors which result in the educated black woman's contingent marital status derive from the marginal position of blacks in American society and from their inability to conform to a number of norms in the family setting which are rooted in patriarchal-focused values. The black male's marginality makes it doubtful he will acquire a professional career; whatever the level of occupation he attains, he will have difficulty in providing a middle-class life-style on his income alone. The educated black woman thus is unlikely to find a mate of similar social rank and education, and it is doubtful she can expect to play the traditional middle-class housewife role played by educated white women.

Lacking the usual guarantee that Prince Charming will come equipped with a good profession and a suburban home, or will come at all, the

[20] Seventy percent of Negro medical students in 1955–56 attended black medical schools as opposed to only 30% who attended white medical schools (Reitzes 1958, p. 28).

162

educated black girl is prepared in both subtle and direct ways to adapt if the dream should fail. The women in our sample reported that their parents did not push them toward marriage, and though they generally married late if they married at all (one-third had not), they did not feel anxious about being unmarried.[21] Although there is some change today, most white girls have internalized enormous pressures to marry and marry early. Not only do black women probably invest less in the good-life-through-marriage dream, there is evidence that a great proportion feel they can do without it.

Bell (1971, p. 254) suggests that "marriage has limited importance to black women at all educational levels" and that it is also possible that "if education were held constant at all levels, black women would show a greater rejection of marriage than would white women." At lower-class levels it is clear that the rejection of marriage comes because it is perceived as unreliable, and at upper-class levels because of the small pool of eligible men and the competition for husbands.

Although the white college-educated woman is strongly deterred from focus on a career when she marries (though she may work), the black woman who marries a black college-educated man cannot consider withdrawing from the marketplace. She knows that her husband's education is no guarantee of his financial success. It has been clearly established that the discrepancy in income between white and black male college graduates is wider than the gap between incomes of those who are less well educated (Sheppard and Striner 1966, p. 24). Educated black women, like other black women who seem able to trim their expectations to the realities of their lives, know they will have to share the financial responsibilities for a middle-class standard of living. One-half of the college-educated black women studied by Fichter (1964, p. 81) said they preferred to combine their family role with an occupational role. This made them twice as likely as Southern white women or the comparable group of other white women in a national NORC sample to select a combination of marriage, child rearing, and employment.

It seems probable, too, that black women view careers differently than white women who expect to combine marriage and career. White women like to view their work as supplemental to the husband's. They tend not to think of their work as a career growing out of their own life aims. Black women tend less to view their work as a "hanger-on" activity. One gets the feeling in interviews with them that the quality of their lives is determined by their own endeavor and is less a response to their husband's occupation situation. Perhaps this is a function of their relatively high

[21] But generally women in the male-dominated professions marry late and a substantial proportion are unmarried (see Epstein 1970a, p. 905).

self-confidence. White women lawyers I studied who practiced with their husbands typically referred to their work as "helping their husbands" and not in terms of a real career (Epstein 1971). Of course, black women have less opportunity to reason so circuitously. They are not in any structure where they could work for a husband. None of the lawyers had lawyer husbands, and only one of the doctors had a husband who was a physician. All of the doctors made more money than their husbands. There was almost no occupational homogamy and very little occupational-rank homogamy between husbands and wives, contrary to the marriage pattern for white women professionals, in which occupational homogamy is exceptionally strong.[22]

Our respondents, following a pattern common to other educated black women,[23] often married down occupationally. Although some white women in my study of lawyers had husbands who earned less than they did, they appeared more threatened by this situation than the black women studied. Some of the white women, faced with developing careers, checked them to assure they would have lower-ranking, lower-paying jobs than their husbands.[24] Black women also consider checking their career progress for this reason, but feel the costs are too great. Although the white woman usually can withdraw from her profession and continue to live at the same economic standard, the black woman who does so pulls the family to a lower standard of living. If the black woman acts like a woman occupationally, she is failing as a mother in helping her family.

The negative rank differential present in most marriages of black professional women has an important effect on their commitment to career. Although black women are probably as hopeful as white women for a long and happy life with their husbands, they face the reality of a higher probability of marital breakup. Divorce and separation rates for blacks

---

[22] Compared by race, marriages tend to be homogamous—husbands and wives coming from similar social, religious, ethnic, and educational background. Within this general similarity, there is some tendency for men to marry a little below their own level, so that they are slightly hypogamous while their wives tend to be slightly hypergamous. The reverse tends to be true for blacks; women tend to marry below their own level (Bernard 1966, p. 90).

[23] Noble reported that more than 50% of the husbands of college-educated black women in her study were employed in occupations of lower socioeconomic level than those of the wives. In more than 60% of this study's cases in which wives reported on their husband's education, the man had a lower level of education than his wife. Noble reports low levels of response for both these items in her questionnaire (1956, p. 51).

[24] Perhaps this is a manifestation of the ambivalence women feel toward success. Matina Horner's work suggests that most women will explore their intellectual potential only when they do not need to compete—least of all with men. They feel success is unladylike and that men will be put off by it (1969, p. 62).

are higher than for whites,[25] and their remarriage rates are lower. Although rates of dissolution for black women professionals are the lowest of any category of black women workers, they are still higher than those for white women in similar jobs (Udry 1968, p. 577). Eight of the 24 women we studied who had ever been married had been divorced.

Caroline Bird suggests that black professional women's deviant place in the structure of marriage expectations "frees" them: "Negro career women are freer than white career women not to marry, to marry outside their race or class. . . . They are . . . much less bound than white women by the role duties most frequently cited as universal and inescapable limitations on the career aspirations of all women forever" (1969, p. 38). Whether or not they are free, it is certainly true that their lack of a safe haven in marriage gives them independence, motivation, and perhaps more reinforcement of self-confidence than the white woman who may retreat to full-time marriage at the first feeling of fear or insecurity as a professional.

MOTHERHOOD

Although getting married may determine whether or not a woman takes her career seriously, it is the demands on her as a mother and how she deals with those demands which become most important in her ability to focus on career.

Having children is costly for a family not only because of what it takes to feed, clothe, and educate them, but because typically the wife leaves the labor force—and her income—for long periods to care for them. And for black families it has been imperative that both wife and husband work to maintain their hold on a middle-class life-style.

Although blacks generally exceed the fertility pattern of whites, the fertility rates of upper-class Negro families are the lowest of any group (Moynihan 1965, p. 758).[26] Noble's study of Negro women college graduates found that although the majority of her sample married, more than 40% were childless and 38% had only one child (1957, p. 17). Of the 24 ever-married women in my study, 17 had children and seven did not. Of those who had children, more than half had two or more. Strikingly, all of those with two or more children were upper-income professionals—an editor, a lawyer, a dentist, and a half-dozen physicians. The sample's only mother of five is a practicing M.D.

[25] Black women appear more likely to encounter marital discord than whites. In 1970, 19% of all black women who at some time had been married were either divorced or separated as contrasted with 6% of white women who had been married (*New York Times*, July 26, 1971, p. 1).

[26] Although there are no data for fertility of women by their own occupation, the

Though black women who have careers can be assumed to reduce demands made on them by having fewer children than their white counterparts, it is more interesting to see the ways in which they handle their role demands as mothers and the unique aspects of the black social structure which help them do so.

The black mothers interviewed seemed far less anxious about their children than whites. They did not insist that it was their sole responsibility to care for their children, nor did they fear that their absence from home during the children's early years would be harmful to their psychic and physical growth. They seemed freer to accept help from relatives (particularly grandparents, who often volunteered it), to leave the children for long periods, and even to let the children accompany them to work if that became necessary. Hill (1971) suggests that black families are generally more adaptable to absorbing new members—other relatives' children, grandchildren, or grandparents—and that often the "new" older members play important roles in caring for young children while the mother works (p. 5).

Black women, whether of Southern or of West Indian origin, share an extended family tradition in which "others" can routinely perform tasks which middle-class white society would see as exclusively the responsibility of the husband and wife. This aspect of the black social structure meshes neatly with the needs of the black professional woman; it makes it possible for her to continue studies or career after having children, and makes combined motherhood and career a rational decision to be made on its merits.

CAREERS

The occupational spread of the 31 women interviewed ranged from physicians (12, including four psychiatrists), to lawyers (eight), dentists (two), a university professor, three journalists, and several in public relations work, business management, and top administrative posts in social services. (One was in library science, a "woman's field" except in administration; this woman was in charge of a noted collection.) We excluded nursing, social work, and teaching, which are not only women's fields but are low in prestige and considered professions almost solely by the United States census.

An early decision to go into professional work was characteristic of most of the women in the sample. They share this history with male professionals of both sexes (Rogoff 1957, p. 111) and with other black women

---

percentage of nonwhite wives of professional men who were childless in 1950 was 33% (Whelpton, Campbell, and Patterson 1966, p. 153).

professionals (Ostlund 1957; Brazziel 1960). Considering the years of preparation, both in terms of anticipatory socialization and formal educational requirements, early deciders have an advantage over those who choose late.

Blacks, however, suffer from having fewer real role models in their decision matrix, although doctors (in particular) and lawyers have always been held in high esteem in the black community. Until recently, physician was the highest status occupation a black person could hold, but the absolute number has been, and remains, small. In 1956 New York City had only 305 black physicians, the largest number of any city in the country, and in 1960 the total census figure for the United States was 5,038, of whom 487 were women.[27]

In contrast to the strong family encouragement of professional careers already noted, most black women recall, as do white women, being urged by primary and high school teachers and guidance counselors to go into schoolteaching or social work. This advice was based on their racial and sex statuses, although black men, too, are sometimes directed into these occupations because of the barriers they face in the more prestigious professions. But the significant messages for them were from their parents, who were encouraging them to be whatever they wanted and who did not raise objections to their trying a white, male profession.

Eight of the physicians went to "white" medical schools (NYU, New York Medical College, Boston University, Philadelphia Women's) or to elite white schools (Columbia's Physicians and Surgeons and Yale).

Despite their educational credentials, most of the doctors work in the black community. Elite medical careers require not only degrees from good schools but a status sequence of internships at elite training hospitals which are hard for any black to get, and which most of the women did not get, or which they did not seek because they felt their chances were nonexistent. None of the women who went to a black medical school was able to work within the medical "establishment," although a few had some contact with it under new programs pairing private teaching hospitals with municipal hospitals.

The lawyers interviewed went exclusively to white law schools; four to Columbia, one to the University of Michigan, two to NYU, and one to Brooklyn Law School, a lower-ranking school with an evening program.

[27] Michel Richard figured that by interviewing 98 black physicians in New York in 1965 he had a sample of about 28% of all black doctors in New York City, using an estimate of 355 for 1965 (1969, p. 21). By doing a little creative statistical calculation, we figured that using the national percentage of black women doctors (9.6% of black doctors) would mean that there are about 28 black women doctors in New York. We interviewed 12, which would be about 40% if one allowed for a general increase in the total number of black doctors by 1968–69, when most of these interviews were done.

Two of the lawyers who achieved elite establishment careers did so after a top-rank legal education during which they had performed at the top of their class. Following another typical route for the ethnic minorities, the Brooklyn Law School graduate achieved a high-ranking position within the city government. Nearly all of the women interviewed found, regardless of educational attainment, that some professional gates were simply locked. It was one thing to get admitted to school, another to find a job.

Like blacks and women, following the negative effect of holding "inappropriate statuses," they tended to go into protected work settings. Most of the doctors and lawyers started in salaried jobs—government work and clinics—where getting clients was not an immediate problem. Many of the doctors took residencies in municipal hospitals and went directly onto the staffs of these same hospitals or into clinics in the black community. Some of the psychiatrists later mixed private practice with their institutional jobs, but only one could be said to have a truly full-time private practice. It was not only the closed opportunity structure which led these women into clinics and municipal hospitals, but also their sense of service and duty to the black community. Later, some with research interests were able to work in private hospitals within the structure of new programs.

Six of the doctors interviewed were on the staff of Harlem Hospital (the hospital has 15 women physicians, a few of whom are white). This was partially the result of sampling by referral and partially because Harlem Hospital is one of the few U.S. hospitals that has any number of black physicians. It is unique in that women doctors are heads of three departments. All of the women interviewed were specialists. In 1952, out of 33,000 medical specialists, only 190 were Negroes (*Negroes in Medicine* [1952], p. 6, cited in Lopate [1968]). With the exception of three (one of whom had done breakthrough research on the "kidney machine") all were in specialties which historically have been relatively open to women and blacks: four were psychiatrists, two were pediatricians, one was in community medicine, and one in dermatology. A few now in psychiatry had been practicing pediatricians. One can see that their specialization and superior training placed them high on the eligibility list. Most black physicians have not had top-rank educations; more than four-fifths of black physicians were graduated from Meharry Medical College and Howard University (Altman 1969, p. 38). The fact that they claimed to work very hard and the somewhat greater tolerance of black men to women's participation in the professions made it possible for black women to get better posts than most white women can aspire to.

The lawyers followed the pattern of protected salaried positions to a lesser degree than the doctors. Three had their own practices, and two had become public figures. One was salaried but had attained the super-elite position of partnership in a Wall Street firm. One was the first woman assistant district attorney in New York, and another was moving from a poverty program into private practice. All had been affected by the social changes in attitudes toward racial discrimination in New York; all were exceptionally attractive or outstanding in some way, all were highly articulate; all had solid educational credentials. With one exception, all worked in the white world. All felt that being black and women gave them additional possibilities than they might not have had as only women or as only black. The lawyers' extremely unique status combination made them highly visible, and in the law, where performance is quite open to the scrutiny of peers, news of one's excellence spreads quickly.

Women lawyers interviewed in my previous study emphasized their need to be better than others so that no one could use incompetence or lack of devotion to work against them. Black women professionals also stressed this motivating factor and were even more passionate about it. Their need to prove themselves and be the best was often tied in with self-consciousness about their visibility and their sense of responsibility for others of their race and sex. These remarks were typical:

> Being a black woman . . . . It's made me fight harder. . . . I think probably one of the strengths of being black or being a black woman is that if you have the native material you really do learn to fight and try to accomplish and all the rest. If I had been white, with the same abilities, I'm not sure the drive would have been the same.

> Women have some advantages as trial lawyers, for one thing they are well remembered, or remembered, well or not, depends on how they perform. The judge is not as likely to forget them if he has ever seen them before, because we women are in the minority. And, of course, for a Negro woman, she is very likely to be remembered. It is always a help, not to be forgotten.

Some of the younger women were well aware of today's emphasis on having women and blacks in hospitals, firms, corporations, and schools. Most spoke of it with irony, but with an air of confidence and a sense that they deserved whatever benefits came out of the new social awareness. Some recognized they were useful because an employer could kill two birds with one stone by hiring a black woman; one said pithily: "I'm a show woman and a show nigger, all for one salary." Some older women felt they had been accepted in their professional work because being a Negro woman was not as bad as being a Negro man. About a third said they believed Negro men were "a threat" to white men or alluded to that belief as if it were well known to all, and that a black woman constituted less of a threat.

Whether or not this is true (and certainly, no data are available on it), the belief may act to discourage black men from seeking entry into white domains and encourage the black woman because she thinks she has more of a chance. Black women doctors and dentists who worked with white patients (one had almost a totally white practice) felt that because most of their patients were children, and therefore brought in by mothers, no "male threat" was operative in their relationship.[28]

Black women probably get "straighter" treatment in white professional setting than do white women. For one thing, white men do not as often see black professional women as romantic partners, or feel the black woman is out "to catch" one of them as a husband, and therefore respect their serious intent. In black settings, the black professional women report suspicious views of their competence and career involvement similar to those encountered by white women in white male settings, but the fact that the working woman is a more familiar image to the black man, and the "woman as doer" is more familiar to him (as it is for the woman), means that attitudes are more tempered.

Black women professionals also seem to have higher regard for each other than white women professionals. I encountered far less self-hatred among them than among the white women lawyers interviewed earlier. The latter shared the (male) negative stereotypes of women lawyers as excessively aggressive and masculine. The black women interviewed seemed to have a more matter-of-fact attitude toward their sister professionals; they never indicated doubts about the competence of other women, and some said they favored women as colleagues because they were more reliable and more willing to work than the men they knew. Few white women professionals favored other women professionals.

These phenomena in the professional world, which grow out of black women's unique position, probably reinforce their self-confidence and act to motivate them toward a career line similar to that of the white male. However, given the limits imposed by the current social structure, only the most extraordinary black women, those who are intellectually gifted and personally attractive, can make it. The fact that some do indicates that an enormous amount of energy in the social system must be directed to keeping others out.

The chance to become professionals developed out of a structure which narrowed their choices, made them visible and unique. For these few, the

---

28 William J. Goode suggests (personal communication) a general psychodynamic interpretation—that perhaps there is such a cultural emphasis on the fragility of the male ego that the typical traditional male professional may, indeed, play it safe in choosing his colleagues (certainly in choosing someone to act in an authority position over him, as a patient does when he chooses a doctor). The black woman professional may not only face less resistance from a white women client (she might prefer a male doctor but certainly would choose a black woman over a black male doctor) but she herself might be willing to challenge the professional setting to a greater extent in attempting to enter the white establishment than the black man because, being a woman, she is not so sensitive to the fear of "losing face" (the woman in American society not being socialized to think she has much face to lose, anyway).

effects of living in a world otherwise beset with limits fed their determination and made them feel the only road to survival lay in occupational success. For those without the special support of family and personal networks of these women, and without their extraordinary ability to drive ahead, the limits of the occupational structure could only be defeating, even to those with ability. The self-maintaining mechanisms of the present stratification system within the professions clearly operate to keep the participation of certain persons low in spite of their possible intellectual contributions. Ironically for this small sample of black women, the effect of mechanisms within the larger stratification system (which operate to keep blacks and women down) served to reinforce their commitment to careers which would be normally closed to them, and by defining them as superunique, made it possible for some to rise within the professional structures. It has become clear that the elaborate filtering system which keeps elite spheres clear of alien groups is costly and self-defeating. It is rare that those who do push through emerge unscathed by the passage. Those who fall on the way are lost to the greater society. But the mechanisms which contribute to the status quo are often not consciously known even by those who participate in their exercise, and only by analyzing the various structural nexus in which they occur can they be isolated and evaluated for what they are.

REFERENCES

Altman, Lawrence K. 1969. "Funds Urged to Attract Negro Doctors." *New York Times,* October 5, 1969.

Bailyn, Lotte. 1964. "Notes on the Role of Choice in the Psychology of Professional Women." *Daedalus* 93 (Spring): 700–710.

Bell, Robert R. 1971. "The Related Importance of Mother-Wife Roles among Black Lower-Class Women." In *The Black Family: Essays and Studies,* edited by Robert Staples. Belmont, Calif.: Wadsworth.

Bernard, Jessie. 1966. *Marriage and Family among Negroes.* Englewood Cliffs, N.J.: Prentice-Hall.

Bird, Caroline. 1969. "Black Womanpower." *New York Magazine* 2 (March): 35–42.

Blake, Elias, Jr. 1971. "Future Leadership Roles for Predominantly Black Colleges and Universities in American Higher Education." *Daedalus* 100 (Summer): 745–71.

Bond, Horace Mann. 1966. "The Negro Scholar and Professional in America." In *American Negro Reference Book,* edited by John P. Davis. Englewood Cliffs, N.J.: Prentice-Hall.

Brazziel, William F., Jr. 1960. "Occupational Choice in the Negro College." *Personnel and Guidance* 39:739–42.

Brimmer, Andrew. 1971. "Economic Outlook and the Future of the Negro College." *Daedalus* 100 (Summer): 539–72.

Cogan, Lee. 1968. *Negroes for Medicine.* Baltimore: Johns Hopkins Press.

Cruse, Harold. 1967. *The Crisis of the Negro Intellectual.* New York: Apollo Editions.

Cuthbert, Marion. 1942. "Education and Marginality." Ph.D. dissertation, Teachers College, Columbia University.

Epstein, Cynthia F. 1968. "Women and Professional Careers: The Case of the Woman Lawyer." Ph.D. dissertation, Columbia University.

————. 1970a. "Current and Emerging Occupation-centered Feminine Life-Career Patterns and Trends." *Annals of the New York Academy of Science* 175:898–909.

————. 1970b. "Encountering the Male Establishment." *American Journal of Sociology* 75:965–82.

————. 1970c. *Woman's Place: Options and Limits of Professional Careers.* Berkeley: University of California Press.

————. 1971. "Law Partners and Marital Partners: Strains and Solutions in the Dual-Career Family Enterprise." *Human Relations* 24 (December 1971): 549–64.

————. Forthcoming. *The Woman Lawyer.* Chicago: University of Chicago Press.

Fichter, Joseph H. 1964. *Graduates of Predominantly Negro Colleges—Class of 1964.* Public Health Services Publication, no. 1571. Washington, D.C.: Government Printing Office.

Ford Foundation. 1970. *The Black American Doctorate.* New York: Office of Reports, 320 E. 42 St.

Ginzberg, Eli, and Dale L. Hiestand. 1966. "Employment Patterns of Negro Men and Women." In *American Negro Reference Book,* edited by John P. Davis. Englewood Cliffs, N.J.: Prentice-Hall.

Glazer, Nathan, and Daniel Patrick Moynihan. 1963. *Beyond the Melting Pot.* Cambridge, Mass.: Harvard University Press and M.I.T. Press.

Goode, William J. 1957. "Community within a Community: The Professions." *American Sociological Review* 22:195–200.

Hall, Oswald. 1948. "The Stages of a Medical Career." *American Journal of Sociology* 53:327–36.

Hill, Robert. 1971. "Strengths of the Black Family." Mimeographed. Washington, D.C.: National Urban League.

Horner, Matina. 1969. "A Bright Woman Is Caught in a Double Bind." *Psychology Today* 3 (November): 36, 62 ff.

Hughes, Everett C. 1962. "What Other." In *Human Behavior and Social Processes,* edited by Arnold Rose. Boston: Houghton Mifflin.

Hyman, Herbert. 1969. "Black Matriarchy, Reconsidered." *Public Opinion Quarterly* 33 (Fall): 346–47.

Johnson, Charles S. 1938. *The Negro College Graduate.* Chapel Hill: University of North Carolina Press.

Ladner, Joyce. 1971. *Tomorrow's Tomorrow.* New York: Doubleday.

Lopate, Carol. 1968. *Women in Medicine.* Baltimore: Johns Hopkins Press.

McGrath, Earl. 1965. *The Predominantly Negro Colleges and Universities in Transition.* New York: Teachers College, Columbia University.

Mack, Delores E. 1971. "Where the Black Matriarchy Theorists Went Wrong." *Psychology Today* 4 (January): 24, 87 ff.

Marshall, Paule. 1959. *Brown Girl, Brownstones.* New York: Random House.

Merton, Robert K. 1957. *Social Theory and Social Structure.* Glencoe, Ill.: Free Press.

Merton, Robert K., George Reader, and Patricia Kendall. 1957. *The Student Physician.* Cambridge, Mass.: Harvard University Press.

Moynihan, Daniel Patrick. 1965. "Employment, Income and the Ordeal of the Negro Family." *Daedalus* 94 (Fall): 745–70.

Noble, Jeanne L. 1956. *The Negro Women's College Education.* New York: Stratford.

————. 1957. "Negro Women Today and Their Education." *Journal of Negro Education* 26 (Winter): 15–21.

Ostlund, Leonard A. 1957. "Occupational Choice Patterns of Negro College Women." *Journal of Negro Education* 26 (Winter): 86–91.

Ploski, H. 1967. *The Negro Almanac.* New York: Bellwether.

Reitzes, Dietrich C. 1958. *Negroes and Medicine.* Cambridge, Mass.: Harvard University Press.

Richard, Michel. 1969. "Ideology of Negro Physicians: A Test of Mobility and Status Crystallization Theory." *Social Problems* 17:20–29.

Rogoff, Natalie. 1957. "Decision to Study Medicine." In *The Student Physician,* edited by Robert K. Merton, George Reader, and Patricia Kendall. Cambridge, Mass.: Harvard University Press.

Shea, John, Ruth S. Spitz, and Frederick A. Zeller. 1970. *Dual Careers: A Longitudinal Study of Labor Market Experience of Women*. Vol. 1. Columbus: Center for Human Resources Research, Ohio State University.

Sheppard, Harold L., and Herbert E. Striner. 1966. *Civil Rights, Employment, and the Social Status of American Negroes*. Report of the U.S. Commission on Civil Rights. Washington, D.C.: Government Printing Office.

Silberman, Charles. 1964. *Crisis in Black and White*. New York: Random House.

Udry, J. Richard. 1968. "Marital Instability by Race, Sex, Education, Occupation, and Income, Using 1960 Census Data." In *Selected Studies in Marriage and the Family*, edited by Robert F. Winch and Louis W. Goodman. New York: Holt, Rinehart & Winston.

United Negro College Fund. 1964–65. "Statistical Information, UNCF Office of Development and Educational Services." Report of member institutions of UNCF. New York: United Negro College Fund.

U.S., Bureau of the Census. 1963. *1960 Subject Reports. Occupational Characteristics*. Final Report PC (2)–7A. Washington, D.C.: Government Printing Office.

————. 1967. *Current Population Reports*. Series P-60, No. 60. Washington, D.C.: Government Printing Office.

————. 1970. *Current Population Reports*. Series P-60, No. 75. Washington, D.C.: Government Printing Office.

U.S., Department of Commerce. 1968. *Statistical Abstract, 1968*. Washington, D.C.: Government Printing Office.

————. 1969. *Changing Characteristics of the Negro Population*. Washington, D.C.: Government Printing Office.

————. 1970. *Statistical Abstract, 1970*. Washington, D.C.: Government Printing Office.

U.S., Department of Commerce and Department of Labor. 1970. *The Social and Economic Status of Negroes in the United States, 1970*. BLS Report No. 394, and Current Population Reports, Series P-23, No. 38. Washington, D.C.: Government Printing Office.

U.S., Department of Labor. 1967. *Negro Women in the Population and the Labor Force*. Washington, D.C.: Government Printing Office.

————. 1970. *Handbook of Women Workers 1969*. Women's Bureau Bulletin No. 294. Washington, D.C.: Government Printing Office.

Whelpton, Pascal K., Arthur A. Campbell, and John E. Patterson. 1966. *Fertility and Family Planning in the United States*. Princeton, N.J.: Princeton University Press.

Women and Social Stratification: A Case of Intellectual Sexism[1]

Joan Acker
University of Oregon

In the last 10 years, empirical studies and speculative discussions on the disadvantaged status of women have increased rapidly. Although social inequality is the subject matter of social stratification studies, little of this work on the position of women has been done by sociologists in the field of social stratification.[2] Indeed, sex has rarely been analyzed as a factor in stratification processes and structures,[3] although it is probably one of the most obvious criteria of social differentiation and one of the most obvious bases of economic, political, and social inequalities. Very few sociologists have even recognized that we have, with the exception of the study of the family, constructed a sociology that tends to deal with only the male half of humanity.

The inclusion of the female half of humanity and of sex as a central dimension in the study of society would lead to a more accurate picture of social structure and to a better understanding of process. However, serious

---

[1] Revision of a paper read at the annual meeting of the Southwestern Sociological Association (1971), Dallas, Texas.

[2] Sociologists in other areas have made a number of recent contributions which are relevant to problems of stratification. For example, Epstein (1970) discusses the salience of sex status in the professional careers of women in the higher professions. Oppenheimer (1968) examines the basis for the sex labeling of jobs in the American work force. Wilensky (1968) explores the relationships between the position of women, economic growth, and democratic ideology. Etzioni (1969) investigates the relationship between sex status and occupation in the semiprofessions. Some earlier, but isolated, analyses were Hacker (1951) and Myrdal (1944, Appendix 5) both of whom discuss women as a minority group: Hughes (1949) who places nontraditional, career women in the role of "marginal men"; Ellis (1952) who studied correlates of mobility among career women; and Caplow (1954) who devotes a chapter to women in the world of work. There have been other sociological discussions of the position of women (Komarovsky 1950, 1953; Bernard 1966, 1968), but these analyses have not been integrated into the studies of social stratification.

[3] Lenski (1966) is one of the few who recognized this problem in the field of stratification. In *Power and Privilege* he states, "Another much neglected aspect of the distributive systems of modern societies is the class system based on sex." He also observes that, "in analyses of advanced industrial societies, it is impossible to ignore or treat as obvious the role of sex in the distributive process." Even Lenski, however, does little analysis. He concludes his brief discussion of the position of women (mentioned on 13 pages out of a total of 446 pages in the book) with the comforting thought that, "for the vast majority of women, the battle for equality has been won." There may be some contradiction between the statements that the battle for sex equality has been won and that sex is still an important factor in the distributive process. However, this book was published pre–women's lib, in 1966, when such inconsistencies, although frequent, were relatively invisible. This contradiction reflects the difficulties of stratification theory in dealing with the status of women.

consideration of sex as a central social factor will require reconceptualization in many areas of sociology. Problems of concept and method which arise in the field of social stratification when women are assumed to be significant participants in society are the subject of this paper. I discuss, first, the assumptions in stratification literature about the social position of women; second, some problems of reconceptualization; and, third, some contributions to the understanding of society which may result from studying women in the stratification system.

ASSUMPTIONS ABOUT WOMEN AND STRATIFICATION

In stratification literature, six assumptions are made, sometimes explicitly and sometimes implicitly, about the social position of women. These are most clearly stated by the functionalists but are present also in the work of nonfunctionalists and Marxists.[4] These assumptions are:

1. The family is the unit in the stratification system.

2. The social position of the family is determined by the status of the male head of the household.

3. Females live in families; therefore, their status is determined by that of the males to whom they are attached.

4. The female's status is equal to that of her man, at least in terms of her position in the class structure, because the family is a unit of equivalent evaluation (Watson and Barth 1964).

5. Women determine their own social status only when they are not attached to a man.

6. Women are unequal to men in many ways, are differentially evaluated on the basis of sex, but this is irrelevant to the structure of stratification systems.

The first assumption, that the family is the unit in stratification, is basic to the other five. Together, these assumptions neatly dispense with the necessity for considering the position of women in studies of social stratification or considering the salience of sex as a dimension of stratification.[5] To put it another way, the fate of the female in the class system is determined by the fate of the male. Therefore, it is only necessary to study males.

How adequate are these assumptions? There are, I believe, deficiencies of both logic and validity which I will discuss briefly.

[4] See, e.g., two recent studies of class structure in Poland and Czechoslovakia (Machonin 1970; Wesolowski and Slomczyński 1968) which explicitly make the assumptions outlined here.
[5] Lenski (1966) makes the same point: "This neglect [of women] has been due in large measure to the tendency of sociologists to treat families, rather than individuals, as the basic unit in systems of stratification" (p. 402).

Joan Acker

1. *The family is the unit in the stratification system.*—The choice of the
family as the unit may be based on the belief that all persons live in
families. This is obviously not true, since 11% of the population over age
18 is categorized as unattached individuals in 1970 data.[6] This assumption
also rests on the validity of the other five assumptions, which I examine in
the following paragraphs.

2. *The social position of the family is determined by the status of the*
male head of the household.—This is a researchable question which has
been little researched. Instead, empirical researchers often imply an answer
to this question in their choice of indicators of class or status position.
Thus, if family income is chosen as an indicator, there is an implication
that total family resources determine standing. If class placement is measured by occupation alone or an index including occupation, the occupation
of the male head of household is invariably used, implying that his position
does decide that of the family.[7]

There is one situation in which the second assumption is clearly invalid.
The position of the family cannot be determined by the male head if there
is no male head of the household. This is the case in a substantial proportion of American families. On the basis of the 1960 census, Watson and
Barth (1964) estimated that approximately two-fifths of the households
in the United States do not have a male head, in the sense implied by the
traditional model of the small nuclear family. They found that two-fifths
of the households were either "females or female headed households or
husband-wife families in which the husband is retired or otherwise not in
the labor force, is unemployed, or is working only part time."

3. *Females live in families; therefore, their status is determined by that*
of the males to whom they are attached.—This assumption may be challenged on the grounds that all females do not live in families. Further, the
assumption that a woman's status is determined by that of the man to
whom she is attached implies that women have no status resources of their
own. In a society in which women, as well as men, have resources of education, occupation, and income, it is obviously not true that women have no
basis for determining their own status. If women do have such resources,
why do we assume that they are inoperative if the woman is married? It is
inconsistent to rank an unmarried woman on the basis of her education
and occupation and then maintain that these factors are of no importance
to her social status or class placement after she gets married the next day.[8]

[6] Calculated from table 6, 8, and table 44, p. 36, *Statistical Abstract of the United*
States, 1971 (U.S., Bureau of the Census 1971).
[7] Hofstetter (1970) explores this problem. She concludes that class self-placement by
college student respondents may be determined by the combined resources of father
and mother, rather than by those of father alone.
[8] Many of these points have also been made by Watson and Barth in a penetrating
critique of some assumptions in stratification theory and research published in 1964.

However, such an abrupt alteration of the criteria of class placement at the time of a shift in marital status is necessary if we are to accept the assumption that only women without men determine their own social status.

4. *The female's status is equal to that of her man.*—Once we question the assumption that the woman's status is determined by the man, we must also question the assumption that the status of the female is equal to that of her male. Of course, wife and husband may be equal, but equivalent evaluation can no longer be assumed.

Even if all females had no independent, status-creating resources, the equality of their status with that of their husbands would still be in question. Equality can be assessed on numerous dimensions. Prestige in the community, style of life, privileges, opportunities, association with social groups, income, education, occupation, and power might all be considered in evaluating the equality of husband and wife in the class structure. Occupation, equated by the functionalists with full-time, functionally important social role, is often used as the indicator of position for men. However, the full-time occupation of many women, that of housewife-mother, is never considered as a ranking criterion in stratification studies. Are we to conclude that this role is either not functionally important or not a full-time activity, or are we to conclude that only those activities which are directly rewarded financially can bestow status upon the individual or the family? Perhaps this is another question which could be explored through empirical research. There is some research evidence to suggest that housewives whose husbands work in a given occupation have less prestige than women who themselves are employed in the same occupation (Haavio-Mannila 1969). However, the evidence to support or refute the assumption of equal status in regard to the class structure is unfortunately sparse.

5. *Women determine their own social status only when they are not attached to a man.*—This assumption can be interpreted as a way of coping with the inconvenient fact that some women are not married or living in the household of a male relative.

6. *Women are at a disadvantage in hierarchies of wealth, power, and prestige, but this fact is irrelevant to the study of stratification systems.*— This assumption is implicit in the stratification literature. I draw this conclusion from, on the one hand, the scant attention to the situation of women in the stratification literature, and, on the other hand, the existence of ample evidence that women are excluded from the higher positions of power, that they earn less than men, and that they are present in very small proportions in the more prestigious occupations.

But, perhaps, the position of women is irrelevant to the structure of the larger system. I don't think so. For example, female-headed households account for almost 40% of those below the poverty line (Ferriss 1970). This statistic suggests that the economic and social disadvantages of being female may have an impact on class differentials in family structure. When stratification theorists talk about some classes, they are talking about women to a large extent. It is possible that some of the differences they discuss are sex rather than class differences. These differences may, for example, have an effect upon mobility patterns and the permeability of class boundaries, thus affecting the larger system in complex ways.

In sum, it is not adequate or useful to assume that females have no relevant role in stratification processes independent of their family roles and their ties to particular men. If this conclusion is reasonable, a reconsideration of sex status and stratification is indicated.

As a first step in such a reconsideration, I make the following assumptions:

1. Sex is an enduring ascribed characteristic which (a) has an effect upon the evaluation of persons and positions, and (b) is the basis of the persisting sexual division of labor and of sex-based inequalities.

2. The sex dichotomy cuts across all classes and strata. (This is also true of ethnicity and race.)

MODELS OF STRATIFICATION AND SEX

A number of conceptual issues arise when sex is considered a relevant stratification variable. One of these issues is, Can inequalities based on sex be integrated into a conceptual model of stratification systems? The traditional view of classes as aggregates occupying similar positions in relationship to the means of production or similar positions in one or more hierarchies of wealth, power, or prestige has made it difficult to deal with inequalities which cut across class lines. It has been easier to assume, as Watson and Barth point out, that the family is a unit, that all members of the family are equally evaluated, and that, therefore, it is not important to investigate the status of women.

Some current developments in the study of social stratification may make it easier to give serious consideration to sex inequalities. For example, there is a trend toward expanding the study of stratification to include a wide variety of structured social inequalities (Heller 1969). Similarly, there is a trend away from exclusive concern with the classic definitions of class and toward a concern with the individual as a unit. Although this trend began a number of years ago, it now seems to have establishment blessing even in the person of Parsons. A recent review article notes, "he [Parsons] also poses some serious objection to the relevance of classic definitions of class in the analysis of modern societies, arguing . . . that the unit of class stratification can no longer be usefully taken to be the family but a man's complex of ascribed and achieved collectivity memberships, including his organization memberships" (Laumann 1970).

Using the individual rather than the family as a unit, it may become possible to integrate sex into models of stratification systems in at least two ways: (1) as a dimension in stratification which cuts across class lines and produces two interrelated hierarchies of positions or persons, or (2) as a basis of evaluation which affects the placement of individuals in particular hierarchies.

An alternative solution to the problem of integrating sex-based inequalities into conceptual models of stratification systems would not require abandoning classic definitions of class. Females can be viewed as constituting caste-like groupings within social classes.[9] Female castes, using this approach, may have certain common interests and life-patterns. In addition, they may share certain disabilities and inequities. At the same time, female castes are imbedded in the class structure and each is affected by the class which envelops it. Class differences in ideology, life-chances, and life-style may obscure the identical nature of many structural factors affecting female castes.

STATUS AND CLASS: CONCEPTUAL AND EMPIRICAL PROBLEMS

An additional conceptual problem can be stated as follows: If women are to be seen as persons rather than as appendages to males, how do we define their social status, particularly if they are not working for pay and cannot be categorized on the basis of their own occupation and income? Can value be assigned to productive work which is not paid labor?[10] This is a broader problem which also arises in trying to define the status of retired persons, of young people who are still students, of volunteers, and of the unemployed. It may eventually become a problem even in determining the status of adult men who are in the work force. If long-range predictions about the declining centrality of work and the increasing importance of nonwork activities in cybernated societies become reality, the relevance of paid occupation for class placement may decline, and other, unpaid activities may become more important as a source of social identity.

In the interim, one solution to the problem of defining women's social status is to view "housewife" as an occupation and to give it some sort of ranking in the hierarchy of occupations. Although the rankings of occupational status in current use, such as the North-Hatt Scale, do not include housewife as a category, new scales could be developed. I assume that this

[9] Both Myrdal (1944; Appendix 5) and Hacker (1951) drew the parallel between women and blacks, suggesting that women occupy a caste position similar to that of blacks. As noted above, their work, among that of others, has remained peripheral to the mainstream study of stratification in all theoretical perspectives.

[10] Exercises along this line can be found in ladies' magazines and in women's lib literature. However, they have not been seriously pursued, so far as I know, by sociologists.

occupation would have a rather low ranking. This raises the interesting question of whether, and under what conditions, marriage constitutes downward social mobility and/or reduced mobility opportunities for women. At the same time, the value of "housewife" may vary with the socioeconomic stratum within which the position occurs. For example, the position of upper-class housewife may be much more highly valued in the overall structure than the position of lower-class housewife. It may be that the valuation of this position rises as its functions become more symbolic and less utilitarian.[11] Or, to put it another way, the value may rise as functions become centered more around consumption and less around productive activities. Within classes, however, the evaluation of housewife relative to other occupations open to females may vary in other ways.

Another partial solution to the problem of defining the status of women is to explore more thoroughly the notions of conferred status and deference entitlement (Shils 1968). Shils points out that "relative proximity to persons in powerful roles is [another] deference entitlement." Applied to the family, this means that the social position of the most powerful person in the family is, to an extent, reflected onto the other members of the family. Dependent women are among the most obvious recipients of this type of deference entitlement. This concept should not be confused with that of equivalent evaluation of all family members, based on the evaluation of the male head. There is no necessary implication that only the male family head determines status or class placement of family members. Some men may achieve entitlement to deference through their close relationship with a prestigious wife or mother. In addition, conferred status does not imply equivalent status. The status which is gained through close association with another person is probably a different order of deference entitlement than that which is gained more directly through characteristics or achievements of the individual herself. The recipient of conferred status in most cases probably does not have deference entitlements equivalent to those of the person whose proximity confers deference. With fewer status resources available, the recipient usually cannot reciprocate, and consequently as long as status is conferred must remain unequal to the person with greater resources.[12] This relationship between the bestower of status and the recipient is, in all probability, reflected in differential social evaluations.

To summarize, the position of the nonemployed wife may be determined by a combination of the ranking of housewife, conferred status, and premarriage deference entitlements belonging to the woman herself.

---

[11] Thorstein Veblen, in *The Theory of the Leisure Class* ([1899] 1953), of course, makes the same point.
[12] This idea derives most directly from Blau (1964).

TOWARD A MORE ACCURATE VIEW OF AMERICAN SOCIETY

The incorporation into sociology of the insight that sex does affect standing in the social structure would contribute to a more accurate picture of our society. Questions about social mobility and about power structures which are suggested when sex is taken as a salient variable illustrate this point.

Generalizations about social mobility patterns and trends on a societal level are based primarily on studies of white males (Blau and Duncan 1967). Since this group does not comprise even one-half of the population, the validity of the generalizations might be questioned. Of course, the choice of males as the proper subjects in the study of mobility is related to the assumption that female mobility is tied to male mobility. This derives from the assumptions discussed above and also pervades the literature. For example, Lopata (1971, p. 14) states, "The occupational ranking of the husbands of the women interviewed is generally higher than that of their fathers; thus the women had experienced upward mobility."

If the assumptions of female dependence were dropped, different patterns might emerge. For example, it would be interesting to look at intergenerational occupational mobility patterns of females, using the mother's status as the point of origin and using housewife as an occupational category. The findings from studies of this type might then be usefully combined with studies of mobility patterns and trends among white males to produce a much more complex and complete view of American mobility processes.

The few studies of intragenerational female mobility which have been made (Rubin 1968, 1969; Scott 1969; Elder 1969) focus on mobility through the contracting of a marriage. It would be just as reasonable to study mobility as the consequence of the dissolution of a marriage. Is there, for example, a greater probability of downward mobility for the woman who is divorced, deserted, or widowed than for the woman whose marriage is not disrupted? Some historical studies on this problem might also help to dissolve the notion that, even though the ideal nuclear family is not universal today, it was almost universal at some mythical time in our past. Although widespread divorce is a fairly recent phenomenon in the United States, dissolution of the nuclear family through death and desertion has probably always been with us. The deserving widow working hard in the boardinghouse to put her boys through school is a well-known mythical figure. It may be that the female-headed household was more prevalent in our past than we generally think. It may also be that, in some cases, this type of downward mobility for the woman contributed to the mobility strivings in her children.

A more complex and complete understanding of the structure of power and power relationships might also result from the recognition of the

Joan Acker

relevance of sex. For example, there may be a relationship between the position of women and the type of power system. This might be examined at the level of the local community as well as the level of the nation-state. In addition, cross-national comparisons of the position of women in societies which are undergoing rapid changes in class structure and the distribution of power might contribute to our understanding of larger social systems.

Conclusion: I have briefly indicated a number of conceptual and empirical questions which arise if we consider sex-based inequalities as salient to the structure of stratification systems. As the traditional nuclear family becomes less and less the dominant form in our country, the contribution which sex makes to the class and caste structure and to the social status of the individual will become more visible. In addition, as women become more powerful through greater participation in the labor force and through political organization as women, their position in the total social structure will become a more legitimate problem for the sociologist.

REFERENCES

Bernard, Jessie. 1966. *Academic Women*. Cleveland: World.
―――. 1968. *The Sex Game*. Englewood Cliffs, N.J.: Prentice-Hall.
Blau, Peter M. 1964. *Exchange and Power in Social Life*. New York: Wiley.
Blau, Peter M., and O. Dudley Duncan. 1967. *The American Occupational Structure*. New York: Wiley.
Caplow, Theodore. 1954. *The Sociology of Work*. Minneapolis: University of Minnesota Press.
Elder, Glenn H., Jr. 1969. "Appearance and Education in Marriage Mobility." *American Sociological Review* 34 (August): 519–32.
Ellis, Evelyn. 1952. "Social Psychological Correlates of Upward Mobility among Unmarried Career Women." *American Sociological Review* 17 (October): 558–63.
Epstein, Cynthia. 1970. "Encountering the Male Establishment: Sex Status Limits on Women's Careers in the Professions." *American Journal of Sociology* 75 (May): 965–82.
Etzioni, Amitai, ed. 1969. *The Semi-Professions and Their Organizations*. New York: Free Press.
Ferriss, Abbott L. 1970. *Indicators of Change in the American Family*. New York: Russell Sage.
Haavio-Mannila, E. 1969. "Some Consequences of Women's Emancipation." *Journal of Marriage and the Family* 31 (February): 123–34.
Hacker, Helen Mayer. 1951. "Women as a Minority Group." *Social Forces* 30 (October): 60–69.
Heller, Celia S. 1969. *Structured Social Inequality*. New York: Macmillan.
Hofstetter, Heather N. 1970. "The Problem of Family Status Arrangements in Stratification Analysis." Unpublished dissertation, University of Oregon.
Hughes, Everett C. 1949. "Social Change and Status Protest: An Essay on the Marginal Man." *Phylon* 10 (First Quarter): 58–65.
Komarovsky, Mirra. 1950. "Functional Analysis of Sex Roles." *American Sociological Review* 15 (August): 508–16.
―――. 1953. *Women in the Modern World*. Boston: Little, Brown.
Laumann, Edward O., ed. 1970. "Stratification Theory and Research." *Sociological Inquiry* 4 (Spring): 3–12.
Lenski, Gerhard. 1966. *Power and Privilege*. New York: McGraw-Hill.

Lopata, Helena Z. 1971. *Occupation: Housewife*. New York: Oxford University Press.

Machonin, Pavel. 1970. "Social Stratification in Contemporary Czechoslovakia." *American Journal of Sociology* 75 (March): 725–41.

Myrdal, Gunnar. 1944. *An American Dilemma*. New York: Harper.

Oppenheimer, Valerie Kincade. 1968. "The Sex-Labeling of Jobs." *Industrial Relations* 7 (May): 219–34.

Rubin, Zick. 1968. "Do American Women Marry Up? *American Sociological Review* 33 (October): 750–60.

————. 1969. "Reply to Scott." *American Sociological Review* 34 (October): 727–28.

Scott, J. F. 1969. "A Comment on 'Do American Women Marry Up?'" *American Sociological Review* 34 (October): 725–27.

Shils, Edward. 1968. "Deference." In *Social Stratification,* edited by J. A. Jackson. Cambridge: Cambridge University Press.

U.S., Bureau of the Census. 1971. *Statistical Abstract of the United States, 1971.* Washington, D.C.: Government Printing Office.

Veblen, Thorstein. (1899) 1953. *The Theory of the Leisure Class.* New York: New American Library, Mentor Books.

Watson, Walter B., and Ernest A. Barth. 1964. "Questionable Assumptions in the Theory of Social Stratification." *Pacific Sociological Review* 7 (Spring): 10–16.

Wesolowski, Wlodzimierz, and Kazimierz Slomczyński. 1968. "Social Stratification in Polish Cities." In *Social Stratification,* edited by J. A. Jackson. Cambridge: Cambridge University Press.

Wilensky, Harold L. 1968. "Women's Work: Economic Growth, Ideology, Structure." *Industrial Relations* 7 (May): 235–48.

Demographic Influence on Female Employment and the Status of Women[1]

Valerie Kincade Oppenheimer

University of California, Los Angeles

In spite of the growing interest in the social consequences of demographic phenomena, the study of the interrelationships between demographic and social variables is still not very advanced from a sociological point of view. The sociologist-demographer, to be sure, is concerned with the interaction of demographic and sociological variables, particularly with regard to fertility. But, as a demographer, his/her professional commitment has usually been to explain *demographic* rather than *sociological* phenomena. And even when the analyses point up important sociological consequences of population changes, the findings seldom receive much attention outside of the field of demography itself. On the other hand, sociologists proper have usually expressed little real interest in or knowledge of demography beyond the most rudimentary principles. They have tended to view demographic phenomena either as largely irrelevant to most of their social analyses or else as annoying variables to be "controlled" out of the picture. Even the recent popular surge of interest in the social consequences of demographic variables has not been particularly evident among sociologists. Furthermore, this growing interest has been confined largely to a concern for the social and economic consequences of one particular type of demographic phenomenon—rapid population growth. Yet there are other, more subtle, ways in which demographic phenomena have considerable relevance for societies—ways which have little or nothing to do with "the population problem."

To the extent that social systems operate within a certain demographic context, then, a much neglected area of sociological analysis is the social system consequences of both long- and short-run demographic changes. This paper is devoted to the analysis of a particular example of this kind of demographically associated social change—the changing nature of women's social roles in American society, particularly their work roles. The objective is to discuss the rather subtle way in which socioeconomic and demographic factors have interacted over time to produce changing patterns of female labor-force participation. The basic argument is that, because of a variety of demographic factors, significant changes in female

[1] This article is a revised version of a paper presented at the 1970 meetings of the American Association for the Advancement of Science in Chicago, Illinois. The research in this paper was partially financed by a grant from the Russell Sage Foundation to study work in the lives of American women.

labor-force participation became necessary for the occupational utilization of women after World War II to remain similar to that before the war. Required were not only a substantial *overall* increase in female work rates but also major changes in the relationship between women's work experiences and their family life cycles.

Let us start by briefly reviewing just what major changes have been occurring in women's labor-force participation since the turn of the century. First of all, the *extent* to which women have contributed to the economy outside their homes has changed considerably over the past 70 years. The change has been particularly great since 1940, when an accelerated growth in women's labor-force participation began. By 1970, 50% of American women 18–64 were in the labor force compared with 30% in 1940 and 20% in 1900 (Oppenheimer 1970, p. 3; U.S., Bureau of Labor Statistics 1971, p. A-10). Even more impressive is the changing relationship between female labor-force participation and the family life cycle. In 1900 if the average woman worked at all during her lifetime—and not many did—it was only before marriage and children; the proportion employed declined steadily with age (fig. 1). By 1940, the rates showed some changes in the *degree* of labor-force participation, but the *pattern* by age was very similar to that of 1900. Starting in the 1940s, however, this traditional pattern was transformed. The first great departure was the entry or reentry of women past 35 into the labor force—those whose children, by and large, had reached school age. The 1950 census shows a sharp increase over the 1940 Census in the work rates of women over 35. This pattern of ever higher work rates among women past 35 has persisted, so we find that in 1970 between 49% and 54% of women in the 35–59 age groups were in the labor force (U.S., Bureau of Labor Statistics 1971, p. A-10).

A second trend, starting in the 1950s but picking up momentum since then, has been the increased labor-force participation of younger married women, including women with preschool children. The 1950 work rates for married women in the 20–34 age groups (husbands present) indicated that work in this period was a rather rare occurrence: at age 20–24 only 26% of women were in the labor force. However, by 1970, work rates ranged from 38% for women 25–29 to 47% for women 20–24 (U.S., Bureau of Labor Statistics 1971, p. A-10). Furthermore, rapid increases in the work rate were shared by wives with preschool children as well as childless wives and those with older children. The proportion of working married women 20–24 (husbands present) with preschool children increased from 13% in 1951 to 33% in 1970. From 1960 to 1969 alone, these rates rose by 82%, from 18% to 33% (U.S., Bureau of Labor Statistics 1961, p. A-13; 1971, p. A-15). Increasingly, then, work is

Valerie Kincade Oppenheimer

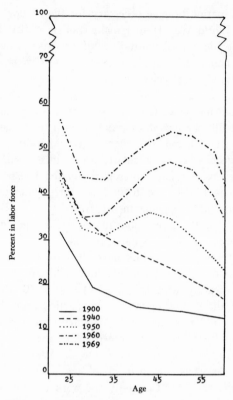

FIG. 1.—Female labor-force participation by age, 1900–1969. Sources: Oppenheimer (1970, p. 8); U.S. Bureau of Labor Statistics (1970a, table A-2).

becoming an important and continuing part of women's lives, not just before they marry and start raising children.

These trends raise a number of interesting questions. First, why have they occurred? Second, will they continue? Third, how will they affect the status and aspirations of American women? What I plan to do is to explore the extent to which a demographic socioeconomic analysis can contribute to our understanding of these questions.

THE DEMAND FOR FEMALE LABOR

In brief, my argument is that continued economic development in our society has increased the demand for female labor, which, combined with demographically induced shifts in the supply of women, has resulted in the considerable post–World War II rise in women's labor-force participation.

There must have been a rise in the demand for labor in the post–World

186

War II period because the percentage of women employed rose considerably. An important question, however, is whether there has been a *general* rise in the demand for labor that could have been met by either male or female labor or whether there has been a rising demand for *female* labor in particular. Although men and women are used interchangeably in some jobs, most demand for labor has usually been sex specific. In another work (Oppenheimer 1970, pp. 64–77) I investigated the sex composition of the detailed occupations listed by the censuses for 1900–1960. The data showed conclusively that the distribution of women throughout the occupational system has been far from random. For example, while in 1960 women constituted 33% of the total labor force, 81% of all women workers were in occupations where women were overrepresented. If these occupations had each been 33% female, they would have accounted for only 38% of the female labor force (Oppenheimer 1970, p. 69). Historically, women have been concentrated in occupations not only where they were overrepresented but where they were actually in the majority. A low estimate for 1960 indicates that at least 59% of the female labor force was in occupations where women were 70% or more of the workers (Oppenheimer 1970, p. 75).

Census data for 1970 are not yet available, but a comparison of the distribution of women by major occupation group in the 1959 and 1970 samples of the Current Population Survey (CPS) shows no decline in the concentration of women in the traditional female occupations. If anything, the concentration may even be greater. For example, the proportion of employed women who were clerical workers rose from 30% in 1959 to 35% in 1970, and women as a proportion of all clerical workers went up from 68% to 74% (Oppenheimer 1972).

The existence of female occupations reflects long-standing norms regarding the sex labeling of jobs. The evidence for these norms—from studies of hiring practices and other studies—is overwhelming (Oppenheimer 1968; 1970, pp. 77–120).

American employers have not only demanded women for certain jobs, but, in the past at least, they typically demanded particular types of women. In general, in the pre–World War II period employers preferred young and unmarried women. Studies of public policy and practice and of private employers' hiring preferences all indicate that in the 1930s and 1940s there was considerable job discrimination against both older and married women (Oppenheimer 1970, pp. 35-52 and 127–39).

There is little doubt that discrimination against older women and married women has declined considerably since then. Their greatly increased rates of labor-force participation are ample evidence of this. Studies of hiring policies of the 1950s and 1960s also attest to declining discrimination (Oppenheimer 1970). The question is, Why has there been

Valerie Kincade Oppenheimer

a reduction in job discrimination against older and married women? The answer is tied up with the explanation of the rise in female employment in general. Both are most fruitfully approached by analyzing what turns out to be a divergence in the demand for female labor compared with the supply of the traditionally preferred female worker. We can get a good idea of this divergence in demand and supply by comparing estimates of the demand for female workers with the supply of various types of females in the population.

ESTIMATES OF THE DEMAND FOR FEMALE WORKERS

As any estimate of the demand for female labor will necessarily be rough, I constructed three, based on assumptions ranging from the most conservative to the most liberal (Oppenheimer 1970, chap. 5). As the most liberal, I used the number of women actually employed at that date. This estimate assumes, in effect, that every job in which a female happens to be employed has a feminine sex label attached to it. It is thus a maximum estimate of demand.

The second demand estimate is based mainly on the number of women in occupations which are at least 70% female—those I have called female occupations. This is an effort to create a more realistic estimate than the one based on total female employment. However, as the data are too crude to accurately measure the number of women in female occupations, this represents a conservative estimate of the demand for female labor (Oppenheimer 1970, pp. 66–76).

The third series of estimates uses the proportion of women employed in 1900. Although it overestimates demand in the early decades of the century, this series greatly underestimates demand after 1940 and is used to provide a minimum estimate of demand in recent years.

The three series of demand estimates shown in table 1 and figures 2 and 3 portray a very rapid increase in the demand for female labor, particularly in the 1950–69 period. The projections for 1980–2000 show a continued rapid rise in the demand for female labor. This is particularly noteworthy, as the projections of demands 2 and 3 were based on the assumption that there would be no increase over 1969 in the proportion of women employed. As the work rates of women have been going up almost continuously throughout the century, the projections undoubtedly underestimate the future demand for female labor.

The major reason for the rapid rise in the demand for female labor is that by the early 20th century women workers had monopolized several occupations which were destined to expand enormously with the continued industrial growth of our society, particularly in the economic surge after 1940. Thus, by the turn of the century, women were already 70% or

TABLE 1

Various Estimates of the Demand for Female Workers: 1900–2000

(In Thousands)

Estimates of Demand	1900	1920	1930	1940	1950	1960	1969	1980	1990	2000
Demand estimated on proportion of females 18–64 years old employed in 1900*	3,965	5,813	7,024	8,018	9,051	9,815	11,145	13,420	14,733	16,474
Demand estimated on number of women in female occupations†	2,607	3,935	5,727	7,278	8,819	12,382	17,012‡	20,464‡	22,482‡	25,122‡
Demand equated with size of employed female population 18–64 years old* ..	3,965	6,997	8,884	10,782	14,849	19,517	27,003	32,482§	35,686§	39,876§

SOURCES.—Oppenheimer (1970, p. 166); U.S., Bureau of Labor Statistics (1970a, table A-2); U.S., Bureau of the Census (1970c, table 2).
* The number of employed females in the 1900–1930 period was estimated using Lebergott's estimates of total employment in these years.
† Female occupations are those where 70% or more of the workers were female. The number of women in such occupations was increased by one-fifth to allow for the industry factor in the sex labeling of jobs.
‡ Estimated for 1969–2000, using ratio of demand based on number in female occupations in 1960 to demand based on number of employed females in 1960. This ratio was .63.
§ Estimated, assuming the same proportion employed as in 1969.

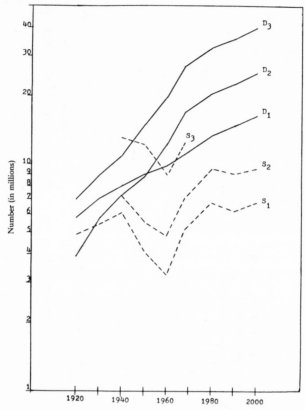

FIG. 2.—Pools of women, 18–34 years old, compared with various estimates of the demand for female workers, 1920–2000. Source: tables 1 and 2. D_1 = demand based on proportion of females employed in 1900; D_2 = demand based on number of women in female occupations; D_3 = demand equated with the employed female population; S_1 = single women 18–34 years old; S_2 = women 18–34 years old, unmarried and married (husband absent); S_3 = women 18–34 years old, except for married women (husband present) with preschool children.

more of nurses, teachers, librarians, telephone operators, stenographers, secretaries, typists, and many other clerical occupations (Oppenheimer 1970, pp. 78–79). Economic development characteristically shifts the demand for labor of both sexes from farming and manufacturing toward service occupations and industries (Clark 1947; Leibenstein 1957). However, this shift has been most characteristic of female workers and occurred at an earlier point in time—primarily, I believe, because of their early monopolization of a number of white-collar occupations such as teaching and clerical work. Many of these occupations were not of great numerical importance as a source of work even for women in 1900, but they were destined to grow rapidly, and with them the demand for female labor.

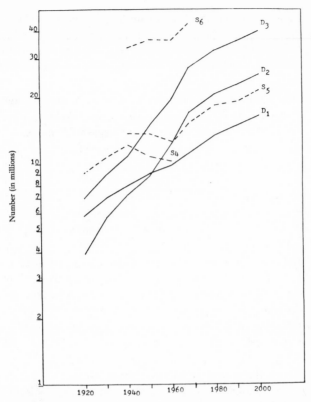

Fig. 3.—Pools of women, 18–64 years old, compared with various estimates of the demand for female workers, 1920–2000. Source: tables 1 and 2. D_1, D_2, D_3: see legend to fig. 2. S_4 = unmarried women 18–64 years old; S_5 = women 18–64 years old, unmarried and married (husband absent); S_6 = women 18–64 years old, except for married women (husband present) with preschool children.

ESTIMATES OF THE SUPPLY OF POTENTIAL FEMALE WORKERS

In order to investigate trends in supply, I have constructed six pools of women representing the population groups from which various types of female workers are drawn (Oppenheimer 1970, chap. 5). In general, my aim was to construct pools that are defined in terms of various employer and family norms regarding what types of women are preferred as workers.

The first three pools are constructed from the population of young women—those 18–34 years old—while the second three pools are based on the population of women in the broader 18–64 age groups. Within each of these age groups, I have constructed three pools, primarily on the basis of marital and family status. Pools 1 and 4 are defined in terms of the unmarried. Pool 1—young single women aged 18–34 corresponds to employer preferences for young single women, as expressed in studies of the 1940s, and is also an estimate of the supply of the typical female worker around the turn of the century. Pool 4—unmarried women 18–64 years old—is a fairly good approximation of the typical female worker of 1940.

Pools 2 and 5 add separated women to pools 1 and 4 in order to estimate the total number of women who were least likely to have men to support them. Pool 2—young unmarried and separated women—is another effort to measure the supply of young women preferred by employers in the 1940s, deducting those less likely to have been available for employment in 1940—namely, married women living with their husbands. Pool 5—the 18–64-year-old unmarried and separated women—measures the population group from which the typical female worker of 1940 came. In fact, 70% of the female labor force came from the group defined by pool 5 (Oppenheimer 1970, p. 169).

Pools 3 and 6 are an effort to get at maximum estimates of the supply of potential female workers—maximum, that is, in terms of compatibility with traditional family norms opposing the employment of mothers of preschool children. These pools primarily exclude only those married women living with their husbands who also have preschool-age children. The women excluded were a group which, even in 1970, had much lower work rates than women at any other point in the family life cycle; in 1940 very few of them were employed (Oppenheimer 1970, p. 170; U.S., Bureau of Labor Statistics 1971, p. A-15). From all the pools 18–19-year-old girls enrolled in school were also deducted.

These pools will greatly overestimate the number of women who are actually available for paid employment outside the home because they make no allowance for those who could not realistically be drawn into the labor force. For example, if we consider single women 18–34—the group with the highest work rates—only 67% were in the labor force in 1960 (Oppenheimer 1970, p. 170). However, since we are trying to investigate whether shortages in the supply of various types of female workers have been developing, *over*estimates of supply should lead to a conservative conclusion.

COMPARISON OF DEMAND AND SUPPLY: 1900–1960

Table 2 and figures 2 and 3 show the trends in our six pools of women; four out of the six pools declined between 1940 and 1960. The decline for young single women was particularly noteworthy—a decrease of about 2.8 million or 46% between 1940 and 1960. Thus, in a period when the demand for female workers was rising steeply, the supply of young women—those who would be the most eligible for employment—under-

TABLE 2

POOLS OF POTENTIAL FEMALE WORKERS: 1900–2000 (IN THOUSANDS)

Pools*	1900	1920	1930	1940	1950	1960	1969	1980	1990	2000
Women 18–34 years old:										
Single women	4,131	4,880	5,407	6,114	4,148	3,284	5,151	6,759	6,209	6,773
Unmarried and married women (husbands absent)†	‡	‡	‡	7,236	5,564	4,853	7,108	9,525	9,109	9,552
All women 18–34, except for married women (husbands present) with preschool children§	‡	‡	‡	13,037	12,160‖	8,950	12,412	‡	‡	‡
Women 18–64 years old:										
Unmarried women	6,884	9,107	10,578	12,101	10,741	10,311	‡	‡	‡	‡
Unmarried women and married women (husbands absent)†	‡	‡	‡	13,552	13,556	12,565	15,123	18,262	18,909	21,418
All women 18–64, except for married women (husbands present) with preschool children ..	‡	‡	‡	33,141	36,183#	36,133	43,000	‡	‡	‡

Sources.—Oppenheimer (1970, p. 172); U.S., Bureau of the Census (1970a, table 1; 1970b, table 1; 1970c, table 2); U.S., Bureau of Labor Statistics (1970b, tables B, I).

* Girls 18–19 years old enrolled in school were omitted from all six pools.
† Assumed same proportion single at each age for 1980–2000 as in 1969.
‡ Not available.
§ Children under five in 1940 and 1950; under six in 1960 and 1969.
‖ Only women married once with preschool children were excluded.
Only women 18–49, married once, and with children under five excluded. It was assumed that no women 50–64 had children under five.

went a sharp decline. In addition, the supplies of unmarried women 18–64 were also declining in the same period.

A direct comparison of the supply and demand estimates reveals how the two have diverged over time. Around the turn of the century, the supply of young single women (pool 1) could provide the majority of female workers—even if a substantial proportion of single women did not work. In fact, the supply was considerably larger than one of the demand estimates (fig. 2). However, as demand rose, it became progressively more difficult to rely on young single women only, especially after the pool declined so sharply between 1940 and 1960. By 1960 the supply of young single women was only one-third of even the lowest estimate of demand at that date. Pools 2 and 3 were larger than pool 1, but they too had declined so much that our minimum estimate of demand exceeded both of them by 1960. As a consequence of the declining supply of young women, the expansion of the female labor force in the 1940–60 period required the increased utilization of older women. It would have been impossible even to have maintained 1940 depression levels of employment without turning more to older women.

Looking at the trend in the pool of unmarried women in the broader age group, 18–64, we see that until 1940 it was still practical to count on such women to contribute the majority of female workers, provided a fairly substantial proportion of them worked. However, after 1940, the supply of these women declined, by 15% between 1940 and 1960. By 1960, the number barely matched the minimum estimate of demand and was well below the other two estimates. The maximum estimate—the employed female population in 1960—was almost twice as large as this pool. Adding separated women to our pool of unmarried women 18–64 does not help much either. This pool (pool 5) also declined from 1940 to 1960, and by 1960 the minimum estimate of demand was 78% of this pool; the medium estimate was 98%, and the maximum estimate, 155%. In sum, even if practically all unmarried and separated women had been employed, their supply would not have been sufficient to meet the growing demand for female labor. It is only when married women with school-age children are added that we have a group large enough to cover all of our demand estimates.

There are several demographic reasons for the decline in the supply of various types of women in the 1940–60 period. First of all, the secular decline in American fertility and, in particular, the low fertility of the 1930s produced relatively small cohorts of women in their twenties in the 1950s and 1960s. As a consequence, the number of women in the six pools—particularly the pools of young women—came from a relatively, and in some cases absolutely, diminishing segment of the total female population. Second, the higher fertility of the postwar period increased the proportion of women with preschool children, and these women were eliminated from all of the pools. Third, there was a long-run decline in the age at marriage, especially after 1940, and the proportion of women remaining single also decreased. Both trends reduced the number of single women in these pools. A fourth reason for the decline in the pools was the rise in the proportion of girls 18–19 enrolled in school. These were eliminated from all pools (Oppenheimer 1970, pp. 171, 175–77).

Because of the rapid growth of the economy the demand for female labor rose enormously in the first 60 years of the century, particularly after 1940. At the same time that the demand for women workers was expanding most rapidly, the supply of the traditionally preferred unmarried and young women was on the decline because of a variety of demographic trends. Consequently, employers had to start utilizing previously less preferred women—women who had often been discriminated against in the past. This led to the great rise in the work rates of older married women after 1940.

Other possible solutions to shortages in the supply of traditionally preferred women workers—employing men, for example, or substituting machines—were less practical than hiring older and married women. For one thing, the shortage of young females which resulted from low fertility during the Depression was matched by a shortage of young males. Second, the poor pay and poor advancement opportunities for most female occupations made them unattractive to men (Oppenheimer 1968; 1970, pp. 77–102). Machines take time to develop and women have been employed in occupations where it is often very difficult to substitute machines *en masse*. And in very rapidly growing fields, it is hard for increasing productivity to keep pace. All in all, the fastest, least disruptive, and least expensive alternative was to relax policies discriminating against the employment of married and older women.

Pointing out the great importance of a rising demand in the increased labor-force participation of women is not, of course, a complete description of the process. It does not tell us about either the general or particular mechanisms by which rising demand led to a growth in supply. The greater availability of jobs was itself an important factor. Furthermore, shortages in a preferred type of labor induce rising wages, which are an additional incentive for women to enter the labor force. In a regression analysis using annual data for the 1948–62 period, Tella has found that short-term variations in labor supply—and particularly the supply of women—were closely correlated with variations in demand, as measured by employment (Tella 1964; Oppenheimer 1970, p. 161). Bowen and Finegan's cross-sectional analysis using data for Standard Metropolitan Statistical Areas (SMSAs) in 1940, 1950, and 1960 also found a strong relationship between female labor-force participation and estimates of the demand for female labor based on industrial composition of SMSAs (Bowen and Finegan 1965; 1969, chap. 6; Oppenheimer 1970, pp. 161–62). In addition, the studies by Bowen and Finegan, Mincer, and Cain all show that women's labor-force participation is positively related to female earnings (Bowen and Finegan 1969, chap. 7; Mincer 1962; Cain 1966).

COMPARISONS OF DEMAND AND SUPPLY: 1960–2000

If an important factor in the rising work rates of older married women was the demographically induced shortage of young women, then the next question is what effect the baby-boom girls will have on job opportunities for older women in the 1960s and later. Is the increasing supply of young women going to put older and married women out of the job market? Are we about to return to the situation that existed in 1940?

A look at our projections of demand and supply for the 1969–2000 period indicates that this is not likely—both older and married women are in the job market to stay. We do have considerable increases after 1960 in all the pools for which we can make estimates, but the increases have not been and will not be enough to return us to the situation of 1940. Why is this so? For one thing, great as is the growth in the pools, fertility has leveled off and population projections indicate that our pools will do the same (figs. 2 and 3). Second, many of the demographic shifts that created shortages of young women workers are probably irreversible. Thus the trend toward increased schooling will undoubtedly continue, and with the ability to control fertility, it seems unlikely that the age at marriage will again rise to prewar levels. Third, and most important I believe, the level of demand for women workers has risen to such an extent that no demographic changes that are at all likely to occur can return us to the situation that existed in 1940. We have, in my estimation, passed the point of no return. Much as the rather peculiar demographic conditions of the 1940s and 1950s contributed to the shifting patterns of female labor-force participation, these demographic factors only hurried up a transition that was bound to come sooner or later anyway.

There is still to be explained the great increase in the labor-force participation of younger married women, especially women with preschool children. To do this would involve a considerably more detailed analysis than is possible here, but I would like to suggest some of the factors which may be of importance. First, we must remember that our pools of potential women workers greatly overestimated the number of such women who could actually be drawn into the labor force. The pools just measured the population base from which labor is drawn. Hence, even though pool 6 appears very large, a high proportion of these women would actually be unavailable for work. Second, many married women past 35 have few employment skills or have lost the ones they used to have and are thus unemployable. Furthermore, with the decline in discrimination against married women, the job opportunities for young mothers—with their greater education and more recent training—probably increased as much as for older married women. In addition, the more women working, the more feasible work appears to women at all points in the family life cycle. Early marriage has meant, moreover, that many young couples cannot subsist on the husband's earnings alone. Indeed he may still be in school and expect his wife to be the main provider for a while.

CONCLUSION

It is now time to view women's changing work roles within a somewhat broader context and to consider also the implications of these changes for the status of women in American society. Trying first to look at the problem in a broad historical perspective, we may examine the economic role of American women in terms of the industrialization process.

In preindustrial America, most productive work, including that by women, was usually carried out within the context of the family situation. Under such conditions women were often economically dependent, first of all, on their families of orientation and, second, after marriage, on their husbands. As our society industrialized, however, productive labor was increasingly carried on in nonfamilial enterprises. But to take women out of their homes to work undoubtedly posed a threat to traditional family institutions. How could our economy reap the benefits of nondomestic female labor and at the same time preserve its traditional family structure? One "solution" to the problem, or one type of adaptation, was to limit the work period of most women to the years before marriage. Although young single female workers may achieve considerable economic independence of their parents, they will have considerably less economic independence of their husbands if they do not work after marriage.

Normative attitudes which support the employment of single women but discourage the employment of married women (except for the poor) may then be interpreted as representing a partial solution to the problem of integrating the family into the economic system of an industrial society. By choosing this solution, however, a society develops a dependence on female labor to perform certain types of tasks, and, in turn, work organizations come to integrate female workers into their structures in ways that would be difficult to achieve with male workers. In other words, the sex differentiation of roles is carried into the occupational world.

What this paper has endeavored to show is that, if only for demographic reasons, this initial solution to the problem of articulating the family system with the industrial order is inherently unstable. Single females and other unmarried women are in relatively short supply at all times, and, furthermore, the supply cannot be depended upon to remain constant or increase over time. As long as female occupations remain small, the demography of the situation permits such a restricted utilization of women in the labor force. In time, however, with continued economic development and the growing numerical importance of female occupations, a society will find itself facing a demand for female labor in excess of a normatively restricted supply. As this occurs, the next step in the adaptation process is likely to be a more extensive integration of women into the economy at all points in the family life cycle. In fact, the evidence seems to indicate that we have been moving toward just that type of adjustment. This is not to say that all women will eventually work throughout their adult lives as men do, but rather that women's family status may be becoming less important as a determinant of their labor force status than other factors such as economic aspirations, marketable skills, occupational commitments, and the like.

Rising demand for female labor has made possible the start of a transition in women's economic roles and with it the decline in normative restrictions against married women's working (Oppenheimer 1970, pp. 39–63). However, if job opportunities do not expand sufficiently to provide work for all the women who want jobs, then we can expect increasing dissatisfaction with the employment situation. The normative restraints which might curb such reactions or prevent people from actively trying to do something about an unfavorable employment situation will not, as in the past, be operating—or at least not so effectively. If the work of a substantial proportion of married women is already needed by the economy, women who are less fortunate in finding jobs cannot be so easily silenced by the argument that married women should not be working anyway.

We are thus in a difficult transition period for it is not at all clear that the employment situation in the female occupations will continue to favor the same rapid growth in the female labor force as it has in the past 20 years. In fact, while it appears that the expansion of job opportunities in the poorer-paying and less desirable female occupations will be more than adequate within the near future, there is some doubt that expansion of the better female occupations will continue to provide equally good job opportunities for moderately or well-educated women as in the past (Oppenheimer 1972). Furthermore, to the extent that employment is becoming more and more extensive throughout women's lives, there will, in all likelihood, be a growing dissatisfaction with the poor pay and limited advancement characteristic of most female occupations. What was once good enough for an interim activity becomes less and less appealing as women's work roles expand. There should be rising pressures among some women, then, to break out of the traditional female occupations into the male occupational world.

REFERENCES

Bowen, William G., and T. A. Finegan. 1965. "Labor Force Participation and Unemployment." In *Employment Policy and the Labor Market,* edited by Arthur M. Ross. Berkeley: University of California Press.
———. 1969. *The Economics of Labor Force Participation.* Princeton, N.J.: Princeton University Press.
Cain, Glenn. 1966. *Married Women in the Labor Force.* Chicago: University of Chicago Press.
Clark, Colin. 1947. *The Conditions of Economic Progress.* 3d ed. London: Macmillan.
Leibenstein, Harvey. 1957. *Economic Backwardness and Economic Growth.* New York: Wiley.
Mincer, Jacob. 1962. "Labor Force Participation of Married Women: A Study of Labor Supply." In *Aspects of Labor Economics,* National Bureau of Economic Research. Princeton, N.J.: Princeton University Press.
Oppenheimer, Valerie K. 1968. "The Sex Labeling of Jobs." *Industrial Relations* 7 (May): 219–34.
———. 1970. *The Female Labor Force in the United States: Demographic and Economic Factors Governing Its Growth and Changing Composition.* Population Monograph Series, no. 5. Berkeley: University of California.
———. 1972 (in press). "Rising Educational Attainment, Declining Fertility and the Inadequacies of the Female Labor Market." In *Final Research Reports,* Commission of Population Growth and the American Future.
Tella, Alfred. 1964. "The Relation of Labor Force to Employment." *Industrial and Labor Relations Review* 17 (April): 454–69.
U.S., Bureau of Labor Statistics. 1961. *Marital and Family Characteristics of Workers, March 1960.* Special Labor Force Reports, no. 13. Washington, D.C.: Government Printing Office.
———. 1970a. *Employment and Unemployment in 1969.* Special Labor Force Reports, no. 116. Washington, D.C.: Government Printing Office.
———. 1970b. *Marital and Family Characteristics of Workers, March 1968 and 1969.* Special Labor Force Reports, no. 120. Washington, D.C.: Government Printing Office.
———. 1971. *Marital and Family Characteristics of Workers, March 1970.* Special Labor Force Reports, no. 130. Washington, D.C.: Government Printing Office.
U.S., Bureau of the Census. 1970a. *Current Population Reports.* Ser. P-20, no. 198. Washington, D.C.: Government Printing Office.
———. 1970b. *Current Population Reports.* Ser. P-20, no. 206. Washington, D.C.: Government Printing Office.
———. 1970c. *Current Population Reports.* Ser. P-25, no. 448. Washington, D.C.: Government Printing Office.

Income Differences between Men and Career Women[1]

Larry E. Suter
Bureau of the Census
Herman P. Miller
Temple University

This paper attempts to throw further light on the reasons for the differential in earnings between men and women. In 1969, the median earnings of female workers in the United States was $3,100 as compared with $7,300 for male workers. Much of this $4,200 gap can be explained by differences in type of work and extent of employment. Nevertheless, even when the earnings of men and women employed in the same occupation groups throughout the year are compared, sharp differences may be noted. Women who worked throughout 1969 as primary and secondary school teachers earned $7,200, whereas men in this occupation earned $10,000; saleswomen made $3,600, whereas salesmen made $7,400; and female operatives in nondurable goods manufacturing industries earned $4,000, whereas men earned $7,000. There are many factors that could account for these differences among year-round full-time employees in given occupation groups. Women may have less work experience, they may be less productive, they may change jobs more often, and they may have other characteristics that make them less desirable as workers. Their earnings may also be lower because of discrimination; that is, women may be paid less than men for doing the same work. The chief purpose of this paper is to quantify some of the factors that account for the earnings differential between men and women. Particular attention will be paid to the lifetime work experience of women.

It is often alleged that one of the reasons women earn less than men is that they work intermittently during their prime working years (Women's Bureau, 1969). Between the ages of 20 and 40, when nearly all men work full-time, most women either leave the labor force entirely or work only part time while their children are growing up.[2] Therefore, women have accumulated less work experience than men in the same age group and

---

[1] Revision of a paper presented at the 1971 annual meetings of the American Sociological Association in Denver, Colorado. Mr. Leigh Boice conducted the computer programming for the data presented in this paper.

[2] The patterns of women's labor force participation have been changing during the past decade. Married women have been entering the labor force in increased numbers, but women with children are still less likely to work than are single women (see Sweet 1968).

accordingly are less likely to move into higher-paying jobs. In this paper, an analysis is made of new data on lifetime work experience for a panel of approximately 5,000 women aged 30–44 who reported retrospective work experience for each year in their adult life.

Several attempts have been made in the past to account for differences in earnings between men and women. Sanborn (1960) found that nearly 90% of the difference between the income of men and women in 1950 could be accounted for by differences in education, residence, occupation, job turnover, absenteeism, experience, and productivity. He concluded, on the basis of evidence available at that time, that less than 10% of the difference between the incomes of men and women was due to market discrimination.[3] More recently, Fuchs (1971) tried to account for the earnings differential between men and women on the basis of the 1960 Census data. Fuchs found that, on the average, women earned about 60% as much as men in hourly earnings. This ratio was increased to only 61% when the data were adjusted for color, schooling, age, and city size, and to 66% when marital status, class of worker, and the length of the work trip were also taken into account. Similar studies of the minority status of women in professional occupations have appeared in sociological journals; however, the data available to investigators have not been of sufficient detail to separate many factors which may produce the difference in salary between men and women (see LaSorte 1971 for a recent study on income differences between male and female sociology teachers).

In this paper, the wage or salary incomes in 1966 of men 30–44 years of age are compared with those of women in the same age group classified according to education, occupational status, and work experience. The unique aspect of this study is that it identifies a group of women who have worked at least six months out of every year since they left school. By comparing the wages of these women, who apparently have had a major attachment to the labor force throughout their working life, with the wages of men in the same age and occupation groups, it is possible to eliminate that part of the earnings differential between the sexes which is associated with the intermittent labor force behavior exhibited by many women because of child rearing and family responsibilities. The figures for men are based on unpublished data from the March 1967 Current

---

[3] Sanborn's estimates were made by applying indirect standardization procedures to 1940 and 1950 census data of income by detailed census occupational categories (only occupations with sufficient sample cases and which represented similar working conditions for both men and women were used). This method will produce underestimates of the difference in female-male incomes when adjustments are made for several factors at once, since the procedure overadjusts for effects of highly correlated characteristics. Although Sanborn recognized this limitation and attempted to reduce the effect of interaction on his adjustments, the data available to him were sufficient for only a partial correction.

Larry E. Suter and Herman P. Miller

Population Survey, whereas the figures for women are based on the initial survey of a five-year longitudinal study of the career behavior of women 30–44 years of age begun in 1967.[4] The same procedures were used in both surveys to select the samples and to collect the information on income and other socioeconomic variables.

TYPE AND LENGTH OF WORK EXPERIENCE

The survey on women attempted to account for the type and length of all previous work experience of women. Respondents were asked to recall the amount of time worked on every job held since leaving school. Each year in which a woman worked for six months or more was counted as a year of employment, and the total number of years of employment was expressed as a percentage of the total number of years elapsed since leaving school. Thus, women are identified as having worked six months or more in every year since leaving school, as having worked at least six months in 75% of the years, and so on. One serious shortcoming of this classification is that it overestimates work experience somewhat, since it includes some women who worked on a regular part-time basis or who worked more than six months a year (such as some nurses) but less than a full year (such as many schoolteachers). Nevertheless, the classification does move a long way toward identifying those women who have had a continuous and an apparently significant attachment to the labor force for their entire adult life.

Some characteristics of women by amount of lifetime work experience are shown in table 1. Of all 17,620,000 women 30–44 years old in 1967, half (55%) had worked at least six months in their lifetime. Only 7% had worked every year since leaving school, and only about 18% had worked three-fourths of that time. The proportion of single women with a lifetime of work experience is much higher than for married women— 55% of single women, 30% of childless married women, but only 3% of married mothers (who represent 90% of this age group). Surprisingly, however, the absolute number of married women with children who are currently working and who have worked every year since they left school is only slightly smaller than the number of comparable single women. The estimates for career women in this survey are 405,000 mothers, 330,000 childless married women, and 440,000 single women. However, there were

[4] This survey was conducted in 1967 by the Bureau of the Census as one of four cohorts of a longitudinal study of work experience under contract with the Manpower Administration, U.S. Department of Labor. Dr. Herbert Parnes of the Ohio State University is the director of the National Longitudinal Surveys and developed the interview schedules for those surveys and the concept of lifetime work experience employed in this paper.

202

TABLE 1

Wages or Salary Income in 1966 for Males and Females 30–44 Years Old

Subject	Men	Women with Work Experience				
			Percentage of Adult Life Worked*			
		Total	100%	75%–99%	50%–74%	Less than 50%
Persons with income	15,781	8,337	1,059	1,636	1,632	4,010
Median income	$7,221	$2,743	$5,281	$3,950	$3,132	$1,583
Mean income	$7,668	$2,943	$4,891	$3,860	$3,082	$1,927
Ratio of mean to median	1.06	1.07	0.93	0.98	0.98	1.22
Year-round full-time workers:						
Median	$7,529	$4,363	$5,618	$4,727	$4,155	$3,655
Mean	$8,089	$4,362	$5,345	$4,660	$4,035	$3,630
Ratio of mean to median	1.07	1.00	0.95	0.99	0.97	0.99
Education:						
Median income:						
Less than high school 4 years ..	$5,660	$2,227	$3,132	$2,915	$2,680	$1,533
High school 4 years	$7,362	$2,982	$5,511	$3,962	$3,231	$1,726
College 1–3 years	$8,310	$3,135	$5,608	$4,128	$3,421	$1,467
College 4 years or more	$10,726	$5,450	$6,862	$6,085	$5,240	$2,399
Ratio of women to men:						
Total	...	38.0	73.1	54.6	43.4	22.8
Less than high school 4 years ..	...	39.3	55.3	51.5	47.3	27.1
High school 4 years	...	40.5	74.9	53.8	43.9	23.4
College 1–3 years	...	37.7	67.5	49.7	41.2	17.7
College 4 years or more	...	50.8	64.0	56.7	48.9	22.4
Work experience in 1966:						
Median income:						
Full-time jobs	$7,284	$3,398	$5,388	$4,383	$3,572	$2,330
Worked 50–52 weeks	$7,529	$4,362	$5,618	$4,727	$4,155	$3,655
Worked 14–49 weeks	$4,816	$2,352	$3,706	$3,106	$2,640	$1,868
Part-time jobs	$2,684	$863	$1,812	$1,637	$1,284	$550
Ratio of women to men:						
Full-time jobs	...	46.7	74.0	60.2	49.0	32.0
Worked 50–52 weeks	...	57.9	74.6	62.8	55.2	48.5
Worked 14–49 weeks	...	48.8	77.0	64.5	54.8	38.8
Part-time jobs	...	32.1	67.5	61.0	47.8	20.5
Occupation:						
Median income:						
Total	$7,221	$2,745	$5,281	$3,943	$3,134	$1,583
Professional, technical, and kindred	$9,686	$4,602	$6,365	$4,928	$4,521	$2,592
Clerical workers	$6,880	$3,650	$5,460	$4,406	$3,892	$2,014
Operatives	$6,174	$2,931	$3,444	$3,759	$3,148	$2,356
Service workers	$5,416	$1,593	$2,799	$2,269	$2,037	$1,175
Ratio of women to men:						
Total	...	38.0	73.1	54.6	43.4	21.9
Professional, technical, and kindred	...	47.5	65.7	50.9	46.7	26.8
Clerical workers	...	53.1	79.4	64.0	56.6	29.3
Operatives	...	47.5	55.8	60.9	51.0	38.2
Service workers	...	29.4	51.7	41.9	37.6	21.7

TABLE 1—*Continued*

SUBJECT	MEN	WOMEN WITH WORK EXPERIENCE				
			Percentage of Adult Life Worked*			
		TOTAL	100%	75%–99%	50%–74%	Less than 50%
Year-round full-time workers:						
Median income:						
Total	$7,529	$4,362	$5,618	$4,727	$4,155	$3,655
Professional, technical, and						
kindred	$9,868	$6,236	$6,705	$6,013	$6,155	$5,540
Clerical workers	$7,006	$4,743	$5,570	$4,846	$4,531	$4,172
Operatives	$6,452	$3,988	$3,666	$4,556	$4,082	$3,744
Service workers	$5,778	$2,749	$3,272	$3,034	$2,614	$2,688
Ratio of women to men:						
Total	...	57.9	74.6	62.8	55.2	48.5
Professional, technical, and						
kindred	...	63.2	67.9	60.9	62.4	56.1
Clerical workers	...	67.7	79.5	69.2	64.7	59.5
Operatives	...	61.8	56.8	70.6	63.3	58.0
Service workers	...	47.6	56.5	52.5	45.2	46.5
Marital status:						
Full-time workers, median income:						
Single	$5,719	$5,554	$5,793	$5,157	B	B
Married, no children	NA	$5,074	$5,678	$5,006	$4,496	B
Married with children	NA	$4,157	$5,417	$4,657	$4,141	$3,683

NOTE.—Figures are for the civilian noninstitutional population, in thousands. NA = not available; B = base was less than 20 sample cases.
* Number of years worked since leaving school divided by total number of years elapsed since leaving school. Each year in which a woman worked at least six months is considered a year of employment.

approximately 1.8 million mothers who had worked for three-fourths of their adult lifetime compared with about 635,000 single women.

Women with a lifetime of work experience have higher levels of education and higher occupational status than other women. The educational level of career women, regardless of marital status, is about the same as for men; 17% of each have completed four or more years of college, while only 9% of all women have completed college. Working mothers with a lifetime of work experience are more likely to be college graduates than are mothers with less work experience—12% of career mothers compared with 7% of mothers with less experience. Single women with a lifetime of career experience are particularly likely to have graduated from college; 26% have finished four or more years.

Career women are less likely than all women to be working as operatives (factory workers) or service workers and much more likely to be in clerical or professional occupations than are women with less work experience. About 42% are clerical workers, and 24% are in professional occupations, whereas among those who worked only half their adult lives, only 26% are in clerical occupations and less than 10% are professional women. Clerical occupations make up the largest single occupational group of women at any level of work experience.

These data show that women with extensive work experience are better educated and hold occupations of higher status than men or women with less career experience: 30% attended college. Apparently women who spend most of their life working are not unskilled women; they are women with high skills necessary to maintain them in satisfactory, if not high-paying, jobs.

As might be expected, there is a close association between the earnings of women and the length of work experience. Median earnings of women in 1966 ranged from $5,300 for those who worked at least six months in *every* year since leaving school to only $1,600 for those who worked about the same length of time in only half the years since leaving school (table 1). Men, on the other hand, earned $7,200. When expressed as a ratio of the earnings received by all men of the same age, those women who worked every year earned 73% of the amount earned by men, while those who worked in only half the years earned only 23% of the amount earned by men. If the analysis is restricted to women who worked full time, we find that those who worked every year since they left school earned 75% as much as men, while those who worked fewer than half the years earned 49% as much as men.

It should be pointed out that the ratio of the median wages between men and women actually understates the difference in earnings between the sexes. Men are much more likely than women to have wages that fall toward the upper end of the income distribution, while the wages for full-time working women are skewed toward lower income intervals (see first panel, table 1). The income distribution is more skewed among women who have worked every year than for other women. Career women, who receive higher incomes than other women, have difficulty in breaking away from average-paying occupations.

SPECIFIC OCCUPATIONAL GROUPS

The figures just cited relate to all male and female workers without regard to occupation. Significant differences are noted when attention is focused on specific occupation groups. For example, among women employed in professional and technical jobs in 1967, those who worked each year since they left school earned $6,400, as compared with only $2,600 for those who worked in only half of the years since leaving school. The lower earnings for the latter group were undoubtedly related to the fact that they had less work experience. Although the professional and technical women who have been working for most of their adult lives have significantly higher earnings than other women, they earned only 66% of the male average in these occupations. A similar comparison made for clerical workers showed that career women earned 79% as much as men, and among operatives and service workers women earned only about half as much as men.

The figures cited suggest in a rather impressionistic way that when occupation, length of work experience, and age are taken into account, about two-thirds of the difference between the earnings of men and women can be explained, leaving about 33% attributable to all other factors.

ESTIMATING REGRESSION COEFFICIENTS

A more precise way of estimating the combined and independent effects of factors that influence women's income—amount of education, occupational status within broad occupational groupings, number of weeks and hours worked, and lifetime career experience—is by producing estimates of regression coefficients for annual wages and salary income for both men and women. These estimates of regression coefficients can be used to calculate the income women would receive if differences between men and women in education, occupational status, weeks worked, and lifetime career experience were removed.

The linear regression coefficients were estimated with least-squares methods from two 1967 national samples of 10,782 men 30–44 years old with earnings in 1966 (March 1967 Current Population Survey data files) and 2,285 women 30–44 years old with earnings in 1966 (1967 longitudinal study). Most characteristics were entered into the model as continuous variables. Education was scored on a seven-point scale representing steps in the education ladder.[5] Occupations were first coded according to the detailed 1960 Census occupational classification system; then each occupation assigned a prestige score according to Duncan's (1961) socioeconomic index for detailed occupations. The regression of earnings on occupational status will represent the average increase in payment for occupations ranked according to prestige.

Work status for the last year is scored as a "dummy variable" so that persons who worked 50–52 weeks during the income year and who usually worked 35 hours a week or more were scored 1 and others, 0. The proportion of years in which women worked at least six months of the time elapsed since leaving school was treated as a continuous variable. Wage or salary income is scored in actual amount earned in 1966. The zero-order correlation coefficients between each of the variables used is shown in the Appendix. The means of each of these items for men and women are presented in table 2.

[5] The steps are 0–4 years, 5–7 years, 8 years, 9–11 years, 12 years, 13–15 years, and 16 years or more.

TABLE 2

MEANS AND STANDARD DEVIATIONS OF INCOME, EDUCATIONAL ATTAINMENT,
OCCUPATIONAL STATUS, YEAR-ROUND FULL-TIME WORK STATUS, AND
PROPORTION LIFE WORKED FOR MEN AND WOMEN 30–44 YEARS OLD
WITH EARNINGS IN 1966

	MEAN			STANDARD DEVIATION		
	All Men	Black Men	All Women	All Men	Black Men	All Women
Wage or salary income 1966	$7,444	$4,262	$2,875	$4,156	$3,080	$2,200
Education*	4.8	3.8	4.7	1.5	1.6	1.3
Occupational status†	41.2	22.3	36.7	25.2	18.3	20.9
Worked year-round, full-time (×100)	85.1	71.9	42.6	35.6	45.0	49.5
Years worked (%)	...	...	52.8	...	...	32.8

* Education is scored in seven steps of attainment: (1) 0–4 years, (2) 5–7 years, (3) 8 years, (4) 9–11 years, (5) 12 years, (6) 13–15 years, (7) 16+ years.
† Persons working more than 35 hours a week in 1966 and who worked 50–52 weeks were scored 1 and others, 0.

The overall difference between mean wages for men and women is great: the average women's wage ($2,900) was 39% of that received by men ($7,440). Not unexpectedly, men have jobs with somewhat higher status than women (the average SES is 41.0 for men and 36.7 for women), and their educational attainment is also slightly higher. But the differences in average level between these two socioeconomic measures alone do not explain the large difference in income. Women were only about one-half as likely to be working year round, full time during the income year as men, and women have only half the work experience accumulated by men of this age.

From the stepwise regression coefficients for women we can estimate the amount by which the average income of women would be raised if they had the same average education, occupational status, and work experience as men and had retained the present relationship between income and each of these variables.[6] For example, if we assume women had the average educational level of men, their income could have been about $55 higher than it was (see table 3). If both educational level and job status were made the same for women (i.e., by increasing job status of women from 37 to 41 on the Duncan socioeconomic index), women would receive $180 more income. Thus, by adjusting women's income for differences in education and occupational status only, the estimated annual income would be

[6] The procedures for this exercise are described by Duncan (1969). Essentially, the results were obtained by substituting the means for men into the raw-score regression coefficients for women. This process is carried out four times for each equation obtained by inserting first education, then occupational status, then year-round full-time work, and finally percentage of years worked into stepwise regression equations with wages and salary as the dependent variable.

Larry E. Suter and Herman P. Miller

TABLE 3

DIFFERENCE IN MEAN INCOME BETWEEN MEN AND WOMEN WITH RESPECT TO
EDUCATION, OCCUPATIONAL STATUS, YEAR-ROUND FULL-TIME STATUS, AND
LIFETIME CAREER EXPERIENCE OF WOMEN, FOR PERSONS 30–44
YEARS OLD WITH INCOME IN 1966

Components	Expected Mean Income	Increments Due to Each Variable	Ratio of Expected Female Income to Male Income (×100)
Actual mean income (women)	$2,875	...	38.6
Education	$2,930	$55	39.3
Occupational status	$3,054	$124	41.0
Work year-round full-time	$4,015	$961	53.9
Lifetime work experience	$4,616	$601	62.0
Residual	...	$2,828	38.0
Actual mean income (men)	$7,444	...	100.0

increased to 41% of male income. If, in addition, the annual wages of women are adjusted according to differences in work status during the income year (i.e., whether worked year round, full time or not), about $960 would be added to the annual income of women in addition to the education and occupational status adjustment. As a final adjustment, assuming that men have worked at least six months in *every* year since leaving school and adjusting the average career experience of women from 53% to 100% according to the average rate of increase in income with additional years of experience, the annual wages or salary income of women would be about $4,600 rather than $2,900. This level is only 62% of the male income level. The remaining 38% represents the portion of male/female income differences produced by all other factors that have not been taken into account in this study.

Table 4 presents the regression coefficients for wage or salary income for each of the independent variables measured in this study. Coefficients are shown for all men, black men, all women, and "career" women (defined as those who worked in 75% or more of the years since leaving school). Separate equations were computed for "career women" because of a suspected interaction between work experience and all other characteristics. The coefficients in columns 1 and 3 of the bottom panel show that, on the average, women exchange educational level or occupational status for income at less than half the rate achieved by men. Thus, for example, women add $23 to their income for each increase of a point on their SES score, whereas men add $56 when education and work status have been partialed out. When SES is taken into account, women add $223 for each increase of a step in education as compared with $515 for men. However, longer work intervals during the work year tend to produce greater incre-

TABLE 4

REGRESSION COEFFICIENTS FOR SOCIOECONOMIC CHARACTERISTICS OF MEN AND WOMEN,
WITH WAGES AND SALARY AS DEPENDENT VARIABLE, FOR PERSONS
30–44 YEARS OLD WITH INCOME IN 1966

| | RAW-SCORE REGRESSION COEFFICIENT | | | | STANDARD ERROR | | | |
INDEPENDENT VARIABLE	All Men (1)	Black Men (2)	All Women (3)	Career Women* (4)	All Men (5)	Black Men (6)	All Women (7)	Career Women* (8)
Sample size (unweighted)	10,782	1,009	2,285	750	...	...	...	...
Occupational status	60.1	45.5	35.7	42.4	1.8	5.4	2.5	4.6
Education	542.5	371.4	183.6	302.0	29.0	60.9	41.3	73.5
Multiple R^2	.268	.171	.168	.245	...	...	...	...
Occupational status	56.0	41.5	22.7	33.7	1.8	5.4	2.0	4.2
Education	514.8	355.6	222.7	393.8	28.6	59.7	32.4	66.6
Worked year-round, full-time	1,769	1,263	1,963	1,833	96.9	189.9	72.0	143.1
Lifetime work experience	...	...	1,670	1,881	...	...	110.1	854.3
Multiple R^2	.290	.206	.494	.391	...	...	...	...

* Women who worked at least six months in three-fourths of the years since leaving school.

ments in income for women than for men, and lifetime career experience results in a substantial increment of $1,700 for women.

The figures in table 4, column 4, present the same information for career women. If long experience in the labor force increases the ability to use acquired training and status, then the coefficients for these "career" women should look more like those for men than do coefficients shown for all women. The coefficients for "career" women are in fact closer to those for men, but they are far from equal. The coefficient for income in relation to education is 76% as great as that of men, and the coefficient for occupational status is 60% as great. Women are unable to change education and occupational status into earnings at the same high rate as men even when women are full-time workers with considerable lifetime work experience. The inability of women to convert occupational status into income to the same extent as men suggests that much of the remaining unexplained difference in male/female earnings could be attributable to discrimination in payment for jobs with equal status.

Considerable experience in measuring discrimination against Negroes with regression estimates of income on occupational status has accumulated in recent years (Duncan 1969). A lower regression slope of income on occupational status for black men is indicative of discrimination in payment for jobs of equal status. Coefficients for black men 30–44 years old in 1967 from the Current Population Survey are presented in column 2 of table 4. We shall not attempt to interpret all of the differences between the groups in this table; however, the similarity of the coefficients for black men and career women is striking. Yet, both groups of men change occupational status into earnings at a faster rate than women who have had considerable career experience.

The coefficient of determination (R^2) shown in table 4 is higher for women than for men. With three independent variables—educational attainment, occupational status, and extent of employment—29% of the variance in income is explained for men and 49% for women. The fact that this simple regresssion model accounts for only three-tenths of the variation in income for men and about one-half of the variation for women suggests that there are important factors other than those considered in this study, but the effectiveness of the model in predicting the income for women is striking.

MARITAL STATUS AND CHILDREN

Marital status and presence of children may be an important additional factor, since the geographic location of a married woman, and thus her job opportunities, is likely to be limited by the place of employment of her husband. The expectation that marital status directly affects income level is not borne out by the facts, however; the bottom panel of table 1 shows that the measure of lifetime career experience explains a large part of the difference in median income between single and married women. Women who are married and have children earned about 75% as much as single women. However, among women with a lifetime of career experience, married women with children earned 94% as much as single women; the difference between married women without children and single women was even smaller. The remaining difference between married and single women who worked each year may occur because married women would have been more likely to work on part-time jobs during those years.

A multiple regression analysis of wages and salary with marital status added to education, occupational status, labor force participation, and lifetime work experience was carried out. Marital status is treated as a "dummy" variable: married women with children were scored 1 and other women, 0. The partial regression coefficient for marital status shows that the average annual earnings of women with children are approximately $400 less than for other women with the same education, occupational status, and work experience. However, the addition of a marital status variable did not significantly increase the R^2 for the regression model. It appears that once a woman's occupational status and work experience are known, learning that she is married and has children does not significantly improve our ability to predict her income.

CONCLUSION

The analysis of incomes for men and women 30–44 years old in 1967 presented in this paper shows that by considering only educational level, occupational status, and work experience, we can predict the income level for women more confidently than for men. Women's pay is commensurate with effort and education, but incomes tend to cluster around the average rather than varying widely around the regression line. The absence of marked variation means that most women were receiving "just average" wages, regardless of training, job status, or experience. The income distribution of men, on the other hand, tends to be skewed toward higher income levels.

While the relationship of income with socioeconomic characteristics is more consistent for women than for men, women receive decidedly lower increments for equal step increases in educational level and occupational status. Married women earn about the same amount as single women with similar education and work experience. After all factors are considered, the overall difference between the earnings of men and women was about $2,800 in annual wages in 1966 or about 38% of the wages for men.

APPENDIX

CORRELATION COEFFICIENTS BETWEEN SOCIOECONOMIC CHARACTERISTICS OF MEN AND WOMEN 30–44 YEARS OLD WITH INCOME IN 1966

	Education	Occupational Status	Worked Year-round, Full-Time	Wages
Women ($N = 2,285$):				
Education*	...	.604	.025	.310
Occupational status	...	...	.126	.401
Worked year-round full-time†	...	...	...	.564
Lifetime work experience‡	.163	.217	.377	.482
All men ($N = 10,782$):				
Education*	...	.646	.174	.437
Occupational status	...	...	.208	.494
Worked year-round full-time†	...	...	...	.255
Black men ($N = 1,074$):				
Education*	...	.496	.109	.338
Occupational status	...	...	.150	.375
Worked year-round full-time†	...	...	...	.247

* Education is scored in seven steps of attainment: (1) 0–4 years, (2) 5–7 years, (3) 8 years, (4) 9–11 years, (5) 12 years, (6) 13–15 years, (7) 16+ years.
† Persons working more than 35 hours a week in 1966 and who worked 50–52 weeks were scored 1 and others, 0.
‡ Number of years worked since leaving school divided by total years elapsed since leaving school.

REFERENCES

Duncan, Otis Dudley. 1961. "A Socioeconomic Index for All Occupations." In *Occupations and Social Status,* edited by Albert J. Reiss. New York: Free Press.

Larry E. Suter and Herman P. Miller

————. 1969. "Inheritance of Poverty or Inheritance of Race?" In *On Understanding Poverty,* edited by Daniel P. Moynihan. New York: Basic.

Fuchs, Victor R. 1971. "Differences in Hourly Earnings between Men and Women." *Monthly Labor Review* (May), pp. 9-15.

LaSorte, Michael. 1971. "Sex Differences in Salary among Academic Sociology Teachers." *American Sociologist* 6 (November): 304–7.

Sanborn, Henry N. 1960. "Income Differences between Men and Women in the United States." Ph.D. dissertation, University of Chicago.

Sweet, James A. 1968. "Family Composition and the Labor Force Activity of Married Women in the United States." Ph.D. dissertation, University of Michigan.

Waldman, Elizabeth. 1970. "Women at Work: Changes in the Labor Force Activity of Women." *Monthly Labor Review* (June), pp. 10–18.

Women's Bureau. 1969. *Handbook on Women Workers.* Bulletin 294. Washington, D.C.: Government Printing Office.

Women, Work, and Wedlock: A Note on Female Marital Patterns in the United States[1]

Elizabeth M. Havens
University of Texas

Sociological attention often focuses on marriage as both cause and effect of diverse phenomena. Patterns of marriage have been assessed as the results of normative sex-role behavior (Epstein 1970)[2] and as the causes of variation in such phenomena as suicide rates (Gibbs 1969) and birthrates (Bogue 1969). This report is also concerned with marital patterns, as dependent variables. Specifically, the research is addressed to the conjunction between economic status and patterns of marital behavior in the United States, circa 1960. Unlike many previous investigations of the economic aspect of marital patterns, however, this one is primarily concerned with the female population. While female marital patterns are certainly not independent of male patterns, they are not necessarily axiomatic or invariant within socioeconomic categories.

In the recent past, many investigators have concluded that divorce and singleness are inversely related to socioeconomic status. For example, Monahan (1955, p. 324), Goode (1966, p. 382), and Udry (1966, p. 208; 1967, p. 673) have noted an inverse relation between socioeconomic status and divorce. Landis (1965, p. 677) concluded that "a substantial proportion of those who do not marry in the United States today are the feebleminded, the mentally ill, the crippled, the physically handicapped, or those who suffer from chronic ill health." In general, Bogue (1969, p. 346) states that the pattern for the U.S. population is "a pattern of early marriage at the present time, with a low level of bachelorhood."

The marital pattern for the U.S. population is held to be a general high level of marriage with an inverse relation between socioeconomic position and unmarried status (singleness and divorce). But statistics taken from the 1960 U.S. census reports indicate quite different patterns for working

---

[1] Revision of a paper delivered at the 1971 meetings of the Society for the Study of Social Problems.

[2] Indeed, marriage is often projected as the only "normal" sex-role behavior for females. As Cooney succinctly summarizes (1971, p. 5), "The female role is defined primarily as being a good wife and mother." And many writers (cf. Bowman 1970, pp. 89–95; Koos 1958, pp. 293–312; Oliver 1964; Porterfield 1962, pp. 334–40; Sullinger 1960) concerned with marriage seem only tangentially interested in the characteristics of the never-married or divorced populations as they relate to the purported reasons for the "deviance."

females. Moreover, the correlations obtained between economic attainment and unmarried status among females are the reverse of those suggested above.

METHODOLOGICAL CONSIDERATIONS

The following analyses, like those of many researchers on this topic, are based entirely upon 1960 U.S. census data. Tables 1–4 show the percentages of males and of females in certain marital status categories for various occupational and income classes. The percentages given in the tables are based on the total number of females and the total number of males in the respective occupational and income classes. These percentages do not total to 100, because the marital status categories are not inclusive.

The aim of this report is to delineate conjunctions between marital status and economic attainment for females, and to provide a possible interpretation for female patterns based on an assumption of rational behavior. The marital categories reported in the census data have therefore been manipulated to form two categories: (1) married—those presently married with spouse present, and (2) unmarried—those never married or currently divorced. The categories of married with spouse absent and separated have been excluded from direct consideration, as they represent the "gray areas" of marital behavior. The widowed category has also been excluded. While singleness and divorce can be interpreted in terms of a decision-making model, the occurrence of "widowhood" cannot (usually) be so interpreted.

Two age categories have been considered. The occupational activity of males and females is reported for those aged 14 and over and for those 35–44.[3] The more specific age category is given to illuminate possible variations by age. However, results are similar for the two categories.

Finally, I have avoided attempting to posit some sort of "grand norm" of marital behavior for the entire country as a base for comparison. Instead, each occupational and income category is considered as comprising a "normative category" with a particular nexus of values and practices regarding marriage.[4] If one accepts occupation and income as primary indices of socioeconomic class, a definite pattern is apparent in differential levels of female unmarriage among classes.

[3] The subcategory of professionals was included in table 1 on the presumption that persons represented in this category would be interested in the results. The census reports provide information on detailed occupations for this age category. However, the results for the subcategory were not used in computing the correlations.

[4] Occupation (cf. Blau and Duncan 1967) and income (cf. Anderson 1971, pp. 104–5) are often presented as the indices of socioeconomic class, usually with the implication that the divisions correspond to differences in values and behavioral practices. The categorical comparison approach controls, in effect, for differential normative patterns by socioeconomic class.

FINDINGS

Among occupational categories , women earning the most are more likely to be unmarried than men (tables 1 and 2). Udry (1966, p. 208) asserted

TABLE 1

MARITAL STATUS BY OCCUPATIONAL CATEGORY FOR OCCUPATIONALLY ACTIVE FEMALES
AND MALES AGED 14+, UNITED STATES, 1960

TYPE OF OCCUPATIONAL ACTIVITY	MEDIAN FEMALE EARNINGS IN 1959 FOR 50–52 WEEKS	PROPORTION UNMARRIED			PROPORTION MARRIED		
		Female	Male	Difference	Female	Male	Difference
Professional, technical and kindred workers ..	$4,186	36.6	16.0	+20.6	53.4	81.3	−27.9
College presidents, professors, instructors, and NEC*	5,814	55.6	19.0	+36.6	35.3	78.2	−42.9
Managers, officials, and proprietors, except farm	3,800	22.0	6.6	+15.4	58.8	90.2	−31.4
Craftsmen, foremen, and kindred workers	3,555	24.6	11.0	+13.6	59.6	85.3	−25.7
Clerical and kindred workers	3,546	35.1	25.4	+ 9.7	54.9	70.9	−16.0
Operatives and kindred workers	2,911	19.5	18.1	+ 1.4	65.3	77.5	−12.2
Laborers, except farm and mine	2,863	30.7	29.7	+ 1.0	52.5	63.6	−11.1
Sales workers	2,370	24.3	21.9	+ 2.4	61.8	75.1	−13.3
Service workers	2,102	24.5	25.7	− 1.2	54.7	66.7	−12.0
Private household workers	922	30.7	41.4	−10.7	37.2	36.7	+ 1.5
ρ	Median female earnings and:			.95			−.90

SOURCE.—U.S. Bureau of the Census (1963, tables 12 and 16).
* NEC = not elsewhere classified.

that "the relationship between occupational status and marital stability for men is direct and unequivocal." But he concluded that marital rates for females were unexplained,[5] for "these rates cannot be said to be associated with the status level of the occupational group." Yet, if one considers the economic rewards attached to an occupation to be elements of status, then the occupational status of working women can be considered a factor explaining differential levels of marriage for females. The nine occupational categories encompass most of the extrafamilial alternatives available to

[5] Udry (1966, p. 208) includes the following factors in "marital instability": "percentage of those ever married who were divorced, separated, or had been married more than once at the 1960 Census."

TABLE 2

MARITAL STATUS BY OCCUPATIONAL CATEGORY FOR OCCUPATIONALLY ACTIVE FEMALES
AND MALES AGED 35–44, UNITED STATES, 1960

TYPE OF OCCUPATIONAL ACTIVITY	MEDIAN FEMALE EARNINGS IN 1959 FOR 50–52 WEEKS	PROPORTION UNMARRIED			PROPORTION MARRIED		
		Female	Male	Difference	Female	Male	Difference
Professional, technical, and kindred workers ..	$4,186	25.4	8.6	+16.8	67.7	89.5	−21.8
Managers, officials, and proprietors, except farm	3,800	20.6	4.6	+16.0	70.2	93.7	−23.5
Craftsmen, foremen, and kindred workers	3,555	18.6	5.9	+12.7	71.3	91.6	−20.3
Clerical and kindred workers	3,546	21.9	11.9	+10.0	70.7	85.3	−14.6
Operatives and kindred workers	2,911	14.8	7.9	+ 6.9	75.1	88.5	−13.4
Laborers, except farm and mine	2,863	16.6	12.7	+ 3.9	45.6	80.8	−35.2
Sales workers	2,370	10.6	6.5	+ 4.1	82.1	91.4	− 9.3
Service workers	2,102	13.9	13.0	+ 0.9	72.1	81.0	− 8.9
Private household workers	922	18.1	25.9	− 7.8	54.9	50.7	+ 4.2
ρ	Median female earnings and:		.98				−.73

SOURCE.—U.S. Bureau of the Census (1963: table 16; 1966, table 5).

females. A definite pattern appears when these categories are ranked according to median female earnings. The higher the income, the greater the level of female unmarriage in the category.[6]

The results by occupational categories suggest that the income of females may be crucial in explaining patterns of female marital behavior. The delineation of female marital status by income groupings shows a similar, but even more pronounced, relationship between economic level and marital behavior. Table 3 reveals that unmarried status among females is directly related to income. Comparisons of both intraclass levels and simple proportions indicate the same pattern.[7] In addition, it can be noted that female patterns are not only dissimilar to male patterns, they are opposite.

[6] The correlation coefficients between median female income and levels of marriage and unmarriage are given in the bottom row of tables 1 and 2. The data have been analyzed ordinally because of the "gross" measure for income which does not take into account such factors as variability in the value of income cross-sectionally.

[7] The correlation coefficients are given in the bottom row of table 3. The only discrepancy in the pattern for females appears in the gross $10,000+ category. This discrepancy suggests that a curvilinear relation between income attainment and marriage for females might become apparent if the gross upper category could be broken down. This possibility is congenial with ideas about variability in the character of the marital institution itself. In other words, the character of the marital

TABLE 3

MARITAL STATUS BY INCOME GROUPING FOR FEMALES AND MALES AGED 35–44,
UNITED STATES, 1960

INCOME GROUPING	PROPORTION UNMARRIED			PROPORTION MARRIED			PROPORTION OF EVER MARRIED MARRIED MORE THAN ONCE		
	Female	Male	Difference	Female	Male	Difference	Female	Male	Difference
$10,000+	30.0	3.8	+26.2	57.7	94.5	−36.8	20.9	8.8	+12.1
7,000–9,999	42.7	4.5	+38.2	44.3	93.7	−49.4	20.8	10.7	+10.1
5,000–6,999	37.9	6.8	+31.1	51.4	90.7	−39.3	19.8	11.8	+ 8.0
3,000–4,999	24.1	10.8	+13.3	65.0	84.4	−19.4	19.3	13.8	+ 5.5
1,000–2,999	14.1	17.8	− 3.7	71.5	73.5	− 2.0	18.7	16.1	+ 2.6
1–999 or loss ...	8.7	32.2	−23.5	81.1	54.8	+26.3	18.6	17.1	+ 1.5
0	2.6	47.4	−44.8	94.7	34.8	+59.9	11.5	16.0	− 4.5
Income level and:									
ρ	.89	−1.00	.89	−.89	1.00	−.89	1.00	−.89	1.00

SOURCE.—U.S. Bureau of the Census (1966: table 6).

Moreover, contradicting previous conclusions about the socioeconomic correlates of divorce, table 4 reveals a perfect *direct* interclass relation

TABLE 4

PERCENTAGES OF FEMALES AND MALES AGED 35–44 NEVER MARRIED AND DIVORCED,
BY INCOME LEVEL

INCOME GROUPING	MALE			FEMALE		
	N	Never Married (%)	Divorced (%)	N	Never Married (%)	Divorced (%)
With income:						
$10,000+	(1,197,013)	2.6	1.2	(33,491)	17.7	12.3
7,000–9,999	(2,024,150)	3.2	1.3	(86,997)	31.0	11.7
5,000–6,999	(3,401,244)	4.9	1.9	(396,150)	26.3	11.6
3,000–4,999	(2,860,712)	8.0	2.8	(1,561,869)	14.7	9.4
1,000–2,999	(1,435,233)	13.6	4.2	(2,277,597)	7.0	7.1
1–999 or loss	(540,919)	25.8	6.4	(1,943,356)	5.3	3.4
Without income ...	(298,629)	40.0	7.4	(6,036,973)	2.0	0.6
Total	(11,757,900)	8.1	2.6	(12,336,433)	6.1	3.8

SOURCE.—U.S. Bureau of the Census (1966, table 6).

institution may be an important *variable*. Thus, females who have attained a certain economic status may have expectations and orientations regarding a conjugal relationship quite different from the traditional familial expectations and demands regarding marriage. Such a possibility is supported by the interclass correlation for income level and the proportion of ever-married females married more than once (1.00). Unfortunately, any elaboration of this interesting possibility is beyond the scope of this note.

Elizabeth M. Havens

between the income level of females and the proportion of divorced females. A similar, though not perfect, relation is apparent between the income level of females and the proportion of females never married. Some will certainly argue that females who are divorced or never married must, because they are not married, earn more money. However, this "need" factor does not explain why females with high incomes are so disproportionately represented in the unmarried category. Such representation implies preparation for economic activity and, perhaps, an unwillingness to "settle" for the alternative of marriage.

SUMMARY AND INTERPRETATION

Among the working female population in the United States in 1960, evidence reveals diverse marital patterns by socioeconomic class. Furthermore, the major pattern among the female population is one of a strong *direct* relation between economic attainment and unmarried status. This finding casts doubt on the inverse relation cited earlier between socioeconomic status and unmarried status in the United States, circa 1960.

If one rejects the common notion that females with high incomes are simply the "marital rejects" or "pathetic misfits" of society, then a possible interpretation is that these females are less willing to enter into and/or maintain marital commitments. In other words, many of these females may *choose* not to be married.

Causality has certainly not been determined in this simple synchronic analysis, but some fairly impressive "conjunctions" have been illuminated between the economic position of females and marital status. The findings suggest that, the greater the economic independence of females, the greater the likelihood that they will be unmarried. From this datum, one might project that, the higher the economic achievement of females, the less their desire to accept the confining traditional familial sex-role of wife-mother-homemaker or to be evaluated solely in terms of that sex-role. This "rejecting marriage" inference is at least as plausible as the oft-heard "marital reject" explanation for female unmarriage and is deserving of further exploration.

REFERENCES

Anderson, Charles H. 1971. *Toward a New Sociology*. Homewood, Ill.: Dorsey.
Blau, Peter M., and Otis Dudley Duncan. 1967. *The American Occupational Structure*. New York: Wiley.
Bogue, Donald J. 1969. *Principles of Demography*. New York: Wiley.
Bowman, Henry A. 1970. *Marriage for Moderns*. 6th ed. New York: McGraw-Hill.
Cooney, Rosemary S. 1971. "Professional Women: Why So Few? A Social-psychological Approach." Unpublished manuscript, University of Texas at Austin.

Epstein, Cynthia F. 1970. *Woman's Place: Options and Limits in Professional Careers.* Berkeley: University of California Press.

Gibbs, Jack P. 1969. "Marital Status and Suicide in the United States: A Special Test of the Status Integration Theory." *American Journal of Sociology* 74 (March): 521–33.

Goode, William J. 1966. "Marital Satisfaction and Instability: A Cross-cultural Class Analysis of Divorce Rates." In *Class, Status, and Power,* edited by Reinhard Bendix and Seymour Martin Lipset. 2d ed. New York: Free Press.

Koos, Earl L. 1958. *Marriage.* New York: Holt.

Landis, Paul H. 1965. *Making the Most out of Marriage.* New York: Appleton-Century-Crofts.

Monahan, Thomas P. 1955. "Divorce by Occupational Level." *Marriage and Family Living* 17 (November): 322–24.

Oliver, Bernard J. 1964. *Marriage and You.* New Haven, Conn.: College and University Press.

Porterfield, Austin L. 1962. *Marriage and Family Living as Self-Other Fulfillment.* Philadelphia: Davis.

Sullinger, Thomas Earl. 1960. *Neglected Areas in Family Living.* Boston: Christopher.

Udry, J. Richard. 1966. "Marital Instability by Race, Sex, Education, and Occupation Using 1960 Census Data." *American Journal of Sociology* 72 (September): 203–9.

———. 1967. "Marital Instability by Race and Income Based on 1960 Census Data." *American Journal of Sociology* 72 (May): 673–74.

U.S., Bureau of the Census. 1963. *U.S. Census of Population: 1960. Occupational Characteristics.* Final Report PC(2)-7A. Washington, D.C.: Government Printing Office.

———. 1966. *U.S. Census of Population: 1960. Marital Status.* Final Report PC(2)-4E. Washington, D.C.: Government Printing Office.

Impediment or Stimulant?
Marital Status and Graduate Education[1]

Saul D. Feldman
Case Western Reserve University

Higher education in the United States began in 1638 with the founding of Harvard College; yet, it was not until 1837, when Oberlin College admitted four women, that higher education became a reality for American women. Both before and after the founding of Oberlin, controversy raged over how much (if any) education women should receive, what subjects they should be taught, and whether they should be educated along with men. Some worried about the effects of female education upon women, some were concerned about the effects of female education upon men, while still others wondered what the education of women would do to society. Others felt that educating women would price them out of the marriage market, while still others argued that educated women would simply get married and then their education would be wasted.

A traditional rallying point against female education has been that it would be a major force for defeminization. Typical is Erasmus Darwin's (1797, p. 10) argument: "The female character should possess the mild and retiring virtues rather than the bold and dazzling ones; great eminence in almost anything is injurious to a young lady; whose temper and disposition should appear to be pliant rather than robust; to be ready to take impressions rather than to be decidedly mark'd; as great apparent strength of character, however excellent is liable to alarm both her own and the other sex; and to create admiration rather than affection."

With the increasing education of women, a series of studies reported a lower marriage rate among college-educated women. To many, especially those who believed in eugenics, this lower marriage rate was a cause for alarm that could signal the end of the human race. A sociologist (Wells 1909, p. 737) wrote: "To speak plainly, children have become to many

[1] Revision of a paper presented before the 1971 meetings of the Pacific Sociological Association (Honolulu). This article may be identified as publication A-123 of the Survey Research Center of the University of California, Berkeley. An expanded version of this article appears in my *Escape from the Doll's House: Women in Graduate and Professional School Education* (New York: McGraw Hill, 1973). This article is based on data gathered by the National Surveys of Higher Education, sponsored by the Carnegie Commission on Higher Education, and supported in part as a cooperative research project by funds from the United States Office of Education. The interpretations put forward in this article do not necessarily reflect the position of the Office of Education, and no official endorsement of the Office of Education should be inferred. I would like to thank Marie R. Haug and Sandra Acker Husbands for their helpful comments in the revision of this article.

women, a nuisance, or at least unwelcome beings of an alien domestic world which years of intellectual training have unfitted the college women to like and understand." If college women were less likely to marry and have children, those of a weaker biological strain will predominate, bringing about in due course, "race suicide."[2]

On the other hand, some feminists at the turn of the century questioned the utility of marriage for educated women either because of the increased effort it took to maintain both a marriage and a career or because they felt that educated women had the ability and the obligation to be self-supporting.

A contrary viewpoint is that the educated woman can make her greatest contribution by accepting what Philip Slater (1970, p. 62) has called the "Spockian Challenge." This challenge posits that child rearing is the most important task for any woman. Many college undergraduates are accepting this challenge. Fifty-five percent of college women in a 1968 national sample (Cross 1968, p. 10) stated that they expected their life-long satisfaction to come from marriage and the family, while only 18% expected their major satisfactions to come from a career. In another study of over 1,400 female Los Angeles high school seniors, 4% opted for a lifetime career, 48% stated that they planned only to be homemakers, while another 48% stated that they would try to combine both a career and homemaking (Turner 1964, p. 280).

Attempting to combine a career and homemaking appears to be a source of strain for many women (Coser and Rokoff 1971). Marriage may (depending upon the woman's viewpoint) enable or force a woman to drop out of a career (Ginzberg 1966, p. 82). Married women who do remain employed may feel what one writer described as "self-conscious gratitude toward their husbands for helping them to maintain a career" (Lopate 1968, p. 148) and for giving them the emotional support needed to maintain two diverse and potentially conflicting roles. A consistent finding in studies of married professional women is that they view their career as secondary to their husband and their children and see their own career as subordinate to their husband's (cf. Arreger 1966; Hubback 1957; Lopate 1968; Poloma and Garland 1970; Sommerkorn 1966).

Today's discussions of women in higher education are not about race suicide or defeminization; rather, there is concern about the conflict between the spouse role and the student role. This paper examines how the spouse role affects both men and women in graduate education. We will be concerned especially with the effects of divorce, for, if there are conflicts between the two roles, abandonment of the spouse role may alleviate or lessen the conflict.

2 For a review of this controversy, see Goodsell (1923, p. 34–61).

Saul D. Feldman

DEMOGRAPHIC CHARACTERISTICS

Data utilized in this article are from a nationwide sample of graduate students collected under the sponsorship of the Carnegie Commission on Higher Education and consist of approximately 33,000 completed mail questionnaires—a 65% response rate from a Spring 1969 sample of graduate and professional school students in 158 U.S. colleges and universities.

The data were weighted to represent the universe of over 1 million students in American graduate and professional education in the 1968–69 academic year (full details on sampling and weighting may be found in Trow et al. [1971]).

Women in graduate education are less likely to be married than their male counterparts (table 1). Perhaps some women avoid a potential conflict

TABLE 1

MARITAL STATUS BY SEX*

| | MARITAL STATUS | | |
AGE	Single (%)	Married (%)	Divorced or Separated (%)
Males	29	69	2
Females	39	56	6

* Based on entire sample (32,963).

situation by remaining single, while others end their marriages. Unfortunately, since data were gathered in only one time period, I am not able to discover actual motives for remaining single or obtaining a divorce, but am only able to control for marital status and infer possible effects of marriage and divorce.

If women students are married, they are much more likely to have a spouse with graduate education (table 2). Traditionally, it has been deemed unacceptable in our society for a women to dominate her husband in any way—including educationally. Thus, married women are freer to pursue postgraduate education if their spouses have also done so. No such limitations exist for married men. Less than a quarter of married male students have spouses with graduate education as compared with over half the married graduate women. These differences obtain for all age groups; even women who return to graduate school after the age of 40 are more likely to have spouses with graduate education than men of a similar age

One of the major limitations of marriage is enrollment status. Regardless of their marital status, women are less likely to be enrolled full-time than men (table 3). However, while marriage reduces the frequency of full-time enrollment for both men and women, it is more likely to

222

TABLE 2

GRADUATE STUDENTS WHOSE SPOUSES ATTENDED GRADUATE SCHOOL,
BY AGE AND SEX: MARRIED STUDENTS ONLY*

	SEX		
AGE	Males (%)	Females (%)	Ratio (% Female/% Male)
22 or younger	14	63	4.50
23	20	54	2.70
24	22	69	3.14
25	33	63	1.91
26–27	27	64	2.37
28–29	29	70	2.41
30–34	22	58	2.64
35–39	20	64	3.20
40+	24	41	1.71
Total	24	55	2.29

* All married students in sample. Smallest cell (females 22 or younger) has 313 unweighted cases.

TABLE 3

ENROLLMENT STATUS BY SEX AND MARITAL STATUS*

	ENROLLMENT AND STATUS		RATIO—% MARRIED OR DIVORCED FULL-TIME/ % SINGLE FULL-TIME
SEX AND MARITAL STATUS	Full-Time (%)	Part-Time (%)	
Single males	76	24	...
Single females	62	38	...
Married males	51	49	0.671
Married females	29	71	0.468
Divorced/separated males	64	36	0.842
Divorced/separated females	52	48	0.839

* Smallest cell (divorced males) has 408 unweighted cases.

reduce it for women than for men. About half the married men are full-time graduate students, compared with less than one-third of the married women. Divorce on the other hand, affects enrollment status only slightly. While divorced men are more likely to be full-time students, the ratio between men and women is similar.

Since nationality and part-time-student enrollment status may have strong effects upon graduate education, a special subsample was selected of only full-time students who are U.S. citizens.[3] Subsequent analysis will be from this subsample.

[3] This sample of full-time students who are U.S. citizens consists of a one-in-three sample of single men ($N = 1,704$); a one-in-four sample of married men ($N = 1,821$); all single ($N = 2,301$) and married women ($N = 1,382$); and all divorced or separated men ($N = 161$) and women ($N = 227$).

Saul D. Feldman

There are significant differences by marital status in the age distribution of graduate students (table 4). As we might expect, single graduate

TABLE 4

AGE DISTRIBUTION BY SEX AND MARITAL STATUS*

	AGE				
SEX AND MARITAL STATUS	22 or Younger (%)	23–25 (%)	26–29 (%)	30–34 (%)	35 or Older (%)
Single males	24	53	18	3	1
Single females	30	46	13	5	5
Married males	6	38	33	14	9
Married females	12	30	20	10	28
Divorced/separated males	2	14	29	38	18
Divorced/separated females	1	15	30	20	34

* Smallest cell (divorced/separated men) has 161 cases. Each row totals 100% (with rounding errors).

students tend to be younger than married or divorced students, and married students tend to be younger than divorced graduate students. Married or divorced female students tend to be older than their male counterparts. Twenty-eight percent of married female graduate students are over 35, compared with 10% of married men; similarly, 34% of divorced or separated women are over 35, as compared with 18% of men. The fact that married or divorced women tend to be older reflects the fact that they are more constrained by the role of spouse than are men. Unlike women, men do not have to wait until their children are raised or until their spouse has an established career to continue in graduate school.

FINDINGS

Table 5 examines students' stated motivations for attending graduate school, using two measures of intellectual and one of financial motivation. Intellectual motives and financial motives appear to be independent; among men the gamma $= -.093$, while among women the gamma $= .093$.

In all marital statuses, women are more likely to express intellectual motives for attending graduate school than men. Since the traditional role of women has not been one of principal provider, it appears that they are freer to attend graduate school for intellectual reasons. Yet, in their less dependent single and divorced states, they are just as likely as male students to express financial motives for attending graduate school. Among married graduate students, men are more likely than women to state financial considerations for attending graduate school. Financial

224

TABLE 5

MOTIVATIONS FOR ATTENDING GRADUATE SCHOOL, BY SEX AND MARITAL STATUS

	(A) Motivation: "To Continue Intellectual Growth"*			(B) Motivation: "To Study Field for Intrinsic Interest"*			(C) Motivation: "To Increase Earning Power"†		
	SEX			SEX			SEX		
MARITAL STATUS	Males (%)	Females (%)	GAMMA	Males (%)	Females (%)	GAMMA	Males (%)	Females (%)	GAMMA
Single	56	70	.285	29	39	.235	32	33	.017
Married	61	81	.475	33	48	.307	43	37	.127
Divorced/ separated ..	62	78	.388	28	59	.570	48	50	.025

* Strongly agree.
† Strongly agree, and agree with reservations.

motives are strongest among divorced students; men may be under pressure to pay child support and/or alimony, and some women may be striving for a more independent financial state.

Marital status seems to influence the intellectual motives of women but not of men. At all levels of marital status, men similarly express a desire for intellectual growth or to study a field for its intrinsic interest. Among women, however, these motives are lowest among single students and rise noticeably among married and divorced/separated students. I interpret these differences as an expression of freedom from some of the constraints of the marital role. The boredom and routine of housewife duties may create a desire for more intellectual stimulation, especially among college-educated housewives.

Just as sex and marital status influence the motivation to enter graduate school, they also exert an influence on the pressures to drop out of graduate school. Among the single or married students, men are more likely than women to state that they have never considered quitting graduate school for good. Among divorced graduate students, however, women are much more likely than men to express a commitment to remain in school. Similarly, among single or married graduate students, men and women agree equally that "I think I would have been happier if I had not entered graduate school" (table 6, B). Among divorced students, however, women are much more likely than men to strongly disagree with this item. Divorced men are less committed to remain in graduate school and they are unhappier with the graduate-student role than single or married men; divorced women are more highly committed to remain in school and seem happiest with the graduate-student role.

No differences by sex or marital status emerge in a question asking

Saul D. Feldman

TABLE 6

PRESSURES AND ATTITUDES TOWARD DROPPING OUT OF GRADUATE SCHOOL
BY SEX AND MARITAL STATUS

	(A) Never Considered (in the Past Year) Quitting Graduate School for Good			(B) Strongly Disagreeing That They Would Be Happier If They Had Not Entered Graduate School			(C) Stating Emotional Strain Will or May Force Them to Drop out of Graduate School		
	SEX			SEX			SEX		
MARITAL STATUS	Males (%)	Females (%)	GAMMA	Males (%)	Females (%)	GAMMA	Males (%)	Females (%)	GAMMA
Single	61	43	.250	61	57	.046	24	34	.221
Married	65	54	.191	67	66	.022	19	29	-.275
Divorced/ separated ..	38	57	.378	44	73	.472	57	42	.295

whether such things as a job offer or inability to do the work will cause students to drop out. However, among married students, 21% of the women as compared with 9% of the men (gamma of sex differences = .444) state that pressure from their spouse will or may cause them to drop out of school. Single and married women are more likely than men to feel that emotional strain will or may force them to quit their graduate education (table 6, C). As one might expect, emotional strain is highest among divorced students; however, women are less likely to state that this strain may cause them to drop out. In all three parts of table 6, divorced women show a higher degree of commitment to remain in graduate school than do divorced men, while the situation is reversed among single or married students.

EFFECTS OF MARRIAGE ON PROFESSIONAL ATTAINMENT

A large proportion of our sample of full-time graduate students plan a career in college or university teaching, which, for many, will involve publishing articles or presenting papers at professional meetings. Table 7 looks at these activities among graduate students who plan university or college teaching careers. The greatest difference between men and women in publication rates are among married students. Married men seem most productive, while productivity for married women is much lower. The time needed to prepare a manuscript probably cannot be budgeted as easily by married as by divorced or single women. Married men have somebody to cook and care for them and an easily available sexual partner. For married women, who have in addition to their academic responsibilities those of

TABLE 7

GRADUATE STUDENTS PRESENTING A PAPER BEFORE PROFESSIONAL MEETINGS
OR PUBLISHING A JOURNAL ARTICLE, BY SEX AND MARITAL STATUS:
FUTURE COLLEGE OR UNIVERSITY FACULTY ONLY*

	(A) Present Paper			(B) Publish Article		
	SEX			SEX		
MARITAL STATUS	Males (%)	Females (%)	GAMMA	Males (%)	Females (%)	GAMMA
Single	12	12	.000	16	12	.175
Married	19	10	.395	23	13	.343
Divorced/separated	14	13	.040	20	18	.069

* Smallest cell (divorced/separated males) has 79 unweighted cases.

caring for a husband and family, the student role may become secondary; hence, the lower publication rate.[4]

Socialization in graduate school takes place outside as well as inside formal settings such as classrooms or laboratories. Much of the development of commitment and professionalization takes place in informal interaction with fellow students (cf. Becker, Geer, Hughes, and Strauss 1961; Becker and Carper 1956; Fox 1957; Kadushin 1969). To a large extent, married women are denied this type of interaction (table 8, A). Although women in all three marital statuses are less likely than men to see their fellow students socially, the greatest differences are found between married men and women. Presumably, for many couples, most of their socializing is done with friends of the husband or mutual friends—not the wife's fellow students. While this arrangement usually works well for the male graduate student, the married woman is placed at a considerable disadvantage.

Full commitment to the student role involves making all other roles subordinate. The majority of graduate students do not give the student role primacy above all others, but differences between single and married men and women are minimal. Among divorced or separated individuals, sex differences are much greater. Whereas divorced men are least likely to subordinate everything else to their work, divorced women are most likely to do so. Apparently, divorced men are burdened with greater responsibilities than their single or married counterparts, while divorced women have reduced their responsibilities and are thus freer to pursue the student role. Few graduate students place career ahead of family; yet,

[4] Students in higher quality institutions are more likely to publish than those in low quality institutions. Women constitute about a quarter of the total enrollment in high quality, medium quality, and low quality universities.

TABLE 8

INFORMAL PEER INTERACTION AND CAREER PRIMACY, BY SEX AND MARITAL STATUS

| | SEX | | |
| | Males (%) | Females (%) | |
MARITAL STATUS			GAMMA
	A. About How Many of the People You See Socially Are Fellow Graduate Students in Your Department?—Stating "Almost None"		
Single	18	25	.194
Married	23	44	.402
Divorced/separated	19	33	.283
	B. I Tend to Subordinate All Aspects of My Life to My Work.— Strongly Agreeing, or Agreeing with Reservations		
Single	28	25	.136
Married	29	24	.173
Divorced/separated	23	38	.344
	C. My Career Will Take Second Place behind My Family Obligations.—Strongly Disagreeing, or Disagreeing with Reservations		
Single	33	27	.253
Married	30	18	.247
Divorced/separated	34	35	.013

among single and married graduate students, women are more family-oriented than men (table 8, C). By contrast, divorced or separated women are more likely than their single or married female counterparts to place career ahead of family. This pattern leads us to speculate that, in some instances, the conflict between the traditional family role and professional aspirations contributed to her divorce.

MARITAL STATUS AND FUTURE PLANS

Marital status also has an effect on the future plans of graduate students. Those studying in schools close to their homes are more likely than out-of-state graduate students to plan to remain in the state after they complete their graduate education (see table 9). Among single graduate students, 60% of the local men and women plan to remain in the state as compared with 20% of out-of-state men and 27% of out-of-state women. However, among married students, while out-of-state male students feel they are just as free as single men to leave, married women feel constrained to remain in the state of their graduate school. We see marriage having no effect on the plans for spatial mobility of men, while it has a strong effect on women, which may severely limit their job alternatives. On the other hand, among divorced students, male "locals" are more likely to

TABLE 9

FUTURE PLANS BY SEX AND MARITAL STATUS

A. INTENDING TO REMAIN IN STATE AFTER THEY COMPLETE THEIR GRADUATE
EDUCATION BY "I GREW UP IN THIS STATE," SEX, AND MARITAL STATUS*

| | Grew up in State of Graduate School | | | Did not Grow up in State of Graduate School | | |
| | SEX | | | SEX | | |
MARITAL STATUS	Males (%)	Females (%)	GAMMA	Males (%)	Females (%)	GAMMA
Single	59	61	.033	20	27	.201
Married	59	78	.305	22	52	.594
Divorced/separated	74	57	.395	28	52	.472

B. LEANING HEAVILY TOWARD TEACHING (RATHER THAN RESEARCH):
FUTURE COLLEGE OR UNIVERSITY TEACHERS ONLY

| | SEX | | |
MARITAL STATUS	Males (%)	Females (%)	GAMMA
Single	20	33	.216
Married	18	35	.308
Divorced/separated	54	22	.489

* Smallest cell (divorced males—grew up in state) had 51 unweighted cases.

plan to remain than female "locals." Previously, I noted a higher degree of emotional strain and a questioning of commitment among divorced men. It may be that they are better able to find a supportive relationship if they remain at home. Among out-of-state divorced students, women are much more likely to plan to remain in the state than men. They and their children may be more constrained than men by the local attachments they have developed more recently.

In American society, teaching has been deemed as an acceptable female occupation (cf. Epstein 1970, pp. 154–62). Among single or married students who plan careers in college or university teaching, women are more likely than men to be strongly oriented toward teaching than to research. However, there is a reversal among divorced students. Divorced women are the least likely to be strongly oriented toward teaching, while divorced men are most likely to be so. If divorce represents an escape for graduate women from the traditional family-oriented sex role, it may also serve to break the bonds of other aspects of the traditional female role. Divorced men are in a less secure position than married or single men. Under emotional and financial strain, teaching may offer more security than research.

Saul D. Feldman

MARITAL STATUS AND FINANCIAL CONDITIONS

Although marriage may have deleterious effects upon the student role for women, there are certain advantages. The popular stereotype of men being put through graduate school by their wives is somewhat true. Of married men, 60% state that their wife's job offers one source of income. But it is also true that married women are being put through graduate school by their husbands. Seventy-four percent of married female graduate students state that one source of their income is their husband's job.

Single men and women differ little in the perception of their financial situation (table 10, A). Like single graduate students, the majority of both

TABLE 10

FINANCES AND FINANCIAL AID BY SEX AND MARITAL STATUS

| MARITAL STATUS | SEX | | GAMMA |
	Males (%)	Females (%)	
A. Percentage Stating Their Current Finances Are Inadequate or Very Inadequate			
Single	26	30	.096
Married	32	25	.188
Divorced/separated	58	32	.298
B. Receiving a Fellowship during the Current (1968–69) Academic Year			
Single	27	33	.147
Married	28	30	.047
Divorced/separated	23	29	.169
C. Receiving a Teaching or Research Assistantship during Current (1968–69) Academic Year			
Single	31	27	.080
Married	35	29	.125
Divorced/separated	33	24	.221

married men and women tend to see their current financial situation as adequate. Divorced students, however, are far less content, with the men most discontented. Only 32% of the divorced women compared with 58% of the men view their current finances as inadequate or very inadequate.

Marital status appears to have very little effect on the receipt of financial aid. The general pattern is that men are more likely to receive teaching or research assistantships and women are more likely to receive fellowships (table 10, B, C). Decisions concerning financial aid may take into account sex but probably not marital status.

CONCLUSIONS

A consistent pattern appears in our data. There is conflict between the role of wife and the role of full-time graduate student. Married women students are under greater pressure to drop out, and, if they remain in school, they are less likely to engage in the forms of anticipatory or informal socialization that are important facets of graduate-student life. Once they leave graduate school, job opportunities are limited. Married men, on the other hand, feel little conflict between the role of spouse and the role of graduate student. They appear to be quite productive and the best-adjusted of all graduate students.

In comparing single and divorced women, I note that the most committed and active graduate students are divorced women. Once divorced or separated, it is almost as if they were making up for lost time by becoming fully immersed in the student role, despite the fact that almost 70% of the divorced female graduate students have at least one child. It appears that divorce becomes a force for liberation for women students, while it becomes a source of strain for men. Men lose a supportive relationship, while women lose a source of severe role conflict.

My data imply that, for some women, the following sequence occurs: from role conflict between the spouse and student roles, to divorce, to increased commitment to the student role. While I cannot establish causality, it does appear that marital status has an effect upon the student roles of both men and women; greatest "success," that is, ability to adhere to a career-primacy model, obtains among married men and divorced women. Durkheim (1951) wrote about the stabilizing effect of marriage upon men, and my data are consistent with his observations. But, while marriage lessens conflicts for men, it increases them for some women. Some women obviously choose divorce. Others become part-time students (indeed more women are enrolled on a part-time basis than men) and thereby reduce the conflict between their two roles. Others abandon their education.

The student and the marital roles are not independent. In some instances, they conflict, while in other instances they compliment one another. Role relationships do change, however, and the effect of marital status upon the student role depends upon adherence to the traditional spouse role. Less rigidity in adherence to traditional sex roles should limit some of the conflict between marital and student roles.

REFERENCES

Arreger, Constance E. 1966. *Graduate Women at Work*. Newcastle upon Tyne: Oriel.
Becker, Howard S., and James Carper. 1956. "The Development of Identification with an Occupation." *American Journal of Sociology* 61 (January): 289–98.

Saul D. Feldman

Becker, Howard S., Blanche Geer, Everett Hughes, and Anselm Strauss. 1961. *Boys in White*. Chicago: University of Chicago Press.

Coser, Rose Laub, and Gerald Rokoff. 1971. "Women in the Occupational World: Social Disruption and Conflict." *Social Problems* 18 (Spring): 535–54.

Cross, Patricia A. 1968. "College Women: A Research Description." Paper presented at 1968 annual meeting of National Association of Women Deans and Counselors. Mimeographed.

Darwin, Erasmus. 1797. *A Plan for the Conduct of Female Education in Boarding Schools*. Derby: Drewry.

Durkheim, Emile. 1951. *Suicide*. Translated by J. A. Spaulding and G. Simpson. New York: Free Press.

Epstein, Cynthia. 1970. *Women's Place*. Berkeley and Los Angeles: University of California Press.

Fox, Renee C. 1957. "Training for Uncertainty." In *The Student Physician,* edited by Robert K. Merton. Cambridge, Mass.: Harvard University Press.

Ginzberg, Eli. 1966. *Life Styles of Educated Women*. New York and London: Columbia University Press.

Goodsell, Willystine. 1923. *The Education of Women*. New York: Macmillan.

Hubback, Judith. 1957. *Wives Who Went to College*. London: Heinemann.

Kadushin, Charles. 1969. "The Professional Self-Concept of Music Students." *American Journal of Sociology* 75 (November): 389–405.

Lopate, Carol. 1968. *Women in Medicine*. Baltimore: Johns Hopkins University Press.

Poloma, Margaret M., and Neal Garland. 1970. "Role Conflict and the Married Professional Women." Paper presented at 1970 annual meeting of Ohio Valley Sociological Society, Akron. Mimeographed.

Slater, Philip. 1970. *The Pursuit of Loneliness*. Boston: Beacon.

Sommerkorn, Ingrid. 1966. "On the Position of Women in the University Teaching Profession in England." Ph.D. dissertation, University of London.

Trow, Martin A., et al. 1971. Technical Report: National Surveys of Higher Education. Berkeley, Calif.: Carnegie Commission on Higher Education. Mimeographed.

Turner, Ralph H. 1964. "Some Aspects of Women's Ambition." *American Journal of Sociology* 70 (November): 271–85.

Wells, D. Collin. 1909. "Some Questions Concerning the Higher Education of Women." *American Journal of Sociology* 14:731–39.

Performance, Rewards, and Perceptions of Sex Discrimination among Male and Female Faculty

Marianne A. Ferber and Jane W. Loeb
University of Illinois, Urbana

A number of investigators have recently raised questions concerning the relative productivity of men and women on university faculties and their relative rates of compensation (ERIC Clearinghouse on Higher Education 1971). It has generally been found that male and female faculty members are similarly productive, though not always similarly well rewarded (e.g., Loeb and Ferber 1972). Some correlates of productivity and reward among women have also been investigated. Simon, Clark, and Galway (1967), who investigated the relationship of productivity and reward to family responsibilities among women faculty members, found that, contrary to general expectation, married women were at least as productive as single women. Single women, on the other hand, tended to receive higher salaries and to attain higher ranks than married women. The present study relates marital and parental status to productivity, salary, and rank for men and women. In addition, productivity and reward of men and women are related to the percentage of the department which is female. The question here is whether "women's" fields differ from "men's" in either the productivity or the reward of their specialists. Finally, perceptions concerning the existence of sex discrimination in the academic department are related to such factors as marital and parental status, salary, rank, and age.

METHOD

A questionnaire was distributed in spring 1970 to 186 women holding the rank of at least instructor at the Urbana-Champaign campus of the University of Illinois, and to a sample of men matched with them on department and rank. Where several matches were possible, the male was randomly selected. The sample of women represented about half the women at academic rank, and all for whom a matching male was available. The requirement of a matching male eliminated from the sample a number of departments, including home economics, library science, and social work. Returned questionnaires numbered 278, or 75%.

Information requested included department; rank; number of years spent at each rank at the University of Illinois; marital status; number of children; whether spouse was employed by the university; age; sex; number of publications of seven types—books, books edited, bulletins and technical reports, reviews, papers read at meetings, articles, and other

233

Marianne A. Ferber and Jane W. Loeb

publications since 1965; number of professional honors since 1967; salary for the 1969–70 year; whether the respondent felt that women were afforded equal opportunity in his/her department. Those who thought that women were not afforded equal opportunity were asked to specify what kinds of discrimination exist.

The question concerning honors was open-ended, and hence varying types of responses were encountered, including grants, editorial positions, election to office in professional organizations, etc. Some individuals specified exact numbers, while others referred to "several" or "many." Each type of honor encountered was scored from 0 to 2, with a score of 2 meaning simply more than 1; and a "total honors" measure was derived by adding an individual's scores on all types of honors encountered in the sample.

Actual salaries were available for 1968–69 in published form (University of Illinois Board of Trustees 1968). The percentage of women in the department was computed from 1968–69 departmental lists.

Missing data correlations were calculated between all pairs of variables of interest, so that the N for each correlation coefficient consists of all individuals who answered both items being correlated.

RESULTS

Correlations of marital and parental status with publications, honors, salary, and rank are listed in table 1. While there is no relationship between publications and marital status for women, professional honors, higher salary, and rank are slightly but significantly more likely to be awarded to single than to married women. Among men, number of papers read at meetings tends to be correlated with marital status, while honors and rank are unrelated to this variable. Salary, however, bears the opposite relationship to marital status among men as compared with women: single females and married men are predicted to earn higher salaries than those of the same sex but the other marital status. Males are significantly more likely to be married than women.

Among women age is correlated with marital status: older women are more likely than younger ones to be single. Because of this correlation, which might itself account for the lower salaries, ranks, and number of honors of married women, age was partialed out of these correlations of honors, salary, and rank with marital status for the 139 female subjects who answered all five items. With age controlled in this fashion the correlation of marital status with rank was no longer significant, but honors and higher salary were still more likely to be achieved by single than by married women.

For women there is no significant relationship between parental responsi-

234

TABLE 1

RELATION OF MARITAL STATUS AND PARENTAL RESPONSIBILITY TO
PERFORMANCE AND REWARDS

	MARITAL STATUS[a]				PARENTAL RESPONSIBILITY[b]			
	Women		Men		Women		Men	
	N	r	N	r	N	r	N	r
Books	144	−.047	134	.128	143	.097	133	.162
Books edited	144	−.025	134	.105	143	.062	133	.149
Bulletins	144	−.039	134	.087	143	−.145	133	.009
Reviews	144	.016	134	.040	143	.113	133	.032
Papers read	144	−.054	134	.206*	143	−.040	133	.190*
Articles	144	.059	134	.167	143	.022	133	.038
Other publications ..	144	−.042	134	−.120	143	.099	133	−.059
Current salary	139	−.333*	127	.228*	139	−.114	126	.292*
	(139)	(−.275*)[c]						
Honors	144	−.194*	134	.150	143	−.117	133	.145
	(139)	(−.191*)[c]						
Rank[d]	143	−.243*	133	.157	142	−.085	132	.228*
	(139)	(−.152)[c]						
Age	142	−.229*	132	.010	142	.010	131	.148

	Combined		Combined	
	N	r	N	r
Sex[e]	278	.394*	276	.397*

[a] 2 = married; 1 = single.
[b] 1 = children; 0 = no children.
[c] Partial r with age partialed out.
[d] 4 = full professor; 3 = associate professor; 2 = assistant professor; 1 = instructor.
[e] 2 = male; 1 = female.
* Significant at .05 level.

bility and either productivity or reward. For men, number of papers read was correlated with whether a man had children. Men with children tended to earn significantly higher salaries and hold higher ranks than men without children. Finally, men were more likely to have children than were women in the sample.

The relationships between the percentage of the department members who are female and productivity and reward variables are reported in table 2. Women in fields with few women tend to write more bulletins and technical reports than do women in more heavily female fields. Individual salaries and ranks are unaffected by the percentage of women in the field, however. Among married women, those in more heavily female fields tend not to have a spouse at the university; rather, the "faculty wives" tend to be employed by the "men's" departments. Among men, productivity, salary, and rank are unaffected by the percentage of women in the field.

Table 3 reports correlates of perception of unequal treatment of men and women. Among women, married women tend significantly more often than single women to perceive unequal opportunity for women in their

TABLE 2

RELATION OF PERFORMANCE AND REWARDS TO PERCENTAGE OF FEMALES IN DEPARTMENT

	WOMEN		MEN	
	N	r	N	r
Books	144	.080	131	.039
Books edited	144	−.010	131	.108
Bulletins	144	−.237*	131	−.106
Reviews	144	.049	131	.028
Papers read	144	.022	131	.128
Articles	144	−.017	131	.000
Other publications	144	.122	131	−.139
Salary	139	−.019	124	−.060
Spouse at university[a]	71	.242*	112	.042
Honors	141	.038	131	.014
Rank[b]	143	.001	130	−.157
Children[c]	143	−.056	130	.024

[a] $2 =$ no; $1 =$ yes.
[b] $4 =$ full professor; $3 =$ associate professor; $2 =$ assistant professor; $1 =$ instructor.
[c] $1 =$ yes; $0 =$ no.
* $P < .05$.

TABLE 3

CORRELATES OF PERCEPTION CONCERNING EQUAL OPPORTUNITY

	WOMEN		MEN	
	N	r	N	r
Marital status[a]	122	.218*	108	−.015
Salary	119	−.126	102	−.195*
Age	121	−.031	107	−.121
Rank[b]	121	−.091	107	−.179
Salary[c]	122	.105	108	.027
Percentage female in department	122	−.165	105	−.049
Spouse at university[d]	60	−.160	92	.010
Children[e]	122	.137	107	.044

	COMBINED	
	N	r
Sex[f]	230	−.255*

NOTE.—Responses to the question concerning equal opportunity were scored 2 for no, 1 for yes.
[a] $2 =$ married; $1 =$ single.
[b] $4 =$ full professor; $3 =$ associate professor; $2 =$ assistant professor; $1 =$ instructor.
[c] Department mean/rank.
[d] $2 =$ no; $1 =$ yes.
[e] $1 =$ yes; $0 =$ no.
[f] $2 =$ male; $1 =$ female.
* $P < .05$.

departments. For women, this is the only significant predictor of tendency to perceive sex discrimination: age, salary, existence of children, rank, percentage of females in department, spouse at the university (for married women), and the difference between the individual's salary and the average salary for her department and rank were all uncorrelated with perception of sex discrimination. Among men, low salary predicted tendency to perceive sex discrimination, while none of the other variables was significantly related to perceived discrimination. Women were more likely than men to believe that the treatment of the sexes in their department was unequal.

Those subjects who did not believe that women were treated equally were asked to cite evidence of discrimination. A wide variety of symptoms was mentioned, ranging from very specific charges to one comment of "too disgusted to detail problems." Table 4 shows the types of evidence that

TABLE 4

EVIDENCE PERCEIVED OF DISCRIMINATION AGAINST WOMEN IN DEPARTMENT

	Women	Men	Total
Women hired at lower rank, more slowly promoted	32	10	42
Women paid less	30	6	36
Discrimination in hiring	16	13	29
Discriminated against in administrative and committee positions	21	2	23
Special discrimination against faculty wives	11	3	14
Women less likely to be given graduate standing and graduate students	7	0	7
Discrimination against women graduate students	5	1	6
Women given heavier work loads	6	0	6

NOTE.—Total number of women who responded to this question was 117; of men, 110.

were mentioned by more than five subjects. Subjects often mentioned more than one type of discrimination, so the total number of comments listed exceeds the total number of people who answered the question. Most frequent allegations by women included lower salary, slower promotion, and discriminatory assignment to administrative and committee positions for women. The one type of discriminatory practice mentioned nearly as often by men as by women was discrimination in hiring. Other complaints included special discrimination against faculty wives, discrimination against graduate students, and problems concerning the assignment of workloads and steering of thesis students to women.

DISCUSSION

The data reported here suggest that marital and parental status are not the bars to productivity by women that they are often assumed to be. Although married and single women are about equally productive, single women tend to be older and to be awarded more honors and higher rank and salary than married women. With age partialed out, greater honors and salary still tend to accrue to single than to married women. Furthermore, married women are more inclined to subscribe to the statement that women in their departments do not enjoy opportunity equal to that of men. Finally, women on the faculty tend to be single rather than married. The findings of this study are consistent with those of Simon, Clark, and Galway (1967), who noted that (1) although married and single women are about as productive as men, both lag behind men in salary and rank; and (2) single women are closer to men in salary and rank than are married women. Taken together, these data suggest that married women experience greater difficulty in being taken seriously than do single women. The correlation of age with women's marital status might suggest either a recent trend toward greater labor market participation by married women or a tendency for married women to be edged out of academe by such factors as low salary and inadequate recognition.

That current salary and rank are correlated with parental status for men but not women, that salary is higher for married than for single men, and that salary is higher for single than for married women suggest that reward tends to be scaled to perceived financial need. We have done a more detailed analysis (Ferber and Loeb 1972) of the current data which lends further support to this conclusion.

Because of the sampling process employed for the present study, very heavily male and female departments were excluded. Hence all generalizations about the relationship of the percentage of female faculty to productivity and reward apply only to the midrange of departments: those with some but not all female members.

By and large, productivity and reward are uncorrelated for either sex with the percentage of female members in the department. The zero correlation between salary and percentage female argues against the widely heard notion that increasing the number of males in a normally female-dominated field increases its "prestige" and hence its salary level. It is believed that because male salaries have been shown to exceed those of equally qualified females (Loeb and Ferber 1971), mean salaries will increase with proportions of men. However, the present data argue that individual salaries are unlikely to increase.

The significant tendency for women in fields which have a relatively high percentage of female professors *not* to be faculty wives suggests that these fields may be particularly disinclined to give regular appointments to faculty wives, perhaps because of the relatively large numbers of women asking them to do so. Although difficult to interpret with any confidence, this may be an empirical finding which can be quite helpful to investigators wanting to pinpoint particularly troublesome departments on a campus.

Age, salary, rank, and the difference between salary and the mean for a respondent's department and rank are uncorrelated with perception of sex discrimination among women. Rather, the only predictor of such perceptions is marital status. Among women, then, whether one has succeeded within the system does not appear to be related to this variable.

Among men, on the other hand, there seems to be some relationship between success and perception of sex discrimination. The correlation between salary and response to the equal-opportunity item suggests that it may be the less successful men who are critical of the system, while the more successful ones may tend to view merit as the only important determiner of success.

Some of the types of discrimination mentioned have been substantiated elsewhere. We reported evidence of discriminatory differences in the rank and pay of equally qualified men and women (Loeb and Ferber 1971). Interestingly, relatively few men volunteered awareness of these inequities. Similarly, we reported evidence of discrimination in hiring and in appointment to administrative and committee positions (Loeb and Ferber 1972). About as many males as females appear to be aware of the former but not the latter form of bias. Generally, this evidence suggests that women's perceptions of sex discrimination are more realistic than those of their male peers.

In summary, the picture of male and female faculty members that emerges from the current study is as follows. Married women with or without children are no less productive than single ones, yet appear to experience less success in academic life. Marital and, for men, parental status may enter reward decisions as a possible indicator of perceived financial need. Men and women in fields with relatively high concentrations of women appear to experience no deficit in productivity or reward: so-called upgrading of fields by increasing male participation is unlikely to affect individual rewards. In this sample, faculty wives tend to be emloyed in fields which are relatively masculine in hiring practices. Perception of sex discrimination appears to be more accurate among women than men; for example, considerably more women than men seem to be aware of salary and rank inequities which have been documented elsewhere. Among women, married women seem more aware than single women of discrimination, possibly because they have, as suggested earlier, experienced more of it.

REFERENCES

ERIC Clearinghouse on Higher Education. 1971. *Status of Academic Women.* Washington, D.C.: George Washington University.
Ferber, Marianne A., and Jane W. Loeb. 1972. "University Professors: Productivity and Rewards." Manuscript.
Loeb, Jane W., and Marianne A. Ferber. 1971. "Sex as Predictive of Salary and Status on a University Faculty." *Journal of Educational Measurement* 8 (Winter): 235–44.
————. 1972 (in press). "Representation, Performance, and Status of Women on the Faculty at the Urbana-Champaign Campus of the University of Illinois." In

Marianne A. Ferber and Jane W. Loeb

Academic Women on the Move, edited by Alice Rossi. New York: Russell Sage Foundation.

Simon, Rita J., Shirley M. Clark, and Kathleen Galway. 1967. "The Woman Ph.D.: A Recent Profile." *Social Problems* 15 (Fall): 221–36.

University of Illinois Board of Trustees. 1968. "Fifty-fourth Report, 1966–68 Supplement, Internal Operating Budget for 1968–69." *University of Illinois Bulletin,* vol. 66.

Social Relations of Black and White Widowed Women in a Northern Metropolis[1]

Helena Znaniecki Lopata
Loyola University of Chicago

Much social science literature on black Americans is based on Frazier's (1949) and Drake and Cayton's (1945) prewar descriptions of family life and assumes the centrality of a matrifocal structure (Billingsley 1968; Meier 1966). The idea that older black women are usually surrounded by their kin is present even in recent books. Scanzoni (1970, p. 134) asserts that in the black lower class several generations often live together in a family headed by a maternal grandmother. "In brief, this is an enduring and highly solidary group of related women who lean very heavily on one another for aid, comfort, and support" (Scanzoni 1970, p. 311).

That the proportion of black families headed by women is about 30% and that this proportion has increased substantially in the last two decades is true (U.S., Bureau of the Census 1971, p. 107). But it does not follow from these facts that older black widowed women tend to be surrounded by kin. Among black families headed by women, the proportion headed by widows has actually decreased in the last decade, from 42% in 1960 to 30% in 1970 (U.S., Bureau of the Census 1971, p. 131). The purpose of this report is to show that the great majority of older black widowed women are not part of an enduring kinship structure. Their social relationships closely resemble those of older white widows. As far as we know, this research is the first which attempts to contrast the social situation of older black and white widowed women.

This research is based on a modified area probability sample of 296 widows aged 50 and over in a major metropolitan area. The sample included 244 women identified as white and 52 women identified as black. The interviews were conducted in 1968 by researchers, mostly middle-aged, of the National Opinion Research Center for the author's four-year study of changes in roles and life-styles in widowhood. Because of the small number in the sample, the findings must be interpreted with great caution.

[1] This research was supported by Roosevelt University and grant AA-4-67-030-01-A1 from the Administration on Aging, Department of Health, Education, and Welfare. The National Opinion Research Center did the interviewing. I wish to thank Ethel Shanas, Robert Winch, Bernice Neugarten, and the members of the Midwest Council for Social Research on Aging for their help in the initial stages, and E. M. Znaniecki for her work in editing the manuscript. Richard Hill and William Bates helped with the statistical analyses and Paul Zelus, Daryl Chubin, and Frank Steinhart with statistical computations. The final version of this report was edited by Joan Huber.

Helena Znaniecki Lopata

As expected, the two samples showed substantively and statistically significant differences in a number of social characteristics. Almost all of the black women had migrated to Chicago, mostly from the rural South; about half of the white women were born in Chicago. Four-fifths of the blacks, in contrast to two-fifths of the whites, had had no schooling beyond the elementary level. Only about a tenth of the blacks, but almost half of the whites, were high school graduates. Blacks were more likely to be poor; 19% of blacks in contrast to 14% of whites had incomes less than $1,000 per year, while 26% of the white women and none of the black women had incomes higher than $5,000 per year (table 1). The age

TABLE 1

CURRENT INCOME OF BLACK AND WHITE WIDOWS (IN %)

	BLACK		WHITE	
LEVEL OF INCOME	%	N	%	N
Under $1,000	19	(9)	14	(32)
$1,000–$2,999	65	(31)	42	(93)
$3,000–$4,999	17	(8)	18	(41)
$5,000 or more	...	...	26	(57)
Total %	101		100	
Total N		(48)		(223)

distribution of the two samples was very close, but the black women had been widowed at an earlier age (table 2). The length of widowhood was

TABLE 2

CURRENT AGE AND AGE AT WIDOWHOOD OF BLACK AND WHITE WIDOWS (IN %)

	BLACK		WHITE	
AGE	%	N	%	N
Current age:				
50–59	29	(15)	25	(62)
60–69	35	(18)	40	(98)
70–79	31	(16)	25	(60)
80 and over	6	(3)	10	(24)
Total %	101		100	
Total N		(52)		(244)
Age when widowed:				
44 or less	31	(16)	14	(33)
45–54	25	(13)	35	(86)
55–64	27	(14)	34	(81)
65 and over	17	(9)	18	(44)
Total %	100		101	
Total N		(52)		(244)

therefore somewhat longer for the black women (table 3). About half of the black women were currently working, in contrast to about a third of

TABLE 3

LENGTH OF WIDOWHOOD OF BLACK AND WHITE WIDOWS (IN %)

LENGTH OF WIDOWHOOD	BLACK		WHITE	
	%	N	%	N
Less than 1 year to 6 years	42	(22)	39	(96)
7–14 years	17	(9)	35	(86)
15 years or more	40	(21)	25	(62)
Total %	99		99	
Total N		(52)		(244)

the white women. But only 16% of the white women reported that they had never worked, in contrast to 29% of the black women. Of the women who had worked, about half of the white women had been in the better-paid occupations: professional, managerial, clerical, and sales in contrast to less than a tenth of the blacks. About half of the blacks had worked as domestics. The work histories of most of the black respondents, whether as domestics, in laundries, factories, or restaurants, tended to be sporadic with a frequent change of job. Identification with the occupation or work group was rare. Most black respondents expressed sentiments similar to those of the woman who said, "All the work I ever done was hard work with little pay."

In past and present social relationships the two samples showed comparatively few differences. Past and current organizational memberships showed no statistically significant differences (table 4). About half of both groups belonged to no voluntary organizations when their husbands were living, and about two-thirds belonged to none at the time of the study. This relatively low participation is not surprising in view of the educational level and age of the respondents (cf. Komarovsky 1962; Lopata 1971). Blacks are sometimes thought to participate in religious activities more than whites, but in this study the differences in membership and participation in religious groups were slight (table 5). Before widowhood, 51% of the blacks and 43% of the whites had been members of some religious group. After widowhood, a parallel decline in membership occurred; 39% of the blacks and 32% of the whites reported membership at the time of the study. High current activity in religious groups was reported by only 27% of the blacks and 19% of the whites.

Differences in neighboring were slight (table 6). "Casual outdoor talking" is reported "frequently" by 47% of the whites and 36% of the

TABLE 4

PAST AND CURRENT ORGANIZATIONAL MEMBERSHIPS OF BLACK AND WHITE
WIDOWS (IN %)

	BLACK		WHITE	
NUMBER OF MEMBERSHIPS	%	N	%	N
Past:				
None	52	(27)	47	(115)
One	39	(20)	33	(80)
Two or more	10	(5)	20	(49)
Total %	101		100	
Total N		(52)		(244)
Current:				
None	65	(34)	64	(156)
One	25	(13)	14	(58)
Two or more	10	(5)	12	(30)
Total %	100		100	
Total N		(52)		(244)

TABLE 5

RELIGIOUS GROUP MEMBERSHIP AND PARTICIPATION OF BLACK AND WHITE
WIDOWS (IN %)

	BLACK		WHITE	
MEMBERSHIP	%	N	%	N
Before widowhood	51	(27)	43	(106)
Current membership	39	(20)	32	(77)
High current activity	27	(14)	19	(47)

TABLE 6

BLACK AND WHITE WIDOWS' INTERACTION WITH NEIGHBORS (IN %)

	FREQUENTLY		NEVER	
FORM OF NEIGHBORING	Black	White	Black	White
Casual outdoor talking	36	47	2	1
Borrow or lend	5	2	61	72
Drop in homes	12	15	24	31
Visit by invitation	7	10	46	32
Go together to meetings	7	5	68	80
Go out to dinner	2	4	85	70
Other activities	5	7	85	81

blacks, while 15% of whites and 12% of blacks "frequently" drop in at the homes of their neighbors. All other forms of neighboring are reported as "frequent" by less than a tenth of both groups.

In relationships with their siblings the two groups show very slight differences. Almost two-thirds of both groups of widows report little or no contact with siblings (table 7). Whites have a slightly higher rate of con-

TABLE 7

BLACK AND WHITE WIDOWS' CONTACT WITH SIBLINGS (IN %)

	BLACK		WHITE	
AVERAGE CONTACT	%	N	%	N
Little or none	65	(34)	62	(151)
Few times per month	21	(11)	24	(58)
Weekly/monthly	12	(6)	11	(26)
Daily/weekly	2	(1)	4	(9)
Total %	100		101	
Total N		(52)		(244)

tact than blacks. In their life histories the black women often make reference to contact with siblings. Often a sibling lived temporarily with the respondent during crisis situations, but such contacts are not a permanent part of the fabric of social life.

The idea that older black women, more than white, are likely to be surrounded by their children and grandchildren was not true of this sample. Two-thirds of both groups had no children living with them at the time of the study (table 8). A slightly higher proportion of black

TABLE 8

NUMBER OF CHILDREN LIVING WITH BLACK AND WHITE WIDOWS
(IN %)

	BLACK		WHITE	
NUMBER OF CHILDREN	%	N	%	N
None	67	(35)	67	(164)
One	29	(15)	24	(58)
Two or more	4	(2)	9	(22)
Total %	100		100	
Total N		(52)		(244)

women had one child with them, but the white women were more likely to have two or more in the household. The two groups differed considerably, however, in the marital status of the children who were living with them at the time of the study (table 9); 78% of the white children had

TABLE 9

MARITAL STATUS OF CHILDREN LIVING WITH BLACK AND WHITE WIDOWS
(IN %)

MARITAL STATUS	BLACK		WHITE	
	%	N	%	N
Married	33	(6)	16	(16)
Separated or divorced	28	(5)	2	(2)
Widowed	22	(4)	4	(4)
Never married	17	(3)	78	(78)
Total %	100		100	
Total N		(18)		(100)

never been married, in contrast to 17% of the black children, most of whom had been married, separated, divorced, or widowed. The reason for sharing the living quarters appears to differ, but the consequence for the widow's contact with her children is about the same.

The response to a series of questions concerning their attitudes toward their late husbands, toward marriage, their friends, and their children shows that the black women are less likely than the white to associate marriage with personal happiness and are more likely to feel that widows are exploited (table 10). Significantly lower proportions of the black women felt that their husbands had been good men, that their sex relations with their husband had been good, that their marriages had been above average. Almost twice as many black women reported that they had shared few common activities with their husbands. Both groups reported a minority who knew nothing about finances when their husbands died. But black women were much less likely to report that learning to make decisions was the hardest thing a widow had to do.

In contrast to 18% of white widows, 45% of the black widows felt that widows are often sexually propositioned, even by the husbands of their closest friends. That other women, if their husbands were around, were jealous of widows was a belief of 59% of the blacks and 39% of the whites. Although 61% of the blacks in contrast to only 36% of the whites felt that people take advantage of widows, 72% of the blacks felt that remarried widows were often unhappy, a view shared by only 49% of the whites. Fifty percent of the blacks in contrast to only 28% of the whites reported feeling sorry for their married friends because of the loss of freedom marriage involves. Interestingly, only 26% of the blacks and

TABLE 10

BLACK AND WHITE WIDOWS' ATTITUDES TOWARD LATE HUSBAND, MARRIAGE, CHILDREN, AND FRIENDS (IN %)*

| | BLACK | | WHITE | |
ATTITUDES ON SOCIAL RELATIONSHIPS	%	N	%	N
Husband very good man	76	(36)	94	(221)
Marriage above average	62	(30)	76	(172)
Sex relations with husband good	57	(24)	80	(153)
Few common activities with husband	48	(24)	24	(58)
Knew nothing of finances when husband died	29	(14)	25	(58)
Decision making hardest for widow to learn	37	(18)	61	(145)
Widows often sexually propositioned	45	(20)	18	(38)
Other women jealous of widows	59	(29)	39	(87)
People take advantage of widows	61	(30)	36	(84)
Remarried widows often unhappy	72	(36)	49	(98)
Feel sorry for married friends	50	(23)	28	(60)
Want more male companionship	26	(13)	20	(45)
Want more friends	53	(25)	34	(76)
Relatives one's only true friends	35	(16)	26	(80)
Old friends cannot be replaced	88	(44)	72	(160)
Adult children always want help	51	(25)	35	(76)
Sons more help than daughters	24	(12)	32	(60)

* Persons who failed to answer the question are not included in computing the percentages.

20% of the whites expressed a desire for more male companionship, although 53% of the blacks and 34% of the whites said that they would like to have more friends. But 88% of the blacks and 72% of the whites said that old friends could not be replaced, no matter how hard one tried.

Half of the black women, in contrast to about a third of the white, agreed that a big problem with adult children was that they always wanted favors such as baby-sitting, sewing, and the like. This difference is probably the result of the fact that black incomes are so low and black job security is so uncertain that the children of the black women are more likely to need help. Only a minority of both samples, 32% of the whites and 24% of the blacks, agreed that sons were more help than daughters.

That older widowed women tend to be somewhat isolated socially is hardly a startling finding. This research indicates that, contrary to the common assumption that older black widows live full and rich lives surrounded by kin, they are just as isolated as the whites. Almost all of the blacks were migrants from the rural South and had a significantly lower level of education than the whites. Their contacts with neighbors, siblings, and organizations was about the same as that of whites. Two-thirds had little or no contact with siblings, and two-thirds had no children in the home currently. Two-thirds belonged to no organizations, and about three-fifths belonged to no church. Older widows, both black and white, lead lonely lives.

Helena Znaniecki Lopata

REFERENCES

Billingsley, A. 1968. *Black Families in White America*. Englewood Cliffs, N.J.: Prentice-Hall.

Drake, St. C., and Horace Cayton. 1945. *Black Metropolis*. New York: Harcourt, Brace.

Frazier, E. F. 1949. *The Negro in the United States*. New York: Macmillan.

Komarovsky, Mirra. 1962. *Blue-Collar Marriage*. New York: Random House.

Lopata, Helena Znaniecki. 1971. *Occupation: Housewife*. New York: Oxford University Press.

Meier, A. 1966. "Review of 'Marriage and Family among Negroes,' edited by Jessie Bernard." Trans-Action 3 (July–August): 45–46.

Scanzoni, John. 1970. *The Black Family in Modern Society*. Rockleigh, N.J.: Allyn & Bacon.

U.S., Bureau of the Census. 1971. *Special Studies: The Social and Economic Status of Negroes in the United States, 1970*. BLS Report no. 394 and Current Population Reports, Series P-23, no. 38. Washington, D.C.: Government Printing Office.

A Review of Sex Role Research

Arlie Russell Hochschild
University of California, Berkeley

This review is offered as a guide to the questions and theoretical starting points of four types of research on sex roles. The range is both broader and more selective than in most reviews. Most of the articles and books were written after 1960, but I shall mention a few earlier ones when theoretical debates cross the decade. Most are within sociology but some are outside it; a few are about men but most about women; some have hard data, others soft, and still others none at all. Finally, I shall suggest what it would do to the rest of sociology were it to assimilate even a few "token" ideas.

More exhaustive reviews and annotated bibliographies have recently come out covering various aspects of women's role (Sells, in press; Suelzle, in press; Steinmann 1971; Spiegal 1969; Cisler 1972; Biggar 1970; Bruemmer 1970; Whaley 1972; Coelho et al. 1970). There are also specialized bibliographies on women's education (ERIC 1970; Kuvlesky and Reynolds 1970), on work (U.S., Department of Labor 1969, 1970; Hughes 1970; Frithioff 1969; Spiegel 1970a, 1970b) and on both education and work (Radcliffe Institute 1970; Astin, Suniewick, and Dweck 1971; Westervelt and Fixter 1971), on fertility (U.S., Department of Health, Education and Welfare 1970a; Keiffer and Warren 1970), and on marriage (National Council on Family Relations 1970; Laws 1971). In addition, some recent books have good bibliographies (Epstein 1970a; Maccoby 1966; Nye and Hoffman 1963). Theodore has collected 53 articles in her anthology, *The Professional Woman* (1971), and Safilios-Rothschild has collected 31 articles in her recent book, *Toward a Sociology of Women* (1972).

Most research in the social sciences is on male subjects (Holmes and Jorgensen 1971); yet there are significantly different findings on males and females (Carlson and Carlson 1960), which are often ignored. As a corrective, most sex role research is on women. There is little research on men in the family (but see Benson 1968), and less still on men qua men outside it. As measured by sheer volume, most of the traditional research on women has been in the sociology of the family (Bart 1971), and most of that concerns middle-class white women as housewives, college students, and professional workers. We have less on lower-class women (e.g., Rainwater, Coleman, and Handel 1959; Gavron 1966; Komarovsky 1969) or upper-class women (e.g., Domhoff 1970) and almost nothing on single or black women (but see Ladner 1972; Cole 1971).

There seems to be the same mix of methodologies in sex-role research as there is in sociology as a whole; most of it is survey research or secondary analysis of it. There is some content analysis (e.g., Martel 1968; Weitzman et al. 1972), and very little participant observation. In my view, many useful ideas come from nonsociologists. The literary critic Watt (1962), for example, links the step-by-step accounts of courtship in the earliest novels such as *Pamela* (the original female Horatio Alger) to the growing necessity for marriage as single women were pushed out of the parental family to earn a pauper's wage in the textile industry in 18th-century England. Fiedler (1966), in his chapter "Good Good Girls and Good Bad Boys, *Clarissa* as a Juvenile," explores some of the ambiguities of sex roles and social control. Other ideas come from historians (Welter 1966; Bridges 1965; Putnam 1910; Potter 1964) and from journalists. Langer's description of women in the telephone company, for example, is a classic on working women (1970).

In addition, some incidental research is on, but not *about,* sex roles. Some of the work on adolescence, old age, divorce, deviance, crime, small groups, demography, and social movements provides a treasure trove of information and ideas about sex roles. For example, in Neugarten's cross-sectional study based on Thematic Apperception Tests given to 131 men and women in their forties, fifties, and sixties, she found that "women, as they age, seem to become more tolerant of their own aggressive, egocentric impulses; whereas men, as they age, of their own nurturant and affiliative impulses" (Neugarten 1968, p. 71; also see Cumming and Henry 1961; Kagan and Moss 1962). Again, case studies of the families of 24 unemployed men during the Depression show that men with more leisure in which to do household work and child care in fact did even *less* than when they had worked full time. (Bakke 1940, sec. 2, pp. 109–243).

Some research on such social problems as mental illness, juvenile delinquency, and overpopulation focuses on the problems women cause rather than the ones they have. For example, the schizophrenia research of the 1940s and 1950s deals with the domineering "schizophrenogenic mother" (Kohn and Clausen 1956). Lidz, Fleck, and Cornelison in the 1960s link role reversal between mother and father to schizophrenia in the child (1965; but see Caputo 1963). Again, much research focuses on how a mother's work outside the home affects such things as her child's grades or proneness to delinquency. In some research it has a harmful effect, in some a good effect, and in some no effect (Hoffman 1961; Stolz 1960; Siegel and Haas 1963). Interestingly, the term is "maternal deprivation" for women and "father absence" for men.

FOUR TYPES OF RESEARCH

Apart from incidental research, the sociology of sex roles seems to reflect four main perspectives. The first is concerned with *sex differences*. Many of the studies here are done by psychologists, although they are often cited by sociologists. The second is concerned with *sex roles* and the norms which govern them. This is still the most common perspective in the field. The third is concerned with women as a *minority group,* and the fourth, the *politics of caste* perspective, carries the minority perspective in a different direction. Each perspective permits both macro- and microanalysis, a stress on both structural and superstructural variables, on both conflict and consensus; but the blend is in each case different. Some of the assumptions shared by all four perspectives are not shared by sociologists outside the field, but among the four there are differences too. They vary and hold constant different variables.

The first type deals with sex differences; the rest, in different ways, deal more with sex equality. I shall first compare them, focusing on the last three, before discussing how they deal with sex inequality—via role strain (type 2), discrimination, prejudice and segregation (type 3), and power differences (type 4). Most assume a plasticity of human nature; Talcott Parsons and Alice Rossi would at least agree on that. But they have different assumptions about the plasticity of the social structure. Whereas those in the first type, and the Parsonsians in the second, assume the division of labor between men and women, most of the rest take it as the problem to be explained, and focus on its dysfunctions for the society (e.g., the "brain drain") or for the individual ("role strain").

Beyond that, they use different conceptual vocabularies; type 1 analyzes measures of emotive and cognitive "traits"; type 2 discusses roles, role models, role conflict; type 3, prejudice, assimilation, marginality; and type 4, interest and power. Each puts a different construction on the behavior of the two sexes; what to type 1 is a feminine trait such as passivity is to type 2 a role element, to type 3 is a minority characteristic, and to type 4 is a response to powerlessness. Social change might also look somewhat different according to each perspective; differences disappear, deviance becomes normal, the minority group assimilates, or power is equalized.

Each perspective sees the family differently too. Type 2 sees the family as a social system, or as a role set generating its own conflicts or strains. In the minority perspective, the family is less important, since it is precisely here that the analogy to blacks and other minorities breaks down; and in the final perspective, the family is an important area of latent bargains, of profit and loss.

Each of these perspectives has different intellectual roots. The role perspective draws on George Herbert Mead, Charles Cooley, Ralph Linton, Florian Znaniecki, Talcott Parsons, Robert Merton, and Mirra Komarovsky, who have influenced the work of such modern-day sociologists as P. Bart, H. Lopata, and J. L. Blumen. The minority perspective, on the other hand, draws more from R. Park, L. Wirth, and E. Stonequist. Just as G. Berreman brought caste theory from India to American blacks, so Myrdal brought it in 1944 for modern sociology from blacks to women, to be further elaborated in 1951 by Hacker and more recently by Werner, Wellman, and Weitzman (1971), and others. The politics-of-caste perspective, by contrast, draws more directly on feminist theory from J. S. Mill's *The Subjection of Women* (1869), revived by Rossi (1970), through Gilman's work, *Women and Economics* ([1898] 1966) and Simone de Beauvoir's *The Second Sex* (1951) to Alice Rossi's modern classic, "The Equality of Women: An Immodest Proposal" (1964). In addition, feminist writings from Kate Millet and Shulamuth Firestone to Juliet Mitchell have been making their way into sociology through recent generations of female graduate students.

Meanwhile, Marx and Freud have come in from the side to be incorporated into role perspective by Parsons and Bales (1953) and to be refuted (Weisstein 1969) or revised (Firestone 1970; Sampson 1965) or partly incorporated (Collins 1971) by the politics of caste. There is not only the "straight" Freud and the "revised" Freud but the "hip" Freud of Philip Slater, introduced into feminist sociology via Millman (1970), who suggests that society preserves and keeps visible its rejected and denied impulses by depositing them in a special group container which "serves as a kind of safety valve to drain off and confine those impulses which conflict with the conscious dominant values." Thus, man retains his affective neutrality by keeping women's emotional lives in a "psychological zoo" where the animal can be appreciated from a safe distance.

Marx's influence also has a "right" and "left" side, both of which bypass the first two types of research. On the right, Marxist theory supports the notion that class, not sex, is the relevant unit of analysis. On the left, such writers as Juliet Mitchell note that women have their unique relation to the mode of production. Like serfs and peasants, housewives have remained at a preindustrial stage, doing work with "use value" but not "exchange value" (Benston 1969). Via the works of Frederick Engels and Thorstein Veblen, the notion of women as property comes in either as "sexual property" (Gilman 1966; Collins 1971) or as an item of "vicarious conspicuous consumption" (Veblen 1953).

Only in the fourth perspective is the notion of "exploitation" explicit, and there it is ambiguous. As the term passed into sociology with the works of E. A. Ross, Von Wiese, and Howard Becker, its meaning was generalized beyond its original reference to economic exploitation, and it has since fallen into disrepute. Following Gouldner (1960), we might resist dismissing it because of its heuristic overload and use it as in type 4, to mean simply "transactions involving an exchange of things of unequal value."

Underlying the four perspectives are, perhaps, implicit models of equality (Rossi 1969a): a pluralist model which envisages a society which keeps and values race, religious, and sex differences (types 1 and partly 2), an assimilation model which envisages minority groups gradually assimilating to the dominant culture (type 3), and a hybrid model which envisages a change in both the majority and the minority, resulting in a "melting pot" (type 4).

TYPE 1: SEX DIFFERENCES

The sexes differ in the way they think (Maccoby 1966), perceive (Bieri et al. 1958), aspire (Horner 1968; Turner 1964), experience anxiety (Sinick 1956), daydream (Singer 1968), and play competitive games (Uesugi and Vinachke 1963). (Men tend to have an exploitative strategy, women an accommodative one, which even wins some games.)

Some studies document these differences; others try to explain them as due to hormones, chromosomes, internal organs, or instinct, on one hand, or upbringing, on the other. In its popular form, it is Sigmund Freud versus the early Margaret Mead, Lionel Tiger versus the feminist anthropologists, and Erik Erikson (1965) versus Naomi Weisstein (1969) and Kate Millet (1970). Actually, in Erikson's own unpublished replication on Indian children of his "inner and outer space" study, the Indian boys did not build towers.

The literature is so vast that I shall cite only a few examples from the work on cognition. Very young girls exceed boys in verbal ability (talking, reading), they do as well in counting and spatial tasks (form boards and block design) and in analytic tasks, and they do better on certain measures of creativity and not on others. But on virtually every measure, boys sooner or later do better (Maccoby 1966; Bradway and Thompson 1952). These abilities are often linked to various traits such as impulse control, fearfulness, anxiety, aggressiveness, competitiveness, degree of aspiration, and need for achievement (Maccoby 1956; Freeman 1970; Suter 1972). These traits are related, in turn, to measures of "masculinity" and "femininity."[1] However, several studies suggest that analytic thinking, creativity, and high general intelligence are linked to cross-sex typing, that is, boys with "feminine" interests and girls with "masculine" ones (Maccoby 1966).

There are two kinds of debate within this genre of research; the first is between biological and sociocultural explanations for sex differences and the second is between various socialization theories. The biological argu-

---

[1] Rosenberg compares the "masculine" and "feminine" typology to the ancient choleric, sanguine, phlegmatic, or melancholic types also based on biology (Rosenberg and Smith 1972, p. 3).

ment usually grounds itself in selected research on animals, neonates, and hormone experiments (Rosenberg and Smith 1972), whereas the socio-cultural argument selects other research on animals, questions the general relevance to human behavior, and cites the data on cultural variation (Barry, Bacon, and Child 1957; Mead 1935, 1949; but see Thurnwald 1936; Mead 1937; Weisstein 1969). One interesting study suggests cul-ture's effect, not on sex differences, but on female biology itself; the pain of menstrual cramps was significantly higher for Catholics and Jews than for Protestants (Paige 1969).

The second debate is between various socialization theorists. In Mischel's "social learning" view, children early learn to discriminate between "boy things" and "girl things" and later generalize to new situations. According to Kohlberg, on the other hand, socialization stimulates or retards basic male and female modes of cognition, pretty much regardless of what parents do or say (Maccoby 1966). These cognitive modes are based on how the young child categorizes himself or herself, and sex-linked values "develop out of the need to value things that are consistent with or like the self" (p. 165). But we know that girls as they grow up learn to value boys more and girls less (Smith 1939; Kitay 1940; McKee and Sherriffs 1956; Mendelsohn and Dobie 1970).

Thus, beyond social and biological differences are status differences, as yet dimly recognized in much type 1 research. Moreover, how American middle-class boys and girls do block designs has not yet been systematically compared with the efforts of Arapesh and Mundugumor or Arab and Chinese girls and boys. Nor do we have research on the effect of early socialization in the *absence* of later social controls which maintain or accentuate the differences.

TYPE 2: THE ROLE PERSPECTIVE

Role studies usually deal with women in the family and in the economy, and with the "cultural contradictions" of being in both. Many studies of school and college girls try to isolate the cultural ingredients of the career woman and the homebody (Rapoport and Rapoport 1971; Olesen 1961) or to show how such influences as picture books (Weitzman et al. 1972), school counselors, and parents (Aberle and Naegele 1968) socialize girls.

Beyond the few studies of lower-class women and black women men-tioned earlier, most of the research discusses white middle-class wives and mothers, and we have a few comparisons between classes (Rainwater, Coleman, and Handel 1959; Gavron 1966). Lopata's study (1971) of 299 housewives in suburban Chicago in the 1950s is a good biography of the "new" traditional role; nearly all had worked at some point. Other works focus on couples' friendships (Babchuk and Bates 1964), on changes through the life cycle (Bart 1970; Neugarten 1961), and on the parenthood of married (Rossi 1968) and unmarried couples (Vincent 1962).

It is always helpful to have a "devil" and some of these studies have tangled with Parsons's functionalist interpretation of the woman in the family. According to Parsons and Bales (1953), in the nuclear family everywhere there is an "instrumental" role (mediating between the family and the outside) and an "expressive" role (concerned with relations within the family). The father usually takes the first, the mother the second, and this is functional for the children, the parents, and the society. Implicitly the career wife is dysfunctional. Attacking Parsons on one flank through psychoanalytic theory, Slater (1964) shows that such a role differentiation can impede a girl's identification with her mother and a boy's with his father. Rossi attacks from the flank of role theory, drawing from type 1 research (Rossi 1968). Other things being equal, the career wife may well put a strain on the family, but it is precisely the "other things" which role theorists are now examining. Both mother and father, according to Parsons, are more powerful than children; but he says virtually nothing about power differences between husband and wife—the source of another debate between Blood and Wolfe (1960) and Gillespie (1971). Komarovsky, also a functionalist, focuses more than Parsons on the dysfunctions (of role differentiation), and she locates the problems in a different place. For example, she argues that women still bound by the apron strings, but married to men who are not, create "in-law" problems (Komarovsky 1950).

The recent research on women at work has yet to filter into the traditional preserve of family theory. About half of employed women are in jobs such as nursing or clerical work where over 70% of the workers are women (Oppenheimer 1968; also see Baker 1969; Smuts 1971). Most research is on the other half of working women, especially those in "male" professions (Epstein 1970a; Bernard 1964; Mattfeld and Van Aken 1965; Williams 1964; Fava 1960; White 1967; Simon, Clark, and Galway 1967; Rossi 1969b; Astin 1969; Theodore 1971; Hennig 1971).

There is a large body of literature on the "dual roles," much of it, like Myrdal and Klein's *Women's Two Roles: Home and Work* (1956), done in the 1950s, but some, like the Ginzberg studies (Ginzberg and Yohalem 1966), done or published in the 1960s. The "cultural contradictions" of these roles (Komarovsky 1946; Wallin 1950) are explored in Horner's well-known work on women's will to fail (1968), recently replicated by Katz (1972). Only a third of the 1972 sample, compared with two-thirds in the Horner study, showed the motive to avoid success. Another response to the dilemma, of course, is simply not to choose, or to decide to do everything; Rose found that college women, even in the fifties, planned to work full time, to volunteer for church and community work, to entertain, and to raise a large family (1951). This fits with Wilensky's finding that women who work simply add it on to other tasks (1968).

Virtually all the research shows that married career women have—or need—supportive husbands (Rapoport and Rapoport 1971). Bailyn's study (1971) of 200 British women and their husbands shows that men who scale down their career involvement, rather than those who go full steam or those who severely curtail it, have happier marriages. But whatever his career commitment, it seems that a man wants his wife to be more oriented to his than to her work (see Komarovsky in this volume), and this, according to Holmstrom's latest study, even for women Ph.D.s, is how it works out (1971).

TYPE 3: MINORITY PERSPECTIVE

A minority group, as Louis Wirth defined it, is "a group who because of their physical or cultural characteristics, are singled out from others in the society for differential and unequal treatment, and who therefore regard themselves as objects of collective discrimination" (Hacker 1951, p. 60). The research treats both the objective and subjective sides of minority status. Many studies draw the parallel with blacks, ranging from similarities in discrimination and prejudice to subjective traits such as passivity and helplessness to similarities in such things as the meaning of consumption; in the case of blacks, it's the Cadillac and magenta shirt, and in the case of women, the proverbial expensive new hat (Willis 1970). Both women and blacks have been portrayed as the hero, more courageous and noble than the ordinary, unoppressed mortal, and as the sambo, more childlike and stupid. Warner, Wellman, and Wietzman (1971) suggest a third model, the operator, who uses these images to get his or her way. The female operator, as part of the underdog psychopolitical style, has a heightened awareness of her situation and knows more although she disguises her own feelings. Shuffling, playing dumb, playing up, and dissembling are so many manipulative strategies of rational actors in oppressive circumstances.

Many studies deal with the prevailing prejudice and discrimination to which this is a response. In his landmark study of prejudice, Goldberg gave 140 college women six articles in both "masculine" fields (e.g., law and city planning) and "feminine" fields (e.g., art history, dietetics). There were two identical sets of each article signed by J. T. McKay. Some named the author as John T. McKay, others as Joan T. McKay. The students rated the articles for value, persuasiveness, profundity, writing style, professional competence, professional status, and ability to sway the reader. In both the male and female fields, the students thought

John McKay more impressive; out of 54 comparisons, 44 favored John. The experiment illustrates not only the belief that females are inferior and the distorting effect of that belief on judgment, but also the women's *sensitivity* to something as apparently irrelevant as the author's sex (Goldberg 1968).

Using the identical procedure, Pheterson (1969) explored prejudice against women among middle-aged, uneducated women. This time the professional articles were on child discipline, special education, and marriage. The women judged female work to be equal to and even a bit better than male work. In a third study, Pheterson, Kiesler, and Goldberg (1971) reasoned that uneducated women may see an article in print as an achievement in itself, and may overvalue female accomplishment because it is so rare. They then showed eight paintings to 120 female students. Half of the sample thought the artist was a man, half thought it a woman; half thought the painting was just an entry, half thought it a prize-winning painting. Also half thought the artist had faced unusually severe obstacles, and half thought the artist had faced no unusual obstacles. The women judged the female entry less favorably than identical male entries, but judged the female winners equal to identical male winners. Thus, women devalued the work of women in competition until it received recognition, but of course, given the bias against triers, that recognition is hard for a woman to earn.

We can distinguish between paternalistic sex relations in which people "know their place" and in which overt conflict is rare, and competitive sex relations, where people don't know their place and overt conflict is more common (Van den Berge 1966). In the legal system, women, like juveniles, in some ways fit the paternalistic model (Nagel and Weitzman 1971). In the economy, sex relations seem to fit the competitive model, although possibly more in academia or business than in nursing or organized crime, where the paternalistic model may fit better.

In the competitive model, women are more likely to complain of discrimination, and a number of studies examine who does and who does not recognize or experience it. For example, Astin, in her study of women who earned Ph.D.'s in the late fifties, found over a third who said they had experienced discrimination. This third also published more, had gone to more professional meetings, and earned more (Astin 1969). According to Simon's nationwide study, 15% of married women Ph.D.'s reported running into nepotism rules; and, again, these women had published more than the men or other women in the sample (Simon, Clark, and Galway 1967). Another study of 2,500 male and female lawyers found that half the women lawyers said they had been discriminated against (White 1967).

Another approach is to look at those who do the discriminating. Fidell

(1970) sent out 10 job applications to 155 college and university graduate psychology departments, and found that male applications received more offers for associate and full professorships, though not more assistant or lower-status offers.

The "marginal woman" is probably more common in the *almost* all-male preserves than in the predominantly female or integrated occupations (Hacker 1951; Stonequist 1961). Like George Simmel's "stranger," and Thorstein Veblen's intellectual Jew, she faces more contradictions than do women who are less, or more, integrated into the male work world. As the position of women improves (and recently it has not), the proportion of marginal women will probably increase. Yet we know little about how marginality affects, say, a woman lawyer's feelings about housewives or office workers, or how she might compare with the assimilated black bourgeois in relation to his "brother" in the ghetto.

TYPE 4:   THE POLITICS OF CASTE

Despite overlap between the last perspective and this, the politics of caste is newer and less coherently developed; it has a different center and is going in a different direction. Its stress is on power, the different kinds of power, its distribution, use, and expression, in the parlor and in the marketplace.

As in the minority perspective, the *Realpolitik* view assumes that sex differences are due to socialization, and that differences in socialization are linked to differences in status and power. It sees role strain in power terms, and it takes as assumptions many of the questions in the minority perspective: that women are an inferior caste and experience discrimination and prejudice. It also assumes that what women as a stratum gain in resources, men as a stratum lose; thus its research comes closer to a conflict model than types 1 and 2.

As in the minority perspective, there is a social-psychological analogue to its macroanalysis. The balance of power in society is linked, in complex ways not yet understood, to various characteristics of face-to-face interaction. We have such propositions as the following: The subordinate is more "oriented" toward the superordinate. Just as the student "psychs out" the professor, and the child works his or her way around parental mood, so, too, the woman may be more oriented toward her husband than he is to her. The superordinate initiates more interactions, while the subordinate is typically more passive. The superordinate has the right to exercise certain familiarities (touching, whistling, calling, first-naming) which the subordinate cannot do (Brown 1965). The superordinate also maintains more social distance than does the subordinate. The superordinate is less likely to disclose information about him/herself than vice versa, so that "information about oneself flows opposite to the flow of power" (Henley 1972; Jourard and Lasakow 1958; Jourard and Rubin 1968). This contradicts the observation of Warner et al. that the oppressed "operator" disguises his/her feelings and knows *more* about the superordinate than the superordinate knows about him/her (Warner, Wellman, and Weitzman 1971). These behavioral regularities may vary with factors unrelated to differences in status or power—for example, nationality. Furthermore, there is some counter evidence that needs to be examined. For example, Jourard found that whites had higher self disclosure rates than did blacks, although females had higher rates than males (Jourard and Lasakow 1958, p. 95).

Interaction can be verbal or nonverbal, as, for example, in body movement (kinesics), the use of personal space (proximics), and the noncontent aspects of speech (paralanguage). The stress here is not on dominant or submissive personalities but on behaviors, although there is some question about whether these behaviors are related to personality as Maslow (1939) and Sampson (1965) suggest. Erving Goffman has recently applied his grammar of face-to-face interaction to males and females. He has categorized various types of "tie-sign" (the arm lock, hand holding, the back and shoulder embrace, ecological proximity) in body behavior and verbal behavior (e.g., the three-quarter terms such as "honey" and "baby" which men and women can say to each other, and women to women but not men to men). His comparisons with other asymmetrical relations such as parent and child suggest a link to the larger political fabric (Goffman 1972).

Another exploratory study, based on 60 hours of observation of "touch," found that high-status persons (older, white, male) touch lower-status persons (younger, black, female) more than the other way around (Henley 1972). Body position and movement may also have power meanings (e.g., the head tilt and leaning as opposed to a "taut" posture). Self-disclosure, personal space, and touch may be "status reminders" and, as such, forms of informal social control. We do not know to what extent they are indicators or reinforcers of interpersonal control (Spitze 1972). But insofar as they operate in daily life they provide an alternative or supplement to the socialization theory of type 3 (Leffler, Gillespie, and Spitze 1972).

In the macropolitics of caste, Collins's recent article "A Conflict Theory of Sexual Stratification" (1971) stands out. Welding Freud's notion of sexual repression onto a Weberian social-economic history, he outlines a bargaining model of sex stratification (also see Lasch 1967). Theoretically both men and women have the same resources to bargain with—for example, income, sexual attractiveness, or social status. But these resources are not equally available to men and women; men have generally monopolized the wealth, and women, to recoup some power, have made more of a resource of their sexuality by controlling and repressing it, thus making it "cost" something (see Waller 1937). But the pattern varies with history, and with the social control of force. Collins outlines four ideal types of social structure and control of force (for instance, household head or police force), resources available to men and women, sex roles, and ideologies. The old trade of income for sex in the earlier types of social structure changes in the last type, so that women increasingly use income as a resource, and men, increasingly, sexuality. Even in the new distribution and use of resources, however, the market favors men, and the old trade still operates too.

IMPLICATIONS

Despite the diversity, the research in this field yields some questions, data, and ideas (and biases) which can infuse sociology from the ground floor up. It may make sociologists trim their generalizations to size; thus studies of social mobility will have to specify that they concern *male* social mobility, alienation, *man's* alienation. Potter (1964) has done just this specifying of propositions for historical writing. It can also question some key assumptions. For example, most stratification research defines the social class of the family, not the individuals in it; but some estimate that this assumption fails to fit a full two-fifths of American households which consist of females, are headed by females, or are husband-wife families where the husband is retired, unemployed, working part time, or otherwise not in the labor force (Watson and Barth 1964; see also Acker, in this volume).

The sociology of sex roles is not simply adding onto sociology studies about women, though clearly there is a need for this too. Until recently, the research on achievement motivation and birth order was virtually all on male subjects. The sociology of sex roles is research on anyone or anything which reflects, in its assumptions and propositions, one of the perspectives described here, and which takes sex roles in some way to be an important independent variable. This may mean more research on men. Much of the work on dominance gestures is based on a mixed male and female sample. Rossi's (1970) study in the sociology of knowledge focuses on the male biographers of Harriet Taylor Mill.

As a result of some of this work, researchers may even alter their vocabulary. Women have been consistently found to be more "field dependent" (i.e., less able to separate figure from ground); but, as Bart (1972) notes, "it is very useful to be aware of the 'ground' or 'environment.' In any case, not being able to see the forest for the trees [is] not superior to not being able to see the trees for the forest." The term in some research is now "field sensitive."

But most of all this new field means turning former assumptions into new research problems. We don't even know whether, let alone how, women's position has improved with industrialization. According to modernization theorists, as a society develops, the importance of ascription declines, achievement rises, and the position of women improves. As measured by income, education, and occupation, we know women's status (relative to men's) has declined in the last 25 years (Knudsen 1969). But even before that, the picture is unclear. Smith notes a decline from the Puritan era to the 19th century, especially at the end of the 18th century (Smith 1970). And in an excellent economic study of women in the underdeveloped world, Boserup shows that as industrialization rises, the position of women declines (1970; also see Sullerot 1971, p. 35) We also know little about the link between class and caste. The ideology of the companionate marriage to the contrary, is the caste gap greater in the upper classes than in the lower (Goode 1970, p. 21)? Do more rigid class barriers mean less rigid caste barriers, or do these structural rigidities occur in all ways at once? What changes have occurred in the avenues of female mobility? Were witchcraft and spiritualism, for example, early means of female social mobility?

In the study of modern societies or traditional, upper-class or lower-, white or black, now or in the 18th century, the issue of sex roles is the single biggest blind spot in existing sociology. While sociology, like the American government, is gifted at "resistance through incorporation," we may nonetheless move slowly to a sociology of people.

REFERENCES

Aberle, David F., and Kaspar Naegele. 1968. "Middle-Class Fathers' Occupational Role and Attitudes toward Children." In *The Family,* edited by N. W. and E. F. Vogel. New York: Free Press.

Astin, Helen. 1969. *The Woman Doctorate in America.* New York: Russell Sage Foundation.

Astin, Helen, Nancy Suniewick, and Susan Dweck. 1971. *Women, a Bibliography on Their Education and Careers.* Washington, D.C.: Human Service Press.

Babchuk, N., and A. Bates. 1964. "The Primary Relations of Middle Class Couples." *Readings on the Family and Society,* edited by W. J. Goode. Englewood Cliffs, N.J.: Prentice-Hall.

Bailyn, Lotte. 1971. "Career and Family Orientations of Husbands and Wives in Relation to Marital Happiness." In *The Professional Woman,* edited by Athena Theodore. Cambridge, Mass.: Schenkman.

Baker, Elizabeth. 1969. *Technology and Women's Work.* New York: Columbia University Press.

Bakke, E. Wight. 1940. *Citizens without Work.* New Haven, Conn.: Yale University Press.

Barry, Herbert, M. K. Bacon, and Irvin L. Child. 1957. "A Cross Cultural Survey of Some Sex Differences in Socialization." *Journal of Abnormal and Social Psychology* 55 (November): 327–32.

Bart, Pauline. 1970. "Mother Portnoy's Complaints." *Trans-Action* 8 (November-December): 69–74.

Arlie Russell Hochschild

———, ed. 1971. Special Issue: "Sexism in Family Studies." *Journal of Marriage and the Family,* vol. 33 (August).

Benson, Leonard. 1968. *Fatherhood: A Sociological Perspective.* New York: Random House.

Benston, Margaret. 1969. "The Political Economy of Women's Liberation." *Monthly Review,* vol. 21 (September).

Bernard, Jessie. 1964. *Academic Women.* University Park: Pennsylvania State University Press.

———. 1966. *Marriage and Family among Negroes.* New York: Prentice-Hall.

Bieri, J., et al. 1958. "Sex Differences in Perceptual Behavior." *Journal of Personality* 26(1): 1–12.

Biggar, Jeanne C. 1970. *Bibliography on the Sociology of Sex Roles.* Charlottesville: Department of Sociology, University of Virginia.

Blood, Robert Jr., and Donald M. Wolfe. 1960. *Husbands and Wives: The Dynamics of Married Living.* New York: Macmillan.

Boserup, Ester. 1970. *Woman's Role in Economic Development.* New York: St. Martin's.

Bradway, Katherine P., and Clare W. Thompson. 1952. "Intelligence at Adulthood: A 25 Year Follow-up." *Journal of Educational Psychology* 53(1): 1–14.

Bridges, W. 1965. "Family Patterns and Social Values in America, 1825–1875." *American Quarterly* 17 (Spring): 3–11.

Brown, R. 1965. *Social Psychology.* Glencoe, Ill.: Free Press.

Bruemmer, Linda. 1970. "The Condition of Women in Society Today: Annotated Bibliography—Part II." *Journal of the National Association of Women Deans and Counselors* 33 (Winter): 89–95.

Caputo, D. 1963. "The Parents of the Schizophrenic." *Family Process* 2(3): 339–56.

Carlson, Earl, and Rae Carlson. 1960. "Male and Female Subjects in Personality Research." *Journal of Abnormal and Social Psychology* 61 (February): 482–83.

Cisler, Lucinda. 1972. "Women: A Bibliography." 102 West 80th Street, New York, N.Y.

Coelho, George, David Hamburg, Rudolph Moos, and Peter Randolph, eds. 1970. *Coping and Adaptation: A Behavioral Sciences Bibliography.* National Institute of Mental Health; U.S., Department of Health, Education and Welfare; Public Health Service; Health Service and Mental Health Administration. Washington, D.C.: Government Printing Office.

Cole, Johnneta B. 1971. "Black Women in America: An Annotated Bibliography." *Black Scholar* 3 (December): 42–53.

Collins, Randall. 1971. "A Conflict Theory of Sexual Stratification." *Social Problems* 19 (Summer): 3–12.

Cumming, Elaine, and William Henry. 1961. *Growing Old: The Process of Disengagement.* New York: Basic.

Domhoff, G. William. 1970. "The Feminine Half of the Upper Class." In *The Upper Circles.* New York: Random House.

Epstein, Cynthia. 1970a. *Woman's Place.* Berkeley: University of California Press.

———. 1970b. "Encountering the Male Establishment: Sex Status Limits Careers in the Professions." *American Journal of Sociology* 75(6): 965–82.

ERIC Clearinghouse on Adult Education. 1970. *Continuing Education of Women, Current Information Sources,* vol. 32 (September). Syracuse, N.Y.: ERIC Clearinghouse on Adult Education.

Erikson, Erik. 1965. "Inner and Outer Space: Reflections on Womanhood." In *The Woman in America,* edited by Robert Lifton. Boston. Houghton Mifflin.

Fava, Sylvia. 1960. "The Status of Women in Professional Sociology." *American Sociological Review* 25 (April): 271–76.

Fidell, L. S. 1970. "Empirical Verification of Sex Discrimination in Hiring Practices in Psychology." *American Psychologist* 25(12): 1094–98.

Fiedler, Leslie A. 1966. "Good Good Girls and Good Bad Boys, *Clarissa* as a Juvenile." In *Love and Death in the American Novel.* New York: Stein & Day.

Firestone, Shulamuth. 1970. *The Dialectic of Sex*. New York: Morrow.

Freeman, Jo. 1970. "Growing Up Girlish." *Trans-Action* 8 (November-December): 36–43.

Frithioff, Patricia. 1967. *A Selected Annotated Bibliography of Materials Related to Women in Science*. Lund: Research Policy Program.

Gavron, Hannah. 1966. *The Captive Wife: Conflicts of Housebound Mothers*. London: Routledge & Kegan Paul.

Gillespie, Dair. 1971. "Who Has the Power? The Marital Struggle." *Journal of Marriage and the Family* 33 (August): 445–58.

Gilman, Charlotte Perkins. (1898) 1966. *Women and Economics*. New York: Harper & Row.

Ginzberg, Eli, and Alice M. Yohalem. 1966. *Educated American Women: Life Styles and Self Portraits*. New York: Columbia University Press.

Goffman, Erving. 1972. Lecture presented at a meeting of Sociologists for Women in Society, San Francisco.

Goldberg, Philip. 1968. "Are Women Prejudiced against Women?" *Trans-Action* (April), pp. 28–30.

Gouldner, Alvin. 1960. "The Norm of Reciprocity: A Preliminary Statement." *American Sociological Review* 25 (April): 161–78.

Hacker, Helen. 1951. "Women as a Minority Group." *Social Forces* 30 (October): 60–69.

Henley, Nancy. 1972. "Power, Sex and Nonverbal Communication: The Politics of Touch." Psychology Department, University of Maryland, College Park.

Hennig, Margaret. 1971. "Career Development for Women Executives." Ph.D. dissertation, Harvard Graduate School of Business Administration.

Hoffman, L. W. 1961. "Effects of Maternal Employment on the Child." *Child Development* 32 (March): 187–97.

Holmes, Douglas S., and Bruce W. Jorgensen. 1971. "Do Personality and Social Psychologists Study Men More than Women?" *Government Reports Announcements*, December 25.

Holmstrom, Lynda. 1971. "Career Patterns of Married Couples." In *The Professional Woman*, edited by Athena Theodore. Cambridge, Mass.: Schenkman.

Horner, Matina. 1968. "Sex Differences in Achievement Motivation and Performance in Competitive and Non Competitive Situations." Ph.D. dissertation, University of Michigan.

Hughes, Marija Matich. 1970. "The Sexual Barrier: Legal and Economic Aspects of Employment." 2422 Fox Plaza, San Francisco, Calif.

Jourard, S. M., and P. Lasakow. 1958. "Some Factors in Self-Disclosure." *Journal of Abnormal and Social Psychology* 56(1): 91–98.

Jourard, S. M., and J. E. Rubin. 1968. "Self Disclosure and Touching: A Study of Two Modes of Interpersonal Encounter and Their Interreaction." *Journal of Humanistic Psychology* 8(1): 38–48.

Kagan, Jerome, and Howard A. Moss. 1962. *Birth to Maturity: A Study in Psychological Development*. New York: Wiley.

Katz, Marlaine L. 1972. "Female Motive to Avoid Success: A Psychological Barrier or a Response to Deviance?" Manuscript. School of Education, Stanford University.

Keiffer, Miriam, and Patricia Warren. 1970. *Population Limitation and Women's Status: A Bibliography*. Princeton, N.J.: Educational Testing Service.

Kitay, P. M. 1940. "A Comparison of the Sexes in Their Attitudes and Beliefs about Women." *Sociometry* 34(4): 399–407.

Knudsen, Dean. 1969. "The Declining Status of Women: Popular Myths and the Failure of Functionalist Thought." *Social Forces* 48 (December): 183–93.

Kohn, Melvin, and John Clausen. 1956. "Parental Authority Behavior and Schizophrenia." *American Journal of Orthopsychiatry* 26 (April): 297–313.

Komarovsky, Mirra. 1946. "Cultural Contradictions and Sex Roles." *American Journal of Sociology* 52 (November): 185–89.

Arlie Russell Hochschild

———. 1950. "Functional Analysis of Sex Roles." *American Sociological Review* 15 (August): 508–16.

———. 1969. *Blue Collar Marriage.* New York: Random.

Kuvlesky, William, and David Reynolds. 1970. *Educational Aspirations and Expectations of Youth: A Bibliography of Research Literature II.* College Station: Department of Agricultural Economics and Rural Sociology, Texas A and M University.

Ladner, Joyce A. 1972. *Tomorrow's Tomorrow.* New York: Doubleday.

Langer, Elinor. 1970. "The Women of the Telephone Company." *New York Review of Books,* March 26.

Lasch, Christopher. 1967. "Mable Dodge Luhan: Sex as Politics." In *The New Radicalism in America.* New York: Vintage.

Laws, Judith Long. 1971. "A Feminist Review of Marital Adjustment Literature: The Rape of the Locke." *Journal of Marriage and the Family* 33 (August): 483–516.

Leffler, Anne, Dair Gillespie, and Glenna Spitze. 1972. Presentation in graduate seminar, "Sociology of Sex Roles." Sociology Department, University of California, Berkeley.

Lidz, R., S. Fleck, and A. Cornelison. 1965. *Schizophrenia and the Family.* New York: International Universities Press.

Lopata, Helena Zananiecki. 1971. *Occupation: Housewife.* London: Oxford University Press.

Maccoby, Eleanor, ed. 1966. *The Development of Sex Differences.* Palo Alto, Calif.: University of Stanford Press.

McKee, J., and A. Sheriffs. 1956. "The Differential Evaluation of Males and Females." *Journal of Personality* 25 (2): 357–71.

Martel, Martin. 1968. "Age-Sex Roles in American Magazine Fiction 1890–1955." In *Middle Age and Aging,* edited by B. Neugarten. Chicago: University of Chicago Press.

Maslow, A. H. 1939. "Dominance, Personality and Social Behavior in Women." *Journal of Social Psychology* 10 (1): 3–39.

Mattfeld, Jacqueline, and Carol Van Aken. 1965. *Women and the Scientific Professions.* Cambridge, Mass.: M.I.T. Press.

Mead, Margaret. 1935. *Sex and Temperament in Three Primitive Societies.* New York: Dell.

———. 1937. "A Reply to a Review of Sex and Temperament in Three Primitive Societies." *American Anthropologist* 39 (3): 558–61.

———. 1949. *Male and Female.* New York: Mentor.

Mendelsohn, Robert, and Shirley Dobie. 1970. "Women's Self Conception: A Block to Career Development." Manuscript. LaFayette Clinic, Department of Mental Health, Detroit, Michigan.

Millet, Kate. 1970. *Sexual Politics.* New York: Doubleday.

Millman, Marcia. 1970. "Some Remarks on Sex Role Research." Paper delivered at the meeting of the American Sociological Association, Washington, D.C., August 31–September 3.

Myrdal, Alva, and Viola Klein. 1956. *Women's Two Roles: Home and Work.* London: Routledge & Kegan Paul.

Nagel, Stuart, and Lenore Weitzman. 1971. "Women as Litigants." *Hastings Law Journal* 23 (November): 171–98.

National Council on Family Relations. 1970. *Annotated Bibliography, Family Life: Literature and Films.* Minneapolis: Minnesota Council on Family Relations.

Neugarten, Bernice L. 1961. "Women's Changing Roles through the Life Cycle." *Journal of the National Association of Women Deans and Counselors* 24 (June): 163–70.

———, ed. 1968. "Age, Sex Roles, and Personality in Middle Age: A Thematic Apperception Study." In *Middle Age and Aging.* Chicago: University of Chicago Press.

Nye, F. Ivan, and Lois Wladis Hoffman, eds. 1963. *The Employed Mother in America*. Chicago: Rand McNally.

Olesen, Virginia L. 1961. "Sex Role Definitions among College Undergraduates: A Study of Stanford Freshmen." Ph.D. dissertation, Stanford University.

Oppenheimer, Valerie. 1968. "Sex Labelling of Jobs." *Industrial Relations,* vol. 7 (May).

Paige, Karen. 1969. "The Effects of Oral Contraceptives on Affective Fluctuations Asssociated with the Menstrual Cycle." Ph.D. dissertation, University of Michigan.

Parsons, Talcott, and R. F. Bales. 1953. *Family, Socialization and Interaction Process.* Glencoe, Ill.: Free Press.

Pheterson, Gail I. 1969. "Female Prejudice against Men." Connecticut College, New London.

Pheterson, Gail I., Sara B. Kiesler, and Philip Goldberg. 1971. "Evaluation of the Performance of Women as a Function of Their Sex, Achievement and Personal History." *Journal of Personality and Social Psychology* 19 (1): 144–48.

Potter, David M. 1964. "American Women and the American Character." In *American Character and Culture,* edited by J. Hogue. De Land, Fla.: Everett.

Putnam, Emily J. 1910. *The Lady.* New York: Putnam.

Radcliffe Institute. 1970. "Womanpower, Selected Bibliography on Educated Women and the Labor Force." 3 James Street, Cambridge Mass. 02138.

Rainwater, Lee, Richard Coleman, and Gerald Handel. 1959. *Workingman's Wife: Her Personality, World and Life Style.* New York: Oceana.

Rapoport, Rhona, and Robert Rapoport. 1971. "Early and Later Experiences as Determinants of Adult Behavior: Married Women's Family and Career Patterns." *British Journal of Sociology* 22 (March): 16–30.

Rose, Arnold. 1951. "The Adequacy of Women's Expectations for Adult Roles." *Social Forces* 30 (April): 69–77.

Rosenberg, B. G., and Brian Sutton Smith. 1972. *Sex and Identity.* New York: Holt, Rinehart & Winston.

Rossi, Alice. 1964. "The Equality of Women: An Immodest Proposal." *Daedalus* 93 (Spring): 607–52.

———. 1968. "Transition to Parenthood." *Journal of Marriage and the Family* 30(1):26–39.

———.1969a. "Sex Equality: The Beginnings of Ideology." *Humanist* (September–October).

———. 1969b. "The Status of Women in Sociology." *American Sociologist* (Fall).

Rossi, Alice, ed. 1970. *Essays on Sex Equality.* Chicago: University of Chicago Press.

Safilios-Rothschild, Constantina. 1972. *Toward a Sociology of Women.* Lexington, Mass.: Xerox.

Sampson, Ronald V. 1965. *The Psychology of Power.* New York: Pantheon.

Sells, Lucy. In press. *Current Research on Sex Roles.* Published by author. Available from Sociology Department, University of California, Berkeley.

Siegel, A. E., and M. B. Haas. 1963. "The Working Mother: A Review of Research." *Child Development* 34 (September): 513–42.

Simon, Rita J., Shirley Merritt Clark, and Kathleen Galway. 1967. "The Woman Ph.D.: A Recent Profile." *Social Problems* 15 (Fall): 221–36.

Singer, Jerome. 1968. "The Importance of Daydreaming." *Psychology Today* 1 (April): 18–27.

Sinick, D. 1956. "Two Anxiety Scales Correlated and Examined for Sex Differences." *Journal of Clinical Psychology* 12 (4): 394–95.

Slater, Philip. 1964. "Parental Role Differentiation." In *The Family, Its Structure and Functions,* edited by Rose Coser. New York: St. Martins.

Smith, Page. 1970. *Daughters of the Promised Land.* Boston: Little, Brown.

Smith, S. 1939. "Age and Sex Differences in Children's Opinions concerning Sex Differences." *Journal of Genetic Psychology* 54 (1): 17–25.

Smuts, Robert W. 1971. *Women and Work in America.* New York: Schocken.

Spiegel, Jeanne. 1969. *A Selected Annotated Bibliography: Sex Role Concepts.* Washington, D.C.: Business and Professional Women's Foundation.

———. 1970a. *A Selected Annotated Bibliography: Working Mothers.* Washington, D.C.: Business and Professional Women's Foundation.

———. 1970b. *A Selected Annoted Bibliography: Women Executives.* Washington, D.C.: Business and Professional Women's Foundation.

Spitze, Glena. 1972. "Non-Verbal Behavior and Interpersonal Control: An Exploration of Causal Relations." Sociology Department, University of California, Berkeley.

Steinmann, Ann. 1971. *Bibliography on Male-Female Role Research.* New York: Maferr Foundation.

Stolz, Lois Meek. 1960. "Effects of Maternal Employment on Children: Evidence from Research." *Child Development* 31 (4): 749–82.

Stonequist, Everett V. 1961. *The Marginal Man: A Study in Personality and Culture Conflict.* New York: Russell & Russell.

Suelzle, Marijean. In press. *The Female Sex Role.* Urbana: University of Illinois Press.

Sullerot, Evelyn. 1971. *Women, Society and Change.* New York: McGraw-Hill.

Suter, Barbara A. 1972. "Masculinity-Feminity in Creative Women." Ph.D. dissertation, Fordham University.

Theodore, Athena. 1971. *The Professional Woman.* Cambridge, Mass.: Schenkman.

Thurnwald, R. 1936. "Review of *Sex and Temperament in Three Primitive Societies,* by Margaret Mead." *American Anthropologist* 38 (4): 663–667.

Turner, Ralph. 1964. "Some Aspects of Women's Ambition." *American Journal of Sociology* 70 (November): 271–85.

Uesugi, T. K., and W. E. Vinachke. 1963. "Strategy in a Feminine Game." *Sociometry* 26 (1): 75–88.

U.S., Department of Health, Education and Welfare. 1970a. *The Federal Program in Population Research: Inventory of Population Research Supported by Federal Agencies during Fiscal Year 1970.* Washington, D.C.: Government Printing Office.

———. Office of Education, International Organizations. 1970b. *The United States of America—Equality of Access of Women and Girls to Education, 1959–1969.* Prepared for the *International Bureau of Education Bulletin.*

U.S., Department of Labor. 1970. *Women—Their Social and Economic Status.* No. 903.590. Washington, D.C.: Government Printing Office.

———. Wage and Labor Standards Administration, Women's Bureau. 1969. *Handbook on Women Workers.* Women's Bureau Bulletin no. 294. Washington, D.C.: Government Printing Office.

Van den Berge, Pierre. 1966. "Paternalistic versus Competitive Race Relations: An Ideal-Type Approach." In *Racial and Ethnic Relations: Selected Readings,* edited by Bernard E. Segal. New York: Crowell.

Veblen, Thorstein. 1953. *The Theory of the Leisure Class.* New York: Mentor.

Vincent, Clark E. 1962. *Unmarried Mothers.* New York: Free Press.

Waller, Willard. 1937. "The Rating and Dating Complex." *American Sociological Review* 2 (August): 727–34.

Wallin, Paul. 1950. "Cultural Contradictions and Sex Roles: A Repeat Study." *American Sociological Review* 15 (2): 288–93.

Warner, Steve, David Wellman, and Lenore Weitzman. 1971. "The Hero, the Sambo and the Operator: Reflections on Characterizations of the Oppressed." Paper presented at the American Sociological Association Convention.

Watson, Walter, and Ernest Barth. 1964. "Questionable Assumptions in the Theory of Social Stratification." *Pacific Sociological Review* 7 (Spring): 10–16.

Watt, Ian. 1962. *The Rise of the Novel: Studies in Defoe, Richardson and Fielding.* Berkeley: University of California Press.

Weisstein, Naomi. 1969. "Kinder, Küche, Kirche as Scientific Law: Psychology Constructs the Female." *Motive* (March-April).

Weitzman, Lenore, Deborah Eifler, Elizabeth Hokada, and Catherine Ross. 1972.

"Sex Role Socialization in Picture Books for Pre-School Children."*American Journal of Sociology* 77 (May): 1125–50.

Welter, Barbara. 1966. "The Cult of True Womanhood: 1820–1860." *American Quarterly* 18 (Summer): 151–74.

Westervelt, Esther, and Deborah A. Fixter. 1971. *Women's Higher and Continuing Education with Selected References on Related Aspects of Women's Lives.* New York: College Entrance Examination Board.

Whaley, Sara Stauffer. 1972. *Women Studies Abstracts,* vol. 1, no. 1. P.O. Box 1, Rush, New York 14543.

White, James. 1967. "Women in the Law." *Michigan Law Review* 65 (April): 1051–1122.

Wilensky, Harold. 1968. *Women's Work: Economic Growth, Ideology and Structure.* Institute of Industrial Relations, Reprint Series, no. 7. Berkeley: Institute of Industrial Relations, University of California.

Williams, Josephine. 1964. "Patients and Prejudice: Lay Attitudes toward Women Physicians." *American Journal of Sociology* 51 (January): 283–87.

Willis, Ellen. 1970. "Women and the Myth of Consumerism." *Ramparts* (June).

The Woman Book Industry[1]

Carol Ehrlich

University of Maryland, Baltimore County

The publishing business is an amoral industry. If it chances upon a "hot topic," it will grind out everything on that subject which it can find, regardless of scholarly or literary quality. When the hot topic cools off, publishers' doors are gently closed—often regardless of the merit of a particular book.

Starting with the rebirth of the feminist movement in the 1960s, the book industry scrambled to keep up with this interesting new phenomenon. Women were newsworthy—women, a subject population which had been ignored by most scholars (including women themselves) and rejected by most publishers. The obvious exception, of course, was the field of marriage and the family, in which woman as mother, sex object, and wife made her male-defined appearance. But outside the kitchen and the bedroom, women did not exist. (Or so we were all led to believe.) The proper study of mankind was man, said man.

The woman book industry changed all this. Not only can women now gain knowledge about themselves from some source other than the inside of their own heads, but after so many years of having to write mainly about the other sex (surely an exercise in self-estrangement), female scholars can now, if they choose, focus upon women. This cannot fail to be beneficial—and I do not mean this only in the sense of what it will do subjectively for the female intellectual. Just as for years the lack of published research and theory about blacks by blacks helped to perpetuate old myths (disguised as scientific fact) about what the Negro race was really like, so too has the absence of feminist scholarship maintained demeaning and inaccurate stereotypes of women. This silence too has been broken, and all of us will benefit.

But because the publishing business is more interested in profit than it is in quality, the products of the woman book industry are extremely variable. As a feminist scholar, I would like to be able to say that, after several years of semi-indiscriminate production, the 1971–72 crop is all, or mostly all, of high quality. I would like to be able to say it, but I can't. A few of the 17 books to be reviewed here are outstanding; some are simply mediocre; and others seem to have been hastily and opportunistically thrown together to cash in on the lucrative new topic.

The 17 books are all either by female authors or, if co-edited or co-

[1] I would like to thank Howard J. Ehrlich for his invaluable comments and assistance. All the bibliographic information for the books reviewed here is given in the Appendix.

authored, by at least one female. All 17 were issued for the first time in 1971 or 1972, so that none is a reissue of an older work, although all of the collected readings contain at least a few earlier pieces. These 17 works represent only a fraction of the product of the woman book industry in 1971–72, and they range from the best to the worst of this genre. Eleven of the 17 are edited readers; one is a mixture of original text and reprinted articles; and five are full-length analyses.

I·shall begin with the readers. A good reader on any subject should meet four criteria. First and most important, it should present a well-organized selection of outstanding articles that covers what the editor says it is intended to cover. Second, it should have some reason for existence, which means that it should avoid duplicating other readers. Third, if there are explanatory headnotes, these should be both accurate and enlightening. Finally, the introduction should present a coherent statement that justifies the selection of the particular articles in an intelligent and articulate manner. If it also contains an index and/or a good bibliography, so much the better.

In my judgment, two of these readers meet all four criteria, while the others vary from considerable success to none. The first two are *Woman in Sexist Society: Studies in Power and Powerlessness,* edited by Vivian Gornick and Barbara K. Moran, and *Red Emma Speaks,* edited by Alix Kates Shulman. They are very different in scope: the first is a wide-ranging collection of contemporary feminist scholarship; the second is a collection of speeches and writings from one historical figure, Emma Goldman.

Woman in Sexist Society is intended as a handbook for the new field of women's studies. Of its 29 selections, a few are widely reprinted elsewhere (including Naomi Weisstein's constantly evolving "Kinder, Küche, Kirche as Scientific Law/Woman as Nigger/Psychology Constructs the Female"), although most are printed here for the first time or are not readily available. This fact in itself makes it a rare specimen among readers. Most readers seem to blur in one's mind because they contain so much familiar material. It is unfortunate that so much of the source material for this growing new academic field consists of great globs of unexciting pro-feminist, antifeminist, and indifferent prose. Here and there one finds something outstanding and unfamiliar, but at best one often finds the good old standards which lose their excitement the sixth time around. *Woman in Sexist Society,* however, is a happy exception: if one were to select a single reader of contemporary materials, it should be this one.

Since it is impossible to do justice to the many fine selections in anything less than a full-length review, I will limit myself to four. If they are read in sequence, the effect is illuminating—even terrifying. Vivian Gornick, in "Woman as Outsider," Jessie Bernard, in "The Paradox of the

Happy Marriage," Pauline Bart, in "Depression in Middle-aged Women," and Phyllis Chesler, in "Patient and Patriarch: Women in the Psychotherapeutic Relationship," all show how acceptance of the so-called female role can literally make a woman ill.

Gornick sums up the psychological costs of being an outsider—that is, of being excluded from the direct experience of life; of being a stereotype, category, symbol, object, or victim; of having one's existence depend upon relating to the powerful; or of having been traditionally socialized to the female role.

Some may be tempted to call journalist Gornick's work "polemical" or "unscientific" and to look instead to veteran Jessie Bernard for some no-nonsense, hard-headed sociology. But consider this: Bernard summarizes considerable data to support her conclusion that "happily married women" are likely to suffer from poor mental health. They are often depressed, phobic, and passive—a sad condition for those who have achieved the female's Reason for Existence. What has happened to the married woman? Bernard states that marriage is far more restrictive for women than it is for men; thus, for a woman to fit "happily" into marriage she may well have suppressed much of her individual potential. And once into marriage, "considerable well-authenticated data show that there are actually two marriages in every marital union—his and hers—which do not always coincide" (p. 86). And the wife's marriage is more likely to produce psychopathology, because, as Bernard suggests, marriage itself may be "sick."

If a traditionalist finds this sociologist's conclusions upsetting, he or she can always turn to another one. But Pauline Bart's materials may be even more disturbing. Bart's study of depressed middle-aged women in mental hospitals demonstrates compellingly that the "super-mother," the woman who buys the traditional role package of wife and mother, is likely to become pathologically depressed when her children leave home and her maternal role is lost. The "good" wife who is not overtly aggressive, the "good" mother whose whole life is her children, expects a payoff for her years of patience, hard work, and self-denial. "Goodness" brings no intrinsic rewards, and these women who move from the rigid wife-mother institution to the mental institution are, in Bart's words, "casualties of our culture" (p. 115).

Finally, psychologist Phyllis Chesler details the psychological mutilation of the woman as Outsider. In an impressively documented article, Chesler makes the following points:

> 1. That for a number of reasons, women "go crazy" more often and more easily than men do; that their "craziness" is mainly self-destructive; and that they are punished for their self-destructive behavior, either by the brutal and impersonal custodial care given them in mental asylums, or by

the relationships they have with most (but not all) clinicians, who implicitly encourage them to blame themselves or to take responsibility for their unhappiness in order to be "cured."

2. That both psychotherapy and marriage, the two major socially approved institutions for white, middle-class women, function similarly, i.e., as vehicles for personal "salvation" through the presence of an understanding and benevolent (male) authority. In female culture, not being married, or being unhappily married, is experienced as an "illness" which psychotherapy can, hopefully, cure. [P. 252]

Red Emma Speaks is another highly successful, although very different, reader. In the revisions of modern American history, Emma Goldman is assured a place. She is already represented in three of the readers reviewed here, although you will not find her in such popular establishment histories as Morison's *The Oxford History of the American People* (1965) or Morris's *Encyclopedia of American History* (1965). To be sure, Red Emma's "place" may be as a minor figure in the woman's movement, but, as those of an anarcho-feminist, her ideas have found great currency in the strong social-anarchist leanings of some contemporary feminists.

Alix Shulman has provided a truly elegant collection of Goldman's speeches and writings, including much that has generally not been available except to anarchist scholars. Sources are detailed and dated, materials are organized on a specified and rational basis, relevant introductions are provided, and the book is indexed. Shulman's introductions also display a rare and genuine knowledge of anarchist political thought. In her comments she attempts to show the contemporary relevance of Goldman's work and her life. As the Emma Goldman Brigade chanted while marching down New York's Fifth Avenue in August 1970: "Emma said it in 1910./ Now we're going to say it again."

Two distinguished sociologists, Cynthia F. Epstein and William J. Goode, have put together a reader which did not meet my high expectations. In *The Other Half: Roads to Women's Equality,* the introductions to the sections are generally competent, and the selections by and large are relevant, although not always outstanding. However, section 2, a catch-all entitled "Perspectives: Biology, Psychology, the Arts and Women's Destiny," is odd, to say the least. The high point is an introduction about the interplay of science and cultural values. But the five selections! The first, not one of Jessie Bernard's best, leans rather heavily on sexual mythology, so that, for example, we are told that men have a higher level of "sexual restlessness" (p. 44) which must find an outlet, lest the restless male be "uncomfortable." That's the old pressure cooker theory of sexuality, and I thought it had lost steam long ago. The second article, by Florence Ruderman, hauls out that scientific chestnut, "human nature," to validate "sex differences" in—to list only a few of her apparently inexhaustible examples—suicide rates, "creative tension," need for achievement, dominance-submission, sexual initiative, and "mental and emotional drive" (whatever that means). There is even the specter of "female sexual demandingness" causing "problems of male resentment, and even a rise in clinical impotence" (p. 51). *Clinical* impotence? At this point, we careen downhill into Lionel Tiger, and then move to a two-and-one-half-page article by Sandra Shevey on sexism in films, and finally to Kate Millett's explication of Henry Miller. If there is an underlying theme, I missed it.

It would be hard to justify using this reader in an undergraduate course, precisely because of the selections in section 2. Given their intelligent introduction to the section, Epstein and Goode have apparently used Ruderman and Tiger as horrible examples, but since Ruderman and Tiger support our culture's sexist prejudices, the editors should have included a selection or two to balance them. The Bernard piece is simply unequal to the task, and the two articles on the arts do not belong in this part of the reader at all.

There are, however, some good selections elsewhere; and one of the best is Goode's own "Civil and Social Rights of Women," a revised portion of his *World Revolution and Family Patterns*. Unfortunately, the pro-feminist sympathies of Goode-the-anthologized at least partly contradict the complacent "let's blame the woman" attitude of Goode-the-anthologizer. In his "Civil and Social Rights of Women," he cites a Detroit area survey in which "66 per cent of the women said that they would work even if they did not have to do so." Then, he continues, "every study of men's satisfaction with their work shows that the percentage who like their work increases with the level of challenge, prestige, and income, and we can suppose the same pattern applies to women. Thus, the lower-class woman is much more likely to have to work, but is much more willing to stay home if the man's income rises sufficiently to permit her to give up her job" (p. 32). Yet in the introduction to section 1, we are told that, except for upper-middle-class women, "the vast majority of women . . . have always been oriented toward the home." Further, if the woman doesn't want to seize the opportunities open to her, it is at least partly because she "creates her own barriers to opportunity" (p. 9). This assumes, of course, that boring, dirty jobs in factories, telephone companies, and as domestics constitute "opportunity." Surely, why one is unmotivated to be a full professor and why one is unmotivated to be an assembly line supervisor are two different stories. As with so many academics, the editors' middle-class bias is showing.

Another reader edited by a sociologist is *The Professional Woman*. This two-pound paperback by Athena Theodore contains 53 articles—some familiar, some new—which are mostly about women in specific professions. The opening quotation from the 19th-century feminist Julia Ward Howe succinctly states the focus of the book: "The professions indeed supply the keystone to the arch of woman's liberty." In her preface, Theodore states: "Most of the furor and attention addressed to the occupationally disadvantaged sex has not been directly concerned with the lot of the highly educated and trained professional woman. After all, she has had the advantages of an expensive education and a higher income than most non-professional males have. Yet female freedom and equality—the values which are being sought—may never materialize unless some attention is given to the socio-economic role of the highly educated professional woman" (pp. ix–x).

While occupational equality for professional women is certainly a desirable goal, I am unconvinced of the necessary connection between freedom and equality for female sociologists (to pick one professional category) and freedom and equality for all women. And, in fact, Theodore herself says that nothing will really change for professional women until "changes occur which will restore the balance between economic and family structures. The future of the professional woman thus depends to a large extent on the redefinition of sex roles in the society in general and in the family in particular" (p. 35). One need only delete "professional" from the final sentence to extend her point to all women.

If one were to try deliberately to throw together a reader of the most frequently reprinted contemporary articles, one would come up with something very close to *Roles Women Play: Readings toward Women's Liberation,* edited by Michele Hoffnung Garskof. Garskof states that she has collected materials she found "relatively inaccessible when I first set out to teach a course on the psychology of women" (p. vii). Without knowing when that was, I cannot judge the accuracy of her statement. But surely in 1971 there was no need to issue a collection made up almost entirely of materials that are highly accessible to anyone who can read: Rossi, "Equality between the Sexes"; Dixon, "Why Women's Liberation?"; Weisstein; and so forth.

On the other hand, everyone should own a copy of *Notes from the Third Year: Women's Liberation,* edited by Anne Koedt and Shulamith Firestone. It is the third annual collection of radical feminist writing put out by this group, and each one seems to get better. For $1.50, one finds an interesting selection of current writings on a wide range of topics: the 19th-century women's rights movement, women in literature, black feminism, children's books, prostitution, lesbianism, rape, the problems of middle age, legal inequities, women in the labor force, the media, religion, and so on. Many of the articles have been printed before, but few induce the sense of *déjà vu* one gets from the Garskof reader.

Five of the readers are historical in scope. *This Great Argument: The Rights of Women,* edited by Hamida Bosmajian and Haig Bosmajian, is designed for college courses in basic rhetoric, and presents chronologically many arguments for and against the rights of women. The notable figures represented range from Plato to Edith Green; the genres include essays, court decisions, speeches, drama, poetry, and congressional hearings. The book's value lies chiefly in the reprinting of court cases and hearings. The headnotes add little, if anything, to the documents.

Of far higher quality are *Feminism: The Essential Historical Writings,* edited by Miriam Schneir, and *Female Liberation: History and Current Politics,* edited by Roberta Salper. Schneir has collected brief excerpts from 36 documents which appeared between the American Revolution and 1929. She has bypassed writings dealing exclusively with suffrage and focuses instead upon issues which are still alive: marriage, economic dependence, and the development of personal independence. One quibble: the publisher's copy on the back cover is quite misleading. It states: "Many works, long out of print or forgotten in what Miriam Schneir describes as a male-dominated literary tradition, are finally brought out of obscurity and into the light of contemporary analysis and criticism." In fact, there is relatively little material included which is unfamiliar to anyone with even a cursory acquaintance with the history of feminism—nor, in fact, does Schneir claim that there is. Familiar excerpts from Abigail Adams, Mary Wollstonecraft, Sarah Grimké, Margaret Fuller, the Seneca Falls Declaration, Lucy Stone, Veblen, Ibsen, Woolf, and others greet us like old friends. The value of this reader lies in a good introduction, in the thoughtful headnotes which precede each selection, and in the variety and brevity of the materials. It is entirely suitable as a supplementary text for undergraduate courses, for it samples lightly from the old familiar materials and encourages the beginner to dig further.

Salper examines the first and second American women's movements from a socialist feminist perspective. The long introduction consists of a scholarly analysis followed by a statement about her own personal evolution—a combination that comes off quite well. One commendable aspect of the introduction is its handling of the first woman's movement. Typically, this topic is treated in one of two ways: either that it "failed" because its membership became exclusively middle class and focused on winning the vote, or, conversely, that feminists from the very beginning concentrated on suffrage alone. Salper avoids both oversimplifications. She does not ignore the increasing conservatism and drive for respectability of many turn-of-the-century feminists, but by seeing them dispassionately as products of a particular moment in history and of a particular class, she is able both to describe their limitations and to concede their achievements. She takes them on their own terms, while recognizing that those terms precluded the restructuring of the social order which alone could eliminate the second-class status of women.

The headnotes, as well as the introduction, add much to the book, but the selections, by and large, are not up to Salper's own performance. One note: those who are interested in the political migration of Marlene Dixon might want to read "Why Women's Liberation—2?". This sequel to the widely reprinted "Why Women's Liberation?" is published here for the first time; it contains some very interesting ideological changes.

The American Sisterhood: Writings of the Feminist Movement from Colonial Times to the Present, edited by Wendy Martin, is a book that also has its own combination of virtues and defects. In her preface, Martin states, "many of these essays can only be found in special collections or in rare book rooms and have generally been overlooked by most historians and literary scholars" (p. ix). Perhaps. Many of them can also readily be found in other readers in any bookstore. With that reservation, I would say that she has made a reasonably good selection of readings. For one thing, the book includes some excerpts from Anne Hutchinson's trial, which is not generally found in histories of the American women's movement. And Martin's own article, "Seduced and Abandoned in the New World" (also to be found in Gornick and Moran), is a first-rate piece of feminist literary criticism. The headnotes, however, leave much to be desired, for they present little analysis and tend simply toward the biographical. And there are some notable non sequiturs: "Even though Lucy Stone strongly opposed the status conferred on married women, characterized by no property or contract rights, and the acceptance of wife beating, she married Henry Browne Blackwell in 1855" (p. 51). And, "although she [Susan B. Anthony] was admired by many at the academy, the proposals of marriage she received were not accepted" (p. 88). At another point, Martin says that Lucy Stone retained her maiden name in marriage, "refusing to substitute her husband's surname for her own" (p. 51), but then calls her "Lucy Blackwell" (p. 89).

The one reader which has virtually no redeeming value is *The New Feminism in Twentieth-Century America,* edited by June Sochen. For example, the introduction states that "during the first ten years of this century, women still could not sue for divorce, own property in their own right, obtain birth-control information, or generally control their own destinies" (p. viii). In truth, states began passing married women's property acts as early as 1848; in 1850 the Oregon Land Donation Act allotted land to both single and married women, and during the Progressive Era about two-thirds of all divorces were granted to women.

Sochen's "suggestions for additional reading" from the 1960s (pp. 207–8) include a directive to "note especially" Sophonsiba P. Breckinridge, *Women in the Twentieth Century: A Study of Their Political and Economic Activities,* which Sochen then tells us was published in 1952 but which in fact came out in 1933. (Breckinridge, one of the early Chicago sociologists, died in 1948.)

There are also a number of unfortunate examples of sexist bias, such as repeated use of the diminutive, "women's lib"; or the comment that "when women received the vote in 1920, they helped the men elect handsome Warren G. Harding to the presidency" (p. x). Also, women who work see it as "a temporary necessity or as a supplement to their husbands' earnings" (p. x). This partial truth leaves out those women who are single, or women who see what they are doing as a rewarding career instead of simply a job. And finally, there is the description of Erik Erikson's notorious article on "inner space" as a "valuable discussion of the psychology of women" (p. 208). Overall, the readings do not comprise an outstanding selection, and the headnotes veer toward the silly. (My favorite, preceding Naomi Weisstein: "What is a 'social context' and how important is it to the psychological makeup of an individual?" [p. 133].)

Womankind: Beyond the Stereotypes, by Nancy Reeves, is a hybrid: it begins with about 150 pages of original text and concludes with approximately 250 pages of "parallel readings" by other writers. These two sections are bridged by an unusual 15-page photographic essay, which I found to be the high point of the book.

The pictorial essay, entitled "The View From the Sexual Ghetto," illustrates the absence of women from public life. On page after page, one encounters masses of masculine faces—at a NATO meeting, in Nixon's cabinet, at the Houston Space Center, in a large Chinese Communist delegation in 1963, in a grouping of top Russian leaders, at an 11-man summit meeting of African heads of state. The essay makes its point very well.

Strictly speaking, the book is not a sociological analysis of stereotypes. Instead, Reeves looks at the current status of women in the light of logic and of cross-cultural and historical data. Unfortunately, with the exception of the final chapter, it is not done very well; the language and the structure of the book get in the way of the content. Despite the publisher's claim that it is "exceptionally well-written," the flowery, frenetic, and often obscure language is a real barrier to understanding many of the points Reeves is trying to make. What is one supposed to make of the following? "Sententious formulations rest on fragile frames" (p. 15); "revolutionaries of the past sought to mold the new woman along two basic lines: wide range and full function" (p. 30); married women are "swinging monads, suspended from the domestic rafters" (p. 65); or, "seesawing between dust motes and atoms demands an extraordinary acrobat" (p. 70). There is also this interesting aphorism: "Happiness is a state of stretch, not of slack" (p. 37).

In addition to the language barrier, there is a structural problem that makes it a difficult book to read. The "parallel readings" for each of Reeves's chapters are separated by as much as 200 pages from the chapter they are meant to accompany, and are always grouped under a different title from the chapter title. This awkward and irritating arrangement makes it difficult to decide whether the content is worth the trouble it takes to dig it out. For me, it wasn't.

I conclude this review with a look at five full-length texts. *Psychology of Women,* by Judith M. Bardwick, is a textbook-like review of the psychological literature on women. Bardwick appears absolutely ignorant of sociology or of any conception of norms and normative behavior. Although she keeps insisting that she is aware of the social, she is (to use her interpretive language) motivated to ignore it. She is, in short, an individual psychologist who holds an essentially biologically determinist position.

Bardwick develops her perspective: "It will be my thesis that the differences between the sexes have early genetic origins" (p. 12). "Differences in personality characteristics begin to develop *before birth*" (p. 21; italics in original). "I do think that there are fundamental psychological differences between the sexes that are, at least in part, related to the differences in their bodies" (p. 6). "My hunch, and it is no more than that, is that there is a phylogenetic inheritance that makes maternity the most fulfilling role for women, at least when children are young" (p. 211).

However, I think her work is far less grounded in fact than she claims. Almost none of the research she cites is based on representative samples; very seldom does she examine the magnitude of variation within same-sex groups, and comparative designs in which age, class, and sex are controlled seem nonexistent.

In *Psychology of Women* there are "male minds" and "female minds" (for their characteristics see p. 100). But basically, as the old joke says, the mind is located between the legs. "The psychological differences between the sexes are based in part on the genital differences. The important difference is that boys have a visible, sensitive, and accessible organ whereas girls have an inaccessible clitoris and an insensitive vagina" (p. 16). The author claims that this difference is more or less responsible, not only for sex differences in intellectual growth and development, but even for differences in self-esteem (see esp. chap. 2).

Because this text supports the present resurgence of biological thinking in the social sciences—a resurgence based in part on a measure of despair about the present world situation and in part on a quest for certainty—it supports a certain political position. Consider her *sotto voce* manifesto:

> 1. Conformity is normality: *"In the reality of current socialization and expectations, I regard women who are not motivated to achieve the affiliative role with husband and children as not normal."* [P. 162; italics in original]

2. Women who protest their position in society have lost their femininity: "I suspect that the current liberation movement among women is a response to their having accepted and internalized masculine standards." [Pp. 19–20]

3. Motivation patterns, not differences in socialization or the presence of occupational discrimination, is the basis for women's lack of occupational achievement: "One reason for American women's lack of professional participation is the critical salience of affiliative motives." [P. 210]; [no other reason is presented, and nowhere does the author acknowledge the existence of sex-based discrimination.]

Sex and Caste in America, by Carol Andreas, is, in one sense, a direct opposite of *Psychology of Women,* for it stands in explicit contrast to so-called value-free science, which in fact values things as they are. Andreas states at the outset that her book is "an unmasking of the ideological premises by which most of us have lived" (p. 4). Her intention is to examine the ways in which socialization, social class, education, the economic system, religion, the nuclear family, popularized psychology, and the law contribute to the maintenance of sexism.

In contrast with Bardwick, Andreas maintains that culture is extremely variable, both in the higher primates and in "pre-modern" societies, and that "whatever innate differences do exist . . . cannot be known decisively until conditions of equal opportunity are realized" (p. 3). This book also supports a certain political position, but one that is in direct contrast with the pessimism and conservatism of biological determinism. It is an activist approach—one that says that the conditions which limit people can be, at least in large part, alleviated—and that scientists can help by providing their research and analytic skills to the women's movement and to other movements for social change.

Too often, scientists do not help: "In any 'behavioral science,' even if systematic observation is the basis for research, the distinction between what 'is' and what 'might be' is seldom made. Thus, a description of role behavior often appears as a justification or defense of such behavior" (p. 84). Andreas has made a nice beginning on a book that should have gone more systematically and in far greater detail into the issues she raised. Perhaps she herself will undertake to complete this task.

In *Rebirth of Feminism,* Judith Hole and Ellen Levine have written a history and analysis of the current feminist movement in America. Of all the full-length texts reviewed here, it is by far the most satisfactory. It is a detailed, accurate, carefully researched book. They have obviously done their homework and have written well. The book contains an added bonus of a 21-page bibliography compiled by Lucinda Cisler in June 1971, and a 27-page chronology of the American women's movement between 1961 and 1971.

This book is unusual in that it discusses both the early and the contemporary feminist movements in such a fashion that the reader can note their similarities as radical critiques of the social order. The emphasis, however, is definitely on the post-1961 period: Hole and Levine "cover" the earlier movement in only 14 pages. Despite the inevitable oversimplification, the description of the earlier activism includes a great deal in that all-too-short space.

At the outset, the authors distinguish between "women's rights" and "women's liberation," and discuss the activities of both of these major branches of the contemporary women's movement. Essentially, the "women's rights" segment is composed of moderate and conservative feminists who work for reform within existing institutions, the members of NOW, WEAL, and similar organizations. The "women's liberation" segment is defined here as that part of the movement which originated in the student activism of the 1960s. Hole and Levine say that these women are radical feminists who have been engaged mainly in efforts to educate themselves and others about women's oppression, primarily in small consciousness-raising groups.

Hole and Levine distinguish "feminists" from "politicos" within the women's liberation segment, and choose to use "feminist" arguments (sometimes also called "radical feminist") synonymously with "women's liberation." Basically, the "politicos" (or socialist feminists) see the fight against sexism as part of the larger struggle for socialism, while the "feminists" see women's oppression as the primary issue. While the distinction is important because it has plagued the women's movement from its beginnings, within the movement these lines are not always so rigidly drawn. And in trying to stick to this distinction, Hole and Levine sometimes run into procrustean problems. The issues, and the women who state them, often elude classification into such neat categories.

In the discussion of the post-1961 movement, Part I traces the growth of both the women's rights and women's liberation forces, beginning with the establishment of the President's Commission on the Status of Women in 1961. Part II describes and analyzes the ideology and social criticism of the feminists, and Part III delineates the areas in which the most significant feminist actions have taken place: the media (both establishment and feminist), abortion, child care, education, the professions, and the church. From this listing, one can see the major defect of this otherwise fine book: it is solidly middle class in orientation. Partly, it is true, the women's movement has been overrepresented in the middle class, and most of its successes have been with this group and its issues. But lower-class and ethnic-minority women are even more discriminated against, and in this book (indeed, in most books about women) there is very little about them. An example is chapter 7, an otherwise interesting and informative history of the abortion issue. Hole and Levine mention three goals which the different sectors of the women's movement hold concerning abortion: legalization, an end to all legal inequities concerning sex and procreation, and the abolition of the "anti-woman" aspects of the entire health care system (p. 302). Certainly, women will not have the right to control their own bodies until these three goals are met. But you don't have to be a "politico" to realize that these changes will most benefit the middle-class woman, and that until abortions are made available either free or at a nominal charge, poor women will continue to bear unwanted children.

With this reservation, and with some mixed feelings about chapter 3, " 'Biological Differences' Argument" (admittedly a difficult subject to discuss adequately), I would nevertheless recommend this book to anyone who wants to know what has gotten into women in the past 10 years.

Sex, Career, and Family, by Michael P. Fogarty, Rhona Rapoport, and Robert N. Rapoport, is also explicitly class-biased: "The terms of reference underlying this report are concerned with women, and in particular women in top jobs: how to get more of the former into the latter" (p. 17). The women and men studied, both in their surveys and case studies, were almost all college graduates and "highly qualified young men and women in Britain" (p. 182). Committed to some egalitarian form of a nuclear family structure, in addition to their economic and class biases, the authors' interpretations of their data are highly predictable.

For persons seeking a comparative perspective on sex roles and the urban family, the primary data of the book may be useful, as will the authors' review of Eastern European materials (chap. 2), if read carefully. From a feminist perspective, the book is a mass of inconsistencies: egalitarian at times but too often accepting of the sexist beliefs and practices of Western society.

Occupation: Housewife, by Helen Znaniecki Lopata, is a fitting text with which to close a review of the current products of the woman book industry. With some thought, the book might have been a good journal article or two. Instead, it is a book that consists of an overblown analysis with unorganized and redundant writing. Here and there are some rare pieces of information, such as the almost eight pages on women's evaluations of the Chicago *Tribune* (pp. 158–65).

But Lopata has problems with interpretation. For example, she begins her "Conclusions" by asserting: "the basic conclusion of the Chicago studies is that modern women are becoming increasingly competent and creative in their social role of housewife and in the manner in which they combine different roles within their life cycle" (p. 362). She presents no systematic data that may be taken as support for that assertion. A part of her interpretive problem is the problem of her discipline and class identification. Unlike the authors of *Sex, Career, and Family,* Lopata's observations are based on samples that cut reasonably across class lines. But for the author, the highly educated, upper-middle-class woman is clearly the heroine—the standard for assessing role performance. Although the author regularly uses class and residence as independent variables, she neither appears sympathetic with nor provides a formal analysis of the dual problem of lower-class status and female subordination. Understandably, then, one finds no socioeconomic analysis of the position of housewife in the American economic and occupational structure.

I began by indicating that I thought the publishing industry was amoral. Many people, however, do not think so and argue, in fact, that the industry is *im*moral, because it profits from the suffering of others. Several years ago, one of the proposals made by the now invisible Sociology Liberation Movement with regard to the explosion of books on blacks and the black movement was that some of the profits of those publications be allocated to the cause of black Americans. Imagine how much better off women's groups would be if they were financed by profits of an industry that does not function demonstrably to serve women.

APPENDIX

Andreas, Carol. 1971. *Sex and Caste in America.* Englewood Cliffs, N.J.: Prentice-Hall (Spectrum). Pp. xiv+146. $1.95 (paper).

Bardwick, Judith M. 1971. *Psychology of Women.* New York: Harper & Row. Pp. 242.

Bosmajian, Hamida, and Haig Bosmajian, eds. 1972. *This Great Argument: The Rights of Women.* Reading, Mass.: Addison-Wesley. Pp. iv+299.

Epstein, Cynthia F., and William J. Goode, eds. 1971. *The Other Half: Roads to Women's Equality.* Englewood Cliffs, N.J.: Prentice-Hall. Pp. 207. $2.45 (paper).

Fogarty, Michael, Rhona Rapoport, and Robert N. Rapoport. 1971. *Sex, Career, and Family.* Beverly Hills, Calif.: Sage. Pp. 581. $17.50.

Garskof, Michele Hoffnung, ed. 1971. *Roles Women Play: Readings toward Women's Liberation.* Belmont, Calif.: Brooks-Cole.

Goode, William J. 1963. *World Revolution and Family Patterns.* New York: Free Press.

Gornick, Vivian, and Barbara K. Moran, eds. 1971. *Woman in Sexist Society: Studies in Power and Powerlessness.* New York: Basic. Pp. xxi+515. $12.50.

Hole, Judith, and Ellen Levine. 1971. *Rebirth of Feminism.* Chicago: Quadrangle. Pp. xiii+488. $10.00.

Koedt, Anne, and Shulamith Firestone, eds. 1971. *Notes from the Third Year: Women's Liberation.* New York: Notes, Inc. Pp. 152. $1.50 (paper).

Lopata, Helen Znaniecki. *Occupation: Housewife.* New York: Oxford University Press. Pp. xi+387. $9.50.

Martin, Wendy, ed. 1972. *The American Sisterhood: Writings of the Feminist Movement from Colonial Times to the Present.* New York: Harper & Row. Pp. ix+374.

Reeves, Nancy. 1971. *Womankind: Beyond the Stereotypes.* Chicago: Aldine-Atherton. Pp. xii+434.

Salper, Roberta, ed. 1972. *Female Liberation: History and Current Politics.* New York: Knopf. Pp. xi+246.

Schneir, Miriam, ed. 1972. *Feminism: The Essential Historical Writings.* New York: Random House (Vintage). Pp. xxi+360. $2.45 (paper).

Carol Ehrlich

Shulman, Alix Kates, ed. 1972. *Red Emma Speaks*. New York: Random House (Vintage). Pp. 413. $10.00.

Sochen, June, ed. 1971. *The New Feminism in Twentieth-Century America*. Lexington, Mass.: Heath. Pp. xiii+208.

Theodore, Athena, ed. 1971. *The Professional Woman*. Cambridge, Mass.: Schenkman. Pp. xi+769.

A Funny Thing Happened on the Way to the Orifice: Women in Gynecology Textbooks[1]

Diana Scully
University of Illinois, Chicago Circle

Pauline Bart
Abraham Lincoln Medical School, University of Illinois, Chicago

The gynecologist is our society's official specialist on women, legitimately commenting on their psyches as well as on the illnesses of their reproductive tracts (Novak, Jones, and Jones 1970; Green 1971). Nevertheless, gynecologists are overwhelmingly male (93.4% [*Time* 1972, p. 89]); and the tools of the sociology of knowledge suggest that one's perspectives are constrained by one's place in the social structure and thus gynecologists may not adequately represent the worldview and the interests of the group they are supposed to attend and advocate. Indeed, examination of gynecology textbooks, one of the primary professional socialization agents for practitioners in the field, revealed a persistent bias toward greater concern with the patient's husband than with the patient herself. Women are consistently described as anatomically destined to reproduce, nurture, and keep their husbands happy. So gynecology appears to be another of the forces committed to maintaining traditional sex-role stereotypes, in the interest of men and from a male perspective.[2]

The contents of 27 general gynecology texts published in the United States since 1943 were analyzed. Complete lists of texts and authors were obtained from the Index Catalog of the Library of the Surgeon General's Office, National Library of Medicine. We attempted to read all the texts available, rather than to sample (27 books out of 32). To allow for emergent trends based on new information about female sexuality, the books were divided into three periods; pre-Kinsey, 1943–52 (six of nine were used); post-Kinsey, pre-Masters and Johnson, 1953–62 (nine of 10 were used); post-Masters and Johnson, 1963–72 (12 of 14 were used). Only the latest edition of each text was read. The numbers represent authors active in the field rather than total volumes published.

[1] We thank Marlyn Grossman for a careful reading of this paper and valuable criticism. Another version of this paper was presented at the American Sociological Association meetings in 1972. A longer version is available from the authors. This paper is on file at the Women's History Research Center in Berkeley, Calif.
[2] There is a growing literature detailing the emphasis on traditional sex roles in works ranging from children's story and school books through college history and sociology texts and academic disciplines (e.g., Ehrlich 1971; Weitzman et al. 1972).

Diana Scully and Pauline Bart

TABLE 1

FEMALE SEXUALITY AND ORGASM IN THREE DECADES OF GYNECOLOGY TEXTS

	1943–52		1953–62		1963–72	
	N	% of Indexed Item (N)	N	% of Indexed Item (N)	N	% of Indexed Item (N)
Texts which indexed female sexuality	(4)	...	(8)	...	(9)	...
Sex primarily for reproduction* ..	...	25 (1)	...	62 (5)	...	67 (6)
Male sex drive stronger	...	50 (2)	...	62 (5)	...	89 (8)
Women characterized as frigid ...	...	25 (1)	...	37 (3)	...	33 (3)
Female sexuality not indexed	(2)	...	(1)	...	(3)	...
Total texts	(6)	...	(9)	...	(12)	...
Texts which indexed orgasm (clitoral-vaginal)	(4)	...	(4)	...	(4)	...
Vaginal mature response	...	0	...	75 (3)	...	50 (2)†
Not discussed in these terms	...	75 (3)†	...	25 (1)	...	0
Orgasm not indexed	(2)	...	(5)	...	(8)	...
Total texts	(6)	...	(9)	...	(12)	...

* Of those books in which female sexuality was indexed, some had more than one reference area. Therefore the total number of references is greater than the number of books.
† One text in the 1963–72 period indicated the clitoris to be the seat of sensation, and two texts, one in the 1963–72 and one in the 1943–52 period, indicated no difference in clitoral and vaginal orgasm.

1943–53[3]

In this period, prior to the work of Kinsey and Masters and Johnson, there was little empirical data about female sexuality. Of the four books in this group, two did not index female sexuality. One of the four (Janney 1950) presented a strikingly egalitarian approach to sexuality. Two others are characterized by a double standard. Thus Cooke stated: "The fundamental biologic factor in women is the urge of motherhood balanced by the fact that sexual pleasure is entirely secondary or even absent" (Cooke 1943, pp. 59–60). Since women were assumed to be "almost universally generally frigid," while the male "is created to fertilize as many females as possible and has an infinite appetite and capacity for intercourse" (Cooke 1943, p. 60), two texts instruct gynecologists to teach their patients to fake orgasm. "It is good advice to recommend to the women the advantage of *innocent simulation* [italics added] of sex responsiveness, and as a matter of fact many women in their desire to please their husbands learned the advantage of such innocent deception" (Novak and Novak 1952, p. 572; Lowrie 1952, p. 671).

[3] Our analysis is based not only on indexed items but on a general reading of the texts.

Once Kinsey et al. published *Sexual Behavior in the Human Female* (1953), the medical field had an authoritative and definitive (albeit from a nonrandom sample) source of information on the female. For the most part, these texts used Kinsey's report selectively; findings which reinforced old stereotypes were repeated, but the revolutionary findings significant for women were ignored. For example, one often finds in the textbooks that the male sets the sexual pace in marital coitus, but nowhere is it mentioned that women are multiorgasmic, a Kinsey finding which raises questions concerning the gynecologist's belief in the stronger male sex drive.

Though Kinsey is not usually credited with the discovery, he debunked the myth of the vaginal orgasm. "The literature usually implies that the vagina itself should be the center of sensory stimulation but this as we have seen is a physical and physiologic impossibility for nearly all females" (Kinsey 1953, p. 582)

Gynecologists, however, have tenaciously clung to the idea of the vaginal orgasm as the appropriate response and labeled "frigid" and immature those patients who could not experience it. The content analysis (see table 1) showed that no text read in any of the three decades said that portions of the vagina had no nerve endings and lacked sensation (a Kinsey finding); only one, in the 1963–72 decade, said that the clitoris was the seat of sensation; three in the second decade and two in the most current decade said that the vaginal response was the "mature response"; and two, one in the current decade and one in the 1952–63 period, stated the vagina and clitoris were equally sensitive. For example: "Investigators of sexual behavior distinguished between clitoral and vaginal orgasm, the first playing a dominant role in childhood sexuality and in masturbation and the latter in the normal mature and sexually active women. . . . The limitation of sexual satisfaction to one part of the external genitalia is apparently due to habit and aversion to normal cohabitation" (Ruben 1956, p. 77). Indeed as late as 1965, gynecology texts were reporting the vagina as the main erogenous zone (Greenhill 1965, p. 496). In 1962: "The transference of sensations from the clitoris to the vagina is completed only in part and frequently not at all. . . . If there has been much manual stimulation of the clitoris *it* [italics added] may be reluctant to abandon control, or the vagina may be unwilling to accept the combined role of arbiter of sensation and vehicle for reproduction" (Parsons and Sommers 1962, pp. 501–2). But, even if she is "truly frigid . . . the marital relations may proceed without *disturbing* [italics added] either partner" (Parsons and Sommers 1962, p. 494).

Diana Scully and Pauline Bart

1963–72

In the early 1960s reports began to flow from the laboratories of Masters and Johnson, and, though their findings are not generally quoted, there has been some indirect influence. Two-thirds (eight) of the books of that decade failed to discuss the issue of the clitoral versus vaginal orgasm. Eight continued to state, contrary to Masters and Johnson's findings, that the male sex drive was stronger; and half (six) still maintained that procreation was the major function of sex for the female. Two said that most women were "frigid," and another stated that one-third were sexually unresponsive. Two repeated that the vaginal orgasm was the only mature response (Greenhill 1965; Jeffcoate 1967).

Although sex roles are never indexed, we learn from reading the texts that when they deal with the subject, the traditional female sex role is preferred (nine out of 12 in the recent decade). Thus Jeffcoate states: "An important feature of sex desire in the man is the urge to dominate the women and subjugate her to his will; in the women acquiescence to the masterful takes a high place" (Jeffcoate 1967, p. 726). In 1971 we read: "The traits that compose the core of the female personality are feminine narcissism, masochism and passivity" (Willson 1971, p. 43).

So it appears that in gynecology texts the basic underlying image of woman and her "normal adult female role in the marital relationship" (Green 1971, p. 436) has changed little even though new data contradicting such views have been available. A 1970 text states: "The frequency of intercourse depends entirely upon the male sex drive. . . . The bride should be advised to allow her husband's sex drive to set their pace and she should attempt to gear hers satisfactorily to his. If she finds after several months or years that this is not possible, she is advised to consult her physician as soon as she realizes there is a real problem" (Novak, Jones, and Jones 1970, pp. 662–63).

The gynecologist's self-image as helpful to women combined with unbelievable condescension is epitomized in this remark: "If like all human beings, he [the gynecologist] is made in the image of the Almighty, and if he is kind, then his kindness and concern for his patient may provide her with a glimpse of God's image" (Scott 1968, p. 25).

SUMMARY

A review of 27 gynecology texts written from 1943 to 1972 shows that they are written, as a sociology-of-knowledge framework would lead us to expect, from a male viewpoint. Traditional views of female sexuality and personality are presented generally unsullied by the findings of Kinsey and Masters and Johnson, though the latter resulted in some changes in rhetoric.

286

In the last two decades at least one-half of the texts that indexed the topics stated that the male sex drive was stronger than the female's; she was interested in sex for procreation more than for recreation. In addition, they said most women were "frigid" and that the vaginal orgasm was the "mature" response. Gynecologists, our society's official experts on women, think of themselves as the woman's friend. With friends like that, who needs enemies?

REFERENCES

*Behrman, Samuel J., and John R. C. Gosling. 1959. *Fundamentals of Gynecology.* New York: Oxford University Press.
*Benson, Ralph C. 1971. *Handbook of Obstetrics and Gynecology.* Los Altos, Calif.: Lange Medical Publishers.
*Brewer, John I., and Edwin J. DeCosts. 1967. *Textbook of Gynecology.* Baltimore: Williams & Wilkens.
*Cooke, Willard R. 1943. *Essentials of Gynecology.* Philadelphia: Lippincott.
*Crossen, Robert James. 1953. *Diseases of Women.* Saint Louis: Mosby.
*Curtis, A. H. 1946. *A Textbook of Gynecology.* Philadelphia: Saunders.
*Danforth, David. 1971. *Textbook of Obstetrics and Gynecology.* New York: Hoeber.
*Davis, Henry Carl, ed. 1964. *Gynecology and Obstetrics.* 3 vols. Hagarstown, Md.: Prior.
Ehrlich, Carol. 1971. "The Male Sociologist's Burden: The Place of Women in Marriage and Family Texts." *Journal of Marriage and the Family* 33:421–30.
*Gray, Laman. 1960. *A Textbook of Gynecology.* Springfield, Ill.: Thomas.
*Green, Thomas H. 1971. *Gynecology: Essentials of Clinical Practice.* Boston: Little, Brown.
*Greenhill, J. P. 1965. *Office Gynecology.* Chicago: Yearbook Medical Publishers.
*Huffman, John Williams. 1962. *Gynecology and Obstetrics.* Philadelphia: Saunders.
*Janney, James C. 1950. *Medical Gynecology.* Philadelphia: Saunders.
*Jeffcoate, Thomas. 1967. *Principles of Gynecology.* London: Butterworth.
*Kimbrough, Robert A., ed. 1965. *Gynecology.* Philadelphia: Lippincott.
Kinsey, Alfred C., et al. 1953. *Sexual Behavior in the Human Female.* New York: Simon & Schuster.
*Kistner, R. W. 1964. *Gynecology.* Chicago: Yearbook Medical Publishers.
*Lowrie, Robert J. 1952. *Gynecology, Diseases and Minor Surgery.* Springfield, Ill.: Thomas.
*Meigs, J. V., and S. H. Sturgis. 1963. *Progress in Gynecology.* New York: Grune & Stratton.
*Novak, Edmund R., Georgeanna Seegar Jones, and Howard W. Jones. 1970. *Novak's Textbook of Gynecology.* Baltimore: Williams & Wilkens.
Novak, Emil, and Edmund R. Novak. 1952. *Textbook of Gynecology.* Baltimore: Williams & Wilkens.
*Parsons, Langdon, and Sheldon C. Sommers. 1962. *Gynecology.* Philadelphia: Saunders.
*Pettit, Mary DeWitt. 1962. *Gynecologic Diagnosis and Treatment.* New York: McGraw-Hill.
*Reich, Walter, and M. Nechtow. 1957. *Practical Gynecology.* Philadelphia: Lippincott.
*Rubin, I. C., and Josef Novak. 1956. *Integrated Gynecology: Principles and Practice.* New York: McGraw-Hill.
Scott C. Russell. 1968. *The World of a Gynecologist.* London: Oliver & Boyd.

* One of the 27 gynecology textbooks used in this study.

Diana Scully and Pauline Bart

*Scott, William A., and H. Brookfield Van Wyck. 1946. *The Essentials of Obstetrics and Gynecology.* Philadelphia: Lea & Febiger.
*Taylor, Edward Stewart. 1962. *Essentials of Gynecology.* Philadelphia: Lea & Febiger.
Time, March 20, 1972, p. 89.
Weitzman, Lenore J., Deborah Eifler, Elizabeth Hokada, and Catherine Ross. 1972. "Sex-Role Socialization in Picture Books for Preschool Children." *American Journal of Sociology* 77 (May): 1125–50.
*Wharton, L. R. 1943. *Gynecology.* Philadelphia: Saunders.
*Willson, James Robert. 1971. *Obstetrics and Gynecology.* Saint Louis: Mosby.

Introducing Students to Women's Place in Society

Betty Frankle Kirschner
Kent State University

A recent examination of a number of texts in the area of marriage and family showed that the authors generally thought women belong at home (Ehrlich 1971). In order to find out whether introductory sociology texts present the same traditional view of women, I examined 10 books, randomly selected from the list in the current edition of *Books in Print* (1971). All of them were published between 1966 and 1971.

Three criteria were used to decide the extent to which a book presented a traditional view of women. First, I made a count of the number of entries in the index, on the assumption that a topic thought to be important or problematic would appear there. I checked the entries for "women," "sex," and "female," and also "occupation" and "family" for sublistings referring to women. Every reference to women (using these categories) was counted, even if it was a duplication. For example, some authors listed "women" as a subentry of "family" but presented the same page reference again under "women." This procedure overestimates the space devoted to women, but the fact that an item appeared more than once in the index generally meant that it referred not just to a single sentence but perhaps to a paragraph or two; however, evidence on this point is impressionistic. A second criterion was whether the author mentioned the fact that, holding weeks worked and type of occupation constant, women earn about three-fifths of the wages of men. Obviously this fact is central to understanding women's place in a money society. A third criterion was whether the author stated that the American family was egalitarian, as an indication of his/her lack of awareness of the role the husband's occupation plays in determining life style and chances for the entire family. I shall discuss the books in alphabetical order by author.

Biesanz and Biesanz (1969) indexes no reference to women. The authors note that women make up more than one-third of the work force, but they say nothing about wage differentials (p. 530). I could find no explicit statement about equality in the family. But the authors note that if a wife restricts her husband's occupational advancement, he "must feel free to find a more satisfactory partner" (p. 534). The authors also observe that "husbands and wives should follow traditional roles, the husband as provider, the wife as homemaker and mother" (p. 537). A count of the clever cartoons indicated that half of them are at the expense of women.

Neither do Broom and Selznick (1970) index references to women. The occupational distribution and wage differential by sex are not discussed.

Betty Frankle Kirschner

American society is said to have a "matricentric pattern within a formal patriarchalism"; that is, the wife makes most of the decisions about domestic and social life (p. 35). No analysis of this pattern of authority is presented. The table of stratification correlates refers mostly to males, in some instances (marital stability and mortality ratios) only to white males. The only correlate given for women measures their relative obesity (p. 171).

Chinoy's (1967) index refers to women 33 times. He does not mention occupational differentials, although he notes that employment has increased women's independence from their husbands (p. 153). He states that the equalitarian family is characteristic of contemporary America (p. 144). His statements about women are inconsistent. After asserting that the traditional division of labor in the home has "substantially" changed, he adds that a rough division of tasks based on sex persists (p. 163). What is meant by "substantial change" and evidence for such change are not mentioned. Likewise, concerning a biological basis for sex roles, he says in the left column of page 63 that wide cultural variation suggests the possibility that no biological basis exists; in the other column of the same page, he says that widespread differences between the sexes refute the idea of cultural determinism.

The index to Green and Johns (1966), British authors who deal almost exclusively with theory, contains no reference to women. The authors do not refer to occupational differentials or to the distribution of authority in the family. The authors note that "boys are more likely to experience barriers to opportunities than girls because their goals typically include occupational and financial goals whereas girls can restrict themselves to more easily attained marital and familial roles" (p. 143).

Hodges's (1971) index refers 13 times to women. The author also notes that women's income lags behind men's. The husband is said to be accorded greater dominance and superiority not only in the United States but also in China, Sweden, the Soviet Union, and Israel (p. 280). But on the next page the author says that, although the father is "still technically head of the household, he has lost one battle after another as once-submissive women carried out their quest for sexual equality to the public" (p. 281). The author does not specify which "battles" women have won.

The index in Mack and Young (1968) refers to women 14 times. The authors note the increase of women in the work force and the fact that their work is restricted to a limited number of occupations. But the pay differential is not mentioned (p. 384). Nothing is said about a division of authority in the family. The book gives an example of the invisible woman: a series of pictures (pp. 36–37) demonstrates the capacity of children to use their imaginations to multiply the play possibilities of familiar objects. Every child in every picture is a male. In addition, a not very veiled "biology as destiny" argument (p. 104) ends with the following: "People do not expect a girl to be a construction laborer. It just wouldn't be right. Who would want to marry a girl bricklayer?"

McKee (1969) indexes woman 25 times. Role limitations are acknowledged (p. 65), as well as the fact of job discrimination (p. 376). Economic motivation for employment is said to be more important than concern with personal fulfillment, but the world of work is male-controlled and women are predominantly in lower-paying jobs (p. 378). The actual wage differential is not mentioned. Upper-middle-class women for whom a delayed-career pattern is inappropriate or undesired may engage in a busy social and civic life; from the League of Women Voters to the March of Dimes, a wide range of "socially acceptable" functions can absorb the skills and talents of women; increasingly such women are "politically active" and undertake the unpaid tasks that go with politics (p. 377). "Despite quite radical changes, the status of women much more than of men is bound up with the traditional wife and mother role" (p. 375). The author does not explain why, since women's role is still traditional, the changes in status vis-à-vis men should be called "radical."

Merrill (1969) has no entry in the index referring to women. Nothing is said of wage differentials. No direct statement is made about equality in the family. Women are said to have increasing freedom (p. 280), and the structure of the family is said to have experienced important changes because of women's employment (p. 343), but the nature of the "important changes" is not specified.

Rose and Rose (1969) refer to women seven times. They state that most women do not have as great an earning capacity as men, but they do not state the ratio (p. 215). Family democracy is said to have increased; the wife today, both in law and practice, has as much control over family matters as the husband (p. 189). But the book has a nice analysis of rewards for obedience to sex-role status in the chapter on social control.

Vander Zanden's (1970) index contains no reference to women. Nothing is said of occupational differentials. However, we do find that, "highly patriarchal family arrangements are no longer the rule," and "contemporary American marriages are highly equalitarian" (p. 390). "The evolution of the equalitarian family has been closely linked with the economic emancipation of women" (p. 391).

SUMMARY

An examination of 10 randomly selected introductory sociology texts revealed that five of the 10 failed to index a reference to women. Occupational wage differentials were mentioned in two of the books, but neither of these attempted to quantify the differential. Five books specifically

Betty Frankle Kirschner

referred to the basically egalitarian structure of the contemporary American family. None of the other five books presented a systematic analysis, however brief, of factors which contribute to family inequality. The analysis of the role of women in American society is an area which the introductory texts leave impressively unexplored.

REFERENCES

Books in Print. 1971. New York: Bowker.
Ehrlich, Carol. 1971. "The Male Sociologist's Burden: The Place of Women in Marriage and Family Texts." *Journal of Marriage and the Family* 33 (August): 421–30.

INTRODUCTORY TEXTS

Biesanz, John, and Mavis Biesanz. 1969. *Introduction to Sociology.* Englewood Cliffs, N.J.: Prentice-Hall.
Broom, Leonard, and Philip Selznick. 1970. *Principles of Sociology.* From *Sociology: A Text with Adapted Readings.* 1970. New York: Harper & Row.
Chinoy, Eli. 1967. *Society.* New York: Random.
Green, Bryon R., and Edward A. Johns. 1966. *An Introduction to Sociology.* Oxford: Pergamon.
Hodges, Harold, Jr. 1971. *Conflict and Consensus: An Introduction to Sociology.* New York: Harper & Row.
Mack, Raymond W., and Kimball Young. 1968. *Sociology and Social Life.* New York: American.
McKee, James B. 1969. *Introduction to Sociology.* New York: Holt, Rinehart & Winston.
Merrill, Francis E. 1969. *Society and Culture: An Introduction to Sociology.* Englewood Cliffs, N.J.: Prentice-Hall.
Rose, Arnold M., and Caroline Rose, 1969. *Sociology: The Study of Human Relations.* New York: Knopf.
Vander Zanden, James W. 1970. *Sociology: A Systematic Approach.* New York: Ronald.

CONTRIBUTORS

JOAN HUBER is assistant professor of sociology at the University of Illinois, Champaign. She has published several articles, is coauthor of a forthcoming text-reader, and author of a forthcoming monograph in the area of her major interest, stratification and ideology.

HELEN MACGILL HUGHES was the last doctoral candidate of Robert E. Park, who was already emeritus professor at University of Chicago when she took her degree. She worked at a series of part-time jobs: Sociology Fellow of the *Encyclopaedia Britannica,* which the University of Chicago had acquired; news reporting of research in medicine, science, and education for *Time;* and, finally, a 17-year stint with the *AJS* which she describes in this issue. She has also been guest professor at Sir George Williams University and at Wellesley. She now lives in Cambridge where she has just completed a series of compilations of sociological articles for high schools and junior and teachers' colleges.

JESSIE BERNARD is Research Scholar Honoris Causa at Pennsylvania State University. Her most recent books are *The Sex Game: Communication between the Sexes; Women and the Public Interest: An Essay on Policy and Protest; The Future of Marriage;* and *The Sociology of Community.* She is currently working on a book on the future of motherhood. She has also written in the areas of the sociology of knowledge (*Academic Women*), social theory (*Origins of American Sociology*), family (*American Family Behavior; Remarriage, a Study of Marriage; Marriage and Family among Negroes*), community (*American Community Behavior: The Sociology of Community*); and conflict and power.

JO FREEMAN is a Ph.D. candidate in political science at the University of Chicago and is writing her dissertation on the Women's Liberation Movement. She has written extensively on women and women's liberation in anthologies and professional and popular journals.

WALTER R. GOVE is an associate professor of sociology at Vanderbilt University. His major area of interest is the sociology of mental illness. He is at present involved in a 2-year research project studying the effects of population density on human behavior.

JEANNETTE F. TUDOR is doing research on the sociology of health and illness at Central Michigan University and is a consultant for East Central Michigan Health Service, a federally funded corporation developing Health Maintenance Organizations in the Michigan area.

CATHERINE BODARD SILVER is assistant professor in the Department of Sociology at Brooklyn College, The City University of New York. She is the author of *Black Teachers in a Ghetto School System* (Praeger, forthcoming), and is presently completing an interpretation, for the University of Chicago Press, of the work of Frédéric LePlay, the 19th-century pioneer of empirical sociology and family analysis. Her current interests are in the sociology of economies and the historical sociology of the family.

HANNA PAPANEK is a research associate with the Committee on Southern Asian Studies at the University of Chicago and is this year a member of the Social Science Faculty of the University of Indonesia in Djarkarta where she hopes to develop a women's research group with some implications for research in family planning.

MIRRA KOMAROVSKY is professor of sociology at Barnard College. She is the author of *Women in the Modern World* and *Blue Collar Marriage*.

ANNE-MARIE HENSHEL is assistant professor of sociology at York University in Toronto. Her main interests are in social psychiatry and the family.

NANCY GOLDMAN is research associate with the Center for Social Organization Studies at the University of Chicago and is currently engaged in research in community organization and public housing in the Chicago Metropolitan area.

CYNTHIA FUCHS EPSTEIN is associate professor of sociology at Queens College, The City University of New York, and a senior research associate at the Bureau of Applied Social Research at Columbia University and at the Center for Policy Research. She is the author of *Woman's Place* and is currently working on a book about women lawyers. Her research interests at present are on elites, contra-elites, and social supports of the stratification system.

JOAN ACKER is assistant professor of sociology at the University of Oregon. Her main interests are the sociology of women, formal organizations, and the sociology of social welfare. She is doing research on feminism and sex role socialization.

VALERIE KINCADE OPPENHEIMER is assistant professor of sociology at the University of California, Los Angeles. She is the author of *The Female Labor Force in the United States* (1970) and is currently working on a study of the function of work in the lives of American women and their families.

LARRY E. SUTER is acting chief of the Education and Social Stratification Branch in the Population Division of the Bureau of the Census. He is interested in the analysis of longitudinal surveys and is currently conducting studies of changes in the patterns of school enrollment of college students.

HERMAN P. MILLER, author of *Rich Man, Poor Man* and *Income Distribution in the United States,* is adjunct professor of economics at Temple University, and an economic consultant in private practice. From 1966 through June 1972 he was chief of the Population Division of the Bureau of the Census.

ELIZABETH M. HAVENS is a doctoral candidate at the University of Texas at Austin and an assistant professor at Houston-Tillotson College in Austin. She is currently studying the relation between female labor force participation and fertility.

SAUL D. FELDMAN is assistant professor of sociology at Case Western Reserve University. He is co-editor (with Gerald Thielbar) of *Issues in Social Inequality* and *Life Styles: Diversity in American Society*. He is also the author of *Escape from the Doll's House: Women in Graduate and Professional School Education,* a monograph soon to be issued by the Carnegie Commission on Higher Education.

MARIANNE A. FERBER is assistant professor of economics at the University of Illinois, Champaign. Her major interests are in the areas of international economics and comparative systems.

JANE W. LOEB is director, Office of Admissions and Records at the University of Illinois, Champaign. Her major interests are in educational measurement and statistics, and in student personnel.

HELENA ZNANIECKI LOPATA is professor of sociology at Loyola University, Chicago. She is the author of *Occupation: Housewife* and of the forthcoming *Widowhood in an American City*. She is currently editing a book on marriage and the family.

ARLIE RUSSELL HOCHSCHILD is assistant professor of sociology at the University of California, Berkeley. She is the author of the forthcoming *The Unexpected Community*. She edited a special issue of *Trans-Action* (*Society*) entitled "The American Woman."

CAROL EHRLICH is instructor of American studies at the University of Maryland, Baltimore County, where she specializes in women's studies. She is co-producer of "The Great Atlantic Radio Conspiracy," a weekly radio program of New Left political commentary, and a doctoral candidate in American civilization at the University of Iowa.

DIANA SCULLY is a graduate student in sociology at the University of Illinois at Chicago Circle. Her areas of interest include the sociology of sex roles, adult socialization, and deviance.

PAULINE BART is assistant professor of sociology in psychiatry at the Abraham Lincoln School of Medicine of the University of Illinois in Chicago, with a joint appointment in sociology at Chicago Circle Campus. Her areas of interest include the sociology of sex roles and the sociology of knowledge. She is currently researching divorced fathers. A special interest is the effect of sexism on health care.

BETTY FRANKLE KIRSCHNER is assistant professor of sociology at Kent State University, where she also co-coordinates the Women's Project. She is interested in the sociology of women.